Student Loans and the Dynamics of Debt

D1286844

Student Loans and the Dynamics of Debt

Brad Hershbein
Kevin M. Hollenbeck

2015

W.E. Upjohn Institute for Employment Research
Kalamazoo, Michigan

Library of Congress Cataloging-in-Publication Data

Hershbein, Brad.
   Student loans and the dynamics of debt / Brad Hershbein. Kevin M. Hollenbeck.
   pages cm
   Includes index.
   ISBN 978-0-88099-484-2 (pbk. : alk. paper) — ISBN 0-88099-484-3 (pbk. : alk.
paper) — ISBN 978-0-88099-485-9 (hardcover : alk. paper) — ISBN 0-88099-485-1
(hardcover : alk. paper)
   1. Student loans—United States. 2. Finance, Personal—United States. I. Title.
   LB2340.2H47 2014
   378.3'620973—dc23
                            2014043892

The facts presented in this study and the observations and viewpoints expressed are the sole responsibility of the authors. They do not necessarily represent positions of the W.E. Upjohn Institute for Employment Research.

Cover design by Alcorn Publication Design.
Index prepared by Diane Worden.
Printed in the United States of America.
Printed on recycled paper.

To E. R. F., for her patience.

– B. H.

To D. C. H., for her support.

– K. H.

Contents

Acknowledgments

We could not have produced this book—or organized the conference on which it is based—without the help of many people and organizations. In particular, we owe a debt to several individuals who dotted all our i's and crossed all our t's. From the Upjohn Institute, we thank Claire Black for helping handle the logistics of the conference, which is always more complicated than anticipated; Allison Hewitt Colosky for her outstanding editing work in helping us put this volume together; Rich Wyrwa for supervising the publication process; and Randy Eberts for his enthusiastic support for the conference from the very beginning. We also received fantastic organizational assistance for the conference from Julie Monteiro de Castro and Sofia Rosenberg, both of the University of Michigan's Ford School of Public Policy and the Education Policy Initiative housed therein. We offer our gratitude to the Spencer Foundation and the Education Policy Initiative for their generous financial and in-kind support. Finally, we thank all of the conference participants: the authors who have contributed to this volume and our understanding of student debt, the discussants who read the conference papers carefully and provided insightful feedback, and the other participants who availed us of their expertise.

1
Introduction

Brad Hershbein
Kevin M. Hollenbeck
W.E. Upjohn Institute for Employment Research

Student loans are instrumental in broadening access to postsecondary educational opportunities. For many individuals who want to develop their own human capital but who otherwise do not have the means, loans serve as an important supplement to governmental or institutional grants in making educational investments affordable and increasing the educational attainment of the population. The availability of student loans thus has great value for individual students and the country as a whole.

However, the burgeoning volume of debt and repayment difficulties that many people now experience have created a vigorous debate on whether public policy should further intervene in student loan transactions. In economic terms, do the benefits exceed the costs? As with many public policy issues, answering that question is not straightforward. Close examination of the data on cumulative debt, number and characteristics of borrowers, types of institutions, and repayment dynamics raises almost as many questions as it answers. In alignment with its mission of investigating the underlying dynamics of the labor market, a component of which is the educational preparation of the workforce, the W.E. Upjohn Institute for Employment Research organized a conference on student loans to catalyze careful and informed analysis of this understudied, but increasingly important, public policy. This volume includes the papers that were presented at the conference, held in Ann Arbor at the University of Michigan in October 2013.[1] The Spencer Foundation and the Education Policy Initiative at the University of Michigan Ford School of Public Policy cosponsored the event.

THE CONFERENCE BEGINS: MEASURING DEBT BURDENS

Much publicity has focused on the size of outstanding student debt, which has surpassed $1 trillion. However, this aggregate number taken out of context can obscure, rather than enlighten, the policy debate. Measuring debt is complicated and can be done in different ways. Sandy Baum's chapter brings attention to several of them. She starts by examining trends in total student loan debt, number of borrowers, and average balances. In the case of average balances, the denominator matters, as the average could be over all students or over the students who borrow. Interestingly, the former has declined over the past two years.

Further, student borrowers may be pursuing undergraduate or graduate education. Baum documents that both the levels and growth trends in per-student loans are much greater for graduate students than for undergraduates. She suggests that if public policy is to address loan availability or terms for students, it must certainly treat these two types of students differently. Finally, Baum compares nonfederal with federal loans. Both the volume and percentage of students taking out private loans have essentially halved since their peak in the 2007–2008 academic year.

Baum concludes by suggesting that the most pressing public policy concern is for students who may have unmanageable debt levels—in her analyses, these tend to be independent students, students attending for-profit institutions, and African American students—and to institute income-dependent repayment programs that shift risk from students to taxpayers.

Meta Brown, Donghoon Lee, and colleagues at the Federal Reserve Bank of New York document in Chapter 3 trends in aggregate student debt and repayment vis-à-vis other forms of debt. Drawing on a longitudinal database of consumer credit reports that covers the entire country, they show that total education debt tripled between 2004 and 2012, and that it was the only major source of debt (among mortgages, credit cards, auto loans, and home equity lines of credit) that increased during the Great Recession. Commensurate with that finding, they note that the fraction of individuals with education debt and the average balance per borrower both grew unabated between 2004 and 2012. Some of this increase was due to more people pursuing education, but some of it was also due to interest accumulation from low repayment and high delinquency during the recession.

When Lee at al. examine repayment, they find that as of the end of 2012, 17 percent of borrowers are behind on their student loan payments by 90 or more days, surpassing credit card debt in the highest delinquency rate. The situation is even more dire for borrowers who are in active repayment (and not in deferment or forbearance): 31 percent of these borrowers are delinquent by 90 or more days. The rise in student debt and difficulty in repayment may have crowded out access to other forms of credit, the authors surmise, documenting that other debt—especially mortgages—fell sharply from 2005 to 2012 for young student loan borrowers.

REASONS FOR GROWTH

Undeniably, student debt—however you measure it—has been increasing over the past two decades, but it has not been growing at the same rate for all students, or even all graduates. Brad Hershbein and Kevin Hollenbeck in Chapter 4 address the questions of where in the entire distribution of college graduates has debt grown, when was it growing, and what factors, if any, can explain it. Using data from the National Postsecondary Student Aid Study for individuals who earned bachelor's degrees, they find that debt—contrary to popular belief—grew faster over the 1990s than over the 2000s, with the sharpest increase occurring between 1996 and 2000. They also find that the increase that did occur between 2000 and 2008 was mostly concentrated in the top fourth of borrowers and was entirely due to private loans.

Using statistical decomposition techniques, the authors find that increases in tuition and fees and the expected family contribution (a proxy for ability to pay) can explain most of the increase in borrowing in the early 1990s and in the 2000s. The surge in borrowing in the late 1990s, however, is not explained by costs or other observable factors. Instead, the chapter suggests that this growth was due to the introduction of new loan products, particularly unsubsidized Stafford Loans and private loans.

Chapter 5 by Elizabeth Akers, Matthew M. Chingos, and Alice M. Henriques also attempts to explain the surge in student debt over the last 20 years and looks at distributional changes. However, their analyses rely on the Federal Reserve Board of Governors' Survey of Consumer Finances (SCF) and cover the entire American population, not just recent bachelor's graduates. Akers, Chingos, and Henriques reach general conclusions that extremely large debt burdens are exceptional cases, and that rising educational attainment—in particular, graduate education—explains part of the increase in aggregate debt balances. They also find that tuition increases are perhaps the largest explanatory factor for increased debt, but that changes in behavior, such as greater substitution of debt for out-of-pocket financing of postsecondary expenses, also have contributed to the increase.

Akers, Chingos, and Henriques also review a number of recent studies on the return to higher education and note that the extent to which the increase in debt burdens is leading to financial hardship is an unresolved question.

STUDENT BORROWING AT FOR-PROFIT INSTITUTIONS

As noted by Baum in Chapter 2, one of the groups of students most likely to have unmanageable debt consists of individuals who attended for-profit institutions. Stephanie Riegg Cellini and Rajeev Darolia focus on these students in Chapter 6. Their analyses suggest that relatively high and rising tuition coupled with relatively low student financial resources are likely to be the key factors that explain the elevated debt levels of for-profit students relative to students in other higher education sectors. Costs and borrowing patterns in the for-profit sector are similar to those found in four-year nonprofit institutions; however, unlike the nonprofit sector, tuition hikes were not offset by increases in institutional grants.

Cellini and Darolia pose an interesting question: What motivates students to attend for-profit institutions? For the most part, characteristics and educational aspirations of students attending for-profits are similar to those for students attending two-year, nonprofit (public or private) institutions and who have relatively low levels of debt. Yet the financial burdens and loans that the for-profit students bear are most similar to those for students in four-year, nonprofit institutions.

IMPACT OF BANKRUPTCY NONDISCHARGEABILITY

A unique feature of student loans is their presumptive non-dischargeability in bankruptcy. For many years, this feature was limited to government or nonprofit-originated loans. Xiaoling Ang and Dalié Jiménez in Chapter 7 look at the impact of congressional legislation in 2005 that amended bankruptcy laws to make private student loans nondischargeable as well. (Unlike federal student loans, private loans take into account the credit risk of the potential borrower.) The authors suggest that this change in the law has three theoretical implications. It should have, other things equal, 1) increased the volume of private student loans; 2) increased the "riskiness" of the borrowers (i.e., decreased their average credit score); and 3) decreased the interest rate charged to borrowers.

In fact, the analyses by Ang and Jiménez indicate a very large increase in the volume of private loans originated after 2005, which they attribute primarily to the law change. The credit score of borrowers skewed toward the lower end of the distribution, although the mean did not change appreciably. Finally, the average interest rate of private loans at four-year undergraduate institutions increased by 35 basis points. The first two findings confirm the theoretical hypotheses; however, the third finding is opposite of what was expected. While this result received ample discussion at the conference, it remained a puzzle.

DEFAULT AND REPAYMENT BEHAVIOR

Chapter 8 by Lance J. Lochner and Alexander Monge-Naranjo examines default and repayment behavior over the 10 years following graduation for individuals who earned a bachelor's degree. These authors note that outcomes are not as simple as the binary case of repayment or default that is often the focus of media stories and creditors, including the federal government. In particular, they analyze five outcomes: 1) the fraction of undergraduate debt still outstanding; 2) default; 3) nonpayment (default, deferment, or forbearance); 4) fraction of debt in default; and 5) fraction of debt in nonpayment. They relate these outcomes, at both 5 and 10 years after graduation, to individual and family background, college major, postsecondary institution characteristics, amount borrowed, and postschool earnings. Of these variables, they find the most important ones explaining repayment outcomes are the amount borrowed and postschool earnings. Perhaps surprisingly, college major and institutional characteristics are not correlated with repayment behavior once the other factors are accounted for, and among the individual and family characteristics, the only variable that consistently matters is race. As with Baum's chapter, Lochner and Monge-Naranjo's study reveals that African Americans have significant repayment difficulties relative to all other ethnic/racial groups, even after controlling for many other variables.

A somewhat surprising finding in Chapter 8 is that many borrowers who enter a nonpayment status eventually return to good standing. Over half of the individuals in default five years after graduation are in "repaying/fully paid" status five years later; and almost three-quarters of individuals in deferment or forbearance five years after graduation are in good standing five years later. The authors conclude that policy strategies that focus exclusively on short-term default, without considering rehabilitation, may be too narrow.

LONG-TERM OUTCOMES

In addition to causing difficulty for repayment, increased student loan burdens may affect other life-cycle behaviors of young adults as they enter careers or family formation. In Chapter 9, Dora Gicheva and Jeffrey Thompson look at long-term household financial stability. Isolating the causal impact of student loans on future behavior is problematic because the same set of factors that influence student loan behavior may also influence the type of education pursued, academic success, and later earnings. The authors employ an instrumental variable strategy to get around this problem. In particular, they use the national average amount borrowed per full-time equivalent student when an individual was 17 years old to predict that individual's borrowing amount.[2]

Gicheva and Thompson look at four indicators of financial stability after age 30: 1) being denied any type of credit, 2) late payments on loans, 3) bankruptcy, and 4) homeownership. In analyses that control for several demographic characteristics and local economic conditions, the authors find that borrowing amounts are positively related to bankruptcy and negatively related to homeownership and making on-time payments, with especially strong results for individuals who failed to complete college.

LOAN AVERSION

Public perception and the data agree: more and more students are taking on more and more debt. In an interesting twist of emphasis, however, Sara Goldrick-Rab and Robert Kelchen examine loan aversion in Chapter 10. They begin by noting that aversion may include individuals who have a distaste for borrowing, but it also may include students who lack information about loans or students who were not offered loan opportunities in their financial aid packages. In looking at data from a sample of more than 600 first-time undergraduates at Wisconsin public institutions who received a Pell Grant and from which the actual loan package offered was observable, the authors note several findings that accord with intuition and prior evidence, but they also point out several results that may seem surprising.

In particular, Goldrick-Rab and Kelchen find that the following characteristics are associated with greater propensity to turn down an offered loan: Southeast Asian ethnicity, greater parental education, lower net prices and less institutional prestige, family background with less financial strength, longer time horizons of the student, planning to work part-time while in college, and higher levels of social capital. They also document differences in loan aversion rates between survey data (student responses) and administrative data (college records), and these differences also vary across subgroups of students.

Goldrick-Rab and Kelchen's analysis further finds a lack of cor-relation between financial knowledge and borrowing behavior. While this may suggest that increased financial education of students, as some researchers and policymakers have proposed, may not substantively change students' borrowing behavior, the authors caution that their sample of low-income, Pell Grant recipients may not generalize to all undergraduate students.

THE CONFERENCE CONCLUDES: SPECIFIC
POLICY RECOMMENDATIONS

Three chapters in the book have specific policy prescriptions, all touching on the issue of how to improve loan repayment. In Chapter 11, Lauren Asher and Debbie Cochrane, along with their coauthors at The Institute for College Access and Success (TICAS), offer specific recommendations in four areas: 1) consolidation and simplification of federal loans, 2) streamlined repayment options, 3) improvements in loan counseling, and 4) strengthened consumer protections. They advo-cate that the federal government offer a single undergraduate student loan with no fees, a low in-school interest rate, and a fixed rate in repay-ment that cannot rise much beyond the rate paid by current borrowers.

In terms of repayment, the authors present a "Plan for Fair Loan Payments" for all federal borrowers that calls for affordable payments based on income, family size, and total federal debt, and that offers forgiveness after 20 years of payments. They recommend rigorous loan counseling before students commit to borrowing, not just at entrance and exit. Finally, the authors have a number of suggestions in the area of consumer protection, particularly in the area of collections.

Susan Dynarski and Daniel Kreisman also present a specific plan for an income-based repayment system, which they label "Loans for Educational Opportunity." (Chapter 12 contains an abbreviated version of their paper, which was originally commissioned by The Hamilton Project. See Note 1.) They document four facts about student loans and future earnings: 1) a moderate level of debt for the typical student bor-rower, 2) a high payoff to a college education, 3) high rates of default on typical loans, and 4) higher rates of default among young borrowers. They argue that in light of these four facts there is not a *debt* crisis, but rather a *repayment* crisis.

Under their Loans for Educational Opportunity proposal, payments would be automatically deducted from borrowers' paychecks, similar to the payroll tax for Social Security. Instead of paying off loans during a fixed, 10-year period, borrowers would have up to 25 years, although they could opt to pay down the loan more quickly. Dynarski and Kreisman suggest that this system will reduce the administrative costs of the current student loan system. The chapter also addresses how their proposed system would work for self-employed individuals or those who become unemployed.

In Chapter 13, Jason Delisle, Alex Holt, and Kristin Blagg examine how a loophole in the federal government's Pay As You Earn (PAYE) program for student loans can affect graduate and professional students. The authors show that for many of these students, there is a level of borrowing at which increasing the loan balance has no impact on the amount of total repayments under PAYE because of the program's loan forgiveness benefit; the authors call this borrowing level the "no marginal cost threshold." If a borrower could predict this threshold with certainty, then she would have an incentive to increase the size of her loan because doing so would essentially be costless.

Using data from the National Postsecondary Student Aid Study and the American Community Survey, Delisle and his coauthors estimate that the majority of graduate and professional student borrowers will borrow more than the no marginal cost threshold. This suggests that PAYE effectively functions as a form of tuition subsidy. The most significant levels of subsidization occur in conjunction with the Public Service Loan Forgiveness program, in which loans are forgiven after only 10 years of payments if the borrower qualifies under a public service job. As a remedy for the unintended level of subsidy, the authors propose that the period of repayment before forgiveness be lengthened or that the amount that can be forgiven be capped.

CONCLUSION

The conference exceeded expectations. The papers presented there and included in this volume represent the most current research and knowledge about student loans and repayment. The conference agenda included comments from discussants and general discussion after each of the papers was presented. We thought that the discussants' comments and the general discussion added great value to the papers. We thank the discussants, who are listed at the end of this volume, for their thoughtful insights. We hope this volume serves as a valuable reference for researchers and policymakers who seek a deeper understanding of how, why, and which students borrow for their postsecondary education; how this borrowing may affect later decisions; and what measures can help borrowers repay their loans successfully.

We also thank our cosponsors, the Spencer Foundation and the Education Policy Initiative at the Ford School of Public Policy. The opportunity to convene a community of scholars has furthered our collective insights of the behaviors of students who are attempting to finance their investments in higher education.

Notes

1. Chapter 12 has an abbreviated version of the Dynarski and Kreisman paper, which was originally commissioned by The Hamilton Project. The full paper may be accessed from http://www.hamiltonproject.org/files/downloads_and_links/THP_DynarskiDiscPaper_Final.pdf.
2. As might be expected at a conference with a number of economists participating, much discussion took place around the validity of this instrument.

2

The Evolution of Student Debt in the United States

Sandy Baum
Urban Institute

The conversation about student debt in the United States has descended into an alarmist focus on the aggregate amount of education debt (over $1 trillion by some estimates); on stories about individual students who borrowed excessively and are struggling to repay in a weak labor market; on a comparison between credit card debt (which has fallen quite a bit in recent years) and education debt (which has not); and on fears of a "student loan bubble" that might follow the path of the housing bubble. Secretary of Education Arne Duncan said recently that the student loan "crisis" has grown so large that it poses "a threat to the American dream" (Porter 2013).

It's time to take a step back to examine the role of debt in financing postsecondary education, the path over time in postsecondary participation and the accompanying student borrowing, and the basic arguments underlying debt financing of postsecondary education and the government's role in the system. The sections that follow examine some of the perspectives on student loan data that can alter the picture that emerges. Is outstanding debt or annual borrowing more meaningful? Should non-borrowers be included in average debt figures? Does the path of total borrowing tell the same story as the path of borrowing per student? Should we focus on all postsecondary students or only on undergraduates? The goal is not to choose the optimal data on which to rely, but to elucidate the different information emerging from different choices about what to measure.

OUTSTANDING DEBT

Perhaps the most commonly cited student debt figures are those from the Federal Reserve Bank of New York. Table 2.1 reports outstanding household debt of various types from the third quarter of 2003 to the third quarter of 2013. Education debt grew from $250 billion in 2003 to $610 billion in 2008 and to $1.03 trillion in 2013. There is no doubt that this represents rapid growth worthy of attention, but several other facts from these data are also relevant.

- Education debt increased from 3 percent to 9 percent of outstanding household debt over the decade. This is a significant change, but mortgage debt is 70 percent of the total, and home equity revolving credit is another 5 percent. Widespread default on student loans could be a real problem, but even if the government did not hold the vast majority of this debt, the economic impact would obviously be on a different scale from the collapse of the housing market.

- Credit card debt increased by 24 percent between 2003 and 2008 but fell by 22 percent over the following five years, ending the decade $21 billion (3 percent) below its 2003 level. (See Table 2.2.)

- Outstanding education debt increased by 68 percent between 2008 and 2013—less than half the rate of growth between 2003 and 2008. (See Table 2.2)

Perhaps more fundamental is the question of whether the new focus on outstanding student loan debt is the best way to understand the risks facing credit markets; the economy; or past, current, and future students.

Outstanding debt per borrower has not grown nearly as much as total outstanding debt. Enrollment in postsecondary education has increased rapidly in recent years, and the number of borrowers retiring their debt each year is significantly smaller than the number incurring debt for the first time.

Figure 2.1 shows the real growth in total outstanding education debt relative to the growth in the number of borrowers with debt and the growth in average balances from the first quarter of 2005 through the

Table 2.1 Outstanding Household Debt, 2003:Q3 to 2013:Q3 (in billions of dollars and as a percentage of total household debt)

	2003	2004	2005	2006	2007	2008	2009	2010	2011	2012	2013
Mortgage ($)	5.18	6.21	6.91	8.05	8.93	9.29	8.94	8.61	8.40	8.03	7.90
Home equity revolving ($)	0.27	0.43	0.54	0.60	0.63	0.69	0.71	0.67	0.64	0.57	0.54
Auto ($)	0.68	0.75	0.83	0.82	0.82	0.81	0.74	0.71	0.73	0.77	0.85
Credit card ($)	0.69	0.71	0.73	0.75	0.82	0.86	0.81	0.73	0.69	0.67	0.67
Student ($)	0.25	0.33	0.38	0.45	0.53	0.61	0.69	0.78	0.87	0.96	1.03
Other ($)	0.48	0.41	0.41	0.44	0.41	0.41	0.38	0.34	0.33	0.31	0.30
Total ($)	7.56	8.83	9.79	11.11	12.13	12.68	12.28	11.84	11.66	11.31	11.28
	2003	2004	2005	2006	2007	2008	2009	2010	2011	2012	2013
Mortgage (%)	69	70	71	72	74	73	73	73	72	71	70
Home equity revolving (%)	4	5	6	5	5	5	6	6	5	5	5
Auto (%)	9	9	8	7	7	6	6	6	6	7	7
Credit card (%)	9	8	7	7	7	7	7	6	6	6	6
Student (%)	3	4	4	4	4	5	6	7	7	8	9
Other (%)	6	5	4	4	3	3	3	3	3	3	3

SOURCE: Federal Reserve Bank of New York (2013a).

Table 2.2 Percentage Changes in Outstanding Household Debt, 2003–2013

	2003–2008	2008–2013
Mortgage	79	−15
Home equity revolving	157	−23
Auto loan	18	4
Credit card	24	−22
Student loan	146	68
Other	−14	−26
Total	68	−11

SOURCE: Federal Reserve Bank of New York (2013b).

Figure 2.1 Total Outstanding Student Debt, Number of Borrowers with Outstanding Debt, and Average Balance, Relative to 2005 Fourth Quarter, 2005–2012

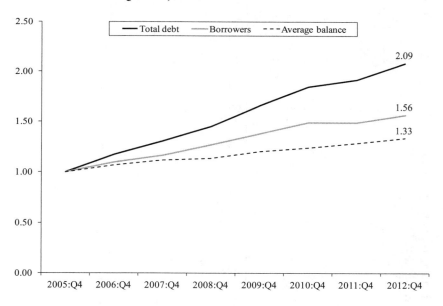

SOURCE: Federal Reserve Bank of New York (2013b).

fourth quarter of 2012. Total outstanding debt was 124 percent higher in constant dollars at the end of 2012 than it had been eight years earlier. In contrast, average balances increased by 33 percent (in 2012 dollars), while the number of borrowers rose by 66 percent. The number of borrowers increased much more rapidly than the average amount borrowed from 2007 through 2010 but did not increase between 2010 and 2011, when average balances continued to grow.

Outstanding balances include debt that was incurred many years ago as well as recent borrowing, borrowing by both students and parents, and borrowing by both undergraduate and graduate students. The accrual of unpaid interest, penalties, and other charges also add to the total outstanding debt.

Solutions for relieving the strains of student debt should certainly include borrowers with old debts who are struggling, and many policy proposals ignore these people. However, developing strategies for the future requires a focus on recent student borrowing patterns. Striking a balance between concern about overdependence on debt for financing postsecondary education and welcoming increases in borrowing as a sign of increased participation by students with limited resources requires more information about borrowing patterns across students on different educational paths, from different socioeconomic backgrounds, and of different ages.

ANNUAL BORROWING

The year-by-year data on federal student loans are more accurate than either estimates of outstanding debt or the data on the total debt levels of students who graduate with different credentials or who leave school without credentials. Those data are based either on samples of students from surveys conducted every four years or on surveys with disappointing response rates completed every year by colleges and universities.

Total annual borrowing, detailed in Table 2.3, has increased dramatically since 1970–1971, when students borrowed $7.6 billion (in 2012 dollars) through education loan programs. Thirty years later, in 2000–2001, total borrowing through these programs had reached

Table 2.3 Total Federal and Nonfederal Loans to Undergraduates, Graduate Students, and Parents of Undergraduate Students, 1970–1971 to 2012–2013, Selected Years (in millions of 2012 dollars)

	Federal loans ($)	Nonfederal loans ($)	Total ($)	Post-secondary enrollment (FTEs)	Total borrowing per FTE student ($)
1970–71	7,622		7,622	7,148,575	1,066
1975–76	7,490	0	7,490	8,479,688	883
1980–81	19,276	0	19,276	8,819,013	2,186
1985–86	21,071	0	21,071	8,943,433	2,356
1990–91	24,403	0	24,403	9,820,205	2,485
1995–96	39,364	2,000	41,364	10,172,987	4,066
2000–01	45,664	6,750	52,414	11,427,001	4,587
2005–06	67,984	20,860	88,844	13,408,264	6,626
2006–07	69,083	23,750	92,833	13,612,494	6,820
2007–08	75,638	25,530	101,168	13,960,922	7,247
2008–09	90,144	12,390	102,534	14,608,127	7,019
2009–10	106,648	9,040	115,688	15,764,432	7,339
2010–11	112,037	8,110	120,147	16,220,701	7,407
2011–12	109,814	8,130	117,944	16,143,133	7,306
2012–13	101,469	8,810	110,279	15,918,548	6,928

NOTE: FTE = full-time equivalent.
SOURCE: College Board (2013).

$52.4 billion, and it more than doubled, to $120.1 billion, over the next decade. As of 2012–2013, however, annual borrowing had fallen from its 2010–2011 peak.

Some of the borrowing changes are due to policy changes. For example, the increase from $24 billion in 1990–1991 to $41 billion in 1995–1996 was to a significant extent the result of the introduction of the unsubsidized Stafford Loan program, which expanded the federal program from one designed only for students with documented financial need to one including all students.

Enrollment growth is another issue. While total borrowing between 2000–2001 and 2012–2013 increased by 110 percent in real terms, from $52.4 billion to $110.3 billion, borrowing per full-time equivalent

(FTE) student increased by 51 percent, from $4,587 (in 2012 dollars) to $6,928.

The decline in both total borrowing and borrowing per student over the last two years may or may not signal a longer-term trend. But these data should serve as a caution to those who have a tendency to predict that when a trend is unfavorable it is likely to continue to be more and more unfavorable. Predictions of doom based on temporary circumstances generate attention-grabbing headlines. But as the economy rises from the depths of the Great Recession, fewer people will enroll in college as the labor market recovers, and students may borrow less as state tax revenues, incomes, and savings rise. Both the upward pressure on tuition prices and the financing strains on families and students are also likely to diminish to some extent.

DEBT PER STUDENT VERSUS DEBT PER BORROWER

Most discussions of average debt levels focus on debt per borrower, setting aside the significant number of college students who do not borrow at all, or at least do not rely on education loans. In 2011–2012, 31 percent of bachelor's degree recipients, 50 percent of associate's degree recipients, and 34 percent of those who earned postsecondary certificates did not have education debt. Including these students may obscure some of the potential problems facing borrowers, but it paints a clearer picture of how students finance their education. For example, in 2011–2012, median debt for bachelor's degree recipients who borrowed was $26,500, and 10 percent borrowed more than $54,900. The median for all bachelor's degree recipients was $16,900, and the 90th percentile was $44,500 (National Center for Education Statistics 2012).

UNDERGRADUATE AND GRADUATE STUDENTS

About 87 percent of all postsecondary students are undergraduate students, while the other 13 percent are graduate students who have already completed bachelor's degrees. Both undergraduate and graduate students are eligible for federal student loans. First-year dependent undergraduate students with documented financial need may be eligible for up to $3,500 in subsidized loans, on which the government pays the interest while the student is in school. These students frequently also take unsubsidized loans, because the total federal student loan borrowing limit is $2,000 higher than the limit for the subsidized program.[1] Since July 1, 2012, graduate students have been eligible only for unsubsidized federal student loans.

Federal loan repayment options are the same for undergraduate and graduate debt. While most students take the default option of making fixed payments every year for 10 years, there are also graduated repayment plans under which payments increase over time, extended repayment plans that allow smaller payments over more years and, of particular importance, income-dependent repayment plans. These plans make the amount owed dependent on the borrower's income, limiting required payments to a manageable portion of discretionary income and forgiving remaining debt after a period of years.

As indicated in Table 2.4 and Figure 2.2, in 2012–2013, federal loans per postsecondary student were $6,374. But focusing only on undergraduate students yields an average of $4,897, while graduate students borrowed over three times as much.

Graduate student debt may be an increasing problem as the gap in earnings between individuals with bachelor's degrees and those with advanced degrees grows, leading more students to continue their stud-

Table 2.4 Average Federal Loans per FTE Student, FTE Undergraduate Student, and FTE Graduate Student, 1992–1993 to 2012–2013

	Federal loans per FTE postsecondary student ($)	Federal loans per FTE UG student ($)	Federal loans per FTE graduate student ($)
1992–93	2,574	1,959	6,968
1997–98	4,007	3,216	9,465
2002–03	4,364	3,406	10,940
2007–08	5,418	3,978	14,937
2012–13	6,374	4,897	16,239

NOTE: FTE = full-time equivalent.
SOURCE: College Board (2013).

Figure 2.2 Average Federal Loans per FTE Undergraduate and per FTE Graduate Student 1992–1993 to 2012–2013 (in 2012 dollars)

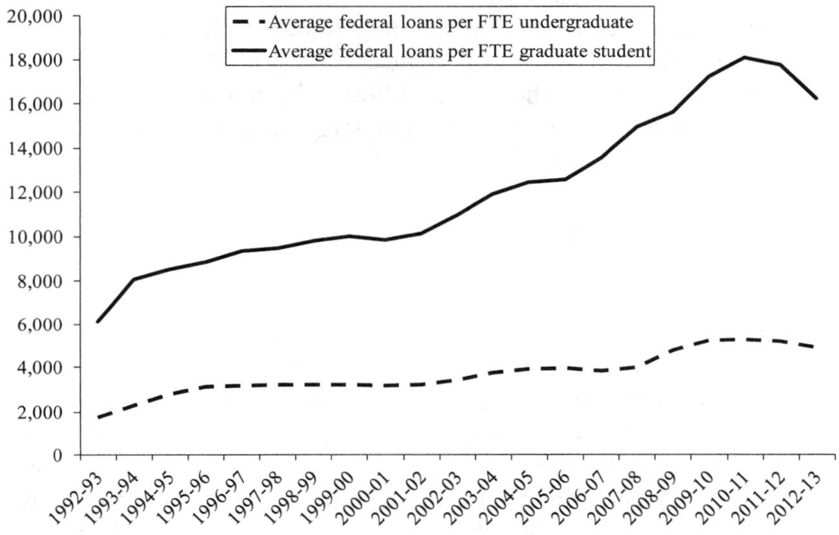

NOTE: FTE = full-time equivalent.
SOURCE: College Board (2013, Figure 3B).

ies.[2] But policy responses to this issue should likely be quite different from those to the undergraduate debt issue. Subsidies for undergraduate students are critical from the perspectives of both equity and efficiency. Some postsecondary education is a virtual necessity for earnings that support a secure lifestyle. There is broad consensus that accidents of birth should not prevent people from having the opportunity to access this education. Failing to provide access also leads to a less productive labor force and to greater reliance on publicly funded income support programs.

The role of public subsidies for graduate education is less clear-cut. Certainly there are social benefits to increased educational attainment at this level, but anyone undertaking graduate study is already a four-year college graduate, and public subsidies come largely from taxpayers with lower incomes at the time students are enrolling, and even more so after they have completed their advanced degrees. Arguments for investing in education only if the financial returns are likely to be high enough to justify the expenditure are stronger in the case of graduate education than in the case of undergraduate education.

There are certainly exceptions and sound arguments for some level of subsidy. However, the argument that graduate student debt, which is held by individuals who have the highest earnings potential of any segment of the population, should be addressed by public policy is much weaker than similar arguments about undergraduate debt.

NONFEDERAL LOANS

Nonfederal loans, from banks and other private lenders and to a lesser extent from states and from colleges and universities, may be a particular concern because they do not come with the repayment protections attached to federal loans. It is not easy to arrange for lower or postponed payments when borrowers hit difficult financial times, and private loans are not eligible for the federal income-dependent repayment plans. Moreover, while the interest rates on federal student loans are limited by law, private loans frequently carry variable interest rates that can reach very high levels.

Figure 2.3 shows that nonfederal borrowing almost doubled, from about $10.5 billion (in 2012 dollars) in 2002–2003 to $25.5 billion in 2007–2008. As was the case in other credit markets, lending standards were less than rigorous. Many of the loans made during this period have not yet been repaid, and concerns over this outstanding debt are probably well placed. But the market collapsed in 2008–2009, and total nonfederal borrowing has been in the $8–$9 billion range since 2009–2010.

In 2007–2008, 14 percent of undergraduates and 11 percent of graduate students relied on the private loan market. By 2011–2012, as shown in Table 2.5, those percentages had declined to 6 percent and 4 percent, respectively (National Center for Education Statistics 2008, 2012). Both supply and demand forces contributed to this change. The tightening of credit markets is evidenced in the decline from 39 percent to 12 percent in the share of undergraduates and from 29 percent to 5 percent in the share of graduate students in for-profit postsecondary institutions taking private loans (National Center for Education Statistics 2008, 2012). But at the same time, federal loan limits for under-

Figure 2.3 Total Nonfederal Education Loans, 1997–1998 to 2012–2013 (in 2012 dollars)

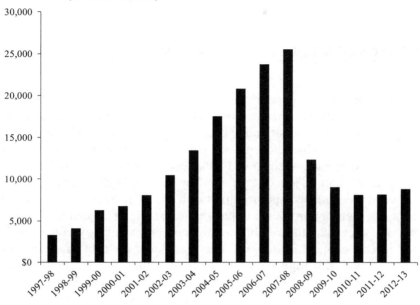

SOURCE: College Board (2013, Table 1).

Table 2.5 Percentages of Undergraduate and Graduate Students Taking Private Loans, 2007–2008 and 2011–2012, by Sector

	2007–08	2011–12
Undergraduate students		
Private for-profit	39	12
Private nonprofit four-year	25	12
Public four-year	14	7
Public two-year	4	2
Total	14	6
Graduate students		
Private for-profit	29	5
Private nonprofit four-year	12	5
Public four-year	6	3
Total	11	4

SOURCE: National Center for Education Statistics (2008, 2012).

graduates have increased, and federal GradPLUS Loans have become available to graduate students.

EVALUATING EDUCATION BORROWING

People tend to compare individuals with student loan obligations to those with similar earnings who do not have the same debt. It is not a surprise that the consumption options of former students who borrowed are more limited than those whose parents paid their way. But what if those students had not borrowed? Chances are they would not have had the same education, job, or earnings. The more important comparison is between the students' opportunities with a college education and some debt and their opportunities if they did not attend college at all.

The fact that students borrow to fund postsecondary education is not in and of itself a problem. The arguments for debt financing for investments with high expected rates of return are straightforward. Between 2008 and 2011, the gap between the median earnings of high school graduates aged 25–34 and those in the same age range with a bachelor's degree or higher declined from 74 percent to 69 percent for men and from 79 percent to 70 percent for women, but the long-term trend is upward. The earnings premium for men rose from 25 percent in 1971 to 56 percent in 1991 and to 69 percent in 2011. For women it rose from 43 percent in 1971 to 56 percent in 1991 and to 70 percent in 2011 (Baum, Ma, and Payea 2013, Figure 1.6). Moreover, the earnings gap is larger for workers at older ages (Baum, Kurose, and Ma 2013, Section 6).

Average debt levels are not alarming. The popular press notwithstanding, the typical bachelor's degree recipient entering the labor market with as much as $30,000 or $40,000 in debt will not have undue difficulty repaying that debt out of the earnings premium from his or her education. But the growing number of borrowers with higher debt levels may struggle, even if they are reasonably successful in the labor market. And labor market outcomes are uncertain. Earnings levels vary quite a bit among people with similar levels of education, and some borrowers with average debt levels might face difficulties, especially if they are attempting to repay their student loans over a relatively short 10-year time period.

The existence of income-dependent repayment options for federal student loans effectively changes the risk of student debt. Many of those with very high debt levels have at least some nonfederal student debt, but the new federal repayment plans shift much of the risk from students to taxpayers, since borrowers are not expected to repay if their earnings are inadequate.

THE FEDERAL ROLE

The logic of education debt and the manageability of average debt levels for typical college graduates do not diminish the very real problems facing a minority of students because they made unwise decisions about their investments in education; because they were, for whatever reason, unable to succeed in meeting their educational goals; or because their labor market outcomes have been less favorable than anticipated. As long as there is a public interest in promoting educational opportunities and attainment, and as long as the federal government is, as it should be, the primary source of student loans, public policy must address these issues constructively.

Some of the concerns about levels of student debt are voiced in the form of recommendations to scale back federal student loan programs. One argument is that the availability of easy credit gives colleges and universities more leeway to raise their prices. This position also reflects the idea that the federal government is inappropriately encouraging students to overborrow.

But in the absence of ample federal credit, many students are likely to turn to the private loan market, which is apt to offer reasonable terms to students enrolled in bachelor's degree programs at selective colleges who have financially secure cosigners. It is less likely to provide favorable terms to the students from low-income, first-generation families borrowing to finance enrollment in community colleges, or to low-income adults seeking credentials that will, for the first time, make them eligible for jobs that pay a living wage. Federal education policy is (or should be) designed to provide opportunities to those students who would otherwise fall through the cracks.

The challenges presented by the prevalence of private student loans between 2002–2003 and 2007–2008 provide a reminder about why the federal government is involved in this market. The private market relies on credit histories and collateral in determining its lending terms. Students tend to have limited credit histories, low incomes, and minimal assets. Many students, including those with weak future prospects, took private loans with high interest rates. When sufficient federal loans were not available to meet their needs, or when they didn't understand their options, they looked elsewhere.

In the current belt-tightening environment, suggestions about risk rating of federal student loans have become surprisingly common. The National Association of Student Financial Aid Administrators (2013) floated the idea in a recent report. Other observers have promoted programs that would modify loan terms based on either the institutions in which students enroll or the characteristics of the students themselves. Some of the suggestions are designed to protect the federal budget (Simkovic 2011), but others are designed to protect students against overborrowing.

It is unrealistic to believe that offering high-risk students loans with higher interest rates is the best public policy for helping them make wise decisions about their educational paths. The national priority on assuring that students with limited means can participate in post-secondary education requires that we make reasonable financing options available to them. Suggestions about incorporating risk rating into the federal loan system generally rely on the assumption that students will respond to market signals and either forgo college or choose alternative programs and institutions when presented with unfavorable loan terms. Both history and the insights of behavioral economics make this seem unlikely.[3] And while there are surely students who would be better off not pursuing further education than attending the institutions in which they enroll, dismantling the system that allows students with limited financial means and uncertain academic futures the chance to improve their prospects is not a prescription for a healthy economy or an equitable society.

WHO IS BORROWING TOO MUCH?

There are two central questions: 1) Who are the students with the highest debt levels, and 2) who are the students with the least manageable debt burdens? These questions are not the same, since students who are in school for a longer time and earn higher degrees are likely to accumulate the most debt—and to have the earnings to repay that debt. Those who enroll for short periods of time and never earn credentials borrow relatively small amounts but also have weak labor market outcomes.

The most recent available data on aggregate debt by demographic and educational characteristics are for 2011–2012. That year, 23 percent of bachelor's degree recipients *with debt* had borrowed more than $40,000. The percentage with no education debt at all was 31 percent. But 44 percent of bachelor's degree recipients from for-profit institutions graduated with $40,000 or more in debt, compared to 18 percent of those from the private nonprofit sector and 10 percent from public institutions. Student loan default patterns also direct attention to the for-profit sector, with 43 percent of FY2011 defaulters coming from these institutions (U.S. Department of Education 2013). The for-profit sector is, and should be, a particular focus of concerns about student borrowing.

Comparisons of the debt levels of bachelor's degree recipients with different demographic characteristics give additional indication of where the problems lie. Independent students borrow more than dependent students. Federal loan limits are higher for independent students, who can now borrow up to $57,500 in Direct Loans for undergraduate study, compared to $31,000 for dependent students whose parents qualify for PLUS Loans. Independent students are also more likely to have responsibilities for supporting families and less likely to have parental support on which to fall back.

As Table 2.6 indicates, among 2011–12 bachelor's degree recipients, 9 percent of dependent students and 24 percent of independent students accumulated more than $40,000 in education debt, with single independent students and those with dependents more likely to fall into this category than those who were married without dependents.

Table 2.6 Percentage Distribution of Aggregate Debt Levels of Bachelor's Degree Recipients by Dependency Status and Dependent Student Family Income, 2011–2012

	No debt	$1–$20,000	$20,001–$40,000	$40,001 or more
All bachelor's degree recipients	31	24	29	16
Dependent	35	27	29	9
Less than $30,000	23	37	31	9
$30,000–$64,999	22	30	39	9
$65,000–$105,999	40	23	26	12
$106,000 or more	46	23	25	7
Independent	26	21	29	24
No dependents, unmarried	25	22	29	24
No dependents, married	34	20	2	18
With dependents	24	2	30	27

NOTE: Includes all loans ever borrowed for undergraduate education in 2011–12 and prior years. Does not include loans to parents of undergraduate students.
SOURCE: National Center for Education Statistics (2012).

Among dependent students, the patterns by family income level are not so clear. Students from higher-income families were more likely not to borrow at all. But among those who borrowed, those from the lowest-income families were most likely to borrow $20,000 or less. Those from families with incomes between $65,000 and $106,000 were most likely to accumulate debts exceeding $40,000, both overall and among those who borrowed.

As Table 2.7 shows, the breakdown of graduates by sector highlights the reality that the students who earn their degrees from for-profit institutions are most likely to have high levels of debt. Within each sector, independent students are more likely than dependent students to be in this situation, and among dependent students, it is middle- or upper-middle-income students who are most likely to borrow more than $40,000 to finance their bachelor's degrees.

It is also notable that, as indicated in Table 2.8, within income groups, there are differences in debt levels by racial/ethnic groups.

Table 2.7 Percentage Distribution of Aggregate Debt Levels of Bachelor's Degree Recipients, by Dependency Status, Dependent Student Family Income, and Sector, 2011–2012

	No debt	$1–$20,000	$20,001–$40,000	$40,001 or more
Public four-year	36	27	27	10
Dependent				
Less than $30,000	27	39	27	7
$30,000–$64,999	25	35	33	7
$65,000–$105,999	47	24	23	6
$106,000 or more	48	22	25	4
Independent	31	25	28	16
Private nonprofit four-year	27	23	32	18
Dependent				
Less than $30,000	12	37	41	10
$30,000–$64,999	14	23	51	13
$65,000–$105,999	27	21	31	21
$106,000 or more	42	23	26	10
Independent	25	20	29	26
For-profit	13	12	32	44
Dependent				
Less than $30,000	0	20	35	45
$30,000–$64,999	9	10	50	31
$65,000–$105,999	26	20	24	30
$106,000 or more	n/a	n/a	n/a	n/a
Independent	13	11	31	45

SOURCE: National Center for Education Statistics (2012).

Small sample sizes make it difficult to include breakdowns by sector, race, and income, but black students are disproportionately likely to enroll in the for-profit sector, while Hispanic students are overrepresented in community colleges.[4] Among 2011–12 black bachelor's degree recipients, 28 percent had at least $40,000 in debt. This compares to 14 percent of white graduates, 16 percent of Hispanic graduates, and 6 percent of Asian graduates. Percentages with high debt were higher for independent students, with 35 percent of independent black bachelor's degree recipients borrowing more than $40,000.

Table 2.8 Percentage Distribution of Aggregate Debt Levels of Bachelor's Degree Recipients, by Dependency Status, Dependent Student Family Income, and Race/Ethnicity, 2011–2012

	No debt	$1–$20,000	$20,001–$40,000	$40,001 or more
White	33	24	30	14
Dependent				
Less than $30,000	20	40	31	9
$30,000–$64,999	21	30	41	7
$65,000–$105,999	39	24	26	12
$106,000 or more	48	21	25	7
Independent	26	21	31	23
Black	16	24	32	28
Dependent				
Less than $30,000	5	36	43	16
$30,000–$64,999	9	25	42	24
$65,000–$105,999	25	30	28	17
$106,000 or more	23	38	31	8
Independent	18	18	29	35
Hispanic	28	27	29	16
Dependent				
Less than $30,000	25	39	31	6
$30,000–$64,999	26	35	28	12
$65,000–$105,999	36	23	31	10
$106,000 or more	28	27	34	11
Independent	28	23	28	22
Asian	53	23	18	6
Dependent				
Less than $30,000	51	27	19	3
$30,000–$64,999	39	27	34	0
$65,000–$105,999	65	18	14	4
$106,000 or more	56	32	11	1
Independent	55	19	13	14

SOURCE: National Center for Education Statistics (2012).

Both differences in enrollment patterns and the reality that black families tend to have lower asset levels than other families with similar incomes make it unsurprising that even within income categories, black bachelor's degree recipients have higher debt levels than members of other racial/ethnic groups (Shapiro, Meschede, and Orsoro 2013). Among dependent students, within racial/ethnic groups, it is middle-income students rather than lower-income students who are most likely to accumulate high levels of debt.

High debt levels don't tell the whole story of at-risk borrowers, because for students who don't earn bachelor's degrees—those who leave school either with associate's degrees or certificates or with no postsecondary credentials—earnings tend to be lower, and lower levels of debt can lead to unmanageable payment requirements. The 84 percent of 2011–12 bachelor's degree recipients who borrowed $40,000 or less are not likely to be at risk, except under unusual circumstances, and as Table 2.9 indicates, very few certificate holders and students who left school without a credential accumulated this much debt. But we know that those who do not complete their credentials are disproportionately likely to default. This pattern may be a function of factors other than debt to earnings ratios, including a reluctance to prioritize the repayment of loans that did not serve their intended purpose. But targeted efforts to diminish student debt problems should certainly include a focus on students with debt levels that do not exceed the overall average.

ENROLLMENT PATTERNS

Tuition and fees, as well as living costs for college students, have risen relative to family incomes over time, even after taking into consideration the role of financial aid in reducing the net price that students actually pay. It is not surprising that students are relying more heavily on borrowing than they did a generation ago. Student loans have become more easily available, and parents seem more willing to shift the responsibility for paying for college onto their children, but the increase in postsecondary participation rates across the population also plays a role.

Table 2.9 Total Student Debt Levels of 2003–04 Beginning Postsecondary Students, by Credentials Earned by 2009 (%)

	No debt	$1–$10,000	$10,001–$20,000	$20,001–$30,000	$30,001–$50,000	$50,001 or more
Total	43	25	16	8	5	2
Bachelor's degree (31%)	36	12	22	14	1	5
Associate's degree (9%)	42	24	18	9	7	1
Certificate (9%)	39	45	12	2	1	0
No degree, still enrolled (15%)	39	27	18	9	5	2
No degree, not enrolled (35%)	52	30	11	4	2	0

SOURCE: College Board (2013, Figure 11C).

Between 2001 and 2011, the total number of postsecondary students grew by 32 percent, from 15.9 million to 21 million. Each student is borrowing more on average, but the growth in debt per student has been slower than the growth in the number of students borrowing. In recent years, because of rapid enrollment growth, total federal loans have grown about twice as fast as federal loans per student. In other words, it isn't so much that students are borrowing more, it's that more students are enrolling and borrowing.

Over the decade from 1983 to 1992, about 30 percent of recent high school graduates enrolling immediately in college were from families in the bottom 40 percent of the income distribution. This percentage increased to an average of about 32 percent from 1993 to 2002 and to 34 percent from 2003 to 2012. The percentage of the new college students whose families were in the highest fifth of the income distribution fell from about 28 percent between 1983 and 1992 to 25 percent from 1993 to 2002, and to 24 percent over the most recent decade.[5] More analysis is necessary to determine the role of the changing economic circumstances of college students, but it seems clear that in order to understand borrowing patterns over time, one should consider the demographic characteristics of students.

CONCLUSION

More students today are borrowing to finance their education than did a generation ago or even a decade ago, and more students are borrowing amounts of money that have the potential to cause them long-term financial difficulties. But this reality does not define a broad "crisis." In order to address the very real problems of students with unmanageable levels of education debt, it is important to focus on the students who are struggling, rather than on students in general. And it is necessary to put education debt into the context of the investment it is financing and the payoff of that investment.

Among bachelor's degree recipients, it is not students from low-income families who accumulate the highest levels of debt. Rather, independent students, most of whom are older than traditional college age, students who attend for-profit institutions, and African American students are more likely than others to accumulate high levels of education debt. These groups of students are also those least likely to earn four-year degrees. Instead, many earn associate's degrees or certificates, or leave school without a credential. Focusing on these students and helping them to make decisions that will more likely lead to positive outcomes is more constructive than generalized panic about student debt.

Much of the hand wringing about student debt stops short of proposing solutions. Viable policy solutions for these particular problems are much more feasible than attempts to have taxpayers cover the entire cost of postsecondary education, or scenarios in which the cost of providing quality education plummets.

Income-dependent repayment programs shift a significant portion of the risk of education debt from the student to the taxpayer, protecting students against unforeseen circumstances. This is critical, given the uncertainty involved in postsecondary investments. The recent focus on potential improvements to these repayment programs is welcome, but care must be taken to balance protecting students with misdirecting subsidies and creating perverse incentives. For example, lowering the percentage of discretionary income required from 15 percent to 10 percent of income exceeding 150 percent of the poverty line provides significant savings only to borrowers with incomes high enough for 5 percent of discretionary income to be a measurable amount. Furthermore, limiting required payments in this way and forgiving outstanding debt after 20 years, when combined with the availability of federal loans for graduate students up to the cost of attendance, creates an unintended windfall for graduate students with very high debt levels, even if their earnings are far above the average for the taxpayers providing the subsidies (see Delisle and Hope [2012]).

Making income-dependent repayment the default option, so that students would not have to have an unusual amount of information, complete a complicated application process, or overcome a series of bureaucratic hurdles in order to benefit, could solve much of the student loan problem. Extending eligibility to students with longstanding debts and limiting the amount of unpaid interest allowed to accrue are also important components of a policy solution.

But such a system will not be feasible if the goal is to prevent students from bearing a reasonable share of the costs of their own education. The system must be carefully designed to target subsidies at students for whom unforeseen outcomes create unmanageable difficulties. It must also be combined with more effective information and guidance in advance of student enrollment and borrowing.

Shifting the burden of repaying loans from students to taxpayers does not diminish the importance of the choices students make about postsecondary study or the support they get to help attain their goals. Many of the problems students face with overborrowing could be prevented if they had more effective guidance about their options and their chances of success. Strategies for diminishing the problems facing future students should include improved support for students—both academic support and assistance with complex decisions. In addition, reforms of the student loan system, both in terms of regulation of the private market and redesign of repayment systems for federal loans, must ameliorate the difficulties facing those who are already in untenable situations as well as protecting future students.

Headline-grabbing statements about high aggregate loan debt do not help the students who need our attention. We should focus on the debt levels of individual students, improve the policies in place to protect them against circumstances beyond their control that lead to repayment problems, and provide incoming students with better information and advice so they don't make poor education and career decisions or borrow excessive amounts.

Notes

1. The limit on subsidized loans for dependent students is $4,500 in the second year and $5,500 in the third year and beyond. The total annual borrowing limit is, in each case, $2,000 higher. Total borrowing for dependent undergraduates may not exceed $23,000 in subsidized loans and $31,000 overall. Independent students (and dependent students whose parents are not eligible for federal parent loans) have the same subsidized loan limits but higher overall limits (studentaid.ed.gov/types/loans/subsidized-unsubsidized).
2. Between 2001 and 2011, the gap in median earnings between full-time working males aged 25–34 whose highest degree was a bachelor's degree and those with only a high school diploma fell from 57 percent to 56 percent. For those with a master's degree or higher, the gap grew from 94 percent to 112 percent (U.S. Census Bureau 2014).
3. For a discussion of the implications of the insights from behavioral economics for the design of the student aid system, see Baum and Schwartz (2013).

4. Hispanic students constitute 18 percent of the students at community colleges but only 13 percent of all students at degree-granting institutions. In 2010, almost half of all Hispanic students across the country were enrolled at community colleges. Black students enroll in disproportionate numbers at for-profit institutions. The share of black students in total enrollment at for-profit institutions (29 percent) was nearly twice as high as the share of black students in total postsecondary enrollment (14 percent) in 2010 (Baum and Kurose 2013).
5. Calculations by the author based on the National Center for Education Statistics (2012).

References

Baum, Sandy, and Charles Kurose. 2013. "Community Colleges in Context: Exploring Financing of Two- and Four-Year Institutions." Background paper in the report, *Bridging the Higher Education Divide*. Washington, DC: Century Foundation.

Baum, Sandy, Charles Kurose, and Jennifer Ma. 2013. *How College Shapes Lives: Understanding the Issues*. New York: College Board.

Baum, Sandy, Jennifer Ma, and Kathleen Payea. 2013. *Education Pays: The Benefits of Higher Education for Individuals and Society*. New York: College Board.

Baum, Sandy, and Saul Schwartz. 2013. "Student Aid, Student Behavior, and Educational Attainment." In *Understanding Student Behaviors: A Prerequisite to Supporting College Enrollment and Success*, Sandy Baum and Robert M. Shireman, eds. Washington, DC: George Washington University Graduate School of Education and Human Development.

College Board. 2013. *Trends in Student Aid, 2013*. New York: College Board. https://trends.collegeboard.org/sites/default/files/student-aid-2013-full -report.pdf (accessed April 24, 2014).

Delisle, Jason, and Alex Hope. 2012. *Safety Net or Windfall? Examining Changes to Income-Based Repayment for Federal Student Loans*. Washington, DC: New America Foundation.

Federal Reserve Bank of New York. 2013a. *Quarterly Report on Household Debt and Credit*. New York: Federal Reserve Bank of New York. http://www.newyorkfed.org/research/national_economy/householdcredit/ DistrictReport_Q22013.pdf (accessed April 24, 2014).

———. 2013b. "Student Loan Debt by Age Group." New York: Federal Reserve Bank of New York. http://www.newyorkfed.org/studentloandebt/ (accessed April 24, 2014).

National Association of Student Financial Aid Administrators. 2013. *Reimagining Financial Aid to Improve Student Access and Outcomes*. Washington, DC: National Association of Student Financial Aid Administrators.

National Center for Education Statistics. 2008. National Postsecondary Student Aid Study, Calculations from Data Lab PowerStats. http://nces.ed.gov/datalab/ (accessed April 24, 2014).

———. 2012. National Postsecondary Student Aid Study, Calculations from Data Lab PowerStats. http://nces.ed.gov/datalab/.

Porter, Nathan. 2013. "College Ranking Plan in the Works as Student Loan Crisis Poses a 'Threat to the America Dream'." *Washington Times*, September 20.

Shapiro, Thomas, Tatjana Meschede, and Sam Orsoro. 2013. "The Roots of the Widening Racial Wealth Gap: Explaining the Black-White Economic Divide." Research and policy brief. Waltham, MA: Institute on Assets and Social Policy, Brandeis University.

Simkovic, Michael. 2011. "Risk-Based Student Loans." *Washington and Lee Law Review* 70(1): 527.

U.S. Census Bureau. 2014. Historical Income Tables: People. Table P-20. Washington, DC: U.S. Census Bureau. http://www.census.gov/hhes/www/income/data/historical/people/ (accessed June 3, 2014).

U.S. Department of Education. 2013. "Comparison of FY 2011 2-Year Official Cohort Default Rates to Prior Two Official Calculations, Calculated July 27, 2013." Washington, DC: U.S. Department of Education. http://www2.ed.gov/offices/OSFAP/defaultmanagement/cdrschooltype2yr.pdf (accessed April 24, 2014).

3
Measuring Student Debt and Its Performance

Meta Brown
Andrew Haughwout
Donghoon Lee
Joelle Scally
Wilbert van der Klaauw
Federal Reserve Bank of New York

Studies continue to indicate that higher education is a worthwhile investment for individuals (Goldin and Katz 2008) and raises the productivity of the workforce as a whole (Moretti 2004). While the rising cost of postsecondary education has not eliminated this "college premium," it has raised new questions about how a growing number of students can make these investments (Archibald and Feldman 2010; Dynarski and Kreisman 2013). One solution to this problem is student loans, which have come to play an increasingly important role in financing higher education. Yet, in spite of its importance, educational debt is not well understood, partly because the currently outstanding stock of student debt includes loans made by both government and private lenders, and there exist few central repositories of information on the characteristics and performance of all student loans. In this chapter, we bring a new data set to bear on this important issue and present a brief analysis of the historical and current levels of student debt and how those debts are performing. We also briefly discuss the implications of student loans for borrowers and the economy.

DATA

Our analysis is based on data drawn from the Federal Reserve Bank of New York Consumer Credit Panel (CCP), which represents a 5 percent random sample of U.S. individuals with credit files as well as all of their household members.[1] In all, the entire data set includes anonymous credit files on more than 15 percent of the population, or nearly 40 million individuals. The panel includes information from the credit reports for those individuals for each quarter during the last 14 years, and we use data for this analysis through December 2012. While the CCP commences in 1999, irregularities in student loan reporting prior to 2004 suggest dropping the 1999–2003 data, and we thus begin our analysis in 2004.

The sampling exploits randomness in the last two digits of individuals' Social Security numbers.[2] The procedure ensures that the panel is dynamically updated in each quarter to reflect new entrants into credit markets. In addition, Equifax, the data provider, matches the primary individual's mailing address to all records in the data to capture information about other members of the primary individual's household. While these individuals are added to the overall CCP sample, in this chapter we focus on the 5 percent primary sample members.

The data set includes detailed data on individual student loans and individual mortgage loans, such as

- month and year the account was opened,
- current balance and payment status,
- origination balance,
- whether the account is individual or joint,
- scheduled monthly payment,
- narrative codes giving details of the account (such as the payment is deferred), and
- industry code indicating the type of the servicer.

In addition, the data set includes somewhat more aggregated data on individuals' other loans, including credit cards, and auto loans, such as

- total number of each type of account (for example, the total number of credit cards);
- credit limit on each type of account (for example, the combined credit limit on all credit cards); and
- total balance on each type of account in each status (for example, the total credit card balance that is current, 30-days delinquent, and so on).

More general information regarding the borrower on the credit report includes

- residential location of the borrower at the census block level and also zipcode level;
- birth year of the borrower;
- indicators for whether the individual has a foreclosure or bankruptcy within the last 24 months, and ever, on the report;
- indicators for whether the individual has any accounts in collection and the amount of collection; and
- a consumer credit score that is analogous to the well-known FICO score.

The data are completely anonymous and stripped of all personal identifiers. Unfortunately, while the vast majority of student loan servicers report to credit bureaus, these data do not distinguish between private and federal loans. Outside reports suggest that private loans account for approximately 15 percent of aggregate student debt. Although a number of reports have pointed to differences in the growth, size, and performance of private and federal loans, this limitation of our data will require a focus on the total student debt burden.

GROWTH OF STUDENT DEBT

Between 2004 and 2012, total student debt in the United States nearly tripled, from $364 billion in 2004 to $966 billion in 2012 (see Figure 3.1). Expressed in annual terms, this means student debt

Figure 3.1 Total Student Loan Balances, by Age Group

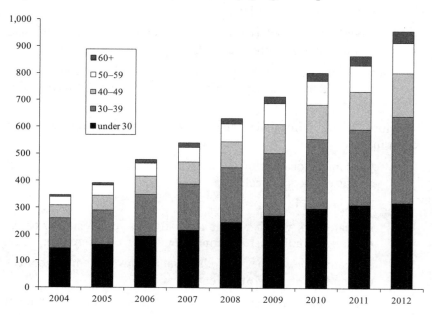

SOURCE: Federal Reserve Bank of New York Consumer Credit Panel/Equifax.

increased by an average of 14 percent per year. As of the end of 2012, about two-thirds of this debt is owed by borrowers under the age of 40, with about one-third of the total being owed by borrowers under the age of 30. Americans older than 40 also have student debt, but their share is much smaller, with 17 percent held by borrowers in their 40s, 12 percent held by borrowers in their 50s, and the remainder held by borrowers 60 and older.

Among the various types of household debt, student debt is unique. While balances on all other forms of household debt—including mortgages, credit cards, auto loans, and home equity lines of credit—declined during and after the Great Recession, student debt has steadily risen, as shown in Figure 3.2 (see Brown et al. [2013] for a discussion of dynamics of other kinds of household debts during the 2000s). In 2010, student debt surpassed credit cards to become the second-largest form of household debt after mortgages, whereas prior to 2008, the student debt was the smallest of household debts.

Figure 3.2 Nonmortgage Balances Reported on Consumer Credit Reports

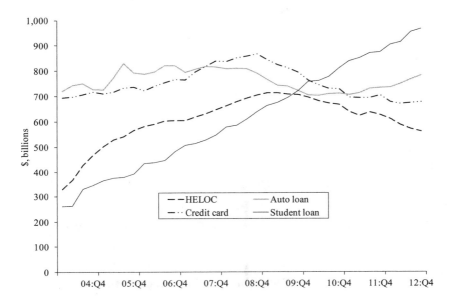

SOURCE: Federal Reserve Bank of New York Consumer Credit Panel/Equifax.

What accounts for the rapid increase of the aggregate student debt in this period? Our research shows that increases in number of borrowers and the average debt per person equally contributed to the growth of total student debt. Between 2004 and 2012, the number of borrowers increased by 70 percent from 23 million borrowers to 39 million (see Figure 3.3). In the same period, average debt per borrower also increased by 70 percent, from about $15,000 to $25,000.

Note, however, that there is actually a great variation in balances among borrowers, as shown in Figure 3.4. Of the 39 million borrowers, about 40 percent have balances of less than $10,000. Approximately another 30 percent owe between $10,000 and $25,000. Only 3.7 percent of borrowers have balances of more than $100,000, with 0.6 percent, or roughly 230,000 borrowers nationwide, having more than $200,000 of debt.

With respect to the rise in the number of borrowers, Figure 3.5 shows that a steadily increasing share of younger people are taking out

Figure 3.3 Number of Borrowers and Average Balances Per Borrower

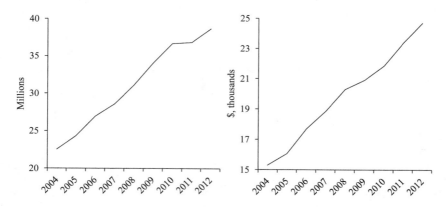

SOURCE: Federal Reserve Bank of New York Consumer Credit Panel/Equifax.

Figure 3.4 Distribution of Student Loan Balances in Q4 2012

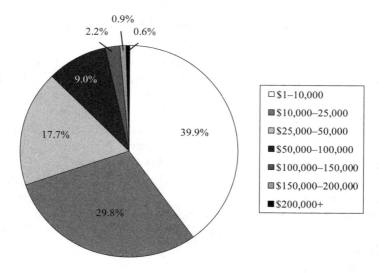

SOURCE: Federal Reserve Bank of New York Consumer Credit Panel/Equifax.

Figure 3.5 Percentage of 25-Year-Olds with Student Debt

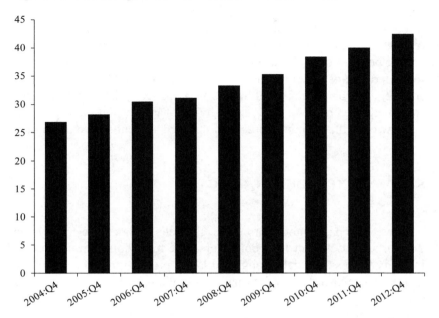

SOURCE: Federal Reserve Bank of New York Consumer Credit Panel/Equifax.

student loans: in 2004, only about 27 percent of 25-year-olds had student debt, while eight years later, in 2012, the proportion of 25-year-olds with student debt increased to about 43 percent.

There are several explanations for these increases. First, more people are attending college, adding to the number of borrowers (National Center for Education Statistics 2013). Second, students are staying in college longer and attending graduate school in greater numbers, and loans to finance graduate study have become more readily available (Gonzales, Allum, and Sowell 2013). Third, it has become cheaper for parents to take out student loans to help finance their children's education.[3] Fourth, the cost of a college education has continued to grow sharply during the period (College Board 2013).

If student borrowers complete their education and quickly start repaying their debt, then the increase in the number of borrowers and in the total amount of student debt would in part be offset by the outflow.

However, as we will discuss in the next section, the repayment rate on student loans is low. This is because many borrowers delay payments through continuing education, deferrals, forbearance, and income-based repayment plans. Some borrowers have difficulty making required payments, become delinquent on their debt, and ultimately default, which for federal loans is defined as falling 270 days behind on payments. In addition, discharging student debt is very difficult; the delinquent debt stays with the borrower, and the high rate of inflow and the low rate of outflow contribute to the increase in the total student debt outstanding.

STUDENT LOAN DELINQUENCY

Over the past eight years there has been an increase in payment difficulties for student loan borrowers. The most common measure of inability to meet the debt obligation is the proportion of borrowers 90 days or more past due on their payments. We refer to this as the "measured delinquency rate."

As of the fourth quarter of 2012, about 17 percent, or 6.7 million borrowers, were 90 days or more delinquent on their student loan payments; see the left panel of Figure 3.6. The measured delinquency rate is higher among borrowers aged 30–49 than it is among younger or older borrowers, which is unexpected since typically younger borrowers have higher delinquency rates. There was a strongly increasing trend in delinquency between 2004 and 2012 among all age groups, with measured delinquency rising from an overall rate of less than 10 percent in 2004 to 17 percent in 2012.

The measured delinquency rate on student debt is currently the highest of any consumer debt product, although for most of the last decade credit card delinquency was even higher.[4] Nonetheless, the measured delinquency rate is somewhat misleading, and the *effective* delinquency rate on student debt (as we define below) is even higher. As noted above, in 2012 the measured delinquency rate among the 39 million borrowers was 17 percent. But many of the remaining 83 percent in fact were not paying down their loan balances. While 39 percent did reduce their balance from the previous quarter by at least one dollar, 14 percent of borrowers had the same balance as the previous quarter.

Figure 3.6 Delinquency Rates for Borrowers Overall and for Those in Repayment (%)

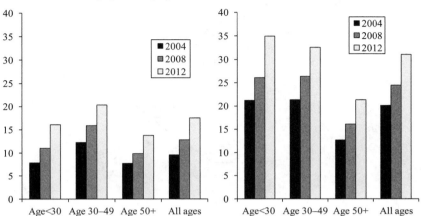

SOURCE: Federal Reserve Bank of New York Consumer Credit Panel/Equifax.

A full 30 percent of borrowers actually saw an increase in their balance. In other words, 44 percent of borrowers were neither delinquent nor paying down their loans.

Those borrowers whose balances did not decline are likely not yet in the repayment cycle, meaning that they were either still in school, in deferral, or in a forbearance period delaying their regular payments. This group may also include some borrowers who participate in income-based repayment plans and make only small payments, which are often insufficient to cover the accumulated interest. In order to have a more accurate picture of the delinquency rate, we calculate the "effective delinquency rate" by excluding this 44 percent of borrowers not in repayment; the result is shown in the right-hand panel of Figure 3.6. This effective delinquency rate is nearly double the measured delinquency rate, with almost one-third of borrowers in repayment being delinquent on their debt. Interestingly, borrowers under 30, who previously appeared to have a lower measured delinquency rate than the 30–49 age group, are now shown to have the highest effective delinquency rate. The fact that fewer of these younger borrowers are in the repayment cycle masks high effective delinquency rates among those who are.

Figure 3.7 Quarterly Transition Rate into Delinquency, Borrowers in Repayment

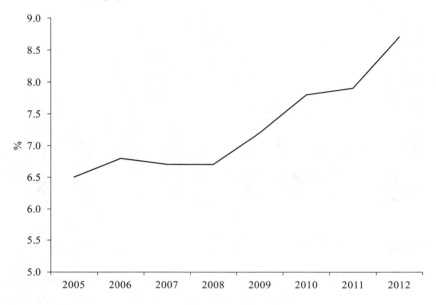

SOURCE: Federal Reserve Bank of New York Consumer Credit Panel/Equifax.

It is important to note that because of the unique character of student debt, an increasing delinquency rate defined either way does not necessarily imply that a greater percentage of new borrowers are falling behind on repayment. Borrowers who became delinquent in the past and remain so are included in the delinquency rate. Some may also default, which, again, is defined as being more than 270 days past due in the case of federal loans. Because student debt is not generally dischargeable, even in bankruptcy, the delinquency rate may continue to increase even when the percentage of borrowers becoming newly delinquent remains constant.

We address this issue in Figure 3.7, which depicts the proportion of borrowers in repayment who became newly delinquent on a quarterly basis. Here we see that in 2005 about 6 percent of nondelinquent borrowers in repayment transitioned into delinquency each quarter, on average. By 2012, that rate had increased to 9 percent. This confirms that indeed there was an increasing trend of borrowers becoming newly delinquent over time.

STUDENT DEBT'S ROLE ON THE HOUSEHOLD BALANCE SHEET

An advantage of our data is that they allow us to look at all the liabilities on each individual's balance sheet and to put educational debt and delinquencies into the broader context of household debt. In this section, we refer to non–student loan debt as "other debt."

Figure 3.8 reports on other debts for borrowers aged 25–30 in 2005 (left panel) and 2012 (right), by their levels of student debt outstanding. In 2005, the average amount of other debt held by student loan

Figure 3.8 Average Non–Student Loan Balances, Borrowers Aged 25–30

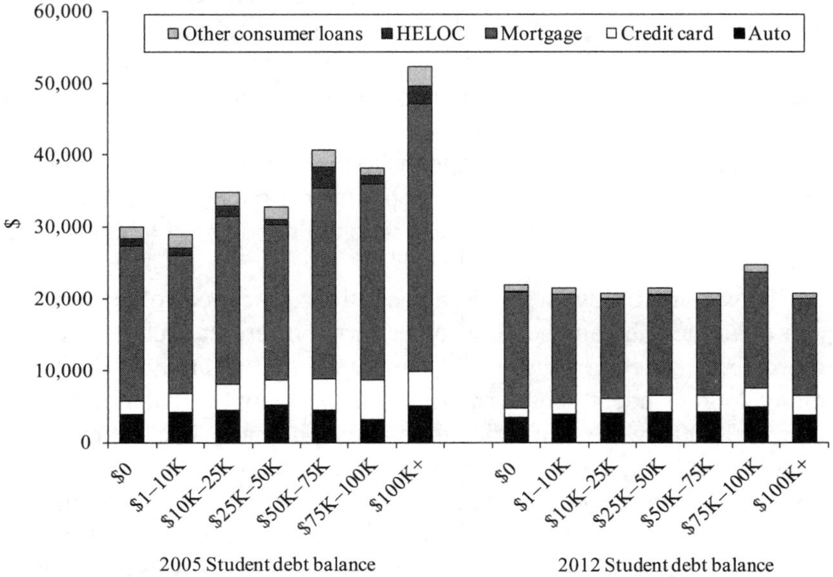

SOURCE: Federal Reserve Bank of New York Consumer Credit Panel/Equifax.

borrowers aged 25–30 exceeded student loan debt, which was $18,200. Interestingly, there was a positive association between student debt and other debt, such as mortgages, credit cards, and auto loans. Borrowers with higher student loan balances used to have more other debt compared to those with lower or no student debt. After all, student debt has historically been an indicator that the borrower has some level of higher education and thus a higher permanent income, so it is perhaps unsurprising to see this reflected in the balances on other debts.

Following the general trend of household deleveraging outside of student debt in the aftermath of the financial crisis (Brown et al. 2013), other debt balances declined for all borrowers between 2005 and 2012. But they declined much more for borrowers with student loans, so that student loan borrowers now have lower other debt at around $20,000, on average. Meanwhile, the average student debt among student loan borrowers increased to $26,500 for those who were between 25 and 30 in 2012. The decline in other debt was especially visible among those with high levels of student debt. As a result, the previous positive association between student and other debts has disappeared.

The shift we observe is an outcome of the interplay between supply and demand factors, and it is difficult to disentangle them. Borrowers with higher student loan balances may have become less confident about their future labor market and income prospects and therefore reduced their demand for credit. On the other hand, lenders may have become more conservative in supplying loans to high-balance student loan borrowers. Likely, both demand and supply factors played a significant role in the sharp reduction in the accumulation of other debt by high student loan borrowers.

Brown and Caldwell (2013) discuss the implications of student debt and delinquencies on access to other forms of credit such as auto and mortgage financing. Figure 3.9 complements that analysis. In 2005, many young student debt borrowers, even those with a balance of more than $100,000, were able to finance a home purchase. The fact that more of these high student loan borrowers did so than those with lower or no student loan balances most likely reflects differences in income and higher postgraduate degree attainments (including holders of professional degrees with good labor market prospects). However, the large homeownership gap between high, low, and no student loan borrowers has since declined considerably.

Figure 3.9 Mortgages among Student Loan Borrowers Aged 25–30

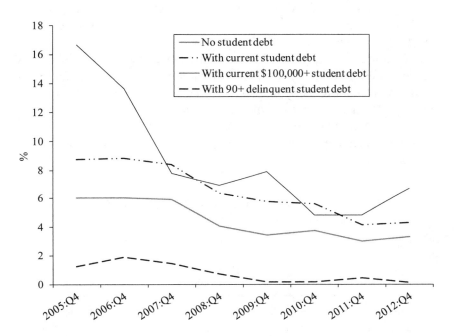

SOURCE: Federal Reserve Bank of New York Consumer Credit Panel/Equifax.

Again, it is difficult to distinguish demand and supply factors, but it appears likely that the sharp decline in mortgage originations among the high student debt borrowers in part reflects a tightening of mortgage eligibility, for example, through maximum debt to income ratio requirements. Brown and Caldwell (2013) provide further evidence of a decline in access to credit by student loan borrowers, showing that while student loan borrowers aged 25 (or 30) used to have average credit scores comparable to those without student debt, by 2012 they had considerably lower average credit scores. This may be attributable in part to the high student debt delinquency rate.

Delinquent student loan borrowers have (perhaps not surprisingly) always been much less likely—or able—to borrow for a home purchase. There are now many more delinquent borrowers than in 2005. In light of the increasing student debt burden and the growth in the delinquency rate, especially among young borrowers, student debt is likely to have an important influence on borrowers' use of other types of credit, particularly mortgage credit.

Figure 3.10 addresses the association between delinquencies on student debt and other debt. Not surprisingly, delinquent student loan borrowers are more likely to also be delinquent on other debts. They are delinquent on 17 percent of their auto loan balances, on 35 percent of their credit card balances, and on 28 percent of their mortgage balances, and these rates are much higher compared to those with no delinquent student debt.

Figure 3.10 Student Loan and Other Debt Delinquency, 25–30-Year-Olds, 2012:Q4

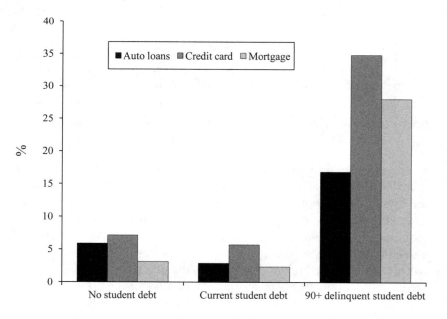

SOURCE: Federal Reserve Bank of New York Consumer Credit Panel/Equifax.

CONCLUSION

Higher education is an important investment among younger individuals to equip them for better job prospects and higher income potential, but over the last several years it has been accompanied by a growing student debt burden. Total student loan balances almost tripled between 2004 and 2012, owing to increasing numbers of borrowers and higher balances per borrower; educational debt is now the second-largest liability on household balance sheets, after mortgages. Nearly one-third of the borrowers in repayment are delinquent on student debt, a fact that is masked by the large numbers of borrowers who are in either deferment or grace periods. While we do not establish causality, it appears that the higher burden of student loans and the associated high delinquency rate negatively affect borrowers' home purchases, other debt payments, and access to credit.

Notes

The views presented here are those of the author and do not necessarily reflect those of the Federal Reserve Bank of New York or the Federal Reserve System. The authors are grateful to Brian Cadena and Raven Molloy for helpful comments.

1. See Avery, Calen, and Canner (2003) for a detailed discussion of the contents, sources, and quality of credit report data.
2. See Lee and van der Klaauw (2010) for further details about the sample design and content of the Federal Reserve Bank of New York Consumer Credit Panel.
3. "Student Loans," accessed February 8, 2014, http://www.finaid.org/loans/parent loan.phtml.
4. See the Federal Reserve Bank of New York's quarterly report on household debt and credit, where delinquency rates are reported as a percentage of outstanding balances rather than as a percentage of borrowers. Available at http://www.new yorkfed.org/microeconomics/data.html (accessed February 10, 2014).

References

Archibald, Robert B., and David H. Feldman. 2010. *Why Does College Cost So Much?* New York: Oxford University Press.

Avery, Robert B., Paul S. Calem, and Glenn B. Canner. 2003. "An Overview of Consumer Data and Credit Reporting." *Federal Reserve Bulletin.* February: 47–73.

Brown, Meta, Andrew Haughwout, Donghoon Lee, and Wilbert van der Klaauw. 2013. "The Financial Crisis at the Kitchen Table: Trends in Household Debt and Credit." *Current Issues in Economics and Finance* 19(2): 1–10.

College Board. 2013. *Trends in College Pricing.* New York: College Board. https://trends.collegeboard.org/sites/default/files/college-pricing-2013-full-report.pdf (accessed May 6, 2014).

Dynarski, Susan, and Daniel Kreisman. 2013. "Loans for Educational Opportunity: Making Borrowing Work for Today's Students." The Hamilton Project Discussion Paper 2013-05. Washington, DC: The Hamilton Project, Brookings Institution.

Goldin, Claudia Dale, and Lawrence F. Katz. 2008. *The Race between Education and Technology.* Cambridge, MA: Harvard University Press.

Gonzales, Leila, Jeffrey R. Allum, and Robert S. Sowell. 2013. *Graduate Enrollment and Degrees: 2002 to 2012.* Washington, DC: Council of Graduate Schools. http://www.cgsnet.org/ckfinder/userfiles/files/GEDReport_2012.pdf (accessed May 6, 2014).

Lee, Donghoon, and Wilbert van der Klaauw. 2010. "An Introduction to the FRBNY Consumer Credit Panel." FRBNY Staff Reports No. 479. New York: Federal Reserve Bank of New York.

Moretti, Enrico. 2004. "Estimating the Social Return to Higher Education: Evidence from Longitudinal and Repeated Cross-Sectional Data." *Journal of Econometrics* 121(1): 175–212.

National Center for Education Statistics. 2013. *Digest of Education Statistics,* (NCES 2014-015), Chapter 3. Washington, DC: National Center for Education Statistics.

4
The Distribution of College Graduate Debt, 1990–2008

A Decomposition Approach

Brad Hershbein
Kevin M. Hollenbeck
W.E. Upjohn Institute for Employment Research

Within the past 21 months, there have been almost as many major news articles on the topic of student debt as there were in the preceding 21 years.[1] Headlines have trumpeted the stories of recent graduates with six-figure debt levels and aggregate loan balances exceeding $1 trillion.[2] A growing number of policy organizations and Web sites have begun to focus and compile information on student debt.[3] And, perhaps in response, President Obama announced in August of 2013 a major initiative to address rising college costs.[4] Despite this increased attention on debt writ large, surprisingly little is known about how student debt has changed for different types of students or what factors can explain it.

Yet, understanding the patterns and factors underlying debt increase is paramount, both for ensuring that students and their families have a realistic, well-informed picture of college finance, and for guiding policymakers toward debt-amelioration strategies for those who need them most. Considerable focus is spent on average debt levels because these are easy to update frequently, but this may be misguided. The distribution of debt is so diffuse, as we show, that changes in the mean are not informative for most students. For example, an increase in borrowing among the top 10 percent of borrowers will increase the mean and total accumulated debt—numbers commonly reported—but leave debt levels for 90 percent of students unchanged. This may seem a convenient hypothetical, but it actually closely resembles how debt evolved for college graduates between 2000 and 2008. In short, factors that influence debt for the median borrower may be quite different from those that influence debt for borrowers in the highest decile. The effectiveness of policy proposals meant to address "rising student debt" rests on how they recognize these phenomena.

In this chapter, we use the National Postsecondary Student Aid Study (NPSAS) to investigate the growing student debt of college graduates—those earning a bachelor's degree. Our focus on this segment of students is not because other groups (graduate students, students with subbaccalaureate degrees, students leaving without any credential) have not experienced rising debt—they have—or because they are unimportant. Rather, the choice is motivated by the recent media interest in college graduates and the desire to limit the analysis to a manageable scale.[5] The data cover the period between 1990 and 2008, and our analysis examines the entire distribution of borrowing among graduates. In addition to documenting how the distribution has changed over time, for all graduates and subgroups, we employ statistical decompositions to apportion the changes by various observable characteristics, such as demographics, attendance patterns, incomes, and costs. Notably, the decompositions allow the role of observable factors to vary at different points of the distribution.

In broad terms, our major findings are that debt profiles increased much more in the 1990s than in the 2000s, with the largest part of this increase occurring in the latter part of the decade. The growth occurred throughout the distribution. Between 2000 and 2008, debt increases were concentrated almost entirely in the top quartile of the distribution and at private institutions, and they stemmed largely from the expansion of private borrowing. About one-third of the overall increase in debt at graduation between 1990 and 2008 is explained by observable characteristics of the students and the schools they attend. Interestingly, we find that observables explain more of the increase at the extensive margin (whether a student ever borrowed) and around the median than they do near the top of the distribution. Of the explained share, roughly half can be attributed to college costs alone, although this still implies that costs account for a small fraction of the total increase in borrowing.

When we look at intermediate time intervals, observables explain most of the increase in borrowing—between 50 and 100 percent, or more—from 1990 to 1996 and 2000 to 2008. While cost structure plays an important role, so do other factors, and again there is a greater role for unexplained factors in the upper tail of the distribution. In contrast, observables explain practically none of the debt increase between 1996 and 2000, and this is true throughout the entire distribution.

We investigate several possibilities that might show up as "unexplained" factors in driving debt increases in the upper tail and throughout the distribution in the late 1990s, including movement from informal to formal loans, redistribution of debt from parents to students, variation in interest rates, increases in federal borrowing limits, the introduction of unsubsidized loans (which are not means tested), and the growing market for private loans. While the first four of these appear to be unimportant, we find suggestive evidence that the latter two may play a prominent role.

We note a number of caveats to our analyses. First, we are not able at this time to examine the distributional changes, if any, that occurred as a result of the Great Recession starting in December 2007.[6] As documented by the College Board (2012a), aggregate borrowing increased significantly during and after this recession. A second caveat is that the NPSAS data contain information only on current and graduating students. As such, they do not contain data on postgraduation labor market experiences or repayment information, and our chapter cannot consider these important outcomes. Third, while the data are quite rich in detail, they do not contain information on previous institutions attended (and the net costs thereof), so differences across students (and over time) in transfer behavior are not captured in the analysis. Finally, the data do not fully document alternative loan sources, including informal loans from friends and family or borrowing against existing assets. Nonetheless, our chapter is the first to investigate distributional changes in borrowing over time and link these to changing characteristics of student attendance.

The chapter is organized as follows. The next section discusses the data source and presents descriptive statistics and distributions from it. We then review the decomposition methods that are used to explain the reasons behind borrowing trends. The results of those decompositions are then presented, followed by a discussion of possible factors that could account for the unexplained portion of the decompositions. Finally, we offer concluding remarks. Two appendices to the chapter describe the data processing in detail and provide an overview of the market for student borrowing, including the structure of terms and borrowing limits, from approximately 1980 through today.

THE NPSAS AND DESCRIPTIVE STATISTICS

The NPSAS is an approximately quadrennial survey of students attending Title IV institutions (those eligible for federal aid) that is conducted by the National Center for Education Statistics. The nationally representative cross-sectional survey is designed specifically to gather information on how different students pay for higher education.[7] It provides student-level information on financial aid provided by the federal government, the states, postsecondary institutions, employers, and private agencies, along with student demographics and enrollment characteristics. The restricted-use version we employ has incredibly rich detail, including administrative data on student financial aid programs merged from both the Free Application for Federal Student Aid and the National Student Loan Data System, the central database for all federal loans. Extensive data about family circumstances, demographics, education and work experiences, and student expectations are collected from students through an interview.

The survey waves are reasonably consistent over time, which is important for our analyses of the debt burdens of graduating seniors from five waves: 1990, 1996, 2000, 2004, and 2008 (the most recent available).[8] The richness of the data is important because our goals are to understand why student debt is growing and for whom. Having cross-sections with large sample sizes and spanning almost two decades allows us to examine the growth in student debt over the entire distribution of college graduates. This allows far more nuanced analyses than are possible by examining means or population totals. (More information about the NPSAS and how we process the data for analysis can be found in Appendix 4A.)

DESCRIPTIVE MEASURES

Table 4.1 summarizes changes in the distribution of student borrowing at graduation. There were substantial increases over the last two decades in both the rate of borrowing for bachelor's degree earners and in the real levels of borrowing. Between 1990 and 2008, the fraction of graduates who borrowed increased by 13 percentage points, from about 55 percent to over 68 percent, with the sharpest increase occurring between 1996 and 2000.

The next panel of the table lists quantiles of borrowing for all graduates, including those who did not borrow at all, in constant dollars. Mean levels have more than doubled over the 18-year horizon, with more than $5,000 of the total $10,000 increase coming between the classes of 1996 and 2000. Since 2000, however, average debt has increased more modestly. This trend of rapid debt increase over the 1990s and milder increases over the 2000s is apparent through at least the 75th percentile. Only in the extreme right tail, above the 95th percentile, has borrowing continued to grow as quickly as it did in the 1990s.

The last panel shows that, among borrowers, the median level of borrowing more than doubled between 1990 and 2000, from about $10,400 to just under $22,000. However, that level remained stable between 2000 and 2008. On the other hand, the mean level of borrowing increased between 2000 and 2008 as the individuals in the upper tail of the borrowing distribution significantly increased their levels of borrowing. Even so, while there have been media suggestions of individuals graduating with six-figure levels of debt, these data suggest that such instances are quite rare, as the 99th percentile of borrowers did not reach that level of borrowing in any of the waves (see also Kantrowitz [2012]).

Table 4.1 thus illustrates two facts that are not well known in either the academic or popular press. First, debt at graduation increased much faster between 1990 and 2000 than it did during 2000 and 2008, and this was true throughout the distribution. Second, the increase in borrowing in the later period was entirely concentrated in the top quartile; the bottom 75 percent of graduates of the class of 2008 had roughly the same debt as the classes of 2000 and 2004. These facts can perhaps be more directly seen in Figure 4.1, which displays the cumulative bor-

Table 4.1 Cumulative Borrowing Statistics from NPSAS, by Wave

	1990	1996	2000	2004	2008
Ever borrow	0.545	0.526	0.636	0.656	0.682
Total borrowing ($000s)					
Mean	7.2	9.2	14.4	14.8	17.2
25th	0.0	0.0	0.0	0.0	0.0
Median	1.9	2.5	10.9	11.6	13.1
75th	11.4	17.7	24.5	23.8	26.6
90th	20.8	25.4	34.8	36.4	42.5
95th	27.3	30.8	42.5	47.7	52.1
99th	48.1	44.9	60.6	65.6	85.0
Total borrowing among borrowers ($000s)					
Mean	13.2	17.6	22.6	22.6	25.2
10th	2.4	5.4	5.6	6.0	5.9
25th	4.8	9.7	12.9	11.9	12.4
Median	10.4	17.0	21.8	20.4	21.3
75th	18.0	23.6	29.3	29.8	33.1
90th	25.7	30.2	38.8	42.6	47.8
95th	32.1	35.1	49.0	51.6	56.0
99th	64.2	51.6	64.5	72.7	90.3

NOTE: Statistics use population weights (of late 2013 vintage) and are for domestic students in the year indicated. Monetary amounts are inflated to year 2012 dollars using the personal consumption expenditures (PCE) index from the Bureau of Economic Analysis. Borrowing is from all sources except friends and family and excludes loans taken out by parents (PLUS Loans).
SOURCE: NPSAS, selected years.

rowing distributions of graduates from each wave of the NPSAS in constant dollars. The remainder of this chapter seeks to gain understanding of the factors that shifted the borrowing distribution so dramatically between 1990 and 2000, and the factors that shifted the upper tail of the distribution between 2000 and 2008.

Our first analysis is entirely descriptive and is meant to isolate changes in debt among certain subgroups. We examine four of these: 1) dependent versus independent students; 2) public versus private, not-for-profit institutions; 3) graduates who took four or fewer years to degree versus those who took five or more years; and, 4) for dependent students, those whose family income is above versus below the

Figure 4.1 Cumulative Borrowing Distribution among College Graduates

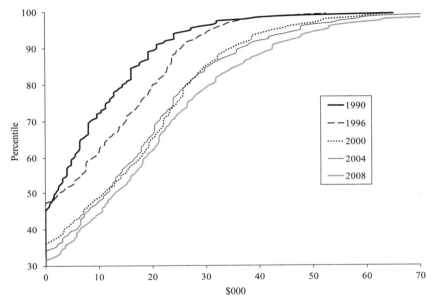

NOTE: All calculations use sample weights, are in constant (year 2012) dollars, and include student-level borrowing from all sources except informal loans from friends and family.
SOURCE: NPSAS, selected years.

median.[9] Figure 4.2 displays the cumulative borrowing distributions for dependent and independent students. As would be expected, the proportion of dependent students with loans is smaller than the proportion of independent students with loans, and the levels of borrowing are much smaller for dependent students in all years of the data. While the distributions for dependent students are qualitatively quite similar to the overall distributions (Figure 4.1), the distributions for independent students show a relatively smooth, monotonically increasing pattern over time. That is, each wave's distribution (first-order) stochastically dominates the preceding wave, which is not at all true for dependent students, whose debt profile in 2004 is smaller than in 2000 for the middle segment of the distribution. Nonetheless, both graphs show substantially larger increases in debt over the 1990s than over the 2000s.

Figure 4.2 Cumulative Borrowing Distribution among College Graduate Subgroups, Dependency

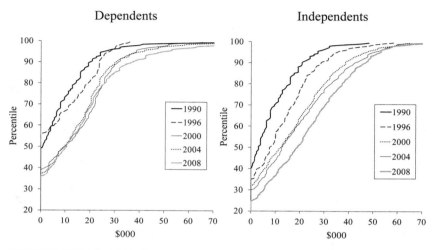

SOURCE: NPSAS, selected years.

Figure 4.3 shows the comparison between public schools and private, not-for-profits. It is not surprising that both the propensity to ever borrow and borrowing levels are greater in all time periods at the latter institutions. What is less well known is the remarkable similarity in the debt profiles at publics across the 2000, 2004, and 2008 waves. Aside from a slight increase between 2004 and 2008 in the upper tail, balanced by a modest decrease between 2000 and 2004 in the middle, the distributions almost lie on top of one another. Although much has been made of the decline in state-level appropriations to public universities during the Great Recession (Lewin 2013), these appropriations had actually fallen by about 15 percent per full-time equivalent student between 2000 and 2004, and they still remained below 2000 levels at the start of the recession (College Board 2012b, Figure 12B; Quinterno and Orozco 2012, Figure 6). Despite these reductions (and concomitant tuition increases), debt of graduating students changed little, especially relative to the large increases over the 1990s. On the other hand, while debt also increased little over the 2000s for the bottom 60 percent at privates, it increased substantially for the top 40 percent, with the size of increase rising with the distribution quantile. Above the 80th percen-

Figure 4.3 Cumulative Borrowing Distribution among College Graduate Subgroups, Sector

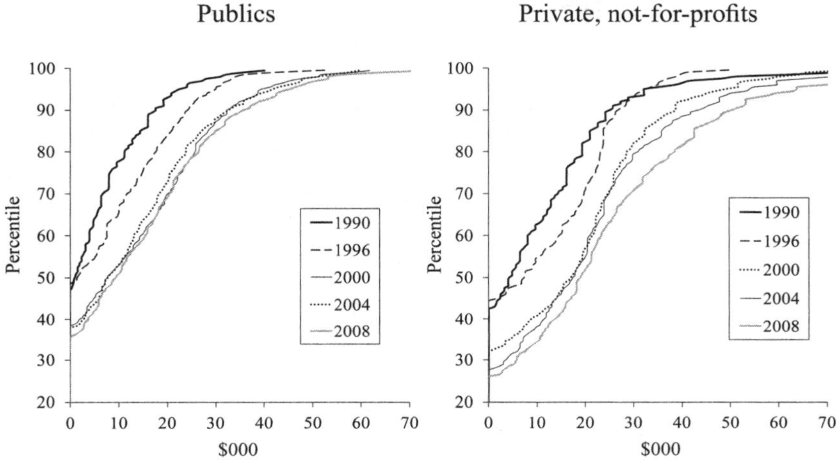

Publics   Private, not-for-profits

SOURCE: NPSAS, selected years.

tile, the debt increase between 2000 and 2008 was comparable to that between 1990 and 2000.

Turning to Figure 4.4, we look at debt distributions by time to degree, although data limitations restrict the analysis to the 1996 and later waves. Students who take longer to finish accumulate more debt, almost mechanically, and as in the previous groups, debt increases faster between 1996 and 2000 than it does over the following eight years. However, for students who graduate on time, debt actually *fell* between 2000 and 2008 through the 80th percentile while rising, often considerably, above that quantile. Among the students who took longer, debt increased modestly but monotonically throughout the distribution.

Finally, we compare dependent bachelor's degree recipients by family income in Figure 4.5. In general, borrowing levels are not that dissimilar across the income groups; although students from wealthier families have more resources, they also tend to graduate from more expensive schools. The standard pattern of fast debt increases during the 1990s is present here, but the most striking trend is that this increase is mostly concentrated between 1990 and 1996 for the lower-income group and (more than) entirely concentrated between 1996 and 2000

Figure 4.4 Cumulative Borrowing Distribution among College Graduate Subgroups, Time to Degree

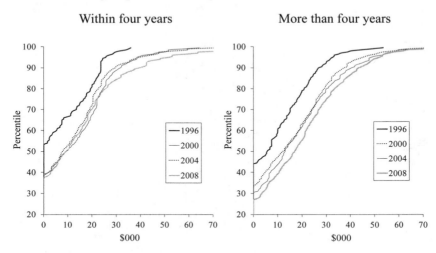

SOURCE: NPSAS, selected years.

Figure 4.5 Cumulative Borrowing Distribution among College Graduate Subgroups, Income of Dependents

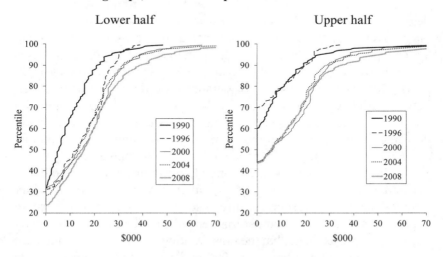

SOURCE: NPSAS, selected years.

for the upper-income group. A related point is that for the latter time period the borrowing rate increased only mildly for the poorer students; however, it increased by 25 percentage points, from 30 percent to 55 percent, for wealthier students. Taken together, these trends imply that changing factors between 1996 and 2000 had a disproportionate impact on student borrowers whose family incomes were above the median and affected borrowing at all levels, not just the top.

A few themes from these comparisons stand out. First, the large increase in debt that occurred throughout the distribution between 1990 and 2000 (Figure 4.1) is common to all the subgroups examined, suggesting that behavioral or policy differences, and not composition effects, are more likely to be the prime suspect. Second, "traditional" graduates (dependents who finish on time) experienced debt increases over the 2000s only in the top portion of the distribution, while "nontraditional" students' debt increases were more uniform.

The next section describes the decomposition methods we employ to systematically unpack changes in the empirical distributions.

DECOMPOSITION TECHNIQUES

To examine the factors behind increases in borrowing, we employ three different econometric decomposition techniques: 1) Oaxaca-Blinder, 2) semiparametric reweighting, and 3) recentered influence functions. While the first of these techniques is common in the literature, it is not suitable for decomposing statistics other than the mean. The second and third techniques, while not as well known, allow for the decomposition of the entire distribution of borrowing. Below we briefly describe each of these techniques, including strengths and weaknesses.

Oaxaca-Blinder

This technique, independently published by Oaxaca (1973) and Blinder (1973), linearly decomposes the average difference in outcomes across groups into differences in observable characteristics and differences in structural factors. Formally, let $Y_i = X_i \beta_i + \varepsilon_i$ for $i = A,B$. Then

(4.1) $E[Y_B - Y_A] = \{E[X_B] - E[X_A]\}\beta^* + \{E[X_B](\beta_B - \beta^*)$
$+ E[X_A](\beta^* - \beta_A)\}.$

The left-hand term represents the average difference between groups A and B. The first term in braces on the right shows the difference in average observables between the groups, multiplied by a common or reference coefficient vector, β. Since X_i is observable for both groups, this component is considered to be what is "explained" by observables. The second term in braces is the difference between the group-specific coefficient vector and the reference coefficient vector, scaled by the observables, for both groups. Since deviations from the reference coefficient are generally not known, this component is considered to be structural or "unexplained."[10] It is common in many economic applications (notably, wage discrimination) to set the reference coefficient β^* to the estimates of either β_B or β_A. In this case, one of the terms in the second pair of braces drops out, and the "unexplained" portion is the (scaled) deviation of one group's estimated coefficient vector from the other's.[11] In other cases, the reference coefficient is set to a weighted average of β_A and β_B, in which the weights depend on the application (see Jann [2008] for an overview).

In practice, Oaxaca-Blinder (O-B) decomposition is straightforward to implement. Ordinary least squares (OLS) regressions are performed on groups A and B, separately, and Equation (4.1) is calculated using estimates of β_A and β_B from these regressions. The technique thus permits detailed decompositions that allow the contribution from each element of X_i (or β) to be estimated, as well as their sum. It is worth noting, however, that the ε_i terms cancel out as a result of the expectations operator (and the standard OLS assumptions). For this reason, O-B decomposition is valid only for the conditional mean function.

In this chapter, we use the O-B decomposition to investigate changes in the extensive margin of having ever borrowed at the time of college graduation as well as mean borrowing levels. Our choice of reference coefficients is the set from the earlier time period in the comparison, although we consider the sensitivity of our results to other sets of base coefficients.

Semiparametric Reweighting

Proposed by DiNardo, Fortin, and Lemieux (1996) in their analysis of changes in the wage distribution, this technique reweights observations from one group so that the joint distributions of the X_i are similar for both groups. By dealing with the joint distributions of the X_i, this reweighting technique overcomes the linearity restriction of O-B and allows the construction of a counterfactual distribution, not just the counterfactual mean. Thus, quantiles and other distributional statistics such as variances or Gini coefficients can be compared.[12]

Semiparametric reweighting is implemented by performing a logit or probit regression on the pooled sample, with the dependent variable being equal to one if an observation is in group A and equal to zero if it is in group B.[13] The right-hand-side variables include all the elements of X, and in some cases interaction terms as well. Fitted values, $\hat{p}$, from this regression are used to construct propensity weights, $\frac{\hat{p}}{1-\hat{p}}$, for group B; weights for group A are set equal to one. If data are sample weighted, the propensity weights can be multiplied by the sampling weights to create composite weights. Distributional statistics for the two groups can be compared by using these composite weights for each group.

We employ this approach to compare the cumulative distributions of borrowing across time periods while controlling for the joint distribution of observables. However, a shortcoming of the reweighting is that it does not easily allow attribution to a specific (marginal) component of X. While it is possible to perform the reweighting multiple times, leaving out one element of X each time, to isolate the contribution of that particular X element on the borrowing distribution, doing so is somewhat cumbersome and tedious for a nontrivially dimensioned vector of X. This drawback motivates the third decomposition technique.

Recentered Influence Functions

This technique, suggested by Firpo, Fortin, and Lemieux (2009), is an extension of O-B for statistics beyond the mean, particularly unconditional quantiles. For any quantile q, define the recentered influence function (RIF) as

$$(4.2) \quad RIF_q = Y_q + \frac{q}{f(Y_q)} - \frac{1}{f(Y_q)} \times \mathbf{1}(Y \leq Y_q),$$

where Y_q is the value of Y at quantile q, $f(Y_q)$ is the density of Y at q and needs to be estimated, and $\mathbf{1}(Y \leq Y_q)$ is an indicator function that equals one if, for a given observation, Y is less than or equal to Y_q and zero otherwise. Note that RIF_q takes on only two values determined by whether Y exceeds Y_q. The RIF has the interesting property that $E[RIF_q]$ = Y_q.[14] Firpo, Fortin, and Lemieux (2009) show that performing O-B on the RIF can recover decompositions at the unconditional quantiles of Y.

While it is easy to estimate Y_q in a sample, it is more challenging to estimate $f(Y_q)$. The density is commonly estimated using kernel density methods, and these are somewhat sensitive to bandwidth choices, particularly for distributions, like those for cumulative borrowing, that are not unimodal and roughly symmetric. On the other hand, the similarity to O-B allows the marginal contribution of specific elements of X to be analyzed much more easily than in the case of semiparametric reweighting.

The Observables

The usefulness of each of the decomposition methods depends on the set of observed variables. Fortunately, the NPSAS data are especially rich. In addition to core demographics such as age, dependency status, sex, ethnicity, and marital status, the set of controls include parents' education, the student's state of permanent residence, the region of the school, whether the student is in state, whether attendance is full or part time and full or part year, the type of institution attended, a set of majors, and whether the student changed schools during the last year.[15] In addition to these variables, all of which are binary or categorical, we include a quartic in expected family contribution (EFC) interacted with dependency status, a quartic in list tuition (or cost of attendance), a quartic in grants, and full interactions of the cost and grant measures.[16] We have chosen to include costs and grants with interactions separately, instead of a simple polynomial in net cost (e.g., tuition less grants) because the former approach is more flexible and allows behavioral considerations (such as a response to nominal instead of net prices) while still nesting the more traditional assumption of net cost.[17]

Despite this detail, the data are not quite ideal. The cross-sectional design of NPSAS limits what is observed about attendance history. While it would be useful to know the cost, financial-aid structure, and attendance intensity for all years before graduation, we see only the final year and must use these data as a proxy for the entire undergraduate experience. Subject to this caveat, summary statistics of these variables, by wave, are presented in Appendix Tables 4C.1 (for continuous measures) and 4C.2 (for categorical measures). We will often refer back to these measures in our discussion of the decomposition results.

DECOMPOSITION RESULTS

Oaxaca-Blinder and Ever Borrowed

We first seek to explain the sharp increase in the propensity of having ever borrowed that occurred between 1996 and 2000. As this is a binary outcome, and we are interested in the mean change, we use Oaxaca-Blinder and focus across different time intervals that span the borrowing spike. In each of the time intervals, the reference coefficients are set equal to those from the earlier period. The composition effects thus capture changes in the joint means of the observables, assuming that the relationship between the observables and borrowing was the same in the later period as it was in the earlier period. This implies that decompositions with different starting periods are not strictly comparable, but they may still be informative. For ease of presentation, we group the observable variables into seven more aggregate categories: 1) age and dependency status; 2) sex, marital status, and ethnicity; 3) both parents' education level (including missing); 4) state of permanent residence, region of school, and in-state status; 5) institutional sector, attendance intensity, and major; 6) EFC; and 7) tuition and grants and interactions.[18] The first panel of Table 4.2A looks at the 1990–2000 time period, during which the borrowing rate increased by 9 percentage points. The decomposition shows that about 4 percentage points (45 percent) of the increase was due to observable factors, with most of the effect concentrated in EFC (the mean of which fell in this time period) and tuition (which rose). The remaining share of the increase was due

Table 4.2A Oaxaca–Blinder Decompositions of Ever Borrowed, Using Tuition

	1990–2000		1990–2008		1996–2000		1996–2008	
Mean difference (percentage points)	9.03	(1.40)	13.64	(1.42)	10.99	(2.02)	15.60	(2.05)
Composition effects due to:								
Age/dependency status	0.27	(0.33)	−0.81	(0.44)	−0.09	(0.39)	1.12	(0.79)
Sex, marital status, ethnicity	0.86	(0.49)	0.99	(0.55)	0.85	(0.52)	1.27	(0.65)
Parental education	−0.42	(0.30)	−0.43	(0.46)	0.98	(0.69)	1.31	(0.93)
Location, in-state status	−1.01	(0.67)	−1.75	(0.66)	0.41	(0.83)	0.49	(0.87)
School sector, attendance, major	−0.01	(1.99)	0.68	(1.09)	1.75	(0.69)	0.86	(1.05)
Expected family contribution	1.09	(0.28)	0.64	(0.41)	−1.08	(0.84)	−2.44	(1.15)
Tuition and grants	3.40	(1.81)	6.75	(1.98)	−0.73	(1.33)	2.30	(1.92)
Total	4.05	(1.51)	6.08	(2.38)	2.07	(2.16)	4.91	(2.96)
Structural effects due to:								
Age/dependency status	3.07	(1.57)	5.77	(1.59)	−0.08	(2.54)	0.33	(2.65)
Sex, marital status, ethnicity	−4.04	(4.58)	−5.43	(4.31)	11.94	(5.59)	10.25	(5.10)
Parental education	1.51	(1.34)	0.36	(1.09)	1.13	(1.97)	−0.37	(1.59)
Location, in-state status	1.72	(2.05)	1.55	(2.15)	−1.77	(2.95)	−2.76	(3.03)
School sector, attendance, major	−1.94	(11.85)	−2.01	(10.65)	−5.92	(6.25)	−4.28	(5.73)
Expected family contribution	−6.33	(2.34)	−1.65	(2.12)	9.90	(3.53)	15.49	(3.14)
Tuition and grants	0.90	(5.41)	−2.20	(6.25)	−4.20	(8.18)	−6.99	(9.60)
Constant	10.08	(14.51)	11.16	(14.40)	−2.07	(11.54)	−0.99	(11.44)
Total	4.98	(1.57)	7.55	(2.24)	8.93	(2.02)	10.69	(2.68)

NOTE: Each column refers to the later period less the earlier period. Oaxaca-Blinder decompositions are based on coefficients from the base period reference and are estimated via OLS (with sample weights). Standard errors robust to heteroskedasticity and intracollege correlation are in parentheses. Borrowing is from all sources except friends and family and excludes loans taken out by parents (PLUS Loans). Results change trivially if time to degree is included for the latter two panels.
SOURCE: Authors' calculations from selected years of NPSAS.

Table 4.2B Oaxaca-Blinder Decompositions of Ever Borrowed, Using Cost of Attendance

	1990–2000		1990–2008		1996–2000		1996–2008	
Mean difference (%-points)	9.03	(1.41)	13.64	(1.43)	10.99	(2.02)	15.60	(2.05)
Composition effects due to:								
Age/dependency status	0.28	(0.32)	−0.76	(0.43)	−0.15	(0.39)	1.12	(0.78)
Sex, marital status, ethnicity	0.91	(0.49)	1.11	(0.55)	0.87	(0.50)	1.29	(0.65)
Parental education	−0.41	(0.30)	−0.50	(0.46)	0.90	(0.67)	1.18	(0.91)
Location, in-state status	−1.02	(0.68)	−1.81	(0.66)	0.48	(0.86)	0.50	(0.90)
School sector, attendance, major	−0.51	(0.72)	0.32	(0.82)	1.75	(0.67)	0.81	(1.05)
Expected family contribution	1.18	(0.30)	0.77	(0.43)	−1.08	(0.86)	−2.51	(1.16)
Attendance cost and grants	4.14	(0.94)	8.21	(1.34)	0.50	(1.53)	4.36	(1.86)
Total	4.57	(1.44)	7.34	(1.93)	3.27	(2.26)	6.75	(2.94)
Structural effects due to:								
Age/dependency status	3.12	(1.57)	5.56	(1.60)	−0.43	(2.57)	−0.30	(2.67)
Sex, marital status, ethnicity	−4.94	(4.61)	−6.80	(4.30)	12.78	(5.59)	10.69	(5.14)
Parental education	1.25	(1.33)	0.25	(1.08)	0.84	(1.98)	−0.53	(1.61)
Location, in-state status	1.22	(2.05)	1.85	(2.21)	−1.51	(3.00)	−1.69	(3.09)
School sector, attendance, major	−1.34	(3.91)	−2.99	(3.69)	−6.68	(6.15)	−6.57	(5.76)
Expected family contribution	−7.37	(2.33)	−2.98	(2.12)	9.15	(3.50)	14.55	(3.12)
Attendance cost and grants	−22.89	(9.03)	−3.57	(10.88)	−0.31	(13.41)	19.22	(15.59)
Constant	35.42	(10.88)	14.99	(11.93)	−6.11	(15.16)	−26.54	(16.99)
Total	4.47	(1.54)	6.30	(1.82)	7.73	(2.11)	8.88	(2.60)

NOTE: Each column refers to the later period less the earlier period. Oaxaca-Blinder decompositions are based on coefficients from the base period reference and are estimated via OLS (with sample weights). Standard errors robust to heteroskedasticity and intracollege correlation are in parentheses. Borrowing is from all sources except friends and family and excludes loans taken out by parents (PLUS Loans). Results change trivially if time to degree is included for the latter two panels.

SOURCE: Authors' calculations from selected years of NPSAS.

to changes in the coefficients relating the observables to the outcome, but the factor-specific estimates are too imprecise to isolate changes in marginal relationships. When examining the longer interval from 1990 to 2008, again 45 percent of the increase is explained, with a slightly greater role for tuition.[19]

The next two panels use 1996 as the base year. While there are slightly larger increases in the percentage borrowing relative to the 1990 base year, the share of the increases attributable to the covariates was smaller, between 20 and 30 percent. Furthermore, the explanatory share in this horizon did not load so heavily on costs but was more diffuse. On the other hand, the estimates on the coefficients for EFC are quite large and statistically significant, suggesting that for a given ability to pay, students were becoming more likely to borrow. However, because the 1996 sample size is relatively small (see Appendix Table 4C.5), these coefficient estimates are less reliable, and we treat them cautiously.

Table 4.2B shows that if we use the broader cost of attendance measure instead of tuition (but leave other variables the same), the picture is similar. A slightly larger share is accounted for by the observables— between 50 and 55 percent for the 1990 base, and 30 and 40 percent for the 1996 base—suggesting that increases in nontuition expenses also increased borrowing. In summary, roughly half of the long-term increase in the borrowing rate was due to observable factors, with cost increases explaining the lion's share. This leaves a substantial fraction due to structural changes, and more so if 1996 is used as the base instead. Note that this pattern is consistent with the large increases in the debt profile between 1996 and 2000. The behavioral explanation for this trend is a topic to which we will return.

Semiparametric Decompositions of the Distributions

What would the cumulative distribution of borrowing in 2008 look like if the distribution of covariates were the same as it was in 1990? Figure 4.6 answers this question by plotting the cumulative distribution functions (CDFs) from 1990 and 2008 (as in Figure 4.1) against just such a counterfactual distribution. Reweighting the 2008 distribution shows that just over half of the increased propensity to borrow (the change in density at zero) can be explained by changes in the covari-

**Figure 4.6 Cumulative Distribution Function of Borrowing among
College Graduates, 1990, 2008, and Counterfactual 2008**

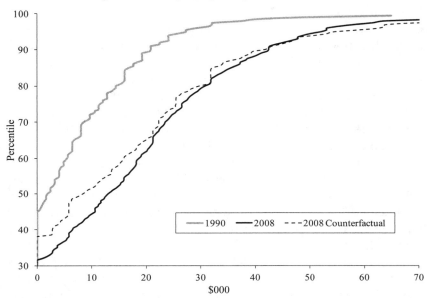

NOTE: The DiNardo, Fortin, and Lemieux (DFL, 1996) reweighting procedure is used
to create a counterfactual distribution for 2008, assuming the distribution of covariates
was the same as in 1990. (See text for the set of covariates used for reweighting.) All calculations use sample weights, are in constant (year 2012) dollars, and include student-
level borrowing from all sources except informal loans from friends and family.
SOURCE: NPSAS, selected years.

ates—very similar to the Oaxaca-Blinder findings despite a quite different methodology. Moving up the distribution, changes in observables
explain approximately half of borrowing levels up to the median, but
they become less and less relevant in the higher quantiles. This result
is not entirely unexpected: changes in borrowing limits, both federal
and private (see Appendix 4B), are not included in the set of covariates, since they vary only over time and not in the cross-section, but we
would anticipate that their effect would be concentrated heavily in the
upper tail of the distribution.

The four panels of Figure 4.7 use the same reweighting approach
across shorter time intervals. By looking at different time horizons,
it is possible to locate when, and where in the distribution, structural

changes were more important in affecting borrowing than covariates. The top left panel reweights the covariate distribution in 1996 to resemble the distribution in 1990. Interestingly, the counterfactual shows a much larger reduction in borrowing rates than actually took place, indicating that structural or policy changes increased the fraction of graduates who borrowed.[20] For levels, the counterfactual for 1996 generally gets more than halfway to the 1990 distribution between the 60th and 90th percentiles, and it is basically identical to the 1990 distribution for the top decile. Observables clearly explain the bulk of the debt increase between 1990 and 1996, and we will subsequently analyze which observables were important to this change.

In contrast, the top right panel of Figure 4.7 illustrates a negligible role for observables between 1996 and 2000. Virtually all the debt increase throughout the entire distribution is due to unexplained or structural factors. Consistent with the Oaxaca-Blinder analysis, the importance for behavioral changes is much greater in the late 1990s than earlier that decade.[21] In fact, the bottom left panel, looking at changes between 1990 and 2000, is almost a composite of the previous two panels, with the counterfactual distribution approaching the halfway point between the actual 1990 and 2000 distributions through the 50th percentile, and roughly a quarter of the way from the 2000 to 1990 distribution at higher quantiles. In some ways, this is reassuring, as it suggests that the earlier results are not just due to small sample issues in the 1996 wave. The last panel focuses on the change between 2000 and 2008, when debt profiles increased relatively little. Here, reweighting the covariates accounts for *all* the change up to the 80th percentile, about half of the change between the 80th and 90th percentiles, and almost none in the top decile.

From these decompositions, it appears that changes in observables were responsible for much of the observed shifts in borrowing between 1990 and 1996 and again from 2000 to 2008. The exceptions are that observables overexplain the lower tail in the early 1990s and underexplain the upper tail in the 2000s. Moreover, observables seem to have no explanatory power during the late 1990s. What policy or behavioral explanations fit with these patterns is a topic we return to in the next section. Before that, however, we turn to recentered influence function decompositions in order to gauge which set of observables mattered most.

**Figure 4.7 Cumulative Distribution Function of Borrowing among
College Graduates, DFL Counterfactuals**

1990, 1996, and Counterfactual 1996   1996, 2000, and Counterfactual 2000

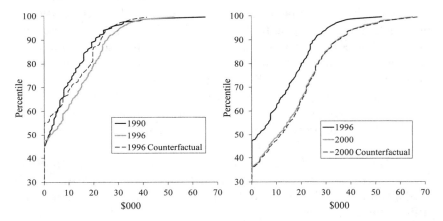

1990, 2000, and Counterfactual 2000   2000, 2008, and Counterfactual 2008

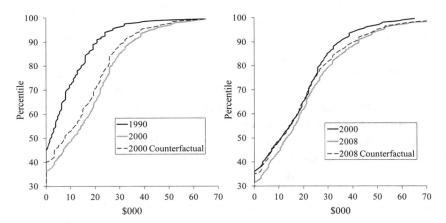

NOTE: The DiNardo, Fortin, and Lemieux (DFL, 1996) reweighting procedure is used
to create a counterfactual distribution for 2008, assuming the distribution of covariates
was the same as in 1990. (See Figure 4.6 for the set of covariates used for reweighting.) All calculations use sample weights, are in constant (year 2012) dollars, and
include student-level borrowing from all sources except informal loans from friends
and family.
SOURCE: NPSAS, selected years.

Recentered Influence Function Decompositions

While the reweighting-based decompositions give a useful graphical overview, the RIF method allows for a greater level of detail of the importance of specific factors. Table 4.3A presents the decompositions over the 1990–2008 period for four statistics: the mean level of borrowing (which uses the Oaxaca-Blinder decomposition), and the 50th, 75th, and 90th percentiles of the distributions of debt. Of the mean difference in borrowing levels of $9,940, only $1,940—or about 20 percent—is explained, a result quite consistent with Figure 4.6. Although the largest component is due to cost structure, the coefficient is imprecise.[22] Smaller, but more precise, effects are due to changes in EFC and attendance patterns.[23]

At the median and 75th percentile, about one-third of the borrowing increase is explained, which is somewhat less than in Figure 4.6 for the median and somewhat more for the higher quantile, but not statistically different in either case. At both quantiles, the factors that were important at the mean are still relevant, as well as a slight role for age due to graduates being more likely to finish in their mid- to late 20s. At the 90th percentile, observables explain essentially nothing, as before, and this appears to be due to the coefficient on cost structure turning negative and canceling out the mostly positive effects from other factors.

Table 4.3B repeats the analysis using the broader cost of attendance measure. The results are similar except for a slightly greater share explained by observables, and this is entirely due to a higher loading on cost structure (which is now statistically significant). Nontuition costs such as room and board matter, particularly in the top decile, where the coefficient is now positive and nearly 30 percent of the increase in borrowing is now explained.

Looking at the bigger picture, between 30 and 40 percent of the debt increase between 1990 and 2008 at both the median and 75th percentiles is explained by observables, and half of this share (15–20 percent of the total increase) is due to changes in the cost structure alone (mostly tuition). At the top decile of borrowing, changes in the tuition and grant structure led to students borrowing *less*, but this reverses once nontuition expenses are accounted for.[24] A small share, between 5 and 7 percent, of the overall rise in borrowing is due to the increased financial resources among dependent students *and* decreased financial resources

Table 4.3A Recentered Influence Function Decompositions of Borrowing: 1990–2008, Using Tuition

	Mean		50th percentile		75th percentile		90th percentile	
Difference (000s of 2012 $)	9.94	(0.27)	11.17	(0.48)	15.19	(0.54)	21.66	(0.53)
Composition effects due to:								
Age/dependency status	−0.16	(0.08)	0.42	(0.14)	0.54	(0.17)	0.21	(0.18)
Sex, marital status, ethnicity	0.11	(0.11)	0.18	(0.14)	0.14	(0.23)	−0.11	(0.25)
Parental education	0.02	(0.10)	0.08	(0.11)	0.27	(0.20)	0.14	(0.20)
Location, in-state status	−0.14	(0.13)	−0.37	(0.30)	−0.18	(0.61)	0.00	(0.63)
School sector, attendance, major	0.63	(0.21)	0.96	(0.54)	0.96	(0.83)	1.65	(1.11)
Expected family contribution	0.26	(0.08)	0.67	(0.22)	1.08	(0.21)	1.28	(0.26)
Attendance cost and grants	1.23	(0.83)	1.32	(1.07)	2.67	(2.03)	−4.06	(2.82)
Total	1.94	(0.86)	3.26	(1.48)	5.48	(2.32)	−0.89	(2.75)
Structural effects due to:								
Age/dependency status	−0.23	(0.45)	0.85	(0.79)	−1.38	(0.83)	−2.86	(1.00)
Sex, marital status, ethnicity	−1.39	(1.00)	−2.75	(1.40)	−2.95	(2.11)	−3.97	(2.09)
Parental education	0.06	(0.25)	0.18	(0.34)	−0.68	(0.44)	−0.29	(0.46)
Location, in-state status	−0.40	(0.85)	−0.63	(0.71)	−0.13	(1.15)	−0.32	(1.45)
School sector, attendance, major	0.75	(1.47)	−2.55	(3.31)	0.98	(2.23)	1.45	(2.86)
Expected family contribution	−0.27	(0.54)	−1.42	(0.67)	0.99	(0.81)	2.89	(1.10)
Attendance cost and grants	4.57	(1.60)	8.51	(3.51)	2.74	(3.19)	9.40	(3.97)
Constant	4.89	(2.48)	5.72	(5.34)	10.15	(4.20)	16.26	(5.69)
Total	8.01	(0.91)	7.91	(1.76)	9.71	(2.35)	22.55	(2.78)

NOTE: Each column refers to the later period less the earlier period. The recentered influence functions and quantiles are calculated with sample weights; the decompositions are based on coefficients from the base period reference and are estimated via OLS (without sample weights). Bootstrapped standard errors (100 replications) are in parentheses. Borrowing is from all sources except friends and family and excludes loans taken out by parents (PLUS Loans).

SOURCE: Authors' calculations from selected years of NPSAS.

Table 4.3B Recentered Influence Function Decompositions of Borrowing: 1990–2008, Using Cost of Attendance

	Mean		50th percentile		75th percentile		90th percentile	
Difference (000s of 2012 $)	9.94	(0.27)	11.17	(0.48)	15.19	(0.54)	21.66	(0.53)
Composition effects due to:								
Age/dependency status	-0.14	(0.07)	0.41	(0.14)	0.46	(0.16)	0.13	(0.17)
Sex, marital status, ethnicity	0.15	(0.10)	0.18	(0.13)	0.14	(0.24)	-0.16	(0.26)
Parental education	0.02	(0.10)	0.08	(0.11)	0.29	(0.20)	0.17	(0.21)
Location, in-state status	-0.17	(0.13)	-0.32	(0.29)	-0.30	(0.60)	-0.04	(0.62)
School sector, attendance, major	0.66	(0.19)	0.96	(0.52)	0.61	(0.79)	1.25	(1.06)
Expected family contribution	0.28	(0.08)	0.61	(0.21)	1.00	(0.21)	1.14	(0.26)
Attendance cost and grants	1.76	(0.35)	2.11	(0.98)	3.71	(1.40)	3.83	(1.93)
Total	2.55	(0.43)	4.03	(1.39)	5.91	(1.78)	6.32	(2.24)
Structural effects due to:								
Age/dependency status	-0.24	(0.45)	1.07	(0.71)	-1.69	(0.80)	-3.29	(0.97)
Sex, marital status, ethnicity	-2.28	(1.06)	-3.26	(1.50)	-4.39	(2.20)	-5.71	(2.28)
Parental education	0.02	(0.25)	0.16	(0.33)	-0.79	(0.44)	-0.39	(0.47)
Location, in-state status	-0.31	(0.88)	-0.37	(0.68)	0.03	(1.13)	-0.31	(1.44)
School sector, attendance, major	-1.29	(1.08)	-2.79	(1.09)	-2.03	(2.08)	-2.08	(2.65)
Expected family contribution	-0.87	(0.54)	-2.63	(0.67)	-0.02	(0.83)	1.93	(1.19)
Attendance cost and grants	11.52	(2.60)	20.82	(5.33)	12.22	(4.65)	5.46	(5.43)
Constant	0.84	(3.15)	-5.85	(4.51)	5.96	(5.33)	19.73	(7.22)
Total	7.39	(0.46)	7.15	(1.68)	9.28	(1.79)	15.34	(2.33)

NOTE: Each column refers to the later period less the earlier period. The recentered influence functions and quantiles are calculated with sample weights; the decompositions are based on coefficients from the base period reference and are estimated via OLS (without sample weights). Bootstrapped standard errors (100 replications) are in parentheses. Borrowing is from all sources except friends and family and excludes loans taken out by parents (PLUS Loans).

SOURCE: Authors' calculations from selected years of NPSAS.

of independent students. This apparent paradox results from fewer dependent students qualifying for need-based grant aid and more independent students not having sufficient outside income to pay for college expenses. In all cases, a large share remains unexplained, with the largest change in coefficients loading on cost structure. That is, not only did costs rise, but for a given set of costs and grants, students borrowed more than they did in the past, conditional on the other observables.[25]

We now break down the decompositions by time period, looking at the 1990s and 2000–2008 periods separately. For the former, a quick glance reveals that, as in the reweighting-based decomposition, observables explain quite little (less than 15 percent) of the debt increase over the 1990s, and this is true throughout the distribution and whether the tuition (Table 4.4A) or cost of attendance measure (Table 4.4B) is used. The reduction in explanatory power relative to that of the longer period stems from the smaller load on cost changes, which is now negligible. This pattern is consistent with relatively small increases in both list tuition and cost of attendance in this time frame (Table 4C.1). While *structural* (coefficient) effects on costs are generally still present, the coefficients representing the constant term, which likely capture omitted variables such as policy reforms, are quite large and statistically significant, especially in upper quantiles.

Before turning to the 2000s, it is helpful to look at the 1990s more granularly, as the reweighting decompositions showed substantial differences in the role of observables between the two. Appendix Tables 4C.3A–4C.4B examine the 1990–1996 and 1996–2000 periods separately. Reassuringly, the RIF estimates are quite consistent with the reweighting decompositions, down to overexplaining the increase in borrowing at the median in the early 1990s.[26] For the earlier period, the change in age composition, cost structure, and EFC all contribute significantly toward greater debt at the median and above, although the explanatory share falls from about one-half to about one-third when moving from the 75th to the 90th percentile, as the roles of cost structure and age diminish at the top of the distribution.[27] In contrast, between 1996 and 2000, the role of age has diminished to negligible levels, and while attendance patterns contribute slightly toward greater borrowing, this covariate is outweighed by the reversal in the relationships of EFC and costs. In short, observables explain more of the debt increase between 1990 and 1996 because the observables that tend to

Table 4.4A Recentered Influence Function Decompositions of Borrowing: 1990–2000, Using Tuition

	Mean		50th percentile		75th percentile		90th percentile	
Difference (000s of 2012 $)	7.13	(0.29)	9.03	(0.61)	13.12	(0.52)	13.96	(0.64)
Composition effects due to:								
Age/dependency status	0.13	(0.07)	0.63	(0.22)	0.81	(0.19)	0.33	(0.21)
Sex, marital status, ethnicity	0.11	(0.10)	0.09	(0.11)	0.05	(0.20)	-0.15	(0.20)
Parental education	-0.01	(0.07)	0.05	(0.07)	0.02	(0.13)	0.14	(0.15)
Location, in-state status	-0.07	(0.14)	-0.88	(0.39)	-0.50	(0.56)	0.07	(0.70)
School sector, attendance, major	-0.02	(0.25)	1.05	(0.65)	-0.01	(0.67)	-0.25	(0.92)
Expected family contribution	0.15	(0.06)	0.49	(0.17)	0.47	(0.11)	0.42	(0.12)
Tuition and grants	0.85	(0.36)	-0.12	(0.45)	0.15	(0.76)	-1.36	(0.92)
Total	1.15	(0.34)	1.32	(0.61)	0.99	(0.89)	-0.80	(0.98)
Structural effects due to:								
Age/dependency status	-0.51	(0.40)	-0.62	(0.84)	0.12	(0.75)	-6.72	(1.26)
Sex, marital status, ethnicity	-1.72	(0.98)	-2.62	(1.88)	-1.21	(2.18)	-4.34	(2.56)
Parental education	0.17	(0.35)	1.37	(0.57)	-0.52	(0.49)	0.11	(0.72)
Location, in-state status	0.23	(0.74)	1.28	(0.85)	0.38	(1.01)	-1.66	(1.53)
School sector, attendance, major	1.37	(1.77)	-5.63	(4.07)	1.80	(2.68)	1.54	(3.83)
Expected family contribution	-1.82	(0.49)	-6.99	(1.15)	-0.09	(0.91)	-0.12	(1.51)
Tuition and grants	2.78	(1.40)	7.15	(2.93)	-0.70	(2.73)	8.73	(3.20)
Constant	5.47	(2.58)	13.42	(5.52)	12.27	(4.77)	17.22	(6.30)
Total	5.99	(0.46)	7.71	(0.99)	12.14	(1.02)	14.75	(1.25)

NOTE: Each column refers to the later period less the earlier period. The recentered influence functions and quantiles are calculated with sample weights; the decompositions are based on coefficients from the base period reference and are estimated via OLS (without sample weights). Bootstrapped standard errors (100 replications) are in parentheses. Borrowing is from all sources except friends and family and excludes loans taken out by parents (PLUS Loans).

SOURCE: Authors' calculations from selected years of NPSAS.

Table 4.4B Recentered Influence Function Decompositions of Borrowing: 1990–2000, Using Cost of Attendance

	Mean		50th percentile		75th percentile		90th percentile	
Difference (000s of 2012 $)	7.13	(0.29)	9.03	(0.61)	13.12	(0.52)	13.96	(0.64)
Composition effects due to:								
Age/dependency status	0.11	(0.06)	0.61	(0.21)	0.70	(0.19)	0.21	(0.21)
Sex, marital status, ethnicity	0.14	(0.09)	0.08	(0.11)	0.04	(0.20)	-0.18	(0.21)
Parental education	-0.02	(0.07)	0.06	(0.08)	0.04	(0.13)	0.15	(0.16)
Location, in-state status	-0.07	(0.14)	-0.84	(0.37)	-0.66	(0.54)	-0.04	(0.68)
School sector, attendance, major	0.21	(0.16)	0.61	(0.42)	0.09	(0.71)	0.12	(0.95)
Expected family contribution	0.17	(0.06)	0.50	(0.17)	0.49	(0.11)	0.43	(0.12)
Attendance cost and grants	0.64	(0.24)	0.31	(0.61)	0.25	(0.70)	0.29	(0.69)
Total	1.17	(0.32)	1.32	(0.67)	0.94	(0.87)	0.96	(0.87)
Structural effects due to:								
Age/dependency status	-0.41	(0.41)	-0.30	(0.79)	-0.17	(0.77)	-6.64	(1.24)
Sex, marital status, ethnicity	-2.26	(0.96)	-2.51	(1.98)	-2.33	(2.17)	-5.63	(2.64)
Parental education	0.13	(0.35)	1.24	(0.57)	-0.66	(0.49)	-0.04	(0.74)
Location, in-state status	0.30	(0.78)	1.23	(0.85)	0.49	(1.01)	-1.60	(1.51)
School sector, attendance, major	-0.52	(1.31)	-4.98	(1.75)	-1.25	(2.65)	-3.27	(3.99)
Expected family contribution	-2.34	(0.51)	-7.80	(1.17)	-0.83	(0.92)	-1.80	(1.58)
Attendance cost and grants	3.27	(1.94)	12.27	(5.94)	0.74	(3.73)	10.76	(5.08)
Constant	7.81	(2.54)	8.56	(5.52)	16.20	(5.36)	21.21	(6.88)
Total	5.96	(0.41)	7.71	(0.97)	12.18	(1.05)	12.99	(1.08)

NOTE: Each column refers to the later period less the earlier period. The recentered influence functions and quantiles are calculated with sample weights; the decompositions are based on coefficients from the base period reference and are estimated via OLS (without sample weights). Bootstrapped standard errors (100 replications) are in parentheses. Borrowing is from all sources except friends and family and excludes loans taken out by parents (PLUS Loans).

SOURCE: Authors' calculations from selected years of NPSAS.

matter the most, cost and EFC, changed more in this period than they did between 1996 and 2000. The apparent puzzle is that the fastest debt growth occurred in a period when list cost barely budged and net cost actually fell.

The contribution of changes in observables over the 2000s, on the other hand, is considerable, and much of this is due to increases in cost. As shown in Tables 4.5A and 4.5B, the RIF approach substantially overexplains the shift in borrowing at the median and 75th percentiles, and more so when cost of attendance is used instead of tuition. Changes in cost often account for half or more of the observable share, although parental education, attendance patterns, and EFC also matter. At the 90th percentile, where the reweighting decomposition found only a modest role for observables, the RIF technique places more weight on them, explaining at least two-thirds of the debt increase, with cost and EFC having the largest impact.[28]

In summary, the RIF decompositions qualitatively resemble the reweighting-based decompositions: a large role for observables in the early to mid-1990s and again between 2000 and 2008, but almost no explanatory power for them in the late 1990s. In both techniques, observables explain less at the very top of the borrowing distribution. The RIF analysis, however, shows that the most important observed factor contributing toward greater borrowing is cost, and this is particularly true over the 2000s, when costs increased relatively quickly. EFC also matters consistently across time periods and quantiles. Smaller but still meaningful effects are found for age composition over the 1990s and attendance patterns and parental education over the 2000s, with all these more prominent in the middle of the debt distribution. Core demographics and geography, despite changing a great deal over time, do not seem to be related to the shift in student debt.

DISCUSSION

Although much of the increase in debt over the 2000s can be explained by changes in student and institutional characteristics, the NPSAS data point to structural, behavioral, or policy shifts underlying the majority of debt increases in the 1990s, particularly the late 1990s,

Table 4.5A Recentered Influence Function Decompositions of Borrowing: 2000–2008, Using Tuition

	Mean		50th percentile		75th percentile		90th percentile	
Difference (000s of 2012 $)	2.81	(0.25)	2.14	(0.50)	2.07	(0.38)	7.71	(0.61)
Composition effects due to:								
Age/dependency status	−0.47	(0.11)	−0.34	(0.12)	−0.25	(0.07)	−0.57	(0.18)
Sex, marital status, ethnicity	0.12	(0.05)	0.26	(0.09)	0.13	(0.05)	0.26	(0.12)
Parental education	0.49	(0.08)	1.16	(0.19)	0.40	(0.08)	0.52	(0.14)
Location, in-state status	−0.05	(0.06)	−0.04	(0.21)	0.02	(0.10)	0.42	(0.23)
School sector, attendance, major	0.22	(0.10)	0.50	(0.28)	0.45	(0.14)	0.92	(0.33)
Expected family contribution	0.22	(0.08)	1.33	(0.17)	0.66	(0.07)	1.30	(0.19)
Tuition and grants	1.09	(0.15)	2.44	(0.41)	1.11	(0.20)	2.15	(0.45)
Total	1.62	(0.24)	5.30	(0.65)	2.52	(0.27)	5.01	(0.61)
Structural effects due to:								
Age/dependency status	0.47	(0.42)	1.61	(0.66)	−1.51	(0.48)	4.31	(1.21)
Sex, marital status, ethnicity	0.20	(0.94)	−0.65	(1.48)	−1.88	(1.05)	0.15	(2.39)
Parental education	−0.57	(0.22)	−2.32	(0.43)	−0.31	(0.30)	−0.92	(0.44)
Location, in-state status	−0.65	(0.59)	−1.36	(0.85)	−0.21	(0.65)	0.85	(1.16)
School sector, attendance, major	−0.19	(0.81)	2.50	(1.14)	−0.30	(0.70)	0.88	(1.48)
Expected family contribution	1.45	(0.54)	4.42	(0.84)	1.02	(0.44)	2.57	(0.80)
Tuition and grants	1.07	(1.39)	0.35	(2.66)	4.86	(1.52)	−4.19	(3.03)
Constant	−0.58	(1.88)	−7.70	(3.21)	−2.12	(2.10)	−0.96	(3.79)
Total	1.20	(0.30)	−3.16	(0.75)	−0.46	(0.45)	2.70	(0.90)

NOTE: Each column refers to the later period less the earlier period. The recentered influence functions and quantiles are calculated with sample weights; the decompositions are based on coefficients from the base period reference and are estimated via OLS (without sample weights). Bootstrapped standard errors (100 replications) are in parentheses. Borrowing is from all sources except friends and family and excludes loans taken out by parents (PLUS Loans).

SOURCE: Authors' calculations from selected years of NPSAS.

Table 4.5B Recentered Influence Function Decompositions of Borrowing: 2000–2008, Using Cost of Attendance

	Mean		50th percentile		75th percentile		90th percentile	
Difference (000s of 2012 $)	2.81	(0.25)	2.14	(0.11)	2.07	(0.38)	7.71	(0.61)
Composition effects due to:								
Age/dependency status	−0.43	(0.11)	−0.30	(0.11)	−0.23	(0.06)	−0.55	(0.17)
Sex, marital status, ethnicity	0.11	(0.04)	0.24	(0.09)	0.12	(0.05)	0.24	(0.12)
Parental education	0.46	(0.08)	1.11	(0.19)	0.38	(0.08)	0.48	(0.14)
Location, in-state status	−0.06	(0.06)	0.02	(0.21)	0.08	(0.10)	0.59	(0.24)
School sector, attendance, major	0.14	(0.10)	0.37	(0.27)	0.33	(0.13)	0.60	(0.30)
Expected family contribution	0.23	(0.08)	1.40	(0.17)	0.70	(0.08)	1.42	(0.20)
Attendance cost and grants	2.08	(0.18)	4.29	(0.40)	2.34	(0.21)	4.61	(0.63)
Total	2.53	(0.24)	7.13	(0.62)	3.72	(0.28)	7.39	(0.85)
Structural effects due to:								
Age/dependency status	0.35	(0.40)	1.47	(0.64)	−1.52	(0.47)	3.82	(1.15)
Sex, marital status, ethnicity	−0.12	(0.92)	−0.90	(1.48)	−2.08	(1.03)	−0.29	(2.37)
Parental education	−0.53	(0.22)	−2.18	(0.43)	−0.25	(0.30)	−0.81	(0.45)
Location, in-state status	−0.64	(0.57)	−1.09	(0.81)	−0.17	(0.65)	0.71	(1.17)
School sector, attendance, major	−0.46	(0.82)	2.18	(1.13)	−0.60	(0.73)	1.72	(1.52)
Expected family contribution	1.35	(0.52)	3.88	(0.85)	0.62	(0.46)	3.02	(0.86)
Attendance cost and grants	7.29	(2.52)	6.06	(5.04)	12.58	(3.17)	−6.37	(5.70)
Constant	−6.97	(2.95)	−14.41	(5.47)	−10.23	(3.50)	−1.48	(5.99)
Total	0.28	(0.29)	−4.99	(0.71)	−1.66	(0.44)	0.32	(1.15)

NOTE: Each column refers to the later period less the earlier period. The recentered influence functions and quantiles are calculated with sample weights; the decompositions are based on coefficients from the base period reference and are estimated via OLS (without sample weights). Bootstrapped standard errors (100 replications) are in parentheses. Borrowing is from all sources except friends and family and excludes loans taken out by parents (PLUS Loans).

SOURCE: Authors' calculations from selected years of NPSAS.

when debt profiles increased faster than in any other period. In this section, we review several possible explanations and weigh the evidence for each.

Formal Loans Crowding Out Informal Loans

The analysis above considers formal loans in which a promissory note has been signed and repayment shows up in credit reports. Informal loans from friends and family also occur, although it is unclear whether these are actually intended to be repaid (with or without interest). A possible "structural" explanation for debt increase is that formal loans have displaced informal loans over time. The NPSAS asked about informal loans only through 2000, but that covers the period in which observables have little explanatory power. Figure 4.8 plots CDFs of borrowing for 1990, 1996, and 2000, both with and without informal borrowing. The thinner or paler lines reflect the distributions of formal borrowing from Figure 4.1, while the thicker lines add in informal borrowing. If displacement were occurring, we would see the difference between total and formal borrowing shrink over time. In fact, we see the opposite: while informal borrowing is rare in 1990, it expands by 1996 and is of a similar magnitude in 2000. We can thus rule out this story.

Parents Transferring Loan Burden to Children

Our analysis also has focused on debt in the student's name and thus has excluded borrowing directly by parents in the form of PLUS Loans. While the terms of student-level loans are more generous than parent-level PLUS Loans (see Appendix 4B), parents are often in a better financial position with which to make repayment. However, if parents have become less willing or able to borrow for their children than in the past, the transference of the burden could explain increases in student-level borrowing. Figure 4.9 shows that this is not the case. The lighter-line CDFs in the figure again show the distributions of borrowing taken from Figure 4.1, while the heavier lines add in cumulative PLUS borrowing of parents (data for 1990 are unfortunately unavailable). Rather than decreasing over time, PLUS borrowing has increased substantially and become more pronounced further down the distribution. Thus, the intergenerational transfer explanation, at least through PLUS Loans, does not work, either.[29]

Figure 4.8 Cumulative Distribution Function of Borrowing among College Graduates with Informal Loans

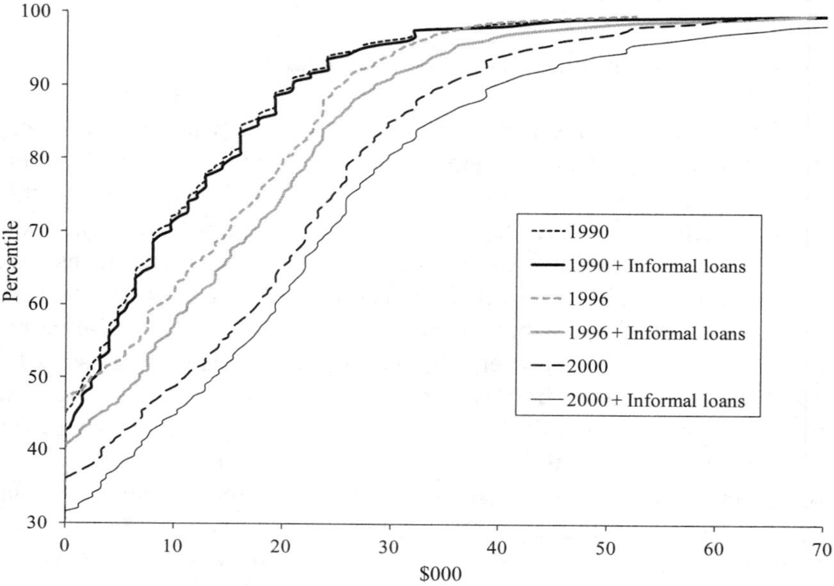

NOTE: All calculations use sample weights and are in constant (year 2012) dollars. Thicker lines include student-level borrowing from all sources *including* loans from friends and family; thinner lines exclude these informal loans, as in Figure 4.1. SOURCE: NPSAS, selected years.

Change in Interest Rates

The prevailing interest rates for student loans (federal and other) have varied over time, and basic economic theory implies that lower interest rates should increase borrowing, all other things being equal. Figure 4.10 presents time series for the interest rates on the predominant federal loan program, the Stafford Loan, as well as the U.S. prime rate, a benchmark for private loans and, at times, federal loans as well. Prior to the early 1990s, Congress periodically set a fixed rate for Stafford Loans (sometimes creating a huge subsidy, as in the early 1980s). Between 1992 and 2006, Stafford rates were tied to market rates before being fixed again.[30] Although interest rates drop by nearly four percentage points in the early 1990s, they are relatively flat over the late 1990s,

Figure 4.9 Cumulative Distribution Function of Borrowing among College Graduates, with PLUS Loans

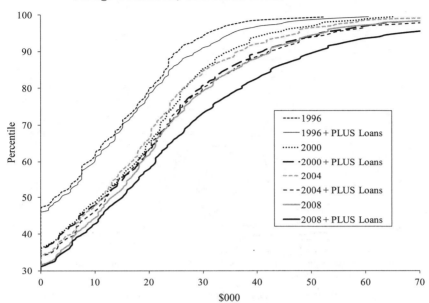

NOTE: All calculations use sample weights and are in constant (year 2012) dollars. Thicker lines include borrowing from parental PLUS Loans; thinner lines exclude PLUS Loans, as in Figure 4.1.
SOURCE: NPSAS, selected years.

and they drop considerably again over the early 2000s recession. This pattern is not consistent with large increases in borrowing during the late 1990s and a flat, or even falling, borrowing profile between 2000 and 2004. It would appear that the borrowing decisions of bachelor's degree graduates are insensitive to the cost of loans, and interest rates therefore cannot explain the observed borrowing patterns.[31]

Borrowing Eligibility

Another set of possible factors deals with increased eligibility to borrow (on both extensive and intensive margins). As Appendix 4B shows, major changes in the student loan market took place over the 1990s, including the introduction of unsubsidized Stafford Loans

Figure 4.10 Interest Rates on New Undergraduate Stafford Loans, 1965–2013

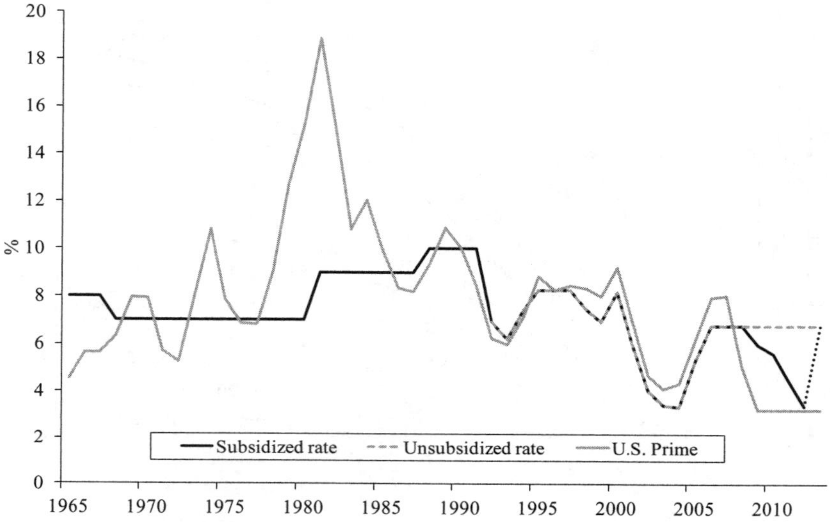

NOTE: All federal loans were subsidized until 1992, when unsubsidized loans became available.
SOURCE: Senate Committee on the Budget (2006); http://www.finaid.org/loans/historicalrates.phtml (accessed April 17, 2014).

(which are more available to higher-income families than are subsidized Stafford Loans), increases in the federal statutory borrowing limits, and the development of private loans. In contrast, there was little structural change in the loan market between 2000 and 2008 (although there was considerable change *after* the 2007–2008 school year).

Except for a brief period in the late 1970s and early 1980s, federal loan eligibility was means tested and subject to a family-income threshold (with the government paying interest while the student was enrolled) until 1992. That year, unsubsidized loans first became available. While interest accumulates on these loans from the time of disbursement, students have access to them regardless of family income. Their availability opened up a large segment of the student population to federal loans, so it would not be surprising if increases in the debt distribution followed. However, Figure 4.5 shows that borrowing increased much faster in the late 1990s than between 1990 and 1996 for wealthier students—the group that would be expected to benefit most from unsubsidized loan eligibility. Why didn't their borrowing increase immediately after 1992? Three reasons suggest that unsubsidized loans became more important in the late 1990s despite becoming available for the 1992–1993 school year. First, total unsubsidized loan volume was quite small initially. In 1992–1993, unsubsidized loan disbursements for *all postsecondary students* totaled $440 million (in 2011 dollars), just 1.9 percent of aggregate loan volume. In 1993–1994, disbursements had increased to $2.7 billion, an 8.9 percent share, and in 1994–1995, the numbers jumped to $9.5 billion, a 26.7 percent share. From this point, the share increased slowly, to 32.5 percent by 1999–2000 (College Board 2012a, Figure 6). Their impact thus would have been muted for the 1996 graduating cohort relative to the 2000 cohort. Second, the Survey of Consumer Finances (Federal Reserve Board of Governors 2012) shows a pronounced jump between 1995 and 1998 (but not between 1992 and 1995) in both the median and mean values of educational loans among families, and these increases were concentrated among families whose heads were college educated, were in managerial or professional occupations, and had income in the second-highest quintile. This pattern is consistent with increased loan volume for the types of households that would benefit most from unsubsidized loans occurring several years after the program's introduction. Third, and perhaps most tellingly, the income distribution among graduates with a Stafford Loan their senior year increased sharply (relative to the income distribution of all graduates) between 1996 and 2000, but not between 1993 and 1996.[32] This is shown in Figure 4.11, with the lighter lines representing the income distributions for Stafford borrowers and the heavier lines those for all graduates.

Furthermore, it is possible to use a back-of-the-envelope calculation to quantify how important unsubsidized loans were to the increase in total borrowing between 1996 and 2000. Figure 4.12 shows the *difference* in senior-year borrowing between 1996 and 2000 by percentile (now on the x-axis). The solid line counts all borrowing, and the dashed line nets out unsubsidized Stafford Loans. Throughout much of the distribution, the gap between the two years is significantly reduced once unsubsidized loans are taken out of the picture.[33] Indeed, the mean gap in the latter case is only 36 percent of the former; the mean squared deviation, 66 percent. (Excluding the area above the 98th percentile, the

Figure 4.11 Cumulative Distribution Function of Family Income, All Graduates and Stafford Borrowers

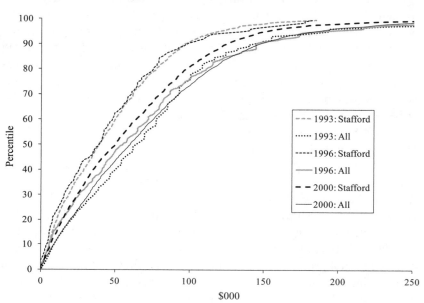

NOTE: All calculations use sample weights and are in constant (year 2012) dollars. Thicker lines represent family income for the set of all graduates; thinner lines represent graduates who took out a Stafford Loan their senior year.
SOURCE: NPSAS, selected years.

two figures are 24 and 23 percent, respectively.) In levels, the mean gap is reduced by $460, and if this pattern held for previous years of enrollment, it could account for roughly $2,500, or about half, of the mean increase in total debt of $5,200 between 1996 and 2000.[34] However, because of the factors mentioned above, this gap in senior-year borrowing probably overstates the gap for earlier years, when unsubsidized loan volume was smaller. But the senior year alone can account for 9 percent of the $5,200 difference, and even conservative estimates for previous class years would bring this share to a quarter.

Thus, unsubsidized loans were important for debt increases in the late 1990s, but what about increases in federal borrowing limits? The annual borrowing limit under the Stafford program, by far the largest federal loan program, was fixed—in nominal terms—between July

Figure 4.12 Difference in Senior-Year Borrowing between 1996 and 2000, with and without Unsubsidized Loans

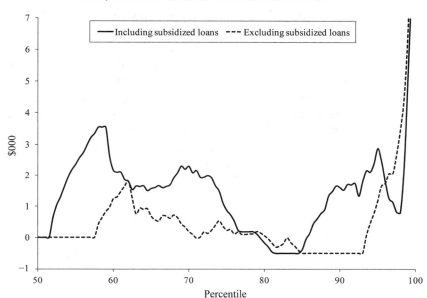

NOTE: All calculations use sample weights and are in constant (year 2012) dollars. Thicker lines represent all formal student-level borrowing in senior year; thinner lines exclude unsubsidized Stafford Loans.
SOURCE: NPSAS, selected years.

1993 and June 2007. The supplementary limits, which raise the maximum borrowing for independent students and some dependent students, were fixed between July 1994 and June 2008. However, the increase in statutory limits in July 1993 applied only for students in their second or higher class year, and the shift in supplementary limits in July 1994 applied only for students in their third or higher year. This means that graduates of the class of 1996 experienced the same nominal limits as the class of 2000; in real terms, borrowing limits declined slightly.[35] Consequently, borrowing limits are not behind the debt increase of the late 1990s.

The other major innovation of that time period was the rise of the private loan sector (Consumer Financial Protection Bureau 2012). Too new to be asked about explicitly in the 1996 NPSAS, private loans in that wave must be inferred by netting out institutional and state-level loans from all nonfederal loans. For graduates of that class, 1.0 percent took out a nonfederal loan their senior year, and most of these were institutional or state loans: just 0.3 percent took out an "other" or private loan. By 2000, the numbers had increased to 6.2 and 4.6 percent, respectively, and they continued to grow through 2008 before retrenching during the recession. The NPSAS data do not break out cumulative borrowing by nonfederal sector, but one can compare cumulative total borrowing to cumulative federal borrowing, and this is done in Figure 4.13 for the 1996 and later waves. The lighter lines represent cumulative total borrowing, as in Figure 4.1, while the heavier lines show cumulative federal borrowing only. The difference between the two captures nonfederal borrowing. For 1996, the gap occurs entirely below the 70th

Figure 4.13 Cumulative Distribution Function of Borrowing among College Graduates, Federal Loans

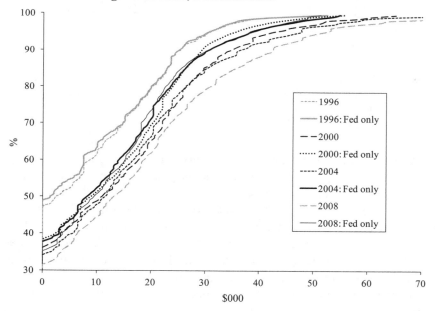

NOTE: All calculations use sample weights and are in constant (year 2012) dollars. Thicker lines represent cumulative formal student-level borrowing from federal loans only; thinner lines include all loans, as in Figure 4.1.
SOURCE: NPSAS, selected years.

percentile and is small, reflecting that most of these nonfederal loans are institutional or state-based and intended for lower-income borrowers.[36] By 2000, the gap has widened, especially above the 75th percentile. In fact, about half of the total increase in borrowing in the top quartile is due to nonfederal—essentially private—loans. (For the same quartile between 1996 and 2008, about three-quarters of the increase is due to private loans, and between 2000 and 2008, all of it is, though much of this latter increase is accounted for by observables.[37])

Broadly speaking, informal loans, PLUS Loans, interest rate changes, and statutory borrowing limits are unlikely to be factors behind the debt increase of the late 1990s. Unsubsidized Stafford Loans and private loans, on the other hand, are probable culprits, at least in part.

Other Explanations

One factor for which we have been unable to control is the use of tax credits, which came into existence in the late 1990s. Nicholas Turner (2012) has shown that the value of educational tax credits is largely capitalized into increases in net tuition (i.e., fewer institutional grants), with suggestive evidence that students compensate by borrowing more. However, the timing of tax credit availability precludes them from being a major factor for the borrowing increases observed during the 1990s. Both the Hope and Lifetime Learning Credits first became available during the 1998–1999 school year (and tax deductions not until the 2002–2003 school year). As the Hope Credit was available only for the first two years of postsecondary education, it could not have benefitted students who graduated during the 1999–2000 school year and took four or more school years to finish. Until 2003, the Lifetime Learning program allowed a (nonrefundable) credit of 20 percent of the first $5,000 in tuition and fees, making its maximum value $1,000.[38] But, according to the NPSAS data, only 20 percent of graduates' families claimed the credit in the 1999 tax year, and only about 20 percent of the claimants qualified for the maximum credit. Even if the credit were completely capitalized into higher borrowing, it could explain only a tiny portion of the increase in debt in the late 1990s.[39]

Another factor we did not examine explicitly is the use of home equity loans and lines of credit for education financing. There is some evidence that these tools became less important over the 1990s. In the

NPSAS, about 4 percent of the class of 1996 claimed to have used them, versus 2.3 percent in 2000. Similarly, the Survey of Consumer Finances shows that in 1989, 0.6 percent of all households were using a home equity loan or line of credit to pay for education expenses; by 1995, the last year in which the purpose can be ascertained, the figure had fallen to 0.4 percent. These levels are probably too small to have had a meaningful impact on student borrowing.

CONCLUSION

Using NPSAS data, we have shown that the entire debt profile of college graduates grew much faster in the 1990s than in the 2000s, and that this growth was concentrated especially in the late 1990s. Between 2000 and 2008, debt was remarkably stable for the bottom three quarters of the distribution—the increase that took place in the top quartile was driven by graduates at private, not-for-profit institutions and stemmed largely from greater private borrowing.

Statistical decomposition techniques consistently indicate that observable characteristics of students and institutions—such as demographics, geography, attendance patterns, income, and costs—explain about one-third of the overall debt increase across the two decades. However, their explanatory power is stronger at the extensive margin and in the middle of the distribution than in the right tail. Moreover, the observables account for more than half of the increase between 1990 and 1996 and approximately all of it between 2000 and 2008, leaving the late 1990s as the period that remains unexplained. Among the observables, cost tends to be the most important factor, often explaining about half of the observable share, but EFC is also important, as is the age structure in the 1990s and parental education in the 2000s.

In trying to unpack the puzzle of the late 1990s, we have ruled out informal loans, PLUS Loans, interest rate changes, and statutory borrowing limits as likely explanations. Instead, the evidence is consistent with the "unobservable" share being driven by the advent of unsubsidized Stafford Loans and private loans. This would imply that much of the debt increase over the 1990s—a much greater increase than over the 2000s—was primarily due to supply-side and not demand-side factors.

Indeed, while nominal costs of college have risen considerably, so has financial aid in the form of grants (Avery and Turner 2012; Greenstone and Looney 2013; see also Appendix Table 4C.1.) Our findings show that changes in costs account for only 20 percent of the increase in distribution-wide borrowing between 1990 and 2008, and this is after capturing the complex interplay between nominal prices and grants.

Of course, the partial-equilibrium analysis we have undertaken does not account for the possible endogeneity between college costs and financial aid. Recent research on the incidence of federal financial aid indicates that in many cases, schools seem to capture much of the benefit: Nicholas Turner (2012) cannot rule out that schools offset one dollar of student tax benefits with one dollar of higher net tuition; Lesley Turner (2012) finds that schools on average reduce institutional grants by $0.16 per dollar of Pell Grants ($0.80 for selective nonprofits); and Cellini and Goldin (2012) conclude that Title IV–eligible for-profits charge tuition 78 percent higher than comparable programs in non-Title IV–eligible for-profits. Whether these results hold specifically for loans, however, is still an open question in which more research is needed.

Notes

1. From January 1, 2012, through September 16, 2013, we found 504 hits of the search term "student debt" across the *New York Times*, the *Los Angeles Times*, the *Washington Post*, the *Wall Street Journal*, *USA Today*, *Time*, *Newsweek*, and *U.S. News and World Report*. For the same outlets, there were 673 hits between 1991 and 2011, inclusive.
2. See Martin and Lehren (2012) and Mitchell and Jackson-Randall (2012).
3. For example, collegerealitycheck.com and collegecompletion.chronicle.com (both by the Chronicle for Higher Education); collegecost.ed.gov/scorecard/ and college cost.ed.gov/catc/ (both by the federal government); projectonstudentdebt.org (by The Institute for College Access and Success); and collegeportraits.org (by the American Association of State Colleges and Universities).
4. See   http://www.whitehouse.gov/the-press-office/2013/08/22/remarks-president -college-affordability-buffalo-ny (accessed April 17, 2014). Congress has also investigated growing debt (Joint Economic Committee 2013).
5. We hope to investigate other groups in subsequent work.
6. The 2012 wave of NPSAS was released in late August of 2013. Although we have requested these data, our analyses are currently limited to 2008 as an endpoint.
7. It also forms the sampling frame for two longitudinal surveys: the Beginning Post-secondary Students study (BPS), which tracks first-time students, and the Bac-

calaureate and Beyond study (B&B), which tracks bachelor recipients. We use the NPSAS rather than the B&B because the former is available earlier and more often.

8. The NPSAS was also fielded in 1993. However, an error in the survey led to many bachelor's degree graduates not being asked the relevant questions on cumulative borrowing, forcing us to exclude this wave.

9. Unfortunately, private, for-profit institutions are too small a group to examine in all but the 2008 wave. Even then, fewer than 4 percent of bachelor's recipients graduated from a private, for-profit institution. Bound, Lovenheim, and Turner (2010) document rising time to bachelor's degree and attempt to explain the factors behind it.

10. Improper specification of the model, such as omitted variables, would show up in this component.

11. For example, in gender-wage discrimination, the reference coefficient is often set to that of men because the exercise is meant to examine how much of the gender gap can be attributable to differences in characteristics under the assumption that the return to those characteristics is the same as men's (the "explained" part) and how much is attributable to "discrimination" (the "unexplained" part, but see Note 10).

12. It is also more robust to functional form violations, such as when Y is a nonlinear function of X. Because this functional form need not be known, the technique is semiparametric. On the other hand, it is more sensitive to the common support requirement that sets of covariate realizations are common to both groups.

13. This setup will make the distribution of X_B resemble the distribution of X_A; switching the coding of the dependent variable will cause the reverse.

14. This follows because fraction q of the population (and sample analogue) has $Y \leq Y_q$, by definition of q.

15. We also experimented with using time to degree, which was available in every wave except 1990. Somewhat surprisingly, the inclusion of this variable, conditional on the others, had a negligible effect on the decompositions. In order to include the 1990 wave, we thus chose to exclude time to degree in the presented results.

16. Expected family contribution measures a student's family's ability to pay for college expenses and is based on family structure, income, and certain assets (excluding home equity). The relationship between borrowing and EFC is likely nonmonotonic, as low EFC levels increase the likelihood of receiving grant aid, and very high EFC levels are associated with a lower need to borrow. The cost of attendance is broader than tuition and fees and also includes room and board, books, travel, and other expenses.

17. A polynomial in net cost implies parameter restrictions in the more flexible model. When we test these restrictions in the relationship between borrowing and cost and aid structure, they are sharply rejected at all conventional significance levels.

18. When the constituent variables diverge in their effects, we make note of it.

19. There is also a slightly positive role from demographics (an increasing minority share) and an offsetting role from location (regional changes in graduates from the Northeast to the South).

20. Indeed, as Appendix 4B documents, unsubsidized Stafford Loans, which are not means tested, became available in 1992, and this would be expected to increase borrowing at the extensive margin.
21. Note that while the Oaxaca-Blinder results showed a small role for observables at the extensive margin during this time period, the estimate was not statistically different from zero.
22. Standard errors are calculated by bootstrapping the entire RIF procedure (with 100 replications) to account for estimation error in the density function.
23. The attendance coefficient is largely driven by a shift from nondoctoral to doctoral public institutions (see Appendix Table 4C.2).
24. For evidence of the growing role of amenities in driving students' attendance decisions, see Jacob, McCall, and Stange (2013).
25. Recall that the cost structure observables include quartics in list prices and grants and their pairwise interactions. These relationships are highly nonlinear and non-monotonic, so it is not quite accurate to say that "costs" rose; we are trading off accuracy for expediency.
26. That borrowing increased less than predicted at this quantile is due to a change in the coefficients on marital status; specifically, married graduates borrowed less than single graduates in 1990, but this relationship reversed in 1996. Since singles increased as a share of graduates between 1990 and 1996 (Table 4C.2), borrowing was predicted to have increased.
27. The explanatory shares of the cost structure are slightly lower when using cost of attendance rather than tuition, reflecting a reduction in nontuition expenses that partially offset tuition hikes over this period (see Appendix Table 4C.1).
28. The difference between the decomposition techniques over this time period may stem from the functional form limitation of the RIF (i.e., linearity). However, isolating the role of specific observables through sequential reweighting yields similar relative magnitudes as RIF.
29. We unfortunately cannot observe direct transfers from parents to students. However, since parents are borrowing more through PLUS Loans, it is very unlikely that the transfer motive has decreased.
30. In late summer of 2013, new legislation passed that will again tie federal borrowing rates to market rates. Although, prior to the legislation's passage, much attention was given to the fact that subsidized rates would double to the unsubsidized rate for the 2013–2014 school year, it was generally unmentioned that the rates had differed at all only since 2009. Note also that, historically, Stafford rates were similar to or below the U.S. prime rate except during and after the Great Recession.
31. There is surprisingly little work on the elasticity of credit demand with respect to price in the higher education context, and it would be a fruitful area for future research.
32. We use the 1993 wave here because the data are for senior-year and not cumulative borrowing. While NPSAS separates survey school year Stafford borrowing by subsidized and unsubsidized status beginning in 1996, it unfortunately does not do so for cumulative borrowing.

33. The notable exception is above the 95th percentile and is probably due to private loans, which are discussed next. The negative section of the lines reflects the nominal annual borrowing cap for Stafford Loans.

34. This assumes a time to degree of 5.5 years, the average for the class of 2000 in the NPSAS data.

35. These statements also apply to lifetime borrowing limits.

36. In 1996, the median recipient of institutional or state loans was below the 30th percentile of the family income distribution of all students; the median recipient of a private loan was at the 70th percentile.

37. That observables can account for most of the change between 2000 and 2008 is likely in large part due to private loans being well established by 2000. An auxiliary analysis that examined the period between 1996 and 2008, with 1996 reference coefficients, found a much smaller role for observables.

38. The threshold was raised from $5,000 to $10,000 in 2003. In all years, the credit was subject to income phase-outs.

39. A back-of-the-envelope calculation that subtracts the real value of the credit from cumulative borrowing—among all students, not just those claiming the credit—shows that debt would have risen by about $500 less at most points of the distribution between 1996 and 2000. At the mean, this is less than 10 percent. At the 90th percentile, it is about 5 percent.

Appendix 4A

NPSAS Data Details

The National Postsecondary Student Aid Study (NPSAS) has been fielded eight times: in 1987, 1990, 1993, 1996, 2000, 2004, 2008, and 2012. In each case, the year references the spring semester or the end of the school year. This chapter employs the restricted-use 1990, 1996, 2000, 2004, and 2008 waves.[1] The 1987 wave was not used because its sampling frame and question bank were significantly different from those of subsequent waves. The 1993 wave was not used because of an interviewing error that caused the cumulative borrowing question—the key outcome of interest—to be not asked of some graduates. Finally, the 2012 wave has only been partially released. (We plan to update the study when the 2012 wave is fully released.)

The longitudinal comparisons in the chapter required that the data be harmonized across waves. Although each wave is similar to the preceding one, there have been many variable name changes and some definition (or universe) changes over time. In most cases, it was straightforward to rename variables or recode values for consistency, although this often necessitated losing some detail for categorical responses. The processing of the most important variables for the analysis is described in this section.[2]

The primary outcome variable is the cumulative borrowing of the student from all sources for undergraduate education. The variable is called BORAMT1 in each of the waves we use, although its construction varies somewhat over time. In 2004 and 2008, BORAMT1 is constructed as the greater of the student's self-reported borrowing total, the cumulative federal borrowing total taken from the National Student Loan Data System plus self-reported private borrowing in the survey school year, or self-reported total borrowing in the survey school year. In each case, the borrowing numbers exclude loans in the name of parents or guardians (e.g., PLUS Loans), as well as informal loans without a promissory note. This is the definition of cumulative borrowing we use in the paper.

In 2000, there are two versions of the BORAMT1 variable: one that matches the 2004 and 2008 definition, and one that also includes informal loans. We use the first version. In 1996, only the version that includes informal borrowing is available. However, a separate variable (FAMLOAN) asks about cumulative loans from friends and family, although this variable is present only for the portion of the sample that conducted a CATI interview (about two-thirds of the overall sample). We revise the BORAMT1 variable in 1996 by subtracting from it FAMLOAN among the CATI part of the sample and use a revised sampling weight (see below) to correct for the smaller sample. In 1990, historical data from National Student Loan Data System was not included. All cumulative borrowing is thus self-reported. After applying the maximizer decision rule used in the 2004 and 2008 waves, PARLOAN is subtracted from BORAMT1, where PARLOAN represents informal borrowing for the 1989–1990 school year. (There is no cumulative informal loan variable in the 1990 NPSAS, so cumulative loan totals, especially near the top of the distribution, may be biased upward.)

The cleaned BORAMT1 variable is converted to year 2012 dollars using the personal consumption expenditures (PCE) deflator from the Bureau of Economic Analysis. We then applied the following five sample restrictions to focus on our population of interest (the 2008 nomenclature of the variable[s] used for the restriction is in parentheses):

1. The respondent was enrolled in the fall term of the survey school year at an institution in the 50 U.S. states or the District of Columbia (COMPTO87 = 1).

2. The respondent was enrolled at a primarily bachelor's (or higher) degree-granting institution (SECTOR9 = 3,4,6,7,9).

3. The respondent was an undergraduate during the survey school year (STUDTYP = 1).

4. The respondent earned a bachelor's degree during the survey school year (COLLGRAD = 1).

5. The respondent was not a foreign or international student on an education visa (SAMESTAT ≤ 2).

Additionally, because construction of a consistent, cumulative borrowing amount in the 1996 wave required variables from the interview component of the survey, the estimation sample for that wave was restricted to respondents with a positive interview weight (CATIWT > 0). The WTA000 sample weights were used for the 2000 and later waves (using late 2013 vintage weights), the WTB000 sample weight was used for the 1996 wave, and the PSKEEPWT sample weight was used for the 1990 wave.

The NPSAS is also used as the sampling frame for two longitudinal studies, the Beginning Postsecondary Study (BPS), which follows first-time postsecondary students, and the Baccalaureate and Beyond (B&B), which follows bachelor's degree recipients. These two studies alternate NPSAS waves, with BPS being drawn from the 1990, 1996, 2004, and 2012 NPSAS waves, and B&B being drawn from the 1993, 2000, and 2008 NPSAS waves. Since the population of interest for the longitudinal studies is oversampled in the NPSAS, the effective sample sizes for college graduates is quite large in 2000 and 2008 and somewhat smaller in 1990, 1996, and 2004. Final sample sizes, rounded to the nearest 10 to comply with rules on disclosure, are found in Appendix Table 4C.5.

The NPSAS is not the only data set that can be used to track how student debt profiles have changed over the last 20 years. Some longitudinal data sets, such as the National Longitudinal Survey of Youth and the Panel Study of Income Dynamics, ask about educational borrowing, as does the repeated, cross-sectional Survey of Consumer Finances. These latter data sets have the advantages of containing information on other forms of debt as well as income and loan repayment information. However, they have a few disadvantages relative to the NPSAS. First, the sample sizes are much smaller. While the NPSAS typically has several thousand college graduates in each wave (or cohort), the other data sets often have only a few hundred per cohort, and this makes examining entire distributions more difficult. Second, the data on college expenses and financing are not as detailed. The NPSAS benefits from the merge with administrative data on exact loan amounts and family financials, and it surveys students immediately after the school year. The other data sets often gather loan data from retrospective questions, introducing the possibility of recall bias.

While we believe NPSAS is the best data set to look at cumulative borrowing at graduation, the other data sets have a comparative advantage when investigating the topics of loan repayment, default, and debt-income ratios, and how and why these have changed over time. These are clearly important topics, but they are beyond the scope of the current chapter.

Appendix Notes

1. These are available by license from the Department of Education's Institute of Education Sciences (IES) after an application process.
2. A complete list of variables used is available by request from the authors.

Appendix 4B

A Primer on Student Loans

FEDERAL LOANS

The primary federal borrowing program for undergraduates is the Stafford program, established in 1965 as part of the Higher Education Act that year, and later named after Senator Robert Stafford in 1988.[1] Originally intended for lower-income students, all Stafford Loans were subsidized until 1992, with the federal government paying the interest while the student was enrolled.[2] Beginning that year, unsubsidized Stafford Loans became available for students regardless of their financial background. These loans accumulate interest while the student is enrolled, although repayment for either type of Stafford Loan does not begin until six months after school leaving.

Stafford Loans account for the vast majority of federal lending to students. Among graduating seniors in the 2007–2008 school year, for example, Stafford Loans accounted for 96 percent of federal borrowing, with about 60 percent of this volume as subsidized loans.[3] While these loans require the student to fill out the Free Application for Federal Student Aid (FAFSA) form, they are not subject to credit checks and do not require a cosigner. There are limits, however, to how much can be borrowed each year and over a student's lifetime, and these limits have changed over time.

The other major undergraduate federal student lending program is the PLUS Loan, which consists of loans to the students' parents (or legal guardians) rather than directly to the student herself. These also require the FAFSA form to be filed. Unlike the Stafford Loan, PLUS Loans are subject to a credit check.

Both the Stafford and PLUS Loans were administered under the Federal Family Educational Loan Program (FFELP) as well as the Direct program. Under FFELP, private lenders made loans to students under the terms set by the federal government and received subsidies to cover interest rate spread and nonpayment. Under the Direct program, the federal government acted as the lender. The FFELP ended in 2010, with all new loans operating under the Direct program. From the point of view of the borrower, there is practically no difference between the two programs, as terms and conditions are identical.

Table 4B.1 shows the annual limits (in nominal dollars) for the Stafford program. Starting in July 2008, these limits were increased by $2,000 for each class year for dependent students (whose parents were not denied a PLUS Loan), but this higher limit was available only as an unsubsidized loan.

For independent students and dependent students whose parents were denied a PLUS Loan, the limits in Table 4B.1 were increased by the amounts shown in Table 4B.2, with these higher limits also available only as unsubsidized loans.

In addition to these annual loan limits, there are also cumulative lifetime limits on Stafford borrowing. Through 1986, this aggregate limit was $12,500. In 1987, the limit was raised to $17,500, and in October of 1992, it was raised again to $23,000. For subsidized loans, this (nominal) cap is still in place. For dependent students (whose parents were not denied a PLUS Loan), the lifetime Stafford limit was increased to $31,000 in July 2008, but amounts beyond $23,000 must be unsubsidized loans. For independent students (or dependent students whose parents were denied a PLUS Loan), the limit was increased to $46,000 in July 1994 and to $57,500 in July 2008, but again the balance beyond $23,000 must be unsubsidized loans.

The PLUS Loan for parents was initially capped at $4,000 per year (and $20,000 per student lifetime), but this changed in 1993, with the annual limit set to the net cost of attendance (list price minus grants) and an unlimited lifetime amount.

PRIVATE LOANS

Private educational lending (not to be confused with FFELP loans, above) was practically nonexistent until the late 1990s, when attendance costs grew enough relative to the federal borrowing limits to create a market for additional lending. Private loans do not require a FAFSA but often do require credit checks and/or a cosigner. Their interest rates and fee structures are generally more variable than federal loans, with terms that are often worse except for the most creditworthy students. While there are no statutory borrowing limits, borrowing is functionally limited by the net cost of attendance as well as creditworthiness.

Among graduating seniors in 2008, 20 percent took out a private loan that year; these loans constituted 34 percent of total borrowing. (These numbers were up from 5 percent and 10 percent, respectively, in 2000.) Private loan volume decreased dramatically after 2008 in the wake of the Great Recession as private capital dried up, but it is expected to grow again as the economy improves, as long as education costs continue to grow faster than federal borrowing limits.

Table 4B.1   Undergraduate Stafford Borrowing Limits, by Calendar Year and Class Standing

	1st year	2nd year	3rd year	4th year +
1977–1986	2,500	2,500	2,500	2,500
1987–June 1993	2,625	2,625	4,000	4,000
July 1993–June 2007	2,625	3,500	5,500	5,500
July 2007–June 2012	3,500	4,500	5,500	5,500

SOURCE: Authors' calculations from selected years of NPSAS.

Table 4B.2   Supplemental Undergraduate Stafford Borrowing Limits, by Calendar Year and Class Standing

	1st year	2nd year	3rd year	4th year +
1986–1994	4,000	4,000	4,000	4,000
July 1994–June 2008	4,000	4,000	5,000	5,000
July 2008– June 2012	6,000	6,000	7,000	7,000

SOURCE: Authors' calculations from selected years of NPSAS.

OTHER LOANS

In addition to the federal and private lending programs, some states and educational institutions themselves have lending programs. These programs, however, are very small relative to federal and private loans. Less than 2 percent of graduating seniors in 2008 received loans from states or educational institutions, and these loans made up less than 2 percent of the total loan volume for the same set of students.

Finally, there are informal loans in which students borrow directly from their parents or other relatives and friends. Because these loans do not appear on credit reports, and because it is uncertain whether they are expected to be repaid, NPSAS stopped collecting data on them after 2000.

Appendix Notes

1. Much of the material in this appendix, including the timeline of changes and statutory borrowing limits, is drawn from www.finaid.org and Dynarski and Scott-Clayton (2013).
2. Except for a brief period between 1978 and 1982, eligibility for subsidized loans has been means tested throughout the life of the program.

3. Almost all of the remaining 4 percent consists of Perkins Loans, which are intended for very low-income students and function similarly to subsidized Stafford Loans with slightly more generous terms. About 6 percent of graduating seniors in 2008 received Perkins Loans, while 51 percent received Stafford Loans.

Appendix 4C

Supplemental Tables

Table 4C.1 Summary Statistics of BA/BS Graduates from NPSAS (continuous variables), by Wave (000s of 2012 $)

	1990	1996	2000	2004	2008
Family income, dependent students					
Mean	94.6	96.7	96.3	97.2	105.5
25th	51.8	49.5	52.6	49.1	53.6
Median	78.8	81.9	85.5	84.8	93.7
75th	116.0	121.4	125.8	125.8	137.3
Family income, independent students					
Mean	30.8	31.1	39.6	39.5	34.3
25th	8.8	7.3	11.2	11.5	9.0
Median	20.2	20.2	26.9	28.5	23.5
75th	46.5	43.3	55.1	56.3	49.4
Expected family contribution, dependents					
Mean	18.9	15.4	16.2	17.2	19.4
25th	5.0	4.4	5.1	4.5	5.1
Median	10.8	11.0	12.0	11.7	14.8
75th	23.3	21.0	23.3	21.8	27.1
Expected family contribution, independents					
Mean	9.9	7.2	8.0	7.9	6.0
25th	2.1	0.4	0.0	0.0	0.0
Median	4.2	3.1	3.9	2.9	2.0
75th	12.5	10.2	11.3	10.1	8.0
List tuition					
Missing (%)	8.4	3.4	4.3	5.5	7.4
Mean	6.3	8.4	8.4	9.4	11.2
25th	1.8	2.8	2.7	3.5	4.2
Median	3.3	4.7	4.8	5.5	7.0
75th	8.5	12.6	10.9	11.8	14.5

(continued)

Table 4C.1 (continued)

	1990	1996	2000	2004	2008
List cost of attendance					
Missing (%)	8.8	3.4	5.6	5.5	7.4
Mean	17.9	17.5	18.4	19.6	22.9
25th	10.0	11.8	11.4	12.3	13.9
Median	15.9	14.8	15.7	17.1	20.0
75th	23.8	22.2	22.7	23.9	29.8
Total grants					
Mean	2.2	2.8	3.4	3.9	4.9
25th	0.0	0.0	0.0	0.0	0.0
Median	0.0	0.3	0.7	1.6	2.2
75th	3.1	3.8	4.7	5.7	7.2
Tuition net of grants					
Missing (%)	8.4	3.4	4.3	5.5	7.4
Mean	4.3	5.6	4.9	5.5	6.2
25th	0.8	1.4	0.9	0.9	1.0
Median	2.4	3.4	3.1	3.6	4.3
75th	5.3	7.4	6.8	7.6	9.3
Cost of attendance net of grants					
Missing (%)	8.8	3.4	5.6	5.5	7.4
Mean	15.7	14.8	14.9	15.7	17.9
25th	8.2	9.3	8.9	9.1	10.2
Median	13.7	13.2	13.4	13.8	16.0
75th	21.0	18.1	18.4	19.6	23.3

NOTE: Statistics use population weights and are for domestic students graduating with a bachelor's degree in the year indicated. Monetary amounts (in $000) are inflated to 2012 using the PCE index from the Bureau of Economic Analysis. Family income is for the calendar year two years prior to graduation year; tuition (and required fees) is for the final year of enrollment for students who attended only one institution that year and is adjusted for attendance intensity. Cost of attendance is tuition plus room and board, books, travel, and other expenses (also adjusted for attendance intensity by NPSAS).
SOURCE: NPSAS, selected years.

Table 4C.2 Summary Statistics of BA/BS Graduates from NPSAS (Categorical Variables), by Wave

	1990	1996	2000	2004	2008
Dependency status					
Dependent	59.0	58.7	58.2	59.1	62.0
Independent	41.0	41.3	41.8	40.9	38.0
Age					
Less than 21	3.9	1.5	2.0	6.1	6.9
21	26.2	26.0	25.0	22.5	23.8
22	26.1	22.9	24.0	23.5	23.6
23	12.1	13.4	12.6	12.4	12.8
24	6.1	6.8	6.3	6.3	6.3
25–29	10.3	16.0	13.5	12.7	12.4
30–34	5.5	4.3	5.7	5.7	4.9
Older than 34	9.9	9.2	10.8	10.9	9.3
Sex					
Male	45.3	43.5	42.5	42.1	42.7
Female	54.7	56.5	57.5	57.9	57.3
Marital status					
Single, divorced, widowed	79.6	84.6	82.2	81.2	84.6
Married	19.7	15.1	16.9	17.5	14.4
Separated	0.7	0.3	1.0	1.3	1.0
Race/ethnicity					
White, non-Hispanic	86.2	82.7	75.6	73.6	70.5
Black, non-Hispanic	5.7	6.0	8.2	9.2	10.0
Hispanic	4.0	4.5	6.8	7.7	9.4
Asian	3.6	5.9	6.2	6.2	7.2
Native American/other	0.4	1.0	3.3	3.2	2.9
Mother's education					
Unknown	7.1	10.3	9.2	2.5	2.7
Less than high school	7.4	5.0	6.8	6.8	6.1
High school/GED	39.2	36.1	31.0	32.1	28.1
Some college	19.6	18.2	19.1	23.5	26.2
Bachelor's	17.3	19.6	22.7	21.9	22.4
Postgraduate	9.4	10.9	11.3	13.2	14.5

(continued)

Table 4C.2 (continued)

	1990	1996	2000	2004	2008
Father's education					
Unknown	9.0	11.4	10.2	4.4	5.0
Less than high school	8.3	6.0	8.0	8.3	7.0
High school/GED	25.2	27.7	25.2	27.7	27.1
Some college	14.7	10.3	14.7	18.8	20.3
Bachelor's	19.8	22.3	23.4	21.9	21.4
Postgraduate	19.4	20.5	18.5	18.9	19.3
Attendance pattern					
Full-time, full-year, 1 school	45.1	55.5	52.4	52.7	54.8
Full-time, full-year, 2+ school	1.3	1.5	2.5	3.3	4.5
Full-time, part-year	16.0	11.9	18.0	13.5	13.1
Part-time, full-year, 1 school	17.3	19.8	15.6	17.9	14.3
Part-time, full-year, 2+ schools	7.0	1.6	0.9	1.3	1.9
Part-time, part-year	13.3	9.8	10.7	11.3	11.4
Years to degree					
Unknown	–	0.7	0.3	0.0	0.0
Fewer than 4	–	1.6	12.6	10.8	8.9
4	–	32.6	34.5	34.5	35.7
5	–	24.4	21.3	22.6	21.0
6	–	11.6	8.0	8.1	9.1
7–9	–	12.6	9.2	9.3	10.9
10 or more	–	16.7	14.0	14.7	14.4
Institution sector					
Public, nondoctoral	29.6	20.1	19.6	21.6	16.8
Public, doctoral	36.4	44.8	46.3	45.8	49.0
Private, NFP,[a] nondoc	19.5	21.9	19.7	17.9	15.0
Private, NFP, doc	13.8	12.6	13.2	12.4	15.0
Private, FP[b]	0.6	0.6	1.3	2.3	4.2
Institution region					
New England	10.8	4.7	6.5	8.2	5.8
Mid East	19.5	19.8	17.9	14.8	17.4
Great Lakes	18.9	18.1	16.6	14.4	14.7

Table 4C.2 (continued)

	1990	1996	2000	2004	2008
Plains	6.7	7.5	8.6	8.3	7.9
Southeast	18.3	22.4	22.7	26.2	25.4
Southwest	8.2	10.9	10.5	8.5	11.5
Rocky Mts.	3.8	2.9	3.7	6.6	4.0
Far West	13.8	13.8	13.5	13.2	13.5
In-state student					
Yes, public	60.1	58.5	58.1	61.5	60.7
Yes, private	22.0	22.5	21.8	22.2	22.2
No	17.9	19.1	20.1	16.3	17.0
Major					
Unknown	6.7	2.3	2.5	1.5	0.8
Humanities	13.9	12.6	13.2	12.5	13.6
Social sciences	14.6	17.3	16.8	15.5	14.7
Life sciences	4.8	10.0	7.2	6.6	9.5
Physical sciences/math	1.8	3.7	2.4	2.6	2.4
Computer science	2.3	2.5	4.4	5.3	2.4
Engineering	7.1	6.1	4.8	5.3	6.3
Education	7.8	8.8	9.2	10.3	8.1
Business	22.5	19.5	20.1	20.5	21.0
Health	8.9	9.4	9.0	6.9	7.8
Other	9.7	8.0	10.4	13.0	13.5

[a] Not for profit.
[b] For profit.
NOTE: Statistics use population weights and are for domestic students graduating with a bachelor's degree in the year indicated. Attendance pattern refers to the final year of enrollment. Years to degree refers to the difference between the calendar year of first postsecondary enrollment and the graduation year indicated. In-state students attend an institution in their state of legal residence.
SOURCE: NPSAS, selected years.

Table 4C.3A Recentered Influence Function Decompositions of Borrowing: 1990–1996, Using Tuition

	Mean		50th percentile		75th percentile		90th percentile	
Difference (000s of 2012 $)	2.01	(0.49)	0.58	(0.47)	6.35	(0.97)	4.55	(0.92)
Composition effects due to:								
Age/dependency status	0.13	(0.13)	0.66	(0.20)	0.92	(0.27)	0.43	(0.24)
Sex, marital status, ethnicity	0.12	(0.06)	-0.02	(0.09)	-0.06	(0.11)	-0.11	(0.12)
Parental education	-0.07	(0.07)	0.16	(0.13)	0.16	(0.16)	0.13	(0.17)
Location, in-state status	-0.24	(0.20)	-0.55	(0.32)	-0.40	(0.40)	-0.24	(0.49)
School sector, attendance, major	-0.11	(0.23)	0.54	(0.64)	-0.23	(0.47)	-0.14	(0.55)
Expected family contribution	0.25	(0.09)	0.72	(0.17)	0.88	(0.21)	0.98	(0.22)
Tuition and grants	1.14	(0.33)	0.72	(0.52)	1.65	(0.51)	0.44	(0.84)
Total	1.22	(0.40)	2.23	(0.57)	2.92	(0.75)	1.49	(1.06)
Structural effects due to:								
Age/dependency status	0.52	(0.67)	1.99	(0.55)	1.63	(1.36)	-3.12	(1.30)
Sex, marital status, ethnicity	-1.90	(2.75)	-3.44	(1.72)	-2.44	(5.09)	-3.83	(4.11)
Parental education	0.29	(0.55)	-0.23	(0.49)	0.18	(1.01)	1.60	(1.07)
Location, in-state status	0.68	(0.81)	0.32	(0.59)	-0.21	(1.39)	-0.05	(1.55)
School sector, attendance, major	1.88	(1.86)	-0.57	(4.95)	5.60	(3.44)	3.36	(3.44)
Expected family contribution	-3.72	(0.85)	-1.23	(0.72)	-5.22	(1.62)	-1.13	(1.41)
Tuition and grants	2.92	(2.07)	-1.76	(2.20)	7.31	(4.27)	9.98	(4.07)
Constant	0.14	(3.78)	3.25	(6.14)	-3.42	(7.98)	-3.76	(6.69)
Total	0.79	(0.50)	-1.65	(0.55)	3.43	(0.95)	3.06	(1.33)

NOTE: Each column refers to the later period less the earlier period. The recentered influence functions and quantiles are calculated with sample weights; the decompositions are based on coefficients from the base period reference and are estimated via OLS (without sample weights). Bootstrapped standard errors (100 replications) are in parentheses. Borrowing is from all sources except friends and family and excludes loans taken out by parents (PLUS Loans).

SOURCE: Authors' calculations from selected years of NPSAS.

Table 4C.3B Recentered Influence Function Decompositions of Borrowing: 1990–1996, Using Cost of Attendance

	Mean		50th percentile		75th percentile		90th percentile	
Difference (000s of 2012 $)	2.01	(0.49)	0.58	(0.47)	6.35	(0.97)	4.55	(0.92)
Composition effects due to:								
Age/dependency status	0.13	(0.11)	0.63	(0.19)	0.76	(0.24)	0.25	(0.23)
Sex, marital status, ethnicity	0.18	(0.07)	-0.02	(0.09)	-0.07	(0.12)	-0.13	(0.14)
Parental education	-0.06	(0.07)	0.17	(0.14)	0.15	(0.17)	0.14	(0.18)
Location, in-state status	-0.26	(0.20)	-0.54	(0.31)	-0.50	(0.41)	-0.32	(0.50)
School sector, attendance, major	0.09	(0.19)	0.12	(0.28)	-0.15	(0.45)	0.12	(0.57)
Expected family contribution	0.27	(0.10)	0.71	(0.18)	0.89	(0.21)	0.95	(0.22)
Attendance cost and grants	0.40	(0.19)	0.94	(0.28)	0.80	(0.41)	0.19	(0.42)
Total	0.73	(0.38)	2.00	(0.52)	1.88	(0.74)	1.19	(0.80)
Structural effects due to:								
Age/dependency status	0.65	(0.67)	1.89	(0.55)	1.73	(1.34)	-3.21	(1.32)
Sex, marital status, ethnicity	-3.02	(2.97)	-4.04	(1.72)	-4.43	(5.37)	-5.87	(4.50)
Parental education	0.39	(0.56)	-0.17	(0.48)	0.42	(1.02)	1.69	(1.09)
Location, in-state status	0.68	(0.84)	0.19	(0.60)	-0.40	(1.39)	-0.25	(1.57)
School sector, attendance, major	0.02	(1.69)	1.54	(1.56)	1.36	(3.46)	-1.73	(3.46)
Expected family contribution	-3.75	(0.85)	-1.58	(0.71)	-6.15	(1.59)	-2.22	(1.43)
Attendance cost and grants	0.72	(2.77)	-9.79	(3.30)	2.93	(6.41)	5.66	(5.47)
Constant	5.60	(4.27)	10.54	(4.09)	9.00	(9.07)	9.30	(7.89)
Total	1.28	(0.49)	-1.43	(0.50)	4.47	(0.96)	3.36	(1.11)

NOTE: Each column refers to the later period less the earlier period. The recentered influence functions and quantiles are calculated with sample weights; the decompositions are based on coefficients from the base period reference and are estimated via OLS (without sample weights). Bootstrapped standard errors (100 replications) are in parentheses. Borrowing is from all sources except friends and family and excludes loans taken out by parents (PLUS Loans).

SOURCE: Authors' calculations from selected years of NPSAS.

Table 4C.4A Recentered Influence Function Decompositions of Borrowing: 1996–2000, Using Tuition

	Mean		50th percentile		75th percentile		90th percentile	
Difference (000s of 2012 $)	5.12	(0.46)	8.45	(0.60)	6.78	(0.83)	9.41	(0.86)
Composition effects due to:								
Age/dependency status	0.04	(0.12)	0.01	(0.04)	−0.05	(0.15)	−0.12	(0.31)
Sex, marital status, ethnicity	0.13	(0.14)	0.07	(0.06)	0.05	(0.21)	0.01	(0.15)
Parental education	−0.04	(0.15)	−0.06	(0.09)	0.08	(0.33)	−0.10	(0.29)
Location, in-state status	0.11	(0.17)	−0.08	(0.15)	0.31	(0.46)	0.03	(0.39)
School sector, attendance, major	0.37	(0.16)	0.35	(0.17)	0.07	(0.53)	0.70	(0.52)
Expected family contribution	−0.32	(0.18)	−0.43	(0.11)	−1.12	(0.31)	−0.68	(0.20)
Tuition and grants	−0.12	(0.32)	−0.52	(0.25)	−0.83	(0.86)	−0.54	(0.85)
Total	0.18	(0.51)	−0.67	(0.33)	−1.50	(1.12)	−0.70	(1.02)
Structural effects due to:								
Age/dependency status	−1.06	(0.63)	−2.65	(0.67)	−1.58	(1.23)	−3.59	(1.21)
Sex, marital status, ethnicity	0.05	(2.69)	1.21	(1.61)	1.38	(4.68)	−0.57	(4.29)
Parental education	−0.02	(0.47)	1.55	(0.49)	−0.92	(0.75)	−1.37	(0.83)
Location, in-state status	−0.39	(0.68)	0.71	(0.82)	0.18	(1.33)	−1.33	(1.43)
School sector, attendance, major	−0.78	(1.46)	−4.91	(1.44)	−3.65	(2.75)	−2.64	(2.69)
Expected family contribution	2.12	(0.88)	−5.55	(0.88)	5.85	(1.62)	1.13	(1.42)
Tuition and grants	−0.31	(1.96)	8.59	(2.09)	−8.68	(3.98)	−2.51	(3.61)
Constant	5.33	(3.58)	10.17	(3.05)	15.69	(7.18)	20.99	(6.40)
Total	4.94	(0.48)	9.13	(0.62)	8.28	(1.13)	10.10	(1.11)

NOTE: Each column refers to the later period less the earlier period. The recentered influence functions and quantiles are calculated with sample weights; the decompositions are based on coefficients from the base period reference and are estimated via OLS (without sample weights). Bootstrapped standard errors (100 replications) are in parentheses. Borrowing is from all sources except friends and family and excludes loans taken out by parents (PLUS Loans).

SOURCE: Authors' calculations from selected years of NPSAS.

Table 4C.4B Recentered Influence Function Decompositions of Borrowing: 1996–2000, Using Cost of Attendance

	Mean		50th percentile		75th percentile		90th percentile	
Difference (000s of 2012 $)	5.12	(0.46)	8.45	(0.60)	6.78	(0.83)	9.41	(0.86)
Composition effects due to:								
Age/dependency status	0.01	(0.12)	0.02	(0.05)	0.01	(0.13)	-0.07	(0.28)
Sex, marital status, ethnicity	0.15	(0.14)	0.08	(0.06)	0.10	(0.20)	0.03	(0.15)
Parental education	-0.07	(0.15)	-0.08	(0.09)	-0.03	(0.34)	-0.16	(0.29)
Location, in-state status	0.13	(0.18)	-0.13	(0.16)	0.11	(0.46)	-0.15	(0.40)
School sector, attendance, major	0.39	(0.15)	0.42	(0.16)	0.39	(0.50)	0.78	(0.51)
Expected family contribution	-0.31	(0.18)	-0.45	(0.12)	-1.19	(0.33)	-0.73	(0.21)
Attendance cost and grants	0.21	(0.35)	-0.37	(0.25)	-0.61	(0.87)	-0.30	(0.82)
Total	0.51	(0.53)	-0.52	(0.35)	-1.22	(1.13)	-0.59	(1.04)
Structural effects due to:								
Age/dependency status	-1.09	(0.63)	-2.23	(0.65)	-1.97	(1.18)	-3.40	(1.20)
Sex, marital status, ethnicity	0.57	(2.88)	1.55	(1.59)	2.11	(4.97)	0.16	(4.56)
Parental education	-0.15	(0.48)	1.39	(0.49)	-1.18	(0.76)	-1.56	(0.83)
Location, in-state status	-0.32	(0.70)	0.87	(0.83)	0.61	(1.32)	-0.92	(1.46)
School sector, attendance, major	-0.80	(1.48)	-6.45	(1.37)	-2.76	(2.94)	-2.31	(2.60)
Expected family contribution	1.61	(0.86)	-5.99	(0.86)	6.10	(1.59)	0.63	(1.45)
Attendance cost and grants	2.58	(2.91)	21.80	(4.11)	-2.13	(5.85)	5.49	(5.57)
Constant	2.21	(4.28)	-1.98	(4.47)	7.20	(8.24)	11.91	(7.62)
Total	4.61	(0.49)	8.97	(0.63)	8.00	(1.12)	10.00	(1.12)

NOTE: Each column refers to the later period less the earlier period. The recentered influence functions and quantiles are calculated with sample weights; the decompositions are based on coefficients from the base period reference and are estimated via OLS (without sample weights). Bootstrapped standard errors (100 replications) are in parentheses. Borrowing is from all sources except friends and family and excludes loans taken out by parents (PLUS Loans).

SOURCE: Authors' calculations from selected years of NPSAS.

Table 4C.5 Sample Sizes

	1990	1996	2000	2004	2008
College graduates	3,270	1,340	12,230	5,170	23,340
Weighted: college graduates	724,000	897,000	1,217,000	1,448,000	1,822,000

NOTE: College graduates are oversampled in 2000 and 2008, as these years represent sampling frames for the Baccalaureate and Beyond longitudinal studies. Sample sizes are rounded to the nearest 10 (thousand for weighted numbers) to comply with disclosure restrictions.
SOURCE: NPSAS, selected years.

References

Avery, Christopher, and Sarah Turner. 2012. "Student Loans: Do College Students Borrow Too Much—Or Not Enough?" *Journal of Economic Perspectives* 26(1): 165–192.

Blinder, Alan S. 1973. "Wage Discrimination: Reduced Form and Structural Variables." *Journal of Human Resources* 8(4): 436–455.

Bound, John, Michael F. Lovenheim, and Sarah Turner. 2010. "Increasing Time to Baccalaureate Degree in the United States." NBER Working Paper No. 15892. Cambridge, MA: National Bureau of Economic Research.

Cellini, Stephanie R., and Claudia Goldin. 2012. "Does Federal Student Aid Raise Tuition? New Evidence on For-Profit Colleges." NBER Working Paper No. 17827. Cambridge, MA: National Bureau of Economic Research.

College Board. 2012a. *Trends in Student Aid, 2012*. New York: College Board.

———. 2012b. *Trends in College Pricing, 2012*. New York: College Board.

Consumer Financial Protection Bureau. 2012. Report to the Senate Committee on Banking, Housing, and Urban Affairs, the Senate Committee on Health, Education, Labor, and Pensions, the House of Representatives Committee on Financial Services, and the House of Representatives Committee on Education and the Workforce. Washington, DC: Consumer Financial Protection Bureau.

DiNardo, John, Nicole M. Fortin, and Thomas Lemieux. 1996. "Labor Market Institutions and the Distribution of Wages, 1973–1992: A Semiparametric Approach." *Econometrica* 64(5): 1001–1044.

Dynarski, Susan, and Judith Scott-Clayton. 2013. "Financial Aid Policy: Lessons from Research." *Postsecondary Education in the United States* 23(1): 67–91.

Federal Reserve Board of Governors. 2012. *Survey of Consumer Finances.* Washington, DC: Federal Reserve Board of Governors.

Firpo, Sergio, Nicole M. Fortin, and Thomas Lemieux. 2009. "Unconditional Quantile Regressions." *Econometrica* 77(3): 953–973.

Greenstone, Michael, and Adam Looney. 2013. "Rising Student Debt Burdens: Factors behind the Phenomenon." Washington, DC: The Hamilton Project, Brookings Institution. http://www.hamiltonproject.org/papers/rising_student_debt_burdens_factors_behind_the_phenomenon/ (accessed June 4, 2014).

Jacob, Brian, Brian McCall, and Kevin Stange. 2013. "College as Country Club: Do Colleges Cater to Students' Preferences for Consumption?" NBER Working Paper No. 18745. Cambridge, MA: National Bureau of Economic Research.

Jann, Ben. 2008. "The Blinder-Oaxaca Decomposition for Linear Regression Models." *Stata Journal* 8(4): 453–479.

Joint Economic Committee. 2013. *The Causes and Consequences of Increasing Student Debt*. U.S. Congress. June. Washington, DC: Joint Economic Committee.

Kantrowitz, Mark. 2012. "Who Graduates College with Six-Figure Student Loan Debt?" www.finaid.org/educators/20120801sixfiguredebt.pdf (accessed June 1, 2013).

Lewin, Tamar. 2013. "Financing for Colleges Declines as Costs Rise." *New York Times*, March 6, A:17.

Martin, Andrew, and Andrew W. Lehren. 2012. "A Generation Hobbled by the Soaring Cost of College." *New York Times*, May 12. http://www.nytimes .com/2012/05/13/business/student-loans-weighing-down-a-generation-with-heavy-debt.html?_r=0.

Mitchell, Josh, and Maya Jackson-Randall. 2012. "Student-Loan Debt Tops $1 Trillion." *Wall Street Journal*, March 22. http://online.wsj.com/news/articles/SB10001424052702303812904577295930047604846.

Oaxaca, Ronald. 1973. "Male-Female Wage Differentials in Urban Labor Markets." *International Economic Review* 14(3): 693–709.

Quinterno, John, and Viany Orozco. 2012. *The Great Cost Shift: How Higher Education Cuts Undermine the Future Middle Class*. New York: Demos.

Senate Committee on the Budget. 2006. "2002 Student Loan Law Takes Effect, Lowers Interest Rates." U.S. Senate Budget Bulletin. August 4. Washington, DC: U.S. Senate.

Turner, Lesley. 2012. "The Incidence of Student Financial Aid: Evidence from the Pell Grant Program." University of Maryland Working Paper.

Turner, Nicholas. 2012. "Who Benefits from Student Aid? The Economic Incidence of Tax-Based Federal Student Aid." *Economics of Education Review* 31(4): 463–481.

5

Understanding Changes in the Distribution of Student Loan Debt over Time

Elizabeth Akers
Brown Center on Education Policy, Brookings Institution

Matthew M. Chingos
Brown Center on Education Policy, Brookings Institution

Alice M. Henriques
Federal Reserve Board of Governors

When outstanding debt passed the $1 trillion mark two years ago, it prompted many to question whether the student lending market is headed for a crisis, with many students unable to repay their loans and taxpayers being forced to foot the bill. Commentators have also expressed concerns that increasing education debt loads are making it more difficult for borrowers to start families, buy houses, and save for retirement (Brown and Caldwell 2013). There is clear evidence that the number of students taking on debt has been increasing and that debt burdens have been growing. However, the large and growing economic return to college education implies that many of these loans are financing sound investments. Consequently, it is not obvious that the growth in debt is problematic. Existing evidence is insufficient to determine what these changes mean for the financial well-being of borrowers and the health of the overall student lending market.

The returns to a college degree are higher than they have ever been. In 2011, college graduates aged 23–25 earned $12,000 more per year on average than high school graduates in the same group, and they had employment rates 20 percentage points higher. Over the last 30 years, the increase in lifetime earnings associated with earning a college degree has grown by 75 percent, whereas costs have grown by 50 percent (Greenstone and Looney 2012). These economic benefits accrue to individuals, but also to society in the form of increased tax revenue, improved health, and higher levels of civic participation (Baum, Ma, and Payea 2013).

Today's students are more likely than their predecessors to borrow and to take out larger loans to pay for tuition, fees, and living expenses while in college. Over the last 20 years, inflation-adjusted published tuition and fees have more than doubled at four-year public institutions and have increased by more than 70 percent at private four-year and public two-year colleges (Figure 5.1). The fact that the total outstanding balance on student loans recently passed $1 trillion, combined with media reports of students with large debts—often in excess of $100,000—have garnered a great deal of public attention. However, the debt picture for the typical college graduate is not so dire. For example, bachelor's degree recipients in 2011–2012 who took on student loan debt accumulated approximately $26,000 in student loan debt ($25,000 at public institutions, and $29,900 at private, nonprofit institutions) (College Board 2013). Debt per borrower is growing rapidly (at an annual rate of 1.2 percent above inflation at nonprofit institutions and 2.1 percent at public institutions), but it is still a manageable burden if the graduate is able to find gainful employment. Extremely high debt levels remain quite rare: in 2012, only 5 percent of borrowers with education debt owed more than $100,000 (College Board 2013).

In the United States, student lending takes place through two channels, the federal lending programs and the private market for student loans. The federal lending program exists because, in the absence of government intervention, the private market would provide too few students access to loans, which would result in underinvestment in education at the national level. The basis for this theory is that, unlike physical capital, human capital—or the skills that one obtains through education—cannot effectively serve as collateral for a loan. This makes student lending inherently risky, because a lender cannot foreclose on a student's education the same way it can foreclose on a home if the borrower goes into default. More generally, the federal loan program ensures that all students have access to higher education, regardless of their ability to pay.

Figure 5.1 Trends in Published Tuition and Fees, 1971–2012

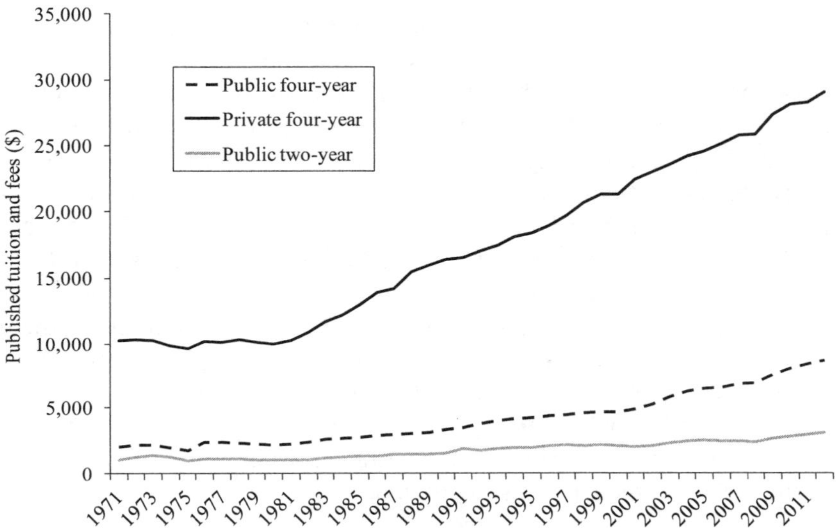

SOURCE: National Center for Education Statistics (2012, Table 381).

Most student lending takes place through the federal government because the interest rates offered in federal lending programs are below those typically offered by private lenders. Interest rates on federal loans are set by legislation and do not depend on the likelihood that a borrower will default. The amount that students can borrow from the government depends on whether they are financially dependent on their parents (as defined by a federal formula) and on their year in college (including whether they are a graduate student). Students from households judged to have more financial need are eligible to borrow a larger portion of their federal loans through the subsidized loan program, in which the government pays interest while the student is in school. Federal student loans carry additional benefits beyond the below-market interest rates and in-school interest subsidies for eligible families. Borrowers who face financial hardship after leaving college are eligible for deferral or reduction of monthly payments, and even forgiveness through a number of repayment programs.

Some students also borrow from private financial institutions, usually after they have exhausted their ability to borrow from the government. Unlike the loans offered in the federal lending programs, private lenders offer loans with interest rates that reflect a borrower's likelihood of default. This means that borrowers from low-income households or borrowers attending colleges with lower completion rates are likely to face the highest rates. In addition, private student loans carry less generous repayment terms than federal loans, an important distinction given that both federal and private student loans are more difficult to discharge in bankruptcy than other types of consumer debt.

Despite the significant role that loans play in our nation's higher education system and the increased attention to rising debt levels, there is little existing empirical evidence that attempts to explain these trends. In this chapter, we examine how education loan balances have evolved over time and measure the extent to which changes in degree attainment, tuition, demographics, and borrowing behavior have contributed to the observed increase in student debt.

BACKGROUND AND DATA

The lack of empirical evidence available to support discussions about perceived problems in the student loan market is at least partly due to the limitations of existing data sources. The primary source of data on student aid is the Integrated Postsecondary Education Data System (IPEDS). These data, which are derived from the Department of Education's survey of all institutions participating in federal student aid programs, report institution-level lending variables, including total outlays within the federal loan program and number of borrowers. While this information is incredibly important, it does not tell the whole story. For instance, we cannot tell how the use of private loans has changed or how much debt students accumulate over time.

In addition to the data available through IPEDS, the Department of Education publishes the findings from a few different longitudinal studies, including Baccalaureate and Beyond and Beginning Postsecondary Students, both of which draw their participants from the National Postsecondary Student Aid Study. These studies track a specific cohort of students for a set number of years. The Baccalaureate and Beyond study collects data for 10 years following graduation from a bachelor's degree program, and the Beginning Postsecondary Students study collects data for 6 years following initial enrollment in postsecondary education. These longitudinal data sources enable us to observe cumulative debt burdens for student borrowers, but only for a select cohort of students. The most valuable feature of these studies for this area of research is that they collect information on both earnings and education liabilities. However, the small number of cohorts available and the relatively short period of observation limit the usefulness of these data.

Two additional data sources not collected by the U.S. Department of Education have been used to answer questions about the evolution of the student loan market. First, the College Board has compiled annual reports that summarize both public and proprietary data on student borrowing from both federal and private sources. The proprietary data are collected through a survey of institutions administered by the College Board. The annual, Web-based survey collects data from nearly 4,000 accredited undergraduate colleges and universities. Although this data set succeeds in filling a void left by federal data, its usefulness is limited by the fact that the data are self-reported by institutions and thus are subject to inconsistencies in reporting and potential manipulation by institutions.

Another data source that has been used to produce evidence on the student loan market is the Federal Reserve Bank of New York's (FRBNY) Consumer Credit Panel. These data, which are based on the proprietary data used in credit bureau reports, capture longitudinal information on the debt portfolio of all individuals who have ever applied for credit. Researchers at the FRBNY have used this resource to compile data on the market for outstanding student loan debt. The primary shortcoming of these data for the purpose of understanding the state of the student loan market is that they do not capture much background information on borrowers, in particular, their level of educational attainment.

The Federal Reserve Board administers a nationally representative survey that generates data with many of the features not available in the previously discussed data sources. The Survey of Consumer Finances (SCF) is administered every three years and collects information on household finances. Unlike the Consumer Credit Panel, the SCF generates cross-sectional data. A key advantage of the SCF is that it links information on liabilities, including outstanding student loan debt, to data on earnings and demographics. Unlike the other data sources, the SCF is a household-level survey. This is advantageous for our analysis. Since financial decision making often takes place at the household level, individual analysis could easily misrepresent an individual's financial well-being. Although the SCF lacks some background variables that would be useful to allow us to more fully understand the decision to take out education loans, it does report educational attainment, which is critical for this work. Since the SCF has been administered in a relatively consistent manner since 1989, it allows for thorough analysis of changes over time for the full U.S. population. However, one limitation of the SCF is that, owing to its sampling procedures, it does not capture the liabilities of young adults living in a household headed by someone else, such as a parent.

We use the SCF from 1989 to 2010 to track changes in student loan debt over time. We measure student loan debt as the total outstanding balance, measured in 2010 dollars, of all education debt held by households, calculated on a per-person basis (that is, we divided household debt by two for households with two adults). We apply survey weights throughout the analysis so that the results are representative of the U.S. population of households.[1]

RESULTS

Trends in Debt over Time

The SCF data show a dramatic increase in education debt among households with an average age between 20 and 40. Table 5.1, with key indicators depicted in Figure 5.2, shows that the share of young U.S. households with education debt more than doubled in 2010, from 14 percent in 1989 to 36 percent. Not only were more individuals taking out education loans, but they were taking out larger loans—not necessarily what you would expect as people cross the margin from being nonborrowers to borrowers. Among households with positive debt, the mean per-person debt more than tripled, from $5,810 to $17,916. Median debt

Table 5.1 Incidence and Amount of Debt over Time, Age 20–40

Year	Incidence (%)	Mean debt ($)	Those with debt		Cell size
			Mean ($)	Median ($)	
1989	14	806	5,810	3,517	971
1992	20	1,498	7,623	3,730	1,323
1995	20	1,475	7,521	3,577	1,429
1998	20	2,539	12,826	8,027	1,362
2001	22	2,881	12,939	6,156	1,307
2004	24	3,402	14,204	7,503	1,246
2007	28	4,583	16,322	9,728	1,144
2010	36	6,502	17,916	8,500	1,865

SOURCE: Authors' calculations using data from the SCF.

Figure 5.2 Trends in Debt over Time, Households with Average Age 20–40, 1989–2010

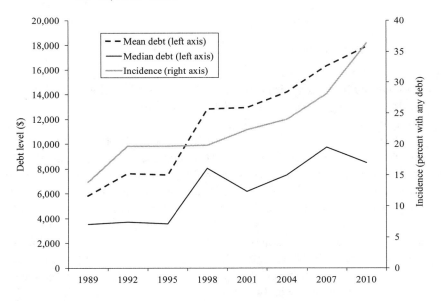

SOURCE: Authors' calculations using data from the SCF.

Figure 5.3 Cumulative Distribution of Education Debt, Households with Average Age 20–40, 1989/1992 and 2010

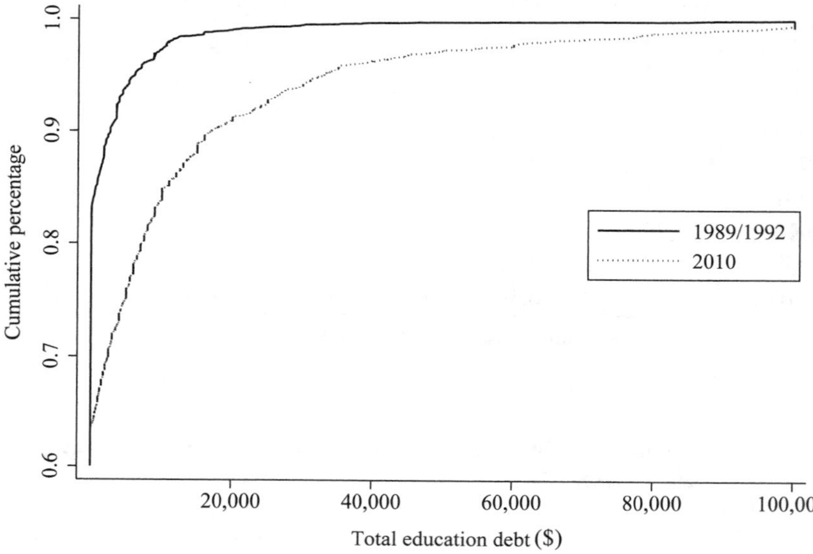

SOURCE: Authors' calculations using data from the SCF.

grew somewhat less rapidly, from $3,517 to $8,500. Among all households, including those with no debt, mean debt increased eightfold, from about $800 to about $6,500.

The change in the distribution of debt between 1989/1992 (combined to increase precision) and 2010 is depicted in Figure 5.3, which shows the cumulative share of households with debt at or below a given level (density plots are shown in Figure 5.4). In the earlier period, not only was the incidence of debt low, but most borrowers had very small loan balances. Only a trivial number of households had more than $20,000 in debt (per person) in 1989/1992, whereas in 2010, about 10 percent of households—or more than a quarter of those with debt—had balances exceeding $20,000. The incidence of very large debt balances is greater now than it was two decades ago, but it is still quite rare. In 2010, 3 percent of all households, or about 8 percent of households with debt, had balances in excess of $50,000.

Figure 5.4 Distribution of Education Debt, 1989/1992 and 2010

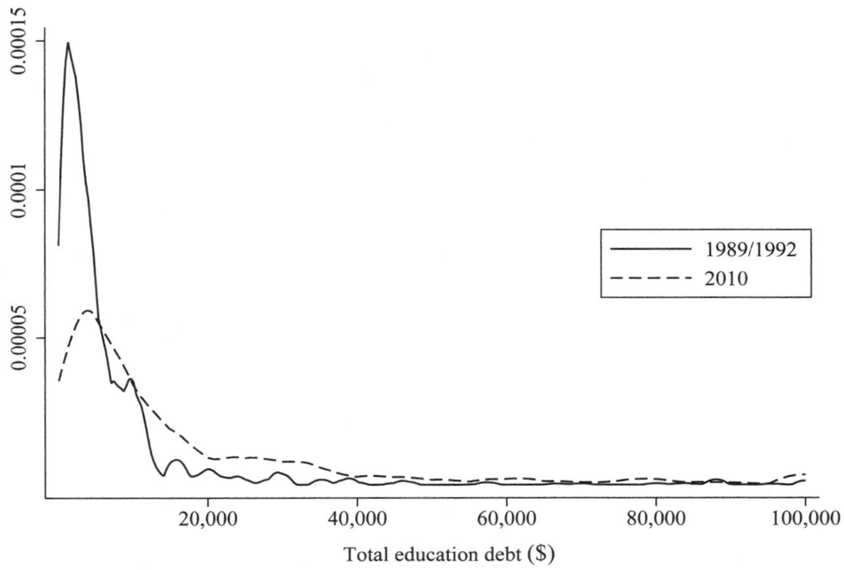

SOURCE: Authors' calculations using data from the SCF.

The focus on the age range 20–40 allows us to examine households that are likely to be within the repayment period of student loans while also capturing individuals who potentially take on graduate as well as undergraduate debt.[2] Because we focus on the remaining total balance of education debt, the trends over time we observe will reflect changes in both borrowing and repayment behavior.[3] In order to examine repayment over time, we would ideally use a panel data set that tracks a cohort of individuals over a long period of time. As a rough approximation using the SCF data, we track a group of age cohorts over time. Specifically, we examine the education loan balances of the group that was aged 20–25 in 1989 or 1992 at three-year intervals through 2007 and 2010, when those cohorts were aged 38–43 (we average over pairs of survey years in order to increase the precision of the results).

The results of this descriptive analysis are shown in Figure 5.5. The share of this group with any education debt declines over time from 28 percent at ages 20–25 to 18 percent at ages 38–43. (The slight

**Figure 5.5 Tracking Cohort Debt over Time, Age 20–25 in 1989/1992
through Age 38–43 in 2007/2010**

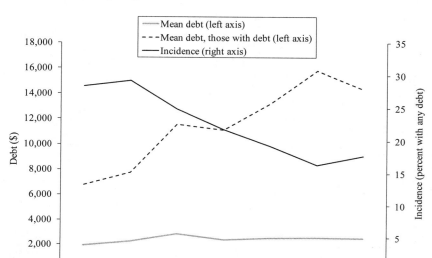

SOURCE: Authors' calculations using data from the SCF.

uptick between ages 35–40 and 38–43 could reflect a small number
of loans taken for children in the household.) Among the remaining
borrowers, mean debt increases dramatically, from less than $7,000 to
more than $14,000. The combination of these two trends results in a
mean debt level (including those without any debt) that increases from
about $2,000 to about $2,500 over the roughly 20-year period that we
observe, an increase of about 25 percent. We interpret these data as
suggesting that many individuals are paying off their education loan
balances during this time period, but some individuals are still taking on
more debt (for graduate school or attending undergraduate programs at
non-traditional ages) as they age, pushing up the balance of those with
any debt.

Explaining Changes in Education Debt

The large increases in education debt levels over the last two decades documented in the SCF data and other data sources are often attributed to the increases in tuition charged by colleges and universities. The tuition trends shown in Figure 5.1 certainly support that theory. But there is also evidence that college students are relying more on debt to finance college costs and paying less out-of-pocket (Greenstone and Looney 2013), suggesting that student behavior is changing in ways that favor loans over other ways of paying for college. Furthermore, there have been shifts in the educational attainment level and demographic characteristics of the U.S. college-age population that could impact observed student borrowing.

We begin by examining the extent to which changes in education debt levels can be explained by changing population characteristics. We primarily focus on educational attainment, given the fact that increased debt due to rising educational attainment may reflect rational human capital investments given the large and growing economic returns to education. Table 5.2 shows that educational attainment of households aged 20–40 rose between 1989 and 2010. The share of households with no college experience fell from 41 to 31 percent, the share with at least one person with a bachelor's degree increased from 20 to 24 percent,

Table 5.2 Summary Statistics, Household Level, Average Age 20–40 (%)

| Year | Race/ethnicity of household head | | | | Maximum education of household | | | | |
	White	Black	His-panic	Other	Couple	High school or less	Some college	BA	Gradu-ate
1989	72	11	11	6	62	41	29	20	9
1992	71	14	10	5	61	37	29	25	9
1995	73	14	9	4	59	36	31	23	10
1998	71	14	11	4	62	36	32	21	11
2001	68	16	12	4	60	38	28	23	11
2004	67	15	14	4	58	34	31	23	12
2007	63	16	15	6	62	33	33	22	12
2010	62	15	17	6	58	31	32	24	13

SOURCE: Authors' calculations using data from the SCF.

and the share with at least one person with a graduate degree increased from 9 to 13 percent.[4]

It is not surprising that education debt levels vary markedly by educational attainment, but debt trends also vary noticeably along this dimension, as shown in Figures 5.6 and 5.7. Among households with some college but no bachelor's degree, the incidence of debt increased from 11 to 41 percent. Households where at least one member holds a bachelor's degree saw an increase from 22 to 50 percent, and households with at least one graduate degree went from 33 to 58 percent. Among those with debt, the average per-person debt load increased 135 and 162 percent among households with some college and a bachelor's degree, respectively. Households with a graduate degree saw an increase of 311 percent, from just under $10,000 to more than $40,000.

Given the rising levels of educational attainment over the 21-year period from 1989 to 1992 and the concentration of debt increases among the more educated, to what extent do the changes in attainment explain the changes in debt? We address this question by calculating what the average debt in 2010 would have been had educational attainment remained at its 1989 level. We do this by calculating a weighted average of mean debt (including those without debt, in order to reflect changes in incidence) in 2010 by educational attainment, using the percentage of borrowers in the educational attainment category in 1989 as the weights. From 1989 to 2010, average debt increased from $806 to $6,502, a change of $5,696. Had attainment (measured as the maximum value in two-person households) remained the same, average debt in 2010 would have been $5,343, a change of $4,538. In other words, the change in attainment explains about 20 percent of the observed change.

We implement this approach for all years of data and report the results in Figure 5.8. As attainment increases over time, the gap between actual debt and the simulated debt with constant attainment grows. These calculations only take into account educational attainment and do so in a simple way by taking the maximum for households. We next implement a multivariate decomposition that allows us to more accurately capture changes in educational attainment of the household and also adjust for race/ethnicity. Table 5.2 shows that, between 1989 and 2010, the white share of the population fell and the Hispanic share rose. To the extent that race and debt are correlated, these changes could also have contributed to (or mitigated) rising debt levels.

Figure 5.6 Incidence of Debt by Educational Attainment, 1989–2010

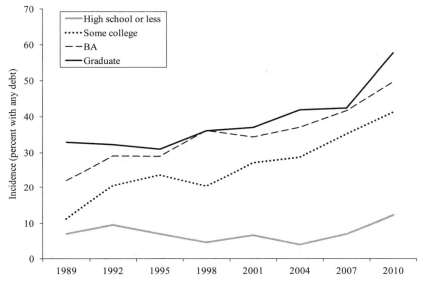

SOURCE: Authors' calculations using data from the SCF.

Figure 5.7 Average Debt by Educational Attainment, among Those with Debt, 1989–2010

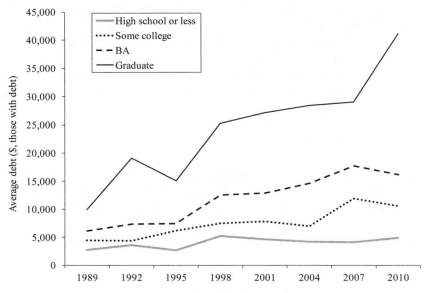

SOURCE: Authors' calculations using data from the SCF.

Figure 5.8 Reweighted (simple method, education only)

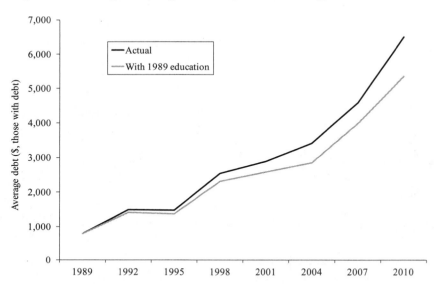

SOURCE: Authors' calculations using data from the SCF and the *Digest of Education Statistics*.

To more carefully account for changes in educational attainment and race, we implement a multivariate decomposition approach along the lines of the one used by Bound, Lovenheim, and Turner (2012). As above, we reweight the 1989 SCF to create a counterfactual distribution of debt in 2010 that captures what student debt would look like if population characteristics had remained constant between 1989 and 2010. To do this, we stack the 1989 and 2010 data and run the following logit regression:

$$I(Year = 1989) = \beta + \delta Ed_{hh} \times Ed_{sp} + \gamma Race_{hh} + \epsilon,$$

where $I(Year = 1989)$ is a dummy variable identifying whether the observation is from the year 1989 (as opposed to 2010), β is a constant, $Ed_{hh} \times Ed_{sp}$ is a vector of dummy variables identifying the full set of interactions between the educational attainment of the household head and the spouse (with one of the spouse education categories identifying households where there is no spouse), $Race_{hh}$ is a vector of dummies identifying the race of the household head, and ϵ is the error term. We then obtain predicted values $\hat{I}$ from the logit regression and calculate a set of weights $\frac{\hat{I}}{(1-\hat{I})}$ (which we combine with the SCF survey weights).[5] We first confirm that the reweighting procedure is working correctly by reporting summary statistics for 1989, 2010, and 2010 with the reweighting. Table 5.3 shows that the reweighting produces summary statistics for 2010 that are nearly identical to the actual statistics for 1989, in all cases to within one percentage point.

We then apply these weights to the 2010 data to calculate an estimate of what debt would have been in 2010 had educational attainment and race remained at their 1989 values. We find that mean per-person debt (among all households) would have been \$4,932 (instead of \$6,502) in 2010 had educational attainment and race remained at their 1989 values. In other words, the variables included in the decomposition exercise explain 28 percent of the observed change.[6]

We next explore how much changes in education debt can be explained by rising college tuition. Ideally, we would implement this as follows: 1) measure how much each individual paid for his or her education; 2) measure how much they would have paid 21 years prior (i.e., the number of years between 1989 and 2010); 3) calculate the causal effect of price on debt; and 4) calculate how much debt they would have taken out had they faced the prices from 21 years prior by multiplying

Table 5.3 Summary Statistics, Household Level, Average Age 20–40 (%)

	1989	2010	2010 reweighted
Maximum education			
High school or less	41	31	42
Some college	29	32	29
BA	20	24	20
Graduate	9	13	9
Race/ethnicity of household head			
White	72	62	72
Black	11	15	11
Hispanic	11	17	11
Other	6	6	6

SOURCE: Authors' calculations using data from the SCF.

the effect of price on debt by the difference between actual tuition paid and the counterfactual tuition (from 21 years prior).

This is not possible for two main reasons. First, the SCF does not contain information on how much respondents paid for their education or even the institutions they attended—only the highest degree obtained. Second, it is far from straightforward to estimate the causal effect of price on debt, and we are unaware of any research on the topic. As a rough substitute, we instead deflate the 2010 distribution of debt to a simulated 1989 level using data on published tuition and fees by year, assuming that the percentage increase in debt is the same as the percentage increase in published tuition.

Specifically, for each individual we calculate counterfactual debt in 2010 as the actual debt multiplied by the ratio of counterfactual tuition (average tuition 21 years prior to when the respondent was age 20) to actual tuition (average tuition when the respondent was age 20).[7] For example, a household with an average age of 34 in 2010 is assigned an actual tuition from 1996 (i.e., at age 20) and a counterfactual tuition from 1975 (i.e., 21 years prior to age 20). Tuition is calculated as a weighted average of published tuition and fees at two-year, public four-year, and private four-year institutions across the country, using enrollment shares as weights (National Center for Education Statistics, various years). We use published tuition and fees, even though net price (tuition and fees less grant and scholarships) would be a better measure because the latter is not available for a sufficiently long period of time.[8] As a result, we likely overstate the contribution of rising prices to growth in debt.

The results of this analysis are reported in Table 5.4. The tuition adjustment explains 58 percent of the 1989–2010 increase in mean debt. Combining the tuition adjustment with the reweighting procedure, which adjusts for changes in educational attainment and race, increases to 72 percent the share of the change explained. Our use of published rather than net price implies that this is an overestimate, but it still leaves 28 percent of the change unexplained. This remaining share of the change could be the result of some combination of changes in characteristics not measured in the SCF data and changes in borrowing behavior.

Table 5.4 Decomposition of Changes in Mean Debt, 1989–2010

	Mean debt ($)	Change from 1989 ($)	Share of change explained (%)
1989 debt	806		
2010 debt			
No adjustment	6,502	5,696	0
Applying 1989 characteristics	4,932	4,126	28
Applying 1989 tuition	3,194	2,388	58
Applying 1989 characteristics and tuition	2,402	1,596	72

SOURCE: Authors' calculations using data from the SCF and the *Digest of Education Statistics*.

CONCLUSION

The media has provided many anecdotes about recent graduates with large amounts of student loan debt who are in financial distress, often living in their parents' basements. Data on the distribution of loan debt, both from the SCF and other sources, indicate that extremely large debt burdens remain exceptional cases. Our analysis of the SCF data also provides some initial estimates of the role that different factors have played in driving up student debt over the last two decades. Rising educational attainment explains some of the trend, and debt data disaggregated by highest degree earned suggest that graduate education has played a particularly important role, especially for the cases of large debt balances.

Tuition is also a likely culprit, although the limitations of historical data on tuition make it difficult to tell exactly how much. Our analysis suggests that inflation in published prices may account for upward of 60 percent of the increase in debt, leaving a significant share of the rise in debt that is unexplained. This fact, coupled with evidence that students are substituting away from paying for college out-of-pocket toward financing (Greenstone and Looney 2013), suggests that behavioral shifts may account for some of the increase in education debt.

These analyses do not shed light on whether the increasing loan burdens taken on to finance education are leading to financial hardship for borrowers. To the extent that increases in attainment are the culprit, at least some of the increase in debt has financed sound investments. But there are surely cases of investments in education that did not pay off or did not even result in a degree. Expanding this analysis to examine debt-to-income ratios and other measures of financial distress is a ripe area for future research.

Notes

1. The use of survey weights in the SCF is particularly important because the sample design oversamples high-income households to properly measure the full distribution of wealth and assets in the United States. This high-income sample makes up approximately 25 percent of households in the SCF.
2. In addition, the SCF does not record the individual associated with loan origination. Therefore, with individuals no older than 40, we are more confident that the loans on their balance sheets are associated with an adult rather than a child in the household.
3. The SCF collects data on the size of loan at origination, but this refers to the date of most recent loan terms, which includes consolidation. Thus, we are not able to measure the size of loans taken out while enrolled for all households.
4. We find similar attainment trends after converting the household-level SCF data into individual-level data (assigning one-half the survey weight to each individual in a two-person household). These summary statistics are available from the authors upon request.
5. Specifically, we use weights that are the product of the weights generated by the logit regression and the original survey weights.
6. These types of reweighting exercises assume that the relative borrowing behavior of demographic groups remains constant over time. This is obviously a strong assumption, and understanding changes in borrowing behavior is left for future research.
7. We calculate the years to use for tuition using the average age of the household rounded to the nearest year.
8. Our tuition data series begins in 1971. We proxy for 1969 and 1970 tuition levels using the 1971 value.

References

Baum, Sandy, Jennifer Ma, and Kathleen Payea. 2013. *Education Pays, 2013*. New York: College Board.

Bound, John, Michael F. Lovenheim, and Sarah Turner. 2012. "Increasing Time to Baccalaureate Degree in the United States." *Education Finance and Policy* 7(4): 375–424.

Brown, Meta, and Sydnee Caldwell. 2013. "Young Student Loan Borrowers Retreat from Housing and Auto Markets." *Liberty Street Economics* blog, April 17. New York: New York Federal Reserve Bank. http://liberty streeteconomics.newyorkfed.org/2013/04/young-student-loan-borrowers -retreat-from-housing-and-auto-markets.html (accessed April 24, 2014).

College Board. 2013. *Trends in Student Aid, 2013*. New York: College Board.

Greenstone, Michael, and Adam Looney. 2012. "Regardless of the Cost, College Still Matters." *Brookings on Job Numbers* (blog), October 5. Washington, DC: Brookings Institution. http://www.brookings.edu/blogs/jobs/ posts/2012/10/05-jobs-greenstone-looney (accessed April 24, 2014).

———. 2013. "Rising Student Debt Burdens: Factors behind the Phenomenon." *Brookings on Job Numbers* (blog), July 5. Washington, DC: The Hamilton Project, Brookings Institution. http://www.brookings.edu/blogs/ jobs/posts/2013/07/05-student-loans-debt-burdens-jobs-greenstone-looney (accessed April 24, 2014).

National Center for Education Statistics. Various years. *Digest of Education Statistics*, 1995–2012. Washington, DC: National Center for Education Statistics.

6

College Costs and Financial Constraints

Student Borrowing at For-Profit Institutions

Stephanie Riegg Cellini
George Washington University,
National Bureau of Economic Research

Rajeev Darolia
University of Missouri

Perhaps no culprit has been more incriminated for the rising levels of student loan debt in the United States than for-profit postsecondary institutions. Two trends have drawn a great deal of attention to this sector. First, students at for-profit institutions disproportionately accrue federal student loan disbursements, leading to concern about the use of public funds and debt burden on students in the sector. Second, student loan default rates are higher at this group of institutions than other sectors on average, calling into question relative employment prospects. There is still much to learn, however, about the student context of these high-level trends, and research on student lending and the for-profit sector remains underdeveloped. Using student-level nationally representative data from the National Postsecondary Student Aid Study (NPSAS), we analyze student borrowing trends over the past decade, with a particular focus on the behavior of students in for-profit institutions compared to students in other sectors.[1]

An impediment to understanding relative student outcomes in the for-profit sector is the unique nature of students served. Descriptive research informs us that the sector disproportionately enrolls financially independent and low-income students (Deming, Goldin, and Katz 2012) such that credit is necessary for many of these students to invest in their human capital. Therefore, we push further than previous research to also ask whether borrowing patterns differ by various measures of financial need and available resources. We further examine preferences for borrowing relative to other available financing options such as working, grants, and family transfers to provide a better understanding of debt behavior in the context of the financial constraints these students face.

As expected, we find that students at for-profit institutions are much more likely to borrow than students in public and nonprofit institutions. We also find that, over the past decade, the incidence of borrowing has risen more steeply than borrowing in other sectors. These high borrowing rates lead to higher average borrowing by students in for-profit institutions than students in public and nonprofit institutions. Published tuition in the for-profit sector has risen substantially over the last decade, following patterns similar to those making headlines in the public and nonprofit sectors. But unlike other sectors, grant aid has not risen with tuition in the for-profit sector, leading to increases in the net price that students pay. In particular, we observe increases in institutional aid in the private nonprofit sector that accompany tuition increases but find little evidence of this type of support in the for-profit sector. Student borrowing in the for-profit sector has risen dramatically to meet the rising net price.

Our examination of financial resources reveals that students attending for-profit institutions have the lowest available personal and family resources to contribute to higher education costs, relative to students in other sectors. Not only do they have the lowest calculated expected family contribution (EFC) according to financial aid formulas, but it is also less likely that they or their parents own a home or have substantial investment or business assets. Given their relative lack of resources, it is not surprising that these students turn to the credit market to finance their education. Students in the for-profit sector also work longer hours and are more likely to work full time than students in the public four-year or private nonprofit sectors (and at levels that are generally similar to public two-year college students). Therefore, the high borrowing rates of for-profit students do not appear to simply reflect preferences for debt over working. Rather, they both seem to be working and borrowing at relatively high rates.

Paradoxically, students in for-profit institutions are most similar to public community college students in the degrees they seek, their demographics, and their financial resources, yet their costs and their debt burdens are on par with students in private nonprofit institutions who typically seek bachelor's degrees from institutions with long-standing reputations and higher expected postcollege incomes. Why are the most disadvantaged students attending relatively expensive for-profit institutions?

We cannot provide an answer here, but our findings highlight the policy importance of the question. An economically rational student will decide whether to attend higher education by comparing the expected benefits of school, such as higher earnings, against expected costs, including tuition and forgone earnings. The answer to the question, therefore, may be that advantages offered by for-profit colleges, such as lower opportunity costs associated with convenient class schedules and streamlined programs, make for-profit education an appropriate choice for judicious and shrewd students. This may be of little concern for policymakers. On the other hand, policymakers may be rightfully concerned if students are making choices while lacking information or being misled.

BACKGROUND ON FOR-PROFITS AND DEBT

Across all sectors of higher education, student borrowing plays an important role in ensuring access to higher education for low- and middle-income students. Yet, evidence that credit constraints affect educational attainment is mixed. Ellwood and Kane (2000) and Belley and Lochner (2007) find some support that credit constraints impact college going, while Cameron and Taber (2004) and Stinebrickner and Stinebrickner (2008) find little evidence in that regard.

Whether students borrow "too much" or "too little" is subject to debate, though analyses of typical debt burdens and returns to college do not indicate that average student borrowing behavior, even at current higher levels, is a serious concern (see Avery and Turner [2012] and Baum and Schwartz [2006] for a more detailed discussion). Loans can promote access to higher education by lowering costs, and research indicates that social benefits to higher education can exceed private benefits (Wolfe and Haveman 2002). Therefore, a robust educational credit market can have both equity and efficiency benefits. On the other hand, debt burdens can lower expected future consumption, since relatively large portions of some borrowers' incomes will be dedicated to making loan payments. Evidence also indicates that high debt can potentially alter choices about early career decisions (Field 2009; Rothstein and Rouse 2011) and other choices (Gicheva 2011).

If not properly managed, student debt can impair access to other credit markets, making it more difficult for students to borrow money to purchase assets such as houses or to guard against income or asset shocks. Debt burdens, therefore, should be considered in relation to the expected benefits associated with borrowing. For student loans, the prominent private benefit is higher expected earnings associated with completed college. For the average student, college earnings premiums have grown, even when taking into account increasing college costs (Avery and Turner 2012). Therefore, modest increases in student borrowing for the average student may not be a source of public concern.

Returns to college investments, however, are heterogeneous across student characteristics and abilities, as well as institutions. Therefore, not every student will earn the average wage premium to college, and students are not evenly stratified across school sectors and types. In fact, several recent studies on the returns to for-profit college attendance suggest that for-profit students generate earnings gains that are lower than those of students in other sectors (Cellini and Chaudhary 2012; Deming, Goldin, and Katz 2012; Turner 2012). Among associate's degree students, estimates of returns to for-profit attendance are generally in the range of 2–7 percent per year of education, compared to upward of 9 percent in the public sector (Jacobson, LaLonde, and Sullivan 2005; Jepsen, Troske, and Coomes 2014).[2] Assessing returns from a different angle, Cellini (2012) calculates that the earnings gains needed to offset the cost of one year of an associate's degree program in a for-profit college must be equal to or greater than 8.5 percent for students to see net benefits. Current estimates fall just short of this threshold. Still, the literature on the returns to for-profit education is quite thin. We know little about how returns have changed over time, and this has important implications for our understanding of the temporal patterns of student borrowing discussed below.

Complicating the policy discussion is that publicly subsidized federal student loans are the most common source of borrowing for college students. Federal loans include Stafford Loans, Perkins Loans, and PLUS Loans for parents. While these loan programs have been widely touted as improving access to higher education for low-income students in "traditional" nonprofit and public institutions, they have come under increasing scrutiny for their role in supporting the growth of the for-profit sector.

For-profit students receive a disproportionate share of federal aid. In recent years, for-profit students composed just over 10 percent of postsecondary enrollment but received about double that proportion of federal Pell Grant and subsidized student loan disbursements (College Board 2013). As we show below, tuition averages about $10,000 per year, and for-profits may be raising tuition to maximize their federal aid (Cellini and Goldin forthcoming). Of course, another explanation for the high aid receipt is that for-profits tend to enroll more disadvantaged students than nonprofits. Deming, Goldin, and Katz (2012) report that among first-time college students, for-profit institutions serve a higher proportion of women, minority students, GED recipients, and single parents than other sectors. Many of these characteristics are associated with lower financial resources. We explore these patterns further using NPSAS data in the analysis that follows.

Disproportionate borrowing alone may not be a problem if disadvantaged students can easily pay back their debt after graduation. More troubling is that student loan default rates are much higher in the for-profit sector than in other sectors. Three-year cohort default rates from 2009 are over 22 percent in the for-profit sector compared to 8.4 percent for public community colleges. Two other estimates produced by the U.S. Department of Education, but not used for Title IV eligibility, yield even higher default rates for for-profit students. Estimates of "cumulative lifetime default rates" based on the number of loans, rather than borrowers, yield a rate of about 31 percent for cohorts graduating between 2005 and 2009. The highest estimate uses dollars, rather than loans or borrowers, to estimate defaults and is used in the president's budget. By this measure, lifetime defaults are around 48 percent for two-year for-profit students (U.S. Department of Education 2011). These patterns have raised the suspicions of policymakers and led the Obama administration to propose new regulations on restricting federal student aid to for-profit institutions (see Darolia [2013b] for further discussion).

There is a small but growing literature on for-profit colleges in economics. Many studies describe student demographics and program offerings at for-profit institutions (Apling 1993; Bailey, Badway, and Gumport 2001; Deming, Goldin, and Katz 2012; Rosenbaum, Deil-Amen, and Person 2006; Turner 2006).[3] Administrative licensing data has added to our knowledge of these institutions in recent years and allowed for causal studies of competition in the two-year college market (Cellini 2009) and a more accurate count of for-profit institutions (Cellini and Goldin forthcoming). And, as noted above, several authors have exploited new sources of student-level data to estimate the labor market returns to a for-profit education (Cellini and Chaudhary 2012; Deming, Goldin, and Katz 2012; Lang and Weinstein 2013; Turner 2013).

Several studies on the relationship between financial aid policy and institutional behavior are particularly relevant to this study. Cellini (2010) finds that for-profit college openings and closings correlate with the generosity of federal aid in the Pell Grant program. Cellini and Goldin (forthcoming) find that for-profit institutions participating in federal grant and loan programs charge tuition that is 78 percent higher than similar programs in institutions that are not eligible for aid. In absolute terms, they find that the dollar value of tuition difference is similar to the value of the aid the institution receives, suggesting that institutions may capture federal student aid. Turner (2013) looks more closely at the incidence of the Pell Grant program and finds that for-profit institutions behave no differently than nonselective nonprofit institutions, capturing around 20 percent of students' Pell Grant awards through reductions in institutional aid. Finally, Darolia (2013a) finds that the loss of federal aid because of high cohort default rates leads to declines in annual enrollment at for-profit colleges that exceed 16 percent. This indicates that the federal government has powerful policy levers at its disposal to determine where and if students attend college by regulating which institutions can disburse aid.

We build on this literature and focus on changes over time in student borrowing in the for-profit sector. We begin to untangle the myriad of possible explanations for the time trends we observe, bringing new data to bear on questions of student resources and work behavior. Our results have important implications for the design of federal student aid policies and the regulation of for-profit colleges.

DATA

To examine trends in postsecondary borrowing and financing behavior of undergraduate students in the United States, we use the four most current available complete waves of the NPSAS. Coordinated by the U.S. Department of Education, NPSAS combines institutional and governmental records with student surveys to produce nationally representative repeated cross-sectional student-level data with information on how students pay for their postsecondary expenses. The advantages of these data are their relatively large sample sizes and particularly detailed information about students' financial backgrounds and college financing strategies.

We use study waves from the 1995–1996, 1999–2000, 2003–2004, and 2007–2008 school years.[4] Each wave contains information on between 41,000 (in 1995–1996) and 105,000 (in 2007–2008) undergraduate students surveyed at random from institutions participating in federal student aid programs under Title IV of the Higher Education Act of 1965.[5] For our analysis, we use measures of borrowing, aid, and other amounts for that year, with all dollars reported in constant 2008 terms. We restrict the sample to undergraduate students but consider yearly figures similarly across the year students are in school and enrollment intensity.

We group schools into four distinct types: 1) for-profit institutions, 2) public institutions that offer programs of two years or less,[6] 3) public institutions that offer four-year programs, and 4) private, nonprofit institutions. Note that both the for-profit and nonprofit groups include all levels of institutions—less-than-two-year, two-year, and four-year—but the composition of the institutions in each sector differs substantially. In 2007–2008 almost 95 percent of private not-for-profit postsecondary institutions were four-year colleges, compared to just 47 percent of for-profit institutions (National Center for Education Statistics 2013, Table 306).[7] We include unweighted counts of observations by year and school sector in Table 6.1.

Table 6.1 Sample Summary

	For-profit (1)	Public two-year (2)	Public four-year (3)	Private nonprofit (4)
Student characteristics (2007–2008)				
Enrolled in a certificate program (%)	32	8	0	2
Enrolled in an associate's degree program (%)	40	79	4	4
Enrolled in a bachelor's degree program (%)	27	2	91	92
Coursework only (no program enrollment) (%)	1	11	2	1
Male (%)	33	44	46	43
Female (%)	67	56	54	57
Minority (%)	53	40	34	33
Age at time of survey	28.3	27.7	23.5	24.4
Age at the start of postsecondary education	22.7	21.4	19.3	19.7
Years delayed entry into postsecondary education	3.6	2.6	0.8	1.2
First-generation immigrant (%)	11	12	9	7
Second-generation immigrant (%)	14	14	13	13
Current or past military service (%)	7	5	3	4
Parent(s) completed high school or higher (%)	83	87	94	94
Parent(s) completed bachelor's degree or higher (%)	19	30	48	52
Independent (%)	76	57	33	34
Single parent (%)	30	17	7	8
Number of dependents	0.9	0.6	0.2	0.3
Risk index	2.9	2.7	1.3	1.3
Sample size (unweighted)				
1995–1996	5,380	7,190	16,070	12,890
1999–2000	4,620	8,770	20,330	11,120
2003–2004	8,900	22,830	19,230	14,200
2007–2008	14,200	31,980	36,880	21,660

NOTE: Survey weights used. Sample sizes rounded to the nearest 10.
SOURCE: NPSAS.

STUDENT FINANCING TRENDS: SIMILARITIES AND CONTRASTS

We begin by describing borrowing behavior over time. In the sections that follow, we examine various explanations for these substantial differences in student borrowing both across sectors and over time within the for-profit sector. The relatively high sticker costs of for-profit colleges and relatively low grant aid and personal financial resources available to students who attend these schools leave a relatively large amount of unmet need for students. While for-profit students appear to be working at comparatively high rates, this behavior does not appear to prevent students from borrowing at high rates or levels.

Borrowing

Table 6.2 presents the average borrowing behavior of students for the 2007–2008 school year. A remarkable 87 percent of for-profit students borrow money of some kind, compared to just 14 percent of public two-year students, 48 percent of public four-year students, and 60 percent of private nonprofit students.[8] Not surprisingly, most student borrowers obtain loans through federal programs. In the for-profit sector, 81 percent of students receive federal loans. Relative to students in other sectors, for-profit students are much more likely to supplement federal borrowing with borrowing from nonfederal sources, but just 6 percent borrowed only from nonfederal sources, as shown in the bottom part of the table.

Figure 6.1 displays the trend of percentage of students who borrow (from any source) from 1996 to 2008. While the relative position of schools in this trend stays constant, and all schools experience a positive upward trend of the percentage of students borrowing, the for-profit sector experienced a 30 percentage point increase in the proportion of students borrowing since 1996, whereas the increase for the other three sectors were all below 15 percentage points. The upward trend in borrowing is notable in the most recent period, climbing from 75 percent in 2004 to 87 percent in 2008.

In addition to the high (and climbing) proportion of students borrowing, the first row of Table 6.2 reveals that for-profit students also

Table 6.2 Average Per Student Borrowing (2007–2008)

	For-profit (1)	Public two-year (2)	Public four-year (3)	Private nonprofit (4)
Rates of student borrowing (%)				
Borrowed any loans	87	14	48	60
Borrowed federal loans	81	11	43	56
Borrowed nonfederal loans	41	5	15	25
Borrowed both federal and nonfederal loans	36	2	10	21
Borrowed federal, but not nonfederal loans	45	9	33	34
Borrowed nonfederal, but not federal loans	6	3	5	4
Average per student borrowing, including all students ($)				
Total loans	7,319	632	3,713	6,530
Federal loans	4,842	457	2,793	4,227
Subsidized federal loans	2,256	253	1,350	2,007
Parent PLUS Loans	485	23	570	1,190
Nonfederal loans	2,477	175	920	2,303
Private loans	2,423	172	856	2,210
Average loan amount for those who borrow each loan type ($)				
Total loans	8,457	4,424	7,769	10,955
Federal loans	5,975	4,053	6,454	7,602
Subsidized federal loans	2,888	2,768	3,870	4,214
Parent PLUS Loans	9,099	7,073	9,558	13,657
Nonfederal loans	6,026	3,586	6,156	9,087
Private loans	5,990	3,652	6,142	9,225

NOTE: Survey weights used. Total loans include parent PLUS Loans.
SOURCE: NPSAS.

have the highest average yearly total loan amounts when considering all students (whether they borrow or not). The for-profit sample has an average debt load of over $7,000 per year, a figure even higher than private nonprofit students, who borrow about $6,500 per year. We display the trend of average student borrowing in Figure 6.2. Per-student borrow-

Figure 6.1 Percentage of Students Borrowing

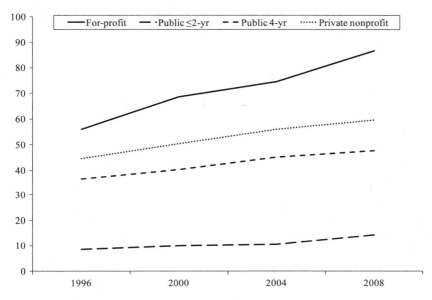

NOTE: Survey weights used.
SOURCE: NPSAS.

ing is increasing in all sectors, but the rate of increase and the relative position of for-profit institutions is the highest among all sectors.

These are annual borrowing figures, such that total debt would depend on the accrual over the whole time the student is in college, and could therefore be lower for for-profit than private nonprofit students overall, as for-profit programs are generally shorter (more on this below). If we assume that the average for-profit student attends for two years and the average nonprofit student attends for four, the total amount borrowed comes to $14,000 for for-profits and $26,000 for nonprofits.[9]

Note that the average per student borrowing in Table 6.2 and Figure 6.2 display averages that are taken across all students rather than just borrowers. Averages conditional on borrowing are listed in the bottom part of Table 6.2. Averages for for-profit student borrowers increase modestly to about $8,400, since almost all students borrow, but the figures become much higher for other sectors because of lower propor-

Figure 6.2 Average Loan Amount

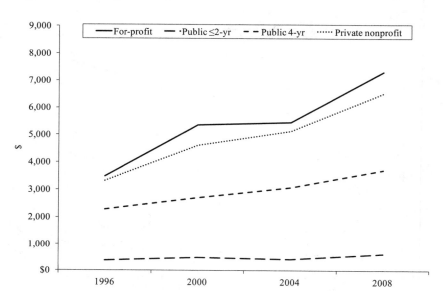

NOTE: All dollars in constant 2008 dollars. Survey weights used.
SOURCE: NPSAS.

tions of borrowers. Notably, when considering loan volume of only the 60 percent of students who borrow in the private nonprofit sector, average loan amounts exceed those of for-profit students, at almost $11,000, while the average loan volume among borrowers in public two-year and four-year institutions remains below that of for-profit students.

Table 6.2 also displays the composition of loans across sectors. In dollar terms, federal loans make up the largest portion of for-profit student borrowing, and just under half of these loans are federally subsidized. About a third of for-profit student loans are from private lenders. Overall, the patterns of for-profit student borrowing look similar to private nonprofit borrowing. Figure 6.3 presents the categorization of student loan types by school sector over time. Although borrowing has increased across all sectors, the for-profit sector saw borrowing increase by the largest loan dollar amount between 1996 and 2008.

It is also worth noting that private loan dollars increased most substantially in the for-profit sector. This trend could be interpreted in a

Figure 6.3 Average Student Loan Borrowing

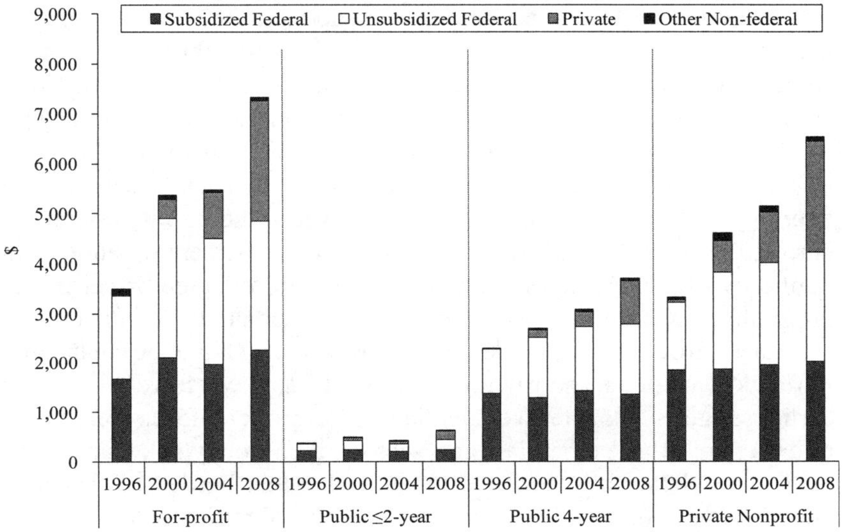

NOTE: All dollars in constant 2008 dollars. Survey weights used.
SOURCE: NPSAS.

couple of different ways. Since private lender loans often have less favorable terms than federal loans, this could be troubling given the expected debt burden on this group of students coming from relatively disadvantaged backgrounds. On the other hand, given some of the concern about public funding at some for-profit institutions, a shift toward more private loans may be welcome to those who believe subsidized public funds should not be used at for-profit institutions. These trends would need to be evaluated after the changes to the federal loan program delivery system in 2010, though more current data similar to that analyzed here is currently not available.

Credential and Demographic Differences

Differences among student bodies present a challenge when comparing financing strategies across school types, as dissimilarities in student demographics and the credentials that students seek may both be important drivers of borrowing behavior. Table 6.1 shows student characteristics across the sector from the 2007–2008 school year.

A number of differences are apparent across school sectors, including the credentials sought by students. About one-third of for-profit students are enrolled in certificate programs, over a third are enrolled in associate's degree programs, and less than a third are enrolled in bachelor's level programs (column 1). This is compared to about 80 percent of students at public two-years that are seeking associate's degrees, and over 90 percent of students at public four-years and private nonprofits enrolled in bachelor's degree programs. Over 10 percent of students at public two-year institutions are not enrolled in a degree or certificate program, compared to just 1–2 percent of students in the other sectors.

These differences in credentials across sectors should be considered in relation to student borrowing behavior. If, as the research described earlier suggests, short-term credentials in for-profit colleges yield lower returns than other credentials and sectors, then policymakers and students should carefully consider whether the debt burden of for-profit attendance is worthwhile. A complicating consideration is that forgone wage costs for a short-term credential could also be expected to be lower. Still, much more research on college wage premia across sectors and for various subbaccalaureate degrees, diplomas, and certificates is needed before assessing whether the debt of the average for-profit student has a reasonable chance of being repaid.

Students vary across sectors demographically, as displayed in Table 6.1. Although for-profit students' borrowing patterns are similar to private nonprofit students', their demographics are a stark contrast. For-profit students are demographically most similar to public two-year students, but even between these two sectors, many important differences remain. For-profits have the highest proportion of female and minority students, and these come from families with the lowest levels of parental education. For example, 83 percent of for-profit students in the sample have at least one parent who completed high school, compared to 94 percent of private nonprofit school students. As well, only 19 percent of for-profit students in the sample have a parent who completed at least a bachelor's degree, as compared to 30 percent of public two-year students, 48 percent of public four-year students, and 52 percent of private nonprofit school students.

Furthermore, for-profit students are, on average, the oldest students in the sample, with the highest age at the start of postsecondary education (22.7), and the longest number of years between secondary and postsecondary studies (3.6). Reflective of their older average age, most for-profit students are independent (76 percent), as compared to public two-year (57 percent), public four-year (33 percent), and private non-profit (34 percent) students. Students who attend for-profit colleges are also the most likely to be a single parent, and they have the highest average number of dependents among the sectors. Taken together, these characteristics suggest that for-profit students may most likely need to support dependents and be less likely to have access to the financial resources of parents, spouses, or other custodians. Access to credit for education may be particularly important for these students. We examine more detailed measures of need, assets, and parental support in subsequent sections.

Finally, NPSAS publishes a "risk index" for each student, which is an index of characteristics potentially related to postsecondary success: delayed enrollment into postsecondary education, enrolling part-time, being an independent student, having dependents, being a single parent, working full time while enrolled, and not having a high school diploma. This index reflects the higher average number of postsecondary risk factors belonging to for-profit students (3.0) and public two-year students (2.7) as compared to public four-year students (1.2) and the private non-profit students (1.3). As we will show in the following sections, these demographic differences are related to differences in resources and constraints of students across school sectors. Therefore, it is important to consider these differences when assessing borrowing behavior across different types of students.

Costs of Education

Perhaps the most obvious explanation for disproportionate borrowing of for-profit students is simply the high cost of for-profit institutions. Table 6.3 displays measures of costs of education for the 2007–2008 school year. Although private nonprofits have average yearly gross costs over $7,000 higher than for-profits (as displayed in column [4]), for-profits have much higher average tuition and fees than either of the public sectors. For example, compared to students at public two-

Table 6.3 Average Per Student Costs, Grant Aid, and Institutional Aid, 2007–2008 ($)

	For-profit (1)	Public two-year (2)	Public four-year (3)	Private nonprofit (4)
Gross tuition and fees	9,807	1,133	5,391	17,519
Tuition and fees minus grants	7,814	700	3,447	10,252
Total grants	2,091	878	2,733	7,629
Total federal grants	1,456	504	838	964
State grants	141	139	681	792
Institution grants	119	77	811	5,069
Outside grants (private and employer)	374	159	403	804
Merit aid	61	57	619	2,414
Veteran and Department of Defense aid	208	93	138	146
Total institutional aid	181	89	899	5,232

NOTE: Survey weights used.
SOURCE: NPSAS.

year colleges, the gross tuition and fees of for-profit students is nearly nine times higher: for-profits average $9,807 of gross tuition and fees, compared to just $1,133 for community colleges. The trend of gross tuition and fees for the sample is included in Figure 6.4. Here we see the highest and most rapid growth at private nonprofits, but for-profits and publics also experienced a fairly steep increase over this period, with for-profit tuition and fees growing about 35 percent for students in the sample.

Grants are perhaps the most important source of nondebt financing, since they lower the net cost of education to the student and do not need to be repaid. Grants can come from a number of different sources. For example, the federal government offers the Pell Grant for low-income students, and other grants are available to targeted groups such as teachers and children of veterans. State governments and individual institutions also make grants available to students based on income, merit, or other characteristics (e.g., sports). Finally, private employers and foundations may provide funds to students of their choosing in order to help subsidize education costs.

Figure 6.4 Average Gross Tuition and Fees

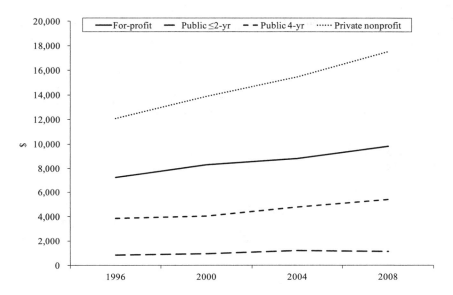

NOTE: All dollars in constant 2008 dollars. Survey weights used.
SOURCE: NPSAS.

As shown in the third row of Table 6.3, for-profit students have the second-lowest level of total grant aid, at $2,091 per year, more than public two-year students and close to the grant aid received by public four-year students. Private nonprofit students receive by far the largest amount of grant aid, at $7,629 annually. The trend of total grants is displayed in Figure 6.5. Given prior observed trends of increasing sticker prices in the private nonprofit sector, the increasing grant aid in this sector is consistent with a "high cost, high subsidy" strategy of college pricing.

Breaking down the sources of grant aid reveals that for-profit students have higher average levels of federal grants than all other sectors but lower levels of every other type of grant aid. For-profit students not only have higher levels of total federal grant aid ($1,456), but they also receive slightly more grant aid through federal veterans and Department of Defense programs, such as the G.I. Bill. For-profit students

Figure 6.5 Average Total Grants

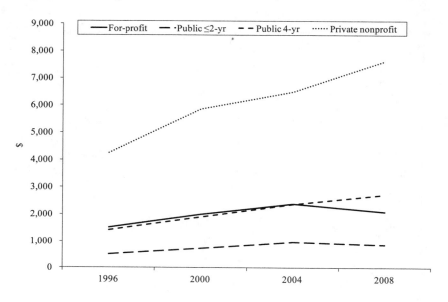

NOTE: All dollars in constant 2008 dollars. Survey weights used.
SOURCE: NPSAS.

receive an average of $208 in veterans and Department of Defense grants compared to $146 in the nonprofit sector, but in relative terms the value of military aid is quite low—just 10 percent of the value of other federal grant aid.

The biggest difference in aid across sectors in Table 6.3 appears to be funding that comes from the institution. For-profit students receive remarkably little institutional aid. Institutional grants average just $119 in the for-profit sector. The same figure is almost 7 times higher for public four-year students and over 40 times higher for private nonprofit students, at $5,069.

The last row of Table 6.3 shows the average of all sources of institutional aid (which can include grants, loans, work-study, and other types of aid) across sectors. Of course, grants make up the largest portion of total institutional aid across all sectors, so again we see a great disparity in the amount of institutional aid provided across sectors. We plot the trend of institutional aid in Figure 6.6. Here we see a large increase in

Figure 6.6 Average Institutional Aid

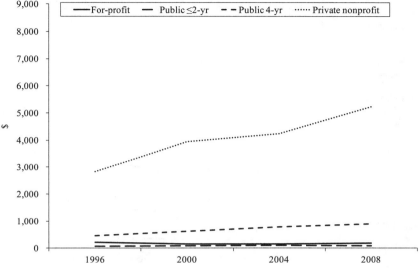

NOTE: All dollars in constant 2008 dollars. Survey weights used.
SOURCE: NPSAS.

institutional aid in the private nonprofit sector and almost no movement in institutional aid in the for-profit sector between 1996 and 2008.

Finally, when accounting for grants, education prices net of grant aid in the for-profit sector remain relatively high, as shown in the second row of Table 6.3 for the 2007–2008 school year. Moreover, the gap between the price of for-profit and public colleges has been increasing over time, as shown in Figure 6.7. Most striking, however, is that the gap between gross prices of for-profit and private nonprofit education closes substantially when taking into account grant aid.

Institutional aid, particularly institutional grants, appear to be filling the gap between cost and need in the nonprofit sector, thereby mitigating the rise in student borrowing for this group of institutions. Presenting difficulty for for-profit students, however, is that the upward trend in this sector's prices is not met by a similarly rapidly increasing trend. While institutions in the nonprofit sector appear to be trying

Figure 6.7 Average Tuition, Net of Grants

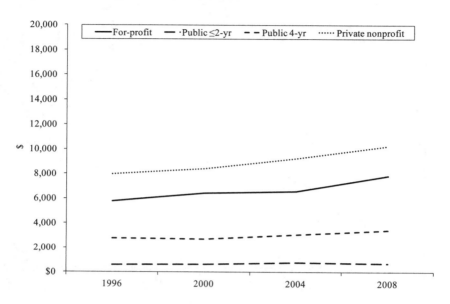

NOTE: All dollars in constant 2008 dollars. Survey weights used.
SOURCE: NPSAS.

to make tuition increases less painful for their students (or at least for some of their neediest students), for-profits have not made the same effort: over the years we observe that they appear more reliant on student debt to cover the high cost of tuition.

Need and Available Financial Resources

Tuition and fees can be considered endogenous if we assume that students have various education options from which to choose. This returns us to the question of why students—particularly disadvantaged students—attend for-profit colleges given their relatively high costs. Here, we examine more closely issues of student need and available financial resources that might explain the patterns of attendance and borrowing that we observe.

Consistent with the demographic patterns described earlier, we observe relatively fewer personal financial resources for students in the for-profit sector, as displayed in Table 6.4. In isolation, the lack of financial resources available to for-profit students may be sufficient to explain why borrowing is so high in the sector, but it does not appear to explain the steep increase in borrowing in the last decade. As shown in Table 6.4, based on need and resources, for-profit students are most similar, but in many ways still less affluent, than public two-year students who pay much lower costs. As noted above, for-profit students pay similar costs to private nonprofit students, but differences in the observed financial positions between for-profit and private nonprofit students are sizable.

Table 6.4 Average Per Student Need and Resources, 2007–2008

	For-profit (1)	Public two-year (2)	Public four-year (3)	Private nonprofit (4)
Expected family contribution ($)	4,759	8,387	12,243	14,367
Student budget minus expected family contribution ($)	15,822	3,423	7,480	16,678
Student budget minus expected family contribution and grants ($)	13,782	2,681	5,188	9,865
Adjusted gross income ($)	31,739	46,225	63,401	72,180
Percent of the poverty line (%)	198	283	350	387
Parent(s) and/or student own a home (%)	46	63	73	76
Parent(s) and/or student own > $10,000 in investments (%)	9	18	24	27
Receive help from parents				
Tuition and fees (%)	47	51	63	74
Other educational expenses (%)	42	49	59	66
Housing (%)	75	79	71	74
Other living expenses (%)	61	61	66	73

NOTE: Survey weights used. Student budget is a measure of "total" direct educational expenses, including tuition, fees, room and board, books and supplies, transportation, and other living expenses. Investments include business and farming assets. Survey responses about help from parents was only solicited from students under 30.
SOURCE: NPSAS.

Students and/or their families' expected family contribution (EFC) to college costs is typically calculated when applying for financial aid. Reflective of their relative lack of resources, for-profit students' average EFC is about half that of public two-year students and less than a third of that of public four-year and private nonprofit students.

We present the trend of EFC in Figure 6.8. Between 1996 and 2008, EFC increased for public four-year and private nonprofit students—perhaps mitigating the need for additional student borrowing in that sector even during times of increasing tuition. In contrast, we observe that EFC stayed effectively stagnant, and even declined, for for-profit students between 1996 and 2008. This trend indicates that the gap between resources available to for-profit students and other sectors may be growing, but it suggests that the increases in student borrowing we observe were likely not driven by the increasing enrollment of needy students in the for-profit sector.

Figure 6.8 Average Expected Family Contribution

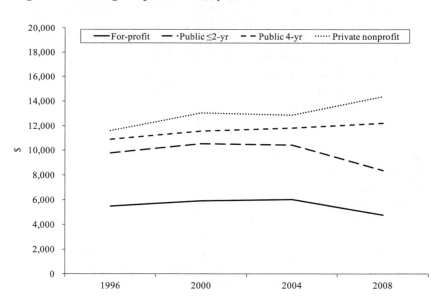

NOTE: All dollars in constant 2008 dollars. Survey weights used.
SOURCE: NPSAS.

Consider students' remaining budgets after taking into account EFC, which gives a measure of how much the typical student will need to cover after subtracting available family resources.[10] Here, we observe that the highest average gaps in costs versus resources (not taking into account grants or other financing strategies) are in the for-profit and private nonprofit sectors, almost five times that of public two-year students and over twice as much as public four-year students. When considering student budget minus both EFC and grants, the picture gets even bleaker, as the high grant aid in the private nonprofit sector allows the for-profit sector to stand alone with the highest average gaps between college costs and resources by some margin.

The measure of EFC described above masks some dispersion of income at the lower end of the income distribution, as students below certain income thresholds are all counted as having a zero EFC; we therefore examine other measures of available financial resources in Table 6.4. For-profit students undoubtedly have fewer assets with which to contribute, or with which to securitize other credit, for educational expenses. For-profit students have by far the lowest average annual household income, at just $31,739, and are closest, on average, to the poverty line. Even public two-year students seem to be much better off than their for-profit counterparts, with incomes averaging $46,225. As well, for-profit students have the lowest homeownership (46 percent vs. 63 percent for community college students) and extremely low personal or business investment rates (just 8 percent own more than $10,000 in investments vs. 18 percent of community college students).

Table 6.4 also reports survey responses of students about the financial assistance they received from their parents. Among respondents, for-profit students are least likely to get help from parents for tuition, fees, other educational expenses, and other living expenses across the sectors. Since for-profit students are most likely to be independent, older, and come from more disadvantaged backgrounds, it is not surprising that aid from parents is relatively low. However, it reinforces the financial challenges faced by many of these students.

Aid Application

Differences in ability to obtain grants, loans, or other types of financial aid can be affected by students' choices to apply for aid, as well as their knowledge of different financing options. In Table 6.5, we provide a summary of survey responses that yield some insight into these differences. Almost all for-profit students apply for financial aid (96 percent) and federal aid specifically (91 percent). Students in the for-profit sector were also least likely to not have information about how to apply for aid or believe they were ineligible for aid.

Therefore, it appears as though for-profit students are obtaining information about aid application. The source of such information may be important, however. Interestingly, for-profit students were most likely to talk with staff about financial aid. This is perhaps not surprising, given the lack of financial resources by many students in the sector. Some have concern, however, that for-profit financial aid offices may not be protecting students' best interests in financing and enrollment decisions (Government Accountability Office 2010). Although the extent of mistreatment is unknown, it may be worth considering the types of incentives involved at for-profit institutions.

An important source of knowledge about financial aid on which many students rely is family and friends, but for-profit students appear

Table 6.5 Financial Aid Application, 2007–2008 (%)

	For-profit (1)	Public two-year (2)	Public four-year (3)	Private nonprofit (4)
Applied for any aid	96	59	79	87
Applied for federal aid	91	43	62	70
Talked with staff about financial aid	71	42	45	51
Discussed financing decisions with family/friends	52	54	71	70
Researched financial aid on the Internet	35	34	45	45
Compared lender options	30	14	25	30
Reason did not apply for aid				
Did not want to take on debt	39	40	42	36
Forms too much work	15	19	19	18
No information on how to apply	16	24	21	17
No need	55	48	54	62
Thought ineligible	53	60	63	64

NOTE: Survey weights used.
SOURCE: NPSAS.

to be soliciting and/or receiving less advice from this group, with about an 18 percentage point lower rate than for the public four-year and private nonprofit students. The rate of discussion of financing with family and friends, as well as researching aid on the Internet, is similar to that of public two-year students, suggesting that information on aid options may be lacking for these students (especially if one assumes college staff to not be operating in the best interests of students). Because of the high unmet need of for-profit students relative to public two-year students, however, this lack of information may be particularly harmful to the former group.

Work Behavior

Working while in school may be an alternative to borrowing for some students. Consider a simple budget equation for students. The most common ways to pay for college costs are grants, savings, parental/family transfers, working, and borrowing. The economically rational student will not turn down grants, since they are relatively cost-free, and we have already shown that students' and families' assets are lower in the for-profit sector, such that these students would be expected to be able to rely less on savings and parental/family transfers than students in other sectors. Therefore, students with resource constraints may be faced with the choice of borrowing and/or working to cover college costs. Could high levels of borrowing simply reflect for-profit students' preferences for debt over working?

Working can have benefits to future labor market outcomes through the accrual of soft skills (Light 2001), although competing evidence shows there could be a penalty to grades (Stinebrickner and Stinebrickner 2003). Moreover, there is evidence that increased working may lead to less credit accrual (Darolia 2014) and therefore potentially longer time to earn a degree. Considering observed relatively high work rates for for-profit students in conjunction with high borrower rates, for-profit students may be uniquely facing challenges associated with both working and borrowing.

Table 6.6 provides average working behavior of students in the sample across the sectors. Interestingly, a similar proportion (76–83 percent) of students work at least some amount (including work-study and all types of employment) while enrolled across all sectors. Differ-

Table 6.6 Average Per Student Employment and Work, 2007–2008

	For-profit (1)	Public two-year (2)	Public four-year (3)	Private nonprofit (4)
Works while enrolled (%)	76	83	76	76
Works full-time while enrolled (%)	41	43	24	26
Earnings from work while enrolled ($)	16,258	16,859	11,429	13,271
Hours worked per week while enrolled	33	33	26	26
Works off campus while enrolled (%)	71	78	64	56
Distance from school to work (miles)	20	17	20	19
Worked in summer prior (%)	80	84	86	86
Job is related to coursework or major (%)	28	31	25	27
Can afford school without working (%)	30	31	42	44
Reason for working				
Minimize debt (%)	51	48	47	44
Pay educational expenses (%)	64	72	68	66
Pay living expenses (%)	85	80	78	71
To send money home (%)	8	7	6	6
Job limits access to campus facilities (%)	35	43	38	32
Job limits class schedule (%)	42	63	53	41
Job limits number of classes (%)	34	58	45	34
Job limits choice of classes (%)	26	47	39	29

NOTE: Survey weights used. Average earnings, hours worked, and distance from school to work include only respondents with values.
SOURCE: NPSAS.

ences become more apparent when examining full-time work behavior. Only about a quarter of four-year students in public and nonprofits work full time, compared to 43 percent and 41 percent in public two-years and for-profits, respectively. As well, among students who work, for-profit and public two-year students work the most average hours per week, almost 25 percent more than their public four-year and private nonprofit counterparts. Reflective of this behavior, these two sectors have the highest earnings from work while enrolled. As shown in Figure 6.9, hours worked by students, as well as work participation rates (not shown), stay relatively flat over the time period examined among all sectors. This suggests that either these students cannot add more work in order to meet debt or that they do not use earnings to substitute for debt. For-profit and public two-year students are also most likely to have jobs off campus, which may increase commuting times and reduce campus integration.

In survey responses, less than a third of for-profit and public two-year students indicate that they can afford school without working (Table 6.6). For-profit students are also most likely to report that they work in an effort to minimize debt. Therefore, even though student loan rates and amounts are high in this sector, students are still working in an effort to lower the amount they have to borrow.

Notably, students in the for-profit sector are among the least likely to report that their job limits access to campus facilities, class schedules, the number of classes the student can take, and the choice of

Figure 6.9 Average Hours Worked

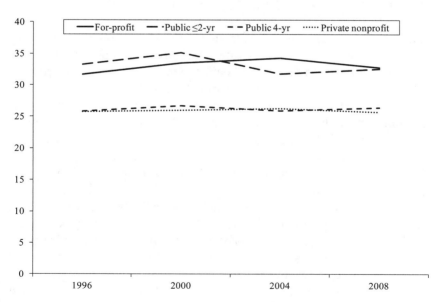

NOTE: Survey weights used.
SOURCE: NPSAS.

classes. These responses may reflect an advantage associated with for-profit colleges, namely, that course delivery is structured in a manner that allows working and schedule-constrained students to attend. These conveniences may be attracting students to this sector, even considering large tuition and fee costs.

Estimations

We have shown that students in the for-profit sector have relatively higher borrowing amounts on average, and that borrowing has risen more sharply for these students in the past decade. Our descriptive analysis suggests that these patterns are driven by high (and climbing) tuition, no commensurate increase in grant aid (as in the nonprofit sector), and the fact that students in the for-profit sector have fewer financial resources than others. To give a picture of relative borrowing after controlling for available resources, we estimate regressions of the following form:

$$Debt = \alpha + \beta Sector + \eta X + \varepsilon.$$

Here, *Sector* is a vector of indicator variables for borrowing at for-profit, public four-year, or private nonprofit institutions (with public two-year colleges as the omitted base group), with parameter vector β; X is a vector of covariates with parameter vector η; α is the intercept, and ε is the error. We make no claims to causal inference in these estimations, and indeed, we would expect many of these decisions to be endogenously determined (for example, the decision to work or borrow). Nonetheless, the results provide some measure of relative debt levels, conditional on observable college costs, financial resources, and student characteristics.

We present estimates of total debt and by federal and nonfederal loan programs in Table 6.7. Column (1) in the table displays estimates including only student characteristics as covariates. In the subsequent columns we add measures of college costs, financial resources, and financing strategies to the vector of covariates.

After accounting for just student characteristics, we observe that for-profit students have the highest levels of debt, over $6,500 more annually than public two-year students (column [1]). When accounting

Table 6.7 Estimations of Debt, 2007–2008

	Total loans		Federal loans	Nonfederal loans
	(1)	(2)	(3)	(4)
For-profit	6,568***	4,118***	2,883***	1,235***
	(64)	(68)	(52)	(43)
Public four-year	1,255***	985***	1,032***	−47
	(77)	(74)	(57)	(47)
Private nonprofit	4,171***	890***	737***	153***
	(84)	(91)	(70)	(58)
Enrolled in a certificate program	−1,533***	−699***	−735***	36
	(216)	(207)	(160)	(131)
Enrolled in an associate's degree program	−1,191***	−358*	−602***	243*
	(211)	(202)	(156)	(128)
Enrolled in a bachelor's degree program	192	645***	55	590***
	(201)	(192)	(148)	(121)
Coursework only (no program enrollment)	−1,545***	−577***	−817***	240*
	(220)	(210)	(162)	(133)
Independent	−454***	−179***	49	−228***
	(52)	(57)	(44)	(36)
Single parent	−177***	−398***	−225***	−174***
	(59)	(57)	(44)	(36)
Tuition and fees ($000s)		275***	140***	135***
		(3)	(3)	(2)
Grants ($000s)		−63***	19***	−82***
		(4)	(3)	(3)
EFC ($000s)		−23***	−17***	−6***
		(1)	(1)	(1)
Parent(s) and/or student own a home		40	−8	48*
		(41)	(32)	(26)
Parent(s) and/or student own > $10,000 in investments		−1,219***	−738***	−481***
		(42)	(33)	(27)
Works while enrolled		355***	177***	178***
		(43)	(33)	(27)
Earnings from work while enrolled ($000s)		−8***	−7***	−1
		(1)	(1)	(1)
Observations (unweighted)	84,890	84,890	84,890	84,890
Adjusted R^2	0.232	0.299	0.228	0.136

NOTE: *$p < 0.10$; **$p < 0.05$; ***$p < 0.01$. Survey weights used. Standard errors included in parentheses. Sample size rounded to the nearest 10. All estimates include controls for credential, age, class level, race/ethnicity, gender, number of dependents, and an indicator for being a first-generation immigrant. Investments include business and farming assets.
SOURCE: NPSAS.

for college costs and financial factors in column (2), we see a decline in this marginal amount to about $4,100. The gap between for-profits and public four-years also declines but remains over $3,000. Accounting for these factors, however, increases the gap between for-profit and private nonprofit students. Columns (3) and (4) split estimates for federal loans and nonfederal loans, with similar apparent trends. Independent students appear to borrow fewer nonfederal loans, but a relatively similar amount of federal loans, with a possible explanation being that they have restricted access to the private educational credit market because of a lack of cosigners.

Unsurprisingly, rising tuition and fees are associated with higher borrowing amounts, while higher EFC is associated with lower borrowing amounts. Higher grants appear to be positively correlated with federal loan amounts but negatively correlated with nonfederal loan amounts, holding all else equal (column [4]). Owning substantial investment or business assets is related to lower borrowing amounts, indicating that students with more assets are unsurprisingly able to borrow less. Interestingly, working while enrolled is associated with higher borrowing, suggesting that students that lack financial resources choose to both borrow and work instead of wholly substituting one for the other. We also observe a small decrease in federal loan amounts associated with increasing earnings.

Many determinants of borrowing and college going are unobserved in the data, and therefore these results should be interpreted with caution. Nonetheless, they provide some evidence that borrowing in the for-profit sector is high relative to the other sectors, even after controlling for a set of plausible, though incomplete, set of explanatory factors, including costs and financial resources that could explain these differences. Potential unobserved explanatory factors could lead to different levels of policy concern. It should be troubling for policymakers and regulators if this higher borrowing is explained by misleading guidance or fraud from the colleges. Less worrying would occur if the unexplained borrowing is driven by preferences for borrowing or other student choices.

DISCUSSION AND CONCLUSIONS

Drawing on data from the NPSAS, we find that for-profit students are much more likely to incur debt to finance their education than students in the public and nonprofit sectors. Nearly 90 percent of students in for-profit institutions borrow and 81 percent participate in federal loan programs. More notable is that the proportion of for-profit students borrowing increased by 30 percentage points between 1996 and 2008, compared to a growth of less than 15 percentage points among students in other sectors.

We document that the borrowing behavior, loan volume, and costs of attendance for for-profit students is most similar to that of private nonprofit students, except that borrowing for nonprofit students did not increase as steeply in the period we observe. Our descriptive analysis suggests that while both sectors experienced steep increases in tuition and fees, the private nonprofit sector mitigated their tuition hikes with increases in institutional grant aid for needy students. We observe no such increase in institutional aid among for-profits. In 2007–2008 the dollar value of institutional grant aid in nonprofit institutions was more than 40 times higher than that in for-profits. The discrepancy may be explained by the structure of the organization: since the profits of for-profit institutions are distributed to shareholders, there is little incentive to provide institutional aid to students or otherwise reinvest those profits back into the institution, as is required of nonprofit institutions.

In contrast to several similarities found between nonprofits and for-profits in college costs and borrowing, the students at for-profit colleges come from much more disadvantaged backgrounds and have fewer financial resources than students in nonprofits. We show that for-profit students appear most similar to public two-year college students in the credentials they seek, their demographics, their financial resources, and their work behavior.

Our analysis leads us to question why disadvantaged and financially constrained students are choosing expensive for-profit colleges over lower-cost community colleges. The answer is not clear.

If we assume that students have full information about their college options and the likely labor market returns to their education, then one possibility is that students choosing for-profits do so because these institutions offer programs, courses, and schedules that better meet their needs than other sectors. Our data on working students, described above, suggest that these students may find for-profit colleges the most convenient option and may be willing to pay a higher price for that convenience. Relatedly, work by Rosenbaum, Deil-Amen, and Person (2006) finds that some top-performing for-profit colleges provide better advising and student services than public sector institutions. This kind of advising may set these colleges apart and justify the high price, at least for some students.

Another possibility is that lower-cost public institutions may be capacity constrained, especially in high-demand fields and in states or localities where public higher education budgets are tight. In this scenario, public institutions may simply not be available for students wishing to pursue certain types of training, leaving for-profit institutions as the only timely option. Indeed, Cellini (2009) finds that infrastructure investments in California community colleges drive out for-profit institutions, providing evidence that public institutions and for-profits compete for students. From a policy perspective, this evidence suggests that investments in public institutions may be worthwhile, especially if they increase capacity to allow more students to access lower-cost, high-quality public education. Without additional public funding, however, for-profit colleges may be the only option for some students in high-demand fields or in geographic areas with few public alternatives.

Still, the high default rates on student loans in the for-profit sector raise concerns that students are borrowing more than they can reasonably expect to repay given the returns to their certificate or degree program. As noted previously, Cellini's (2012) analysis of the costs of a for-profit education suggests that the returns to attendance would need to be over 8.5 percent per year of education to fully offset the cost to students. Adding taxpayer costs to the equation would require 9.8 percent returns. Literature on the returns to for-profit degrees and certificates is still underdeveloped, but recent studies suggest that returns to for-profit associate's degrees are between 2 and 8 percent per year, as of the early 2000s (Cellini and Chaudhary 2012; Turner 2012). Much more research on the returns to education and whether returns have changed over time is needed to fully understand the temporal patterns of student borrowing.

If students were aware of the costs and returns described here, then it would be surprising that so many would choose for-profit institutions. It could be that students are overly optimistic or simply believe, even with knowledge about the distribution of earnings outcomes, that they are above average. More troubling for policymakers, however, is the potential for students to be misinformed or misled about the earnings they can expect after completing their education, or about the true cost of their debt. For example, the Government Accountability Office (2010) documented conversations of for-profit staff misrepresenting starting salaries of graduates and claiming that debt did not have to be repaid. It is unclear how widespread these practices are. Still, our data on financial aid applications reveal that a much higher proportion of for-profit students talked to staff about financial aid (71 percent) than students in other sectors (42–51 percent). Even if college staff members are equally misrepresenting costs and outcomes across all sectors, for-profit students are much more likely to come into contact with them than students in other sectors.

Finally, we must consider the role of federal student aid policy in affecting both the behavior of institutions and the choices of students. Since for-profit institutions are beholden to the (profit-maximizing) interests of shareholders, there is, of course, an incentive to generate as much taxpayer support as possible. For-profit institutions receive about 74 percent of their revenue from federal student aid (Deming, Goldin, and Katz 2012) and are allowed to receive up to 90 percent, under the so-called 90-10 rule. Veterans' benefits do not count toward the 90 percent, so there is an added incentive to recruit military students to capture additional taxpayer dollars. As noted earlier, Cellini and Goldin (forthcoming) find that tuition is much higher in for-profit certificate programs that receive aid relative to those that do not, and Turner (2013) finds additional evidence of aid capture in the Pell Grant program. The patterns we document appear to be consistent with these articles in suggesting that high levels of student borrowing may support high tuition levels and the crowding-out of institutional aid in the for-profit sector.[11]

We suggest that policymakers look closely at student borrowing in the for-profit sector and the incentives created under the current federal student aid system. Given the large public investment in students in the for-profit sector, policymakers should make efforts to ensure that colleges are contributing to positive student outcomes and that students and taxpayers are protected. Recent efforts at regulation based on the "gainful employment" of graduates may be warranted.[12] However, policymakers should think carefully about the metrics used to measure student outcomes. Single measures, such as the amount of borrowing alone, may be too narrow of a metric on which to judge the multi-faceted goals and outcomes of education. And, as we show here, other factors that affect student borrowing behavior, such as backgrounds, resources, and constraints, are not evenly distributed across sectors. As noted previously, whether or not the level of borrowing needed to finance a for-profit college education is a worthwhile investment for the average student depends crucially on the labor market returns to for-profit degrees and certificates. Much more research remains to be done to investigate this issue and answer questions about student choice, cost, debt, and information in the for-profit sector.

Notes

1. The NPSAS is nationally representative of students who attend postsecondary institutions eligible to disburse federal financial aid.
2. Lang and Weinstein (2013) find that for-profit certificate students have lower returns, but associate's degree students have higher returns than students in public community colleges. They attribute the latter finding to a selection problem: students in community colleges are more likely to go on to a bachelor's degree and are not included in their sample.
3. The Integrated Postsecondary Education Data System severely undercounts the number of two-year for-profit colleges in the United States. For many years the survey relied on snowball sampling and did not require their participation. In recent years, greater efforts have been made to track down institutions receiving federal financial aid, but many colleges remain unaccounted for in the data (Cellini and Goldin forthcoming).
4. The full 2011–2012 wave of the NPSAS was not yet available at the time of this writing. Future research will incorporate these data. It is worth noting that the higher education landscape continued to evolve post-2008, such that trends observed after the period analyzed here may lead to an update of the inferences we draw.
5. Note that many for-profit institutions (particularly those that do not offer degrees) do not participate in Title IV programs and are therefore not represented in the NPSAS. See Cellini and Goldin (forthcoming) for a discussion of these institutions.
6. We refer to these institutions in the text as public two-year colleges and community colleges for ease of exposition.

7. Adding students in two-year nonprofit institutions to the public two-year and less-than-two-year group made very little difference in the analysis. We believe that our categorization allows for the cleanest comparisons across institution types.
8. In this and all subsequent tables we use survey weights unless otherwise noted.
9. Calculations of cumulative debt are not straightforward in the NPSAS.
10. "Student budget" is a measure of "total" direct educational expenses in NPSAS, including tuition, fees, room and board, books and supplies, transportation, and other living expenses.
11. We have also considered the role of federal student loan limits in encouraging borrowing, but despite small increases in the limits for freshmen and sophomores around 2007, the aggregate limit on Stafford Loans has remained stable at $23,000 since 1992 (http://www.finaid.org/loans/historicallimits.phtml (accessed April 17, 2013).
12. See the Department of Education's Web site for a discussion of the negotiated rulemaking process for details on the latest proposed regulations: http://www2.ed .gov/policy/highered/reg/hearulemaking/2012/gainfulemployment.html (accessed April 17, 2013).

References

Apling, Richard N. 1993. "Proprietary Schools and Their Students." *Journal of Higher Education* 64(4): 379–416.

Avery, Christopher, and Sarah Turner. 2012. "Student Loans: Do College Students Borrow Too Much—Or Not Enough?" *Journal of Economic Perspectives* 26(1): 165–192.

Bailey, Thomas, Norena Badway, and Patricia J. Gumport. 2001. "For-Profit Higher Education and Community Colleges." Stanford, CA: National Center for Postsecondary Improvement.

Baum, Sandy, and Saul Schwartz. 2006. "How Much Debt Is Too Much? Defining Benchmarks for Manageable Student Debt." New York: College Board.

Belley, Philippe, and Lance Lochner. 2007. "The Changing Role of Family Income and Ability in Determining Educational Achievement." *Journal of Human Capital* 1(1): 37–89.

Cameron, Stephen V., and Christopher Taber. 2004. "Estimation of Educational Borrowing Constraints Using Returns to Schooling." *Journal of Political Economy* 112(1): 132–182.

Cellini, Stephanie Riegg. 2009. "Crowded Colleges and College Crowd-Out: The Impact of Public Subsidies on the Two-Year College Market." *American Economic Journal: Economic Policy* 1(2): 1–30.

———. 2010. "Financial Aid and For-Profit Colleges: Does Aid Encourage Entry?" *Journal of Policy Analysis and Management* 29(3): 526–552.

————. 2012. "For-Profit Higher Education: An Assessment of Costs and Benefits." *National Tax Journal* 65(1): 153–180.

Cellini, Stephanie Riegg, and Latika Chaudhary. 2012. "The Labor Market Returns to a For-Profit College Education." NBER Working Paper No. 18343. Cambridge, MA: National Bureau of Economic Research.

Cellini, Stephanie Riegg, and Claudia Goldin. Forthcoming. "Does Federal Student Aid Raise Tuition? New Evidence on For-Profit Colleges." *American Economic Journal: Economic Policy*.

College Board. 2013. *Trends in Student Aid, 2013*. New York: College Board.

Darolia, Rajeev. 2013a. "Integrity versus Access? The Effect of Federal Financial Aid Availability on Postsecondary Enrollment." *Journal of Public Economics* 106(C): 101–114.

————. 2013b. "Student Loan Repayment and College Accountability." Federal Reserve Bank of Philadelphia Payment Cards Center Discussion Paper Series D-2013. Philadelphia, PA: Federal Reserve Bank of Philadelphia.

————. 2014. "Working (and Studying) Day and Night: Heterogeneous Effects of Working on the Academic Performance of Full-Time and Part-Time Students." *Economics of Education Review* 38, 38–40.

Deming, David J., Claudia Goldin, and Lawrence F. Katz. 2012. "The For-Profit Postsecondary School Sector: Nimble Critters or Agile Predators?" *Journal of Economic Perspectives* 26(1): 139–164.

Ellwood, David T., and Thomas J. Kane 2000. "Who Is Getting a College Education? Family Background and the Growing Gaps in Enrollment." In *Securing the Future*, Sheldon Danziger and Jane Waldfogel, eds. New York: Russell Sage, pp. 282–324.

Field, Erica. 2009. "Educational Debt Burden and Career Choice: Evidence from a Financial Aid Experiment at NYU Law School." *American Economic Journal: Applied Economics* 1(1): 1–21.

Gicheva, Dora. 2011. "Does the Student-Loan Burden Weigh Into the Decision to Start a Family?" Unpublished manuscript.

Government Accountability Office (U.S. GAO). 2010. For-Profit Colleges: Undercover Testing Finds Colleges Encouraged Fraud and Engaged in Deceptive and Questionable Marketing Practices. GAO-10-948T. Washington, DC: GAO.

Jacobson, Louis, Robert LaLonde, and Daniel G. Sullivan. 2005. "Estimating the Returns to Community College Schooling for Displaced Workers." *Journal of Econometrics* 125(1-2): 271–304.

Jepsen, Christopher, Kenneth Troske, and Paul Coomes. 2014. "The Labor-Market Returns to Community College Degrees, Diplomas, and Certificates." *Journal of Labor Economics* 32(1): 95–121.

Lang, Kevin, and Russell Weinstein. 2013. "The Wage Effects of Not-for-Profit and For-Profit Certifications: Better Data, Somewhat Different Results." NBER Working Paper No. 19135. Cambridge, MA: National Bureau of Economic Research.

Light, Audrey. 2001. "In-School Work Experience and the Returns to Schooling." *Journal of Labor Economics* 19(1): 65–93.

National Center for Education Statistics. 2013. *Digest of Education Statistics: 2012*. Washington, DC: U.S. Department of Education.

Rosenbaum, James E., Regina Deil-Amen, and Ann E. Person. 2006. *After Admission: From College Access to College Success*. New York: Russell Sage Foundation.

Rothstein, Jesse, and Cecilia E. Rouse. 2011. "Constrained after College: Student Loans and Early-Career Occupational Choices." *Journal of Public Economics* 95(1): 149–163.

Stinebrickner, Ralph, and Todd R. Stinebrickner. 2003. "Working during School and Academic Performance." *Journal of Human Resources* 38(3): 473–491.

———. 2008. "The Effect of Credit Constraints on the College Drop-Out Decision: A Direct Approach Using a New Panel Study." *American Economic Review* 98(5): 2163–2184.

Turner, Lesley. 2013. "The Incidence of Student Financial Aid: Evidence from the Pell Grant Program." Unpublished manuscript. University of Maryland, College Park. http://econweb.umd.edu/~turner/Turner_FedAidIncidence .pdf (accessed April 18, 2014).

Turner, Nicholas. 2012. "Do Students Profit from For-Profit Education? Estimating the Return to Postsecondary Education Using Tax Data." Working paper. Washington, DC: U.S. Treasury.

Turner, Sarah E. 2006. "For-Profit Colleges in the Context of the Market for Higher Education." In *Earnings from Learning: The Rise of For-Profit Universities*, David W. Breneman, Brian Pusser, and Sarah E. Turner, eds. Albany: State University of New York Press.

U.S. Department of Education. 2011. "Information for Federal Student Aid Professionals." http://ifap.ed.gov/eannouncements/010512DefaultRates 20052009.html (accessed Sept. 25, 2013).

Wolfe, Barbara L., and Robert H. Haveman. 2002. "Social and Nonmarket Benefits from Education in an Advanced Economy." *Conference Series* 47: 97–142.

7

Private Student Loans and Bankruptcy

Did Four-Year Undergraduates Benefit from the Increased Collectability of Student Loans?

Xiaoling Ang
Consumer Financial Protection Bureau

Dalié Jiménez
University of Connecticut School of Law

What effect will a law that virtually eliminates the possibility that a loan will be discharged in bankruptcy have on the pricing and availability of that loan? This chapter seeks to answer that question by investigating the effect of bankruptcy discharge on private student loans (PSLs). We use a unique data set and find some unexpected results.

On April 20, 2005, President Bush signed the Bankruptcy Abuse Prevention and Consumer Protection Act (BAPCPA) into law.[1] The bill was the result of intense political wrangling dating as far back as 1999.[2] Proponents of the bill argued that the significant increases in bankruptcy filing rates were the result of strategic debtors taking advantage of lax bankruptcy rules; a problem that they thought would be solved by increasing the hurdles to a bankruptcy discharge.[3] Opponents argued that the vast majority of debtors filed bankruptcy for reasons largely beyond their control: loss of a job, divorce, medical issues, or a death in the family. Many argued that instead of further limiting bankruptcy protection, Congress should focus on regulating the availability of credit.

Proponents of bankruptcy reform predicted that its effect would be to reduce the cost of consumer credit by reducing the "bankruptcy tax" implicitly spread to all consumers in their cost of credit. Opponents of the bill hypothesized that consumer lenders were providing a rebate of the bankruptcy tax to high credit-scoring borrowers, and thus expected no change in the cost of student loans as a result of BAPCPA.[4] In this chapter, we report on our tests of some of the predictions made by both groups as they relate to the market and pricing of private student loans.

The 2005 amendments added private student loans (PSLs), that is, loans originated by the private market and not insured by any federal or state institution, to the list of debts presumptively nondischargeable in bankruptcy. Through a series of legislative changes that began in 1976 and culminated in 1998, loans made, guaranteed, or insured by the federal or state governments, as well as loans made by nonprofit institutions, were already presumptively nondischargeable before 2005.[5]

This special treatment granted to PSLs ran counter to two of the fundamental policies behind the bankruptcy laws: the equality of treatment of creditors in bankruptcy and the fresh start for the debtor.[6] Neither of these policies has ever been absolute—tax debts and debts obtained by fraud, for example, have both received priority over other unsecured creditors and been nondischargeable as far back as the Bankruptcy Act of 1898.[7] Nonetheless, most of the 19 so-called "rifle-shot" exceptions to discharge exist for strong policy reasons. For example, when domestic support obligations were added to the list of exceptions, the rationale was that this would "provide new protections for parents" and "strengthen their ability to collect child support."[8] The rationale for adding federal and state loans to the list of presumptively nondischargeable debts was to protect the public fisc.

PSLs are very different from the other kinds of student loans that were nondischargeable before the 2005 bankruptcy reform. A brief synopsis of their features is instructive because it highlights how extraordinary the law change was. Unlike federal student loans, PSLs are risk-priced at origination. Only creditworthy individuals (or individuals with creditworthy borrowers) are eligible to obtain PSLs.[9] Since the majority of undergraduate students do not have a significant credit history, most PSLs require students to secure a cosigner who will be responsible for the loan if the student does not repay. In fact, 90 percent of all PSLs required a cosigner in 2011, even if the student had a good credit history or was attending graduate school.[10] The cosigner is liable for the loan as much as the student is, even if the student does not finish school or dies.

PSL borrowers take on the risk of interest rate changes over the typical 15–20 year repayment period. The typical PSL is a variable-rate loan, indexed to LIBOR or similar.[11] Students are offered loans at an "index-plus" variable interest rate. That "plus" (the interest rate charged above the index) is the risk premium, presumed to be closely related to the risk-of-loss that the lender places on that borrower. In this chapter, we refer to that plus as the "margin." All things being equal, a borrower with a higher credit score should receive a loan with a smaller margin than a borrower with a lower credit score. In 2011, initial variable PSL interest rates varied between 2.98 percent and 19 percent for the riskiest borrowers.[12] Finally, funding for PSLs during the period of our study came primarily from the secondary market through asset backed securities.[13]

When BAPCPA became effective on October 17, 2005, every outstanding PSL—no matter when originated—became presumptively nondischargeable for both borrowers and coborrowers. Loans that were originated before BAPCPA presumably priced in the cost of bankruptcy dischargeability in their margins (risk premiums), but those loans became presumptively nondischargeable all the same.[14]

The nondischargeability of PSLs is problematic from at least two perspectives: the concern that billions in outstanding student loans may be stifling the economy and the general lack of protections offered to delinquent borrowers.

Standing at over $1 trillion, student loan debt is the second largest type of debt Americans carry, surpassed only by mortgage debt. In recent years, regulators, policymakers, and academics have worried publicly over the effect this amount of debt has on our economy. PSLs are a small but significant feature of the American postsecondary education finance system and may become more prominent to the extent that other forms of aid do not keep pace with increasing costs of attendance. As of 2011, 15 percent of student loan debt had been originated by for-profit companies (typically, but not exclusively, banks) in the form of PSLs.[15] The current $150 billion in PSL outstandings is especially concerning because of the lack of protections for borrowers who cannot repay.

Outside of bankruptcy, federal student loans have protections for borrowers in financial distress. These include the ability for borrowers to enter into income-based or income-contingent repayment plans, temporarily suspend payments for up to 2 years, and extend the term of the loan for up to 30 years.[16] Federal loans are also eligible for cancellation in the case of total or permanent disability, the death of a student or parent taking out a PLUS Loan, where the school that the student attends closes while the student is enrolled, or in some cases, if the student becomes a teacher or works in public service.[17] None of these features are found in the typical PSL. Student borrowers with federal and private loans will have a difficult time discharging either federal loans or PSLs, but they will have a much tougher time living with delinquent private loans because of the lack of protections for those in default. In addition, some students may have a disproportionate amount of PSL debt relative to federal loans because students need not exhaust their federal loan opportunities before obtaining a PSL. The CFPB found that "more than 54 percent of PSL borrowers do not exhaust their Stafford Loan eligibility, or do not even apply for federal aid."[18]

We would ideally like to be able to compare federal and PSL default rates and bankruptcy filing rates. Unfortunately, it is impossible to compare the default rate of federal loans versus PSLs, owing to differences in the methodology of calculating those rates and the lack of availability of data. The Department of Education (DOE) does not report how many individuals with federal student loans have filed for bankruptcy. The DOE publishes "cumulative lifetime default rates" for loans that enter repayment during a fiscal year and have defaulted through the end of the fiscal year. As an example, for the cohort that graduated or left school in 2006 that had federal student loans, the DOE estimates that 9.2 percent will default over their lifetime.[19] In contrast, what we know about PSL default rates is limited to the origination-year level (also called "vintages") or alternatively to loans outstanding at the end of a year. The CFPB found that lenders' underwriting practices had a significant effect on PSL default rates. While some securitized trusts have "default rates expected to reach 50 percent," some depository institutions that never securitized their loans have default rates of less than 4 percent.[20] The nine lenders in our study had approximately $8.1 billion in cumulative defaults as of 2011, a figure made up of approximately 850,000 distinct loans.[21] Between 2005 and 2011, as few as 0.2 percent of outstanding PSLs and as high as 1.1 percent of all outstanding loans made by the lenders in our study were included in a bankruptcy filing.[22]

This chapter relies on a unique large data set that sheds some light on the typically opaque private student loan market. Per a congressional mandate, the CFPB collected data that have never been available before.[23] Our data set covers loan-level information for all PSL originations made by the nine largest PSL lenders between 2005 and 2011. The data are de-identified but include borrowers' and coborrowers' credit scores, amount borrowed, the student's year in school, and the name of the school the student is attending. We merge these data to DOE administrative data sources that provide school-level information about federal student loans as well as institutional characteristics.

Lenders use most of these variables in their underwriting. Credit scores in particular are highly correlated with loan grants and pricing. However, we do not observe all variables that lenders have available for underwriting purposes. For example, lenders may have asked about coborrowers' employment or income or have included information from a credit report (e.g., the fact that someone has a large number of credit cards) that we do not observe. The granular information from the credit report is "baked in" the credit score number, but income is not.

We find that excluding PSLs from discharge in bankruptcy decreased the average credit score of borrowers and increased the volume of loans but also *increased* the overall cost of loans. This latter finding runs counter to general economic theory as well as the arguments of both proponents and opponents of BAPCPA. Specifically, we find that the credit score composition of borrowers after the law changed skewed toward the lower end of the credit score spectrum, but the average borrower credit score only decreased slightly in practical terms. We also find that the overall cost of PSLs at four-year undergraduate institutions increased by an average of 35 basis points (0.35 percent) as a result of the law change. Finally, we observe that the volume of loans originated tripled after BAPCPA and find that 60 percent of that increase is attributable to the law change.

The first section of this chapter provides some background on PSLs and a brief literature review. The second section describes the competing theories predicting the effect of BAPCPA on credit and bankruptcies. The third section describes our unique data set, its limitations, and our empirical strategy. We report our results in the fourth section. Following that, we attempt to explain our surprising findings and consider welfare implications. We conclude by discussing next steps.

BACKGROUND AND LITERATURE

Since 1976, federal student loans have received some form of bankruptcy protection. The stated purpose when the first restriction on the dischargeability of federal loans passed in Congress was a concern that students were using bankruptcy opportunistically to wipe out their student debt on the eve of a "lucrative career."[24] There has never been empirical evidence of widespread strategic default with regard to student loans. Even as far back as 1977, the evidence pointed to the contrary—strategic defaults are a rarity.[25] Nonetheless, by 1998, federal loans became nondischargeable "unless excepting [them] from discharge . . . would impose an undue hardship on the debtor and the debtor's dependents."[26] In 2005, PSLs were added to the list.[27] In this section, we explain the legal implications of this treatment and put it in context of the empirical studies that have examined its effect to date.

Congress never elaborated on the meaning of "undue hardship." The sole mention of the phrase in the congressional record comes from opponents of the amendments who called it "vague" and argued that the provision itself "may create an undue hardship for good faith bankrupts" because "the standard is a very hard one. It will be very difficult to meet. Worse, it will be variously interpreted by different judges around the country and even in the same judicial district."[28] As we discuss below, there is some evidence that this is what happened.

The nondischargeability provision has been amended five times with the same "undue hardship" language, with no clarification from Congress.[29] In the meantime, courts have settled on two interpretations of the phrase. Almost all courts use the fairly rigid Brunner test to evaluate whether a debtor can overcome the presumptive nondischargeability of student loans.[30] Rebutting the presumption can be a difficult task. To do so, the debtor must file an "adversary proceeding" (effectively a lawsuit) with the bankruptcy court against her student loan creditors. She must convince the court by a preponderance of the evidence that repaying her loans would present an undue hardship.[31] The bankruptcy court must determine whether the debtor has met the threshold for dischargeability, even if the creditor does not respond to the suit.[32] If the debtor loses the lawsuit, or does not file one in the first place, her student loans are unaffected by the bankruptcy.[33]

A handful of empirical studies have examined debtors seeking to discharge student loans in bankruptcy and how they fared in the courts. Three key findings pertain to this study: 1) an almost infinitesimal number of student loan borrowers seek to discharge their student loans in bankruptcy; 2) discharge seekers are outliers—they have high educational debt relative to the population and find themselves in especially miserable situations; and 3) about half of discharge seekers are successful, but the reasons for their success are not entirely explainable by objective factors.

Only a handful of individuals attempt to discharge their student loans in bankruptcy. In the only nationwide study on the subject, Jason Iuliano estimates that of the individuals who filed bankruptcy in 2007, only 0.1 percent had student loans and sought to discharge those loans.[34] That percent amounted to 213 individuals out of the 169,774 who filed a bankruptcy case in 2007 and had a student loan.[35]

Based on Iuliano's study as well as two studies from Rafael Pardo and Michelle Lacey, we can establish a picture of the "typical" discharge seeker.[36] All three studies find that the average discharge seeker is over 41 years old, well past typical college age.[37] Between 62 and 80 percent of discharge seekers were unmarried, but most had one or more dependents, which is suggestive of a number of single-parent households.[38] Fewer discharge seekers tended to be employed at the time they file bankruptcy relative to the rest of the bankrupt population.[39] Unsurprisingly, discharge seekers are in more financial distress. "They make less money, own fewer assets, and have more liabilities, including educational debt" than nondischarge seekers.[40] The average educational debt load varies between $47,137 in the oldest study to $80,476 in the study with the most recent data.[41] Discharge seekers are also in dire straits: more than half of them suffered from a medical condition themselves or had one or more dependents with a condition.[42] The majority of the discharge seekers seem to have tried various avenues to mitigate or resolve their student debt issues before filing bankruptcy.[43]

Discharge seekers are more often than not successful in obtaining at least a partial discharge: 57 percent of the adversary proceedings in Pardo and Lacey's study of bankruptcy cases filed between 2002 and 2006 in the Western District of Washington resulted in at least a partial discharge.[44] In Iuliano's study, 39 percent (or 81 individuals out of the almost 1 million nationwide bankruptcies in 2007) received either a full or a partial discharge of their student loans.[45] This may seem like favorable odds, but it is likely a result of a selection bias. The more downtrodden and unfortunate, the more likely one might be to seek a discharge. These odds are nonetheless hard to predict: Pardo and Lacey argue that the undue hardship standard is not applied consistently.[46] Their 2005 study finds few statistically significant differences between debtors who were granted a discharge of their student loans versus those who were denied.[47] Troubling from an equal justice perspective, Pardo and Lacey also find that "factors unrelated to the command of the law (e.g., the identity of the judge assigned to the debtor's adversary proceeding), rather than factors deemed relevant by the legal doctrine (e.g., the debtor's income and expenses), account for the substantive outcomes" in the case.[48]

Iuliano and Pardo and Lacey's studies do not distinguish between federal and private loans, but they nonetheless give us a sense of who might seek and who might get their student loans discharged. Only one study has examined the effect of the bankruptcy reform on the availability of PSLs.[49] Mark Krantowitz from the Web site FinAid.org issued a report shortly after the law came into effect finding a small expansion in loan availability to borrowers with lower FICO scores.[50] Using data from student loan securitizations,[51] he found a 1.2 percent increase in loans to borrowers with FICO scores less than 650 (typically considered subprime borrowers) after BAPCPA.[52] However, when looking only at loans originated without a coborrower, Krantowitz found that credit contracted after BAPCPA by 1.7 percent for subprime borrowers. He also found a modest increase (5.2 percent) in PSL availability to borrowers with a FICO score between 651 and 710 (generally considered prime).[53] Krantowitz also found that in some of his sample the average FICO score post-BAPCPA dropped from 719 to 715, further indicating a slight credit expansion to borrowers with lower creditworthiness.[54]

Until now, Krantowitz's report has been the only analysis attempting to answer the question of the effect of BAPCPA on the pricing and availability of private student loans. His findings that credit moderately expanded are consistent with the hypotheses we discuss in the next part of this chapter.

ANALYTICAL FRAMEWORK AND HYPOTHESES

Under the dominant legal and economic theory behind the latest round of bankruptcy reform, the "easy" availability of bankruptcy was thought to have one of two effects: increasing the cost of credit for everyone to account for strategic borrowers or rationing credit, leading to a suboptimal amount of available credit. Opponents of bankruptcy reform, on the other hand, argued that there was no empirical evidence for this view: household credit increased dramatically, even as bankruptcy filings were increasing in the late 1990s. In their view, lenders in particular stopped rationing credit as early as the 1980s, just after the Supreme Court effectively lifted usury cap restrictions and after credit scoring had improved enough that lenders were better able to identify high-risk borrowers.[55] Each of these predicted effects yields some intuitions about what might happen to the cost of credit (specifically PSLs) post-BAPCPA. In this part, we develop three models to more formally theorize the expected result from the increased protection of PSLs in bankruptcy. In a later section, we compare the models' predictions to our results and discuss the similarities and (surprising) differences.

The majority of the 2005 bankruptcy reforms were directly responsive to a view of the world that assumed consumers were not only perfectly rational but also engaging in strategic behavior. We refer to this as the "bankruptcy tax" view. According to this view, strategic consumers impose a cost on the system by forcing lenders to either pass on the cost of opportunism to borrowers as a whole or ration credit. Portions of BAPCPA, including the PSL nondischargeable provision, were designed to ameliorate these problems. Some BAPCPA proponents posited that current strategic behavior was causing a "bankruptcy tax" of "$400-a-year on every household in the country."[56] Alternatively or in conjunction with a bankruptcy tax, lenders may ration credit in a world where bankruptcy is easy "in order to maintain underwriting standards."[57] One of the aims of bankruptcy reform was to reduce the number of opportunistic borrowers. In support of BAPCPA, Judge Posner theorized that "by increasing the rights of creditors in bankruptcy . . . [bankruptcy reform] should reduce interest rates and thus make borrowers better off."[58]

We can model this straightforwardly. Let x be a measure of the credit quality of a borrower and $f(x)$ denote the probability with which type x borrowers repay their loans, regardless of the loan amount. Let r be one plus the rate of return of the loan for the creditor conditional on the borrower repaying their loan,[59] and let $c(x)$ be the average recovery rate of loans that are not repaid in full.[60] For these purposes, assume that repayment rates and the average proportion repaid are increasing in x, so $f'(x) > 0$ and $c'(x) > 0$. Let $z(r)$ represent the original balance of a loan a borrower is willing to accept, which depends on the interest rate. Assume also that consumers are risk averse, so that $z'(r)$ and $z''(r) < 0$.

Further assume that the creditor is risk neutral and rational. Then for each borrower of type x, the creditor maximizes expected repayment or recovery net of the loan amount, as shown in Equation (7.1).

$$(7.1) \quad \max_r f(x)z(r)r + (1 - f(x))z(r)c(x) - z(r)$$

A rational, risk-neutral creditor will only originate a loan for which expected repayment net of loan amount is nonnegative such that

$$(7.2) \quad f(x) \geq \frac{1 - c(x)}{r - c(x)}$$

As the average recovery rate of the loans not repaid in full, $c(x)$, increases, the right-hand side of Equation (7.2) decreases, so if repayment rates are increased by BAPCPA, creditors would be willing to make loans to borrowers with lower values of x, so access to credit should expand.

Taking the first order conditions of Equation (7.1) and then differentiating implicitly yields Equation (7.3),

$$(7.3) \quad \frac{dr}{dc(x)} = \frac{-(1 - f(x))z'(r)}{[f(x)(r - c(x)) - (1 - c)]z''(x)} < 0$$

This implies that for any type x borrower, rates of returns conditional on borrowers repaying the loan in full should decrease if bankruptcy protection increases the recovery rate of loans that default, which would correspond to a decrease in interest rates for borrowers of all levels of credit quality, as shown in Figure 7.1, which illustrates the equilibrium price schedule for a PSL of a given size by credit quality. Prior

**Figure 7.1 Effect of BAPCPA on Cost of a PSL of Fixed Size by
Credit Quality**

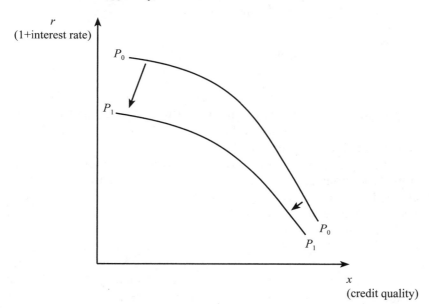

to BAPCPA, P_0 traces out the relationship between the cost of credit, captured by r, and credit quality, x. After BAPCPA, the increase in $c(x)$, the return given less than full payment at a given interest rate, resulting from higher rates of recovery conditional on bankruptcy, should be offset by a decrease in interest rates for borrowers, so the price schedule shifts from P_0 to P_1. Note that the size of the decrease may vary by credit quality.

Consider the case where the borrower is von Neumann-Morgenstern (VNM) rational, as assumed by proponents of bankruptcy reform.[61] In that case, his utility function can be expressed as

$$U(z,r;x) = g(x)u(z,r) + (1 - g[x])v(z,r),$$

where $g(x)$ is the borrower's ex ante belief about the probability that he will repay the loan, $u(z,r)$ is the expected utility from successfully being able to pay back his loan when he borrows z at interest rate $r - 1$, and $v(z,r)$ is his expected utility of not being able to pay back a loan that he borrows at these terms. The larger the loan, the better off he is when he is able to pay it back, so $u_1 > 0$, and the worse off he is when he is unable to pay it back, so $v_1 < 0$. From the first order conditions

$$\frac{g(x)}{1 - g(x)} = \frac{-v_1(z, r)}{u_1(z, r)},$$

which implicitly defines $z(r)$. Note that consumer overoptimism or positive cognitive bias can be captured by $g(x) > f(x)$. In other words, the borrower's belief about his ability to repay the loan is greater than his actual probability of repaying the loan.

The new treatment of PSLs in bankruptcy—making them presumptively nondischargeable and effectively very unlikely to be discharged—makes the consequences of default more severe; a severity that increases with the size of the loan. We model this as the expected utility of not being able to repay a loan, $v(z,r)$, becoming $\hat{v}(z,r)$, and $\hat{v}_1$. Figure 7.2 illustrates the effect of BAPCPA on the supply of and demand for PSL for a borrower of a fixed credit quality, x. Assuming that ability-to-repay conditional on credit quality is not affected by BAPCPA—that is, there is no additional strategic default after BAPCPA—then $g(x)$ is unchanged and

$$\frac{g(x)}{1 - g(x)} = \frac{-v_1(z, r)}{u_1(z, r)} = \frac{-\hat{v}_1(\hat{z}, r)}{u_1(\hat{z}, r)},$$

so $\hat{z} < z$.[62] This implies that the VNM borrower's demand curve shifts down, as illustrated in Figure 7.2. Supply responds as described in Equation (7.3) and shifts from S_0 to S_1.[63] Equilibrium moves from E_0 to $\hat{E}_1$.

Note that the magnitude of this shift is determined by the relationship between the change in the expected utility of not being able to repay a loan and the average recovery rate of loans that are not repaid in full, $c(x)$, so, a priori, it is not possible to determine whether loan sizes will increase, decrease, or remain the same as a result of BAPCPA. Similar to Judge Posner's prediction for the law change, this simple model would thus predict that the price of the loans—in our parlance, the loan margin—will decrease after the law change and the effects on credit quality and volume are an empirical question.

Figure 7.2 Effects of BAPCPA on Supply and Demand of PSL for Consumers of a Fixed Credit Quality

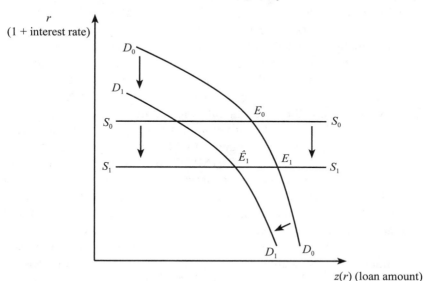

As an alternative model, we also consider credit provision in the private student loan market in a Stiglitz-Weiss model in Appendix 7C.[64] For this model to hold, we assume that there is credit rationing in the private student loan market, as some BAPCPA proponents argued.[65] The Stiglitz-Weiss model predicts that the cost of credit will remain the same (because of rationing); the supply of credit will increase (increased volume of loans originated, as opposed to the ambiguous effect on quantity in the simple model); and that lenders will on average lend to riskier borrowers (in our data, lower credit scores).[66]

Opponents of BAPCPA have argued that the assumptions of strategic rationality on the part of consumers are too simplistic. Incorporating behavioral research findings and empirical research of actual debtors in bankruptcy, Susan Block-Lieb and Edward Janger propose a behavioral model of consumer bankruptcy that relaxes the assumption of consumer rationality but retains the assumption of lender rationality.[67] This is captured by the model presented above, since $f(x)$ and $g(x)$ can differ. Positive consumer biases, including optimism, present bias, and probability neglect, correspond to cases where $g(x) > f(x)$.

If we assume, for example, that borrowers are present biased, then they focus on the interest rate, and do not fully consider their probability of bankruptcy or the consequences of BAPCPA upon bankruptcy.[68] These behaviors could be captured by setting $g(x) = 1$ (assuming that a borrower believes he will definitely repay the loan) or by setting $\hat{v}(z,r) = v(z,r)$ (borrower ignores the consequences of bankruptcy), respectively. This would mean that borrowers' demand curves do not shift in response to BAPCPA. Instead, these loans will appear "cheaper" to borrowers because they are not fully accounting for the costs or are overly optimistic about their likelihood of repayment, and therefore loan originations and loan amounts should increase at any given credit quality, as shown in Figure 7.2. BAPCPA causes the supply curve to shift downward for individuals of credit quality x, which means that the price of credit, r, decreases. In response to this shift, the new equilibrium moves along the demand curve from E_0 to E_1, so the loan size demanded increases, in contrast to the loan size decrease we see in $\hat{E}_1$, the case where borrowers internalize the cost of nondischargeability.

Block-Lieb and Janger go further than this model. They theorize that "consumer lenders already provide a rebate of the bankruptcy tax" to subprime and less credit-worthy consumers.[69] This model is really a special case of the competitive model with present-biased consumer above. If, as Block-Lieb and Janger predict, the charge-off rate does not change post BAPCPA, then $c(x)$ does not change, and so the supply curve does not shift. Also, if consumers understand that $c(x)$ does not change, or if they do not factor in nondischargeability in bankruptcy into $v(z,r)$, the demand curve does not shift. Therefore, prices and borrowing decisions will remain the same.

To summarize, depending on what assumptions we make and what model we use, we would expect a variety of different outcomes for the effect of the change to the bankruptcy laws making private student loans presumptively nondischargeable, as shown in Table 7.1.

Incorporating all of these leads to the following hypotheses, which we test with our analysis:

- H0 — Price, average credit quality or loan amount, and total loan volumes will remain the same.

- H1 — Loan pricing (that is, lender margins) should remain the same or decrease for originations after the law change.

- H2 — Lenders should be willing to lend to borrowers with lower credit quality than they were willing to lend before the law change.

- H3 — Overall loan volumes should increase.

- H4 — Average loan amount should also increase independent of tuition and fees.

Table 7.1 Expectation of Outcomes by Theory

Outcome	Simple Competitive (CP) Model	Stiglitz-Weiss (credit rationing)	CP + Present- Biased Consumer	Block-Lieb & Janger (CP + $\Delta c(x)=0$)[70]
Price	Decrease	No change	Decrease	No change
Credit quality	Decrease	Decrease	Decrease	No change
Loan amount	Ambiguous	Increase	Increase	No change
Loan volume	Ambiguous	Increase	Increase	No change

DATA AND METHODOLOGY

Data

Our data set was created by CFPB economists in preparation for the congressionally mandated report on PSLs issued in 2012.[71] The data set includes PSL originations from the nine largest PSL lenders in the period between the first quarter of 2005 and the last quarter of 2011.[72] The data do not allow us to identify the lender for a given loan, but it does contain origination information at the individual loan level. The variables available in the data set include the loan amount, credit score of the borrower, credit score of any coborrowers, interest rate for fixed-rate loans, margin and the index used for variable rate loans, and the state of residence of the borrower.[73] This data set was merged to two public administrative data sets maintained by the Department of Education: the Integrated Postsecondary Education System (IPEDS) and the Postsecondary Education Participants System (PEPS).[74] IPEDS "gathers information from every college, university, and technical and vocational institution that participates in the federal student financial aid programs."[75] It includes data on "enrollments, program completions, graduation rates, faculty and staff, finances, institutional prices, and student financial aid programs."[76] The PEPS data include school-level data on topics such as school characteristics, cohort default rates, and eligibility status.[77] We used these additional variables in the school-level analysis.

In order to compare PSLs to federal loans for the difference-in-differences (DD) analysis, we also made use of data from the DOE's Title IV Program Volume Reports for Direct Loans and Federal Family Education Loan Program (FFELP) loans at the school level in the 2004–2005 and 2005–2006 academic years.[78]

While the PSL data set includes originations on a variety of school types, for purposes of this study, we restricted the data set to originations for undergraduates at four-year institutions from the first quarter of 2005 and 2006. We limited ourselves to this smaller (though still considerable) sample because we thought the heterogeneity of school and program type (certificate, medical school, law school) might obscure the effect. We also limit ourselves to this time period to avoid conflating the effects of other major policy changes, such as the 2006 implementation of the Higher Education Reconciliation Act of 2005, which modified eligibility and application requirements for Title IV funds, with the effects of BAPCPA.[79]

Our outcome variables include the credit worthiness of student loan applicants (measured by the highest FICO score between the borrower and coborrower), the margins (interest above the index), the lender charged on the loan, the size of the loan, and the total number of loans originated. Table 7.2 presents summary statistics for private student loans originated in the first quarter of 2005 (before the law changed) and the first quarter of 2006 (after the law changed). Of note is the overall small reduction in mean and median FICO scores in 2006; this is true both for borrower FICO scores and for maximum FICO score (if the borrower applied with a coborrower, the maximum of the two scores). The average original balance and the number of loans originated increased; the latter more than tripled in the postperiod.

In Figure 7.3, we plot the distribution of maximum FICO scores before and after BAPCPA. We observe that the distribution shifts slightly to the left, so that FICO scores decrease after BAPCPA.

Table 7.2 Summary Statistics for Loans Originated in the First Quarter of 2005 and First Quarter of 2006

	Before BAPCPA (Q1 2005)		After BAPCPA (Q1 2006)	
	Mean	Median	Mean	Median
Has a coborrower	0.80	1	0.82	1
	(0.40)			
Maximum FICO score	720.34	718	714.96	700
	(47.50)		(47.45)	
Borrower's FICO score	651.02	662	648.65	660
	(65.44)		(67.48)	
Year in school	2.62	3	2.54	3
	(1.15)		(1.15)	
Margin (%)	4.18	4.75	4.63	4.85
	(1.59)		(1.06)	
Original balance ($)	8,614	6,271	10,015	7,650
	(6,956)		(785.4)	
Deferral term (months)	28.67	28	28.67	29
	(15.1)		(14.8)	
Tuition and fees ($)	11,485	7,229	11,091	7,795
	(8,011)		(8,200)	
Loans originated	4,960		15,318	

NOTE: Maximum FICO score is the maximum of the borrower and all coborrower scores. Standard deviations in parentheses. Restricted to loans originated in the first quarter of 2005 and 2006 to undergraduates at four-year institutions for which a borrower or coborrower's FICO score was reported.

Figure 7.4 displays the changes in margins between the first quarter before the law change and the same quarter one year later. Before the law changed, some lenders were originating PSLs that had a zero or below zero margin; in other words, they were not charging a premium above the index for some loans. After the law changed, surprisingly, premium-free or less-than-index loans were no longer being originated, and the distribution shifts toward higher margins.

Figure 7.5 presents the distribution of the original balances of the loans originated in the first quarter before the law changed (Q1 2005) and the same quarter after the law changed (Q1 2006). Original balances are positively skewed in both time periods, but slightly higher after BAPCPA.

Figure 7.3 Distribution of Maximum FICO Scores Shifts toward Less Creditworthy Borrowers in the Post BAPCPA Period

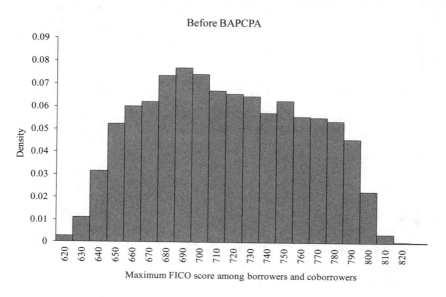

Before BAPCPA

Maximum FICO score among borrowers and coborrowers

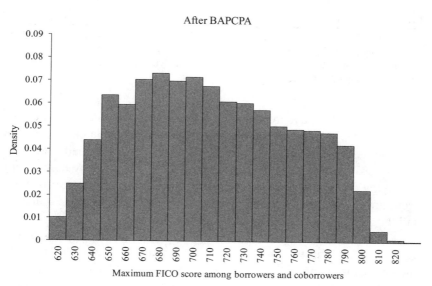

After BAPCPA

Maximum FICO score among borrowers and coborrowers

SOURCE: Authors' analysis of CFPB private student loan data.

Figure 7.4 Distribution of Margins Increased in the Post BAPCPA Period

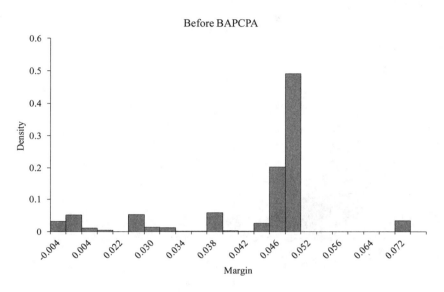

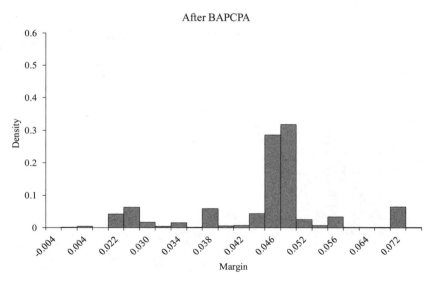

SOURCE: Authors' analysis of CFPB private student loan data.

Figure 7.5 Distribution of Original Balances Increased in the Post BAPCPA Period

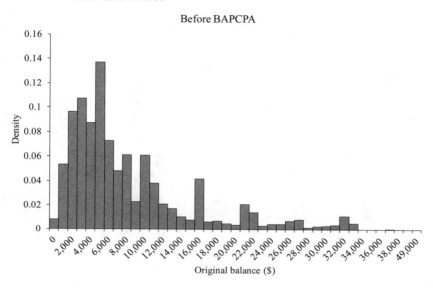

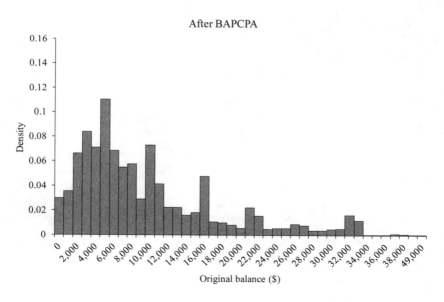

SOURCE: Authors' analysis of CFPB private student loan data.

Limitations

The available data impose some limitations on our analysis. The first limitation is related to the timing of bankruptcy reform, the second with the available data.

First, bankruptcy reforms, including changes to the dischargeability of PSLs, were debated in Congress as early as the mid-1990s, and by 1999 and 2000, the House and Senate had passed bills that included language adding PSLs to the list of presumptively nondischargeable loans in bankruptcy. These bills were vetoed by President Clinton in 2000.[80] The upsurge of Republican congressional members in the 2004 election and the public support of bankruptcy reform by sitting President Bush meant that the bill, as one newspaper phrased it in an opinion piece a month before the bill's passage, "gained the momentum of a runaway freight train."[81] The bill was introduced in the Senate on February 1, 2005, passed by both houses on April 14, 2005, was signed into law by President Bush on April 20, 2005, and became effective on October 17, 2005.[82]

Despite the lack of a "surprise" factor for the law change, lenders are unlikely to have made preemptive changes to their underwriting algorithms, primarily because by doing so they could lose the benefit afforded by the law's protection for at least some of the loans they would originate in anticipation. This is because BAPCPA did not apply retroactively: PSLs were not affected unless and until a bankruptcy case was filed after the law became effective. This means that PSLs only became presumptively nondischargeable for bankruptcies that were filed on or after October 17, 2005, and they became so regardless of when the loans were originated.[83] Prior to that date, the loans were dischargeable like most other forms of unsecured debt, such as credit card debts.

Our earliest data are from Q1 2005, before the law was passed or took effect. The law took effect at the very end of Q3 2005, so we use Q1 2006 as the effective postperiod. Figure 7.6 shows the timeline of the law changes and the available data.

We note one additional limitation to using first-quarter originations. Because the academic year traditionally runs from August to May, many student loans are originated over the summer or the fall. Beyond the fact that there are fewer originations in Q1 than Q3, loans originated in Q1 differ from loans originated in other quarters. Table 7.3

Figure 7.6 Major Events in Bankruptcy Reform and Our Data Set Observations

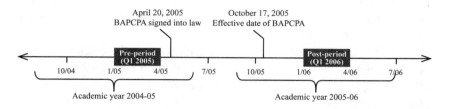

presents a comparison of first quarter 2006 originations to third-quarter originations in 2005 and 2006. Columns (2)–(5) present the results for ordinary least squares (OLS) regressions of the outcome variables with controls for quarter of origination and school fixed effects. Compared to first-quarter loans, third-quarter loans tend to have significantly larger original balances, are more likely to be originated through the school channel, are more likely to be made with coborrowers, and have slightly higher maximum FICO scores. To mitigate these seasonal differences, we restrict our analysis to comparing Q1 2005 data (the first quarter available) to Q1 2006 data.

Empirical Strategy

We analyze changes in loan characteristics—that is, changes in loan amount, debtor credit quality, and margin (risk premium cost)—at the loan level. We implement three methods in this analysis: 1) OLS regression, 2) Blinder-Oaxaca decomposition, and 3) propensity-score matching. We then collapse the data and analyze the volume of loans originated at the school level using the same three methods and also perform a DD analysis using volumes of federal loans as a comparison for PSL volumes.

Loan-level analysis

We can think of the price and terms of credit in terms of the expected returns for the creditor conditional on repayment, the amount of the loan extended, and the credit quality of the borrower. In our data set, these characteristics most closely correspond to margin (the risk premium),[84]

Table 7.3 OLS Regressions Comparing First-Quarter 2006 Originations with Third-Quarter 2006 Originations

	(1) Total originations	(2) Original balance	(3) School channel	(4) Has a cosigner	(5) FICO score
2006 Q1	16,017				
2005 Q3	37,795	1,927***	0.0420***	0.0250***	6.563***
		(78.89)	(0.00388)	(0.00356)	(0.473)
2006 Q3	26,127	2,689***	0.00796**	0.0499***	1.798***
		(74.17)	(0.00365)	(0.00334)	(0.445)
Constant		9,936***	0.248***	0.821***	716.5***
		(61.80)	(0.00304)	(0.00279)	(0.371)
Observations		79,913	79,939	79,939	79,939
R^2		0.148	0.293	0.079	0.098

NOTE:*p < 0.10; **p < 0.05; ***p < 0.01. Standard errors in parentheses. Restricted to four-year undergraduates in the first quarter of 2006 and the third quarters of 2005 and 2006. Columns (2) through (5) represent separate OLS regressions and include school-level fixed effects.

original balance, and the maximum FICO scores among borrowers and coborrowers on a loan.[85] To evaluate how these characteristics changed as a result of BAPCPA, we implement three techniques.

As a first approach, we run OLS regressions of these characteristics, y, on *post*, a dummy variable for receiving a loan after the implementation of BAPCPA, and a vector of control variables, X, that would be included in an underwriting model, such as type of school attended, tuition and fees, credit score, year in school, and a constant, as shown in Equation (7.5).[86] The sample is restricted to individuals with valid FICO scores, as this is the dominant measure of creditworthiness used in the data set.

$$(7.5) \quad y_i = \beta_{post} post_i + \beta_x X_i + \varepsilon_i$$

Note that H2 discussed in the analytical framework implies that the coefficient on $\beta_{post} < 0$ when the outcome under consideration is the maximum credit score among all borrowers and H1 implies that at each maximum credit score, the interest rate should decrease, so $\beta_{post} < 0$.

$$(7.6) \quad y_i = \beta_{post}post_i + \sum_{j=1}^{N} \beta_j x_{ji} + \sum_{j=1}^{N} \beta_{j \times post} x_{ji} \times post_i + \varepsilon_i$$

We also perform this analysis with interactions between school and borrower characteristics, which are observable to the creditor, and an indicator for the postperiod. Let X_i be a vector of school or borrower characteristics, $X_i = [x_{1i} \quad x_{2i} \quad \cdots \quad x_{Ni}]'$. Then the interaction terms can be written as in Equation (7.6). For a borrower with characteristics X_i, the estimated effect of BAPCPA on the outcome variables is given by

$$\beta_{post}post_i + \sum_{j=1}^{N} \beta_{j \times post} x_{ij} \times post_i$$

Effectively, $\beta_{j \times post}$ can be interpreted as the contribution of having one more unit of x_j to the magnitude of the effect of the policy. For example, if two borrowers have identical characteristics except that one has a coborrower and the other does not, we would expect the effect of BAPCPA on their outcomes to differ by $\beta_{coborrower \times post}$ on average.

Since the lender data set only contains data for originated loans, one concern is that the composition of borrowers in the data set may change in response to changes in the loan offers by creditors. In order to separately identify effects due to changes in terms for borrowers who would have received loans in the absence of BAPCPA and the effects of the change in the composition of borrowers, we employ two techniques: the Blinder-Oaxaca decomposition and propensity score matching.

The Blinder-Oaxaca decomposition was initially developed in the context of wage discrimination, where wages are only observed for individuals who are employed.[87] In the context of this study, we consider the group that was exposed to BAPCPA, that is, borrowers who received loans in the first quarter of 2006.[88] First, we run regressions of the outcome variables on their characteristics for both samples restricted to the *pre* group, which received loans before BAPCPA (in Q1 2005), and the *post* group, which received loans after BAPCPA (in Q1 2006), as in Equations (7.7) and (7.8).

$$(7.7) \quad y_i^{pre} = \beta_X^{pre} X_i^{pre} + \varepsilon_i^{pre}$$

(7.8) $y_i^{post} = \beta_X^{post} X_i^{post} + \varepsilon_i^{post}$

An estimate of the difference in average loan terms for the groups due to the changes in the characteristics of the individuals in the group ("endowments") is captured in the first term on the right-hand side of Equation (7.9). An estimate of the effects of the program on the loan terms for individuals who would receive loans in the absence of BAP-CPA is captured by the effect due to coefficients in the second term of the right-hand side of Equation (7.9). The effect due to coefficients can be thought of as the change in how the underlying underwriting model classifies borrowers with a certain set of observable characteristics (e.g., a certain credit score).

(7.9) $\bar{y}^{pre} - \bar{y}^{post} = \beta_X^{pre}(\bar{X}_i^{pre} - \bar{X}_i^{post}) + (\beta_X^{pre} - \beta_X^{post})\bar{X}_i^{post}$

It follows that for margins, the effect due to the program corresponds to an average of the effects characterized by H2. These results are invariant to omitted reference groups when dummy variables are added; that is, the program effect estimates do not vary with the omitted category when we use indicator variables for the values of a categorical variable as controls.[89] Since Kline has shown that the Blinder-Oaxaca decomposition is a reweighting estimator, we can also interpret the Blinder-Oaxaca results causally.[90]

To further isolate the effect of BAPCPA, we use propensity score matching methods to understand its effect on individuals who received loans after BAPCPA but who, based on their observable characteristics, would have been approved for loans in the absence of BAPCPA. We estimate the effects on this population using nearest-neighbor propensity score matching, matching observations from the first quarter of 2006 with a single observation from the first quarter of 2005. This allows us to reduce the bias due to potential confounding variables.

During this time period, underwriting of student loans was largely based on automated underwriting and primarily based on the characteristics we observe—namely, credit score, amount of loan, and school characteristics. In other words, conditional on borrower and coborrower characteristics, approval for a loan is deterministic because lenders are making decisions based on observable characteristics run through an algorithm. We thus have reason to believe that propensity score methods are appropriate because our sample satisfies the strong ignorability and conditional independence assumptions in Equation (7.10), where S is post-BAPCPA status, as discussed in Rosenbaum and Rubin.[91]

$$(7.10) \quad y_i^{pre} \coprod S | X = x, \forall x$$

$$(7.11) \quad \tau = E\left[y_i^{post} | p(x), S = 1\right] - E\left[y_i^{pre} | p(x), S = 0\right]$$

The effect of the program on individuals in the common support of the characteristics of those observed in the pre- and postperiods can be estimated by Equation (7.11), where τ is the treatment effect and p is the propensity score estimated by a probit regression, and $S = 1$ if the individual is observed post BAPCPA and 0 otherwise.[92]

H2 implies that the composition of borrowers may change, owing to the availability of credit to individuals who would not have been offered credit prior to the policy change. Lenders' ex ante assessment of borrower credit quality, x, may be determined by multiple factors, including credit score, school attended, and year in school. Therefore, there may be differences in the observable characteristics of borrowers between the pre- and postperiods. The propensity score analysis thus cannot tell us anything about the type of borrower that is able to get a loan after BAPCPA. It can only tell us the effect of BAPCPA on borrowers in the first quarter of 2006 that would have been approved for a loan before the law changed.

School-level analysis

To test the hypothesis that loan volumes increase because of BAPCPA, H3, we collapse our loan origination data set to the school level. Since our unit of observation is now a school, we are able to use the three methods described above—1) OLS, 2) Blinder-Oaxaca, and 3) propensity-score matching—to examine loan volumes. We also implement a DD strategy using federal loan volumes for comparison.

First we compare the log number of private student loans in the lender data sample at each school in the preperiod to the postperiod. Note that in order to understand the magnitude of the effect, we must exponentiate the coefficients on *post* in the OLS specification and the analogues in the Oaxaca decomposition and the propensity score matching models. We also run a school fixed effects model in order to consider the within school effects. All models are weighted by full-time equivalent enrollments.

We also perform a DD analysis using available information on the volume of both Direct and FFELP Loans at a given school for the 2004–2005 and 2005–2006 academic years. We assume that in the absence of BAPCPA, the change in PSLs would parallel the change in federal loans and that the change in federal loans is proportional across quarters. We can then estimate the effect of the program on loan volumes using a DD strategy. We believe that our assumption of PSL volume moving in a parallel fashion to federal loan volume in the absence of BAPCPA is likely, since they are subject to the same demand shocks, such as enrollments and changes in tuition costs. Although we do not have quarterly data for federal loans, annual average loans per student grew steadily from 2000 through 2005.[93]

We combine Direct Loan and FFELP Loan totals at the institution-year level, append the resultant data set to the school-level origination data, and merge the appropriate IPEDS and PEPS data at the institution-year level. We then consider PSLs the treated group, so the coefficient of interest is $\beta_{psl \times post}$ in Equation (7.12), and the comparison groups are subsidized and unsubsidized Stafford Loans, Parental PLUS Loans, combined Stafford Loans, and all federal loans. We use a similar strategy to estimate the effects of the program on average loan size at a given school by stacking the loan-level origination data with the Title IV Program Volume Reports and weighting by the number of originations.[94]

$$(7.12) \quad y_i = \beta_{post} post_i + \beta_{psl} psl_i + \beta_{post \times psl} post_i \times psl_i + \beta_X X_i + \varepsilon_i$$

One challenge with using federal loans as controls for PSLs arises from the fact that federal loans have defined maximum loan amounts.[95] This means that loan demand for federal loans is effectively top-coded, which leads to downward bias in estimates of $\beta_{post \times psl}$.[96] As a result, as shown in Appendix 7B, we are likely to underestimate the true effect with the DD analysis.

We make two assumptions in our DD analysis. This is necessary, since data on federal loans are only available at the academic-year level. These assumptions are illustrated in Figure 7.6. First, we assume that all of the federal student loans originated in academic year 2004–2005 are originated by April 20, 2005. It is likely that the majority of federal loans are originated by this point in time, since the academic year ends at the close of the second quarter, and the law took effect midway through the second quarter. This allows us to associate academic year 2004–2005 with the pre-BAPCPA period and academic year 2005–2006 with the post-BAPCPA period. Second, we assume that at any given institution, the proportion of the academic year's federal loans originated is constant: if x percent of academic year 2004–2005 federal loans at school y are made in Q1 2005, then x percent of academic year 2005–2006 federal loans at school y are made in Q1 2006. Similarly, we assume either that the absolute difference or the proportional difference in average federal loan size between quarters is constant within schools across academic years, in the specifications that consider average original balance and log original balance, respectively. Academic year volumes are a noisy measure of quarterly volumes, which means our results are biased toward zero, and the true effect is likely larger than what we observe.[97]

RESULTS

We analyzed the loans originated in the first quarters of 2005 and 2006 using OLS regression, Blinder-Oaxaca decomposition, and propensity score matching. These methods produced similar results displayed in Appendix 7A, Tables 7A.1–7A.5. All of the results we discuss in this section are statistically significant to the 95 percent level or higher unless noted.

Loan-Level Analysis

Table 7A.1 uses OLS to estimate Equation (7.5) for tuition and fees, with various combinations of controls for a borrower's year in school, school type, maximum FICO scores, linear splines for FICO scores, and school fixed effects.[98] Once school fixed effects are introduced, the results are stable across specifications. As predicted by H2, lenders are lending to borrowers who have worse credit after the law changed, as evidenced by the 5.3 point average decrease in FICO scores shown in column (3). Contrary to the prediction from H1 that for a given credit quality the consumer price of borrowing will decrease owing to increased collections, the margins increase by 30 basis points in column (5). Mean original balance also increased by $1,189.

Because of their credit quality, some applicants would have been able to receive a PSL both before and after BAPCPA. To understand how BAPCPA may have affected the borrower population through changes in underwriting, we turn to the Blinder-Oaxaca decomposition. The results displayed in Table 7A.2 show a 26 basis-point increase in margin but no significant change in loan amount. In column (2) of Panel A, the 0.398 decrease in credit scores due to endowments suggests that some of the characteristics of borrowers may have changed that resulted in average lower FICO scores. This result is statistically significant at the 0.1 level but disappears when school fixed effects are added in column (3). This suggests that the composition of schools to which the sample creditors are lending may have changed and merits further investigation.

Consistent with the OLS results in Table 7A.1, column (5) of Panel B shows a within-school effect of a 35-basis-point increase in margins, 11 basis points of which are attributable to changes in the composition of students (endowments in Blinder-Oaxaca terminology), and 26 basis points of which are attributable to changes in underwriting (coefficients). Recall that we defined r as one plus the rate of return of the loan for the creditor conditional on the borrower repaying their loan. This suggests that for a given set of borrower characteristics, lenders are increasing r, so, inconsistent with the prediction from H1, lenders increased the price of loans in response to BAPCPA.

Similarly, in Panel C, the overall change in original balance due to BAPCPA is insignificant, but changes in borrower characteristics predict a $116 increase in borrowing due to endowments (changes in the composition of students after the law changed).

Table 7A.3 presents the results from the propensity score matching, where the propensity score is calculated by a probit regression of borrower characteristics on whether or not an individual appears in the post-BAPCPA observations. For each specification, the raw difference in means is reported above the difference in means for the matched pairs, labeled as the average treatment on the treated effect. For maximum FICO scores, these results can be interpreted as the type of students, based on schools attended and school year, that the lenders would have successfully extended credit to pre-BAPCPA. The result in column (3) of a 4.2 point average decrease in FICO scores is consistent with the previous results and suggests that within a given school, lenders are extending credit to individuals with slightly lower credit scores in the postperiod.

For margins and original balances, the results in Table 7A.3 can be interpreted as the effects of the program on the loan terms of individuals who would have been granted loans prior to BAPCPA, based on their characteristics. Consistent with the OLS and Blinder-Oaxaca result, the result in column (5) suggests a 30-basis-point increase in the average margin experienced by a borrower. As also shown in that column, average original balances increased by $1,157 post-BAPCPA.

Overall, these results suggest that credit did expand to some individuals who previously did not have access to private student loans prior to BAPCPA either because of their observable credit quality through their FICO scores or the characteristics of the schools that they attended. This is consistent with H2, and as can be seen from Figure 7.3, it was significant to a number of borrowers with low credit scores. Consistent with the previous methods presented, margins actually increase by a significant amount post-BAPCPA. This is inconsistent with the theoretical prediction of H1 that the price of loans, as captured by the margin, should not increase, since collection given bankruptcy should increase the value of defaulted loans for creditors.

School-Level Analysis

As predicted by H3, when we collapse our data set to the school level, we observe a significant increase in the volume of PSLs after the implementation of BAPCPA. As shown in Table 7A.4, once we control for school characteristics, including tuition and fees, graduation rates, Carnegie classification, log full-time equivalent students, and the percent of the student body that is black and Hispanic, we observe a 174.3 percent increase in PSL originations in the OLS specification in column (6) of Panel A.[99] The corresponding Blinder-Oaxaca decomposition in column (6) of Panel B suggests that a 192.1 percent increase is due to a change in underwriting due to BAPCPA.[100] Similarly, the propensity score matching result yields a 215.2 percent increase in loans due to BAPCPA in column (6) of Panel C.

An OLS regression of log borrowers on BAPCPA with school fixed effects, restricted to students at schools where the creditors issued loans before the policy change, yields an estimate of a 243.0 percent increase in loan volumes. Note that these volumes may be attenuated owing to measurement error and may underestimate the effect of the policy change, since we do not observe other firms that enter due to the construction of the sample.[101]

The DD results for loan volumes in Table 7A.5 are qualitatively similar to estimates in Table 7A.4. With all of our comparison groups, we observe an approximate 60 percent increase in the number of private student loan originations, and a similar increase in the number of distinct borrowers in each loan type. When we compare average original balance to Stafford Loan balances, we observe an effect of the law change of an approximately $600 increase in the average original balance of PSL. This is smaller than our point estimate using other techniques, and we believe that that DD estimate may be biased downward, owing to the loan limits for federal loans.[102]

We add Parent PLUS Loans as comparison in column (4) because they are a close substitute for PSLs, and because PLUS loan eligibility is based on the parents' creditworthiness. Doing so leads us to estimate a $121 decrease in the average size of the PSL. In our sample of PSLs the original rate is negatively correlated with original balance ($\rho = -0.0975$), so it is possible that marginal individuals who would have applied for smaller PLUS Loans in the absence of the policy change make have substituted PSLs for PLUS Loans because of potentially lower interest rates.[103]

DISCUSSION

Recall our hypotheses from Table 7.1. While not every model predicted every outcome of interest, those that did were heading in the same direction. Our prediction was that credit would expand; in other words, borrower credit quality would stay the same or decrease, and average loan amounts as well as the volume of loans would stay the same or increase. Our models predicted the prices would either stay the same or decrease. Our results are mostly consistent with these hypotheses: credit expanded among all dimensions after BAPCPA. The first quarter after the law changed saw a dramatic 309 percent increase in the number of loans originated; we estimate that 60 percent of that increase was caused by BAPCPA.[104] Additionally, borrowers with lower credit scores were moderately more able to obtain PSLs as a result of BAP-CPA. The decrease in the average maximum credit score was small in magnitude, a drop similar to the effect of applying for two credit cards within a few days. Credit also expanded at the loan level; the average original balance of the loans increased by between $1,100 and $1,400, even after controlling for tuition and fees, year in school, having a coborrower, maximum FICO score, and school fixed effects. All of this is not unexpected. The most surprising finding of our study is that contrary to our hypotheses, both from the point of view of reform proponents and opponents, average loan prices (in our parlance, lender margins) *increased* during this period.[105] Our estimates show that margins increased by between 30 and 40 basis points, even for students who would have received a loan before BAPCPA.

An expansion of credit coupled with an increase in price sounds eerily similar to what happened in other consumer credit markets during the pre-Great Recession bubble. The secondary market for all consumer credit—mortgages, credit cards, auto loans, etc.—increased dramatically before the Great Recession. Consumer credit ABS issuances peaked before 2005, but it is widely theorized that, securitization demand drove both an expansion of credit as well as an increase in prices in markets such as housing.[106] One potential story here is that we are not observing BAPCPA so much as securitization demand. This account would be consistent with Block-Lieb and Janger's prediction that lenders would not relax underwriting standards or originate more loans after BAPCPA because they had no reason to expect increased charge-offs after the law changed.[107] If BAPCPA did not cause shifts in supply, then lenders would have only relaxed their underwriting criteria in order to meet the demand from the securitization market. We cannot discount that securitization had an effect on our findings; however, as we discuss below, we find evidence that is inconsistent with this hypothesis.

As shown in Figure 7.7, PSL Asset Backed Securities (PSLABS) outstandings increased in a steep linear fashion between 2003 and 2007. We note that the growth in outstandings in the period we studied (repre-

Figure 7.7 Outstanding Private and Mixed Private/Public Student Loan Asset Backed Securities

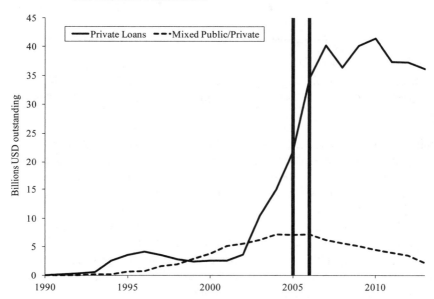

SOURCE: U.S. ABS Issuance and Outstanding, Securities Industry and Financial Markets Association (see Note 108).

sented by the vertical lines in Figure 7.7) is similar to that in the period that came before it (2004–2005) and after 2006–2007. In other words, PSLABS were increasing steadily between 2003 and 2007.

Given this stable increase, we compare our results among our four outcomes of interest (maximum FICO score between borrower or coborrower, margin charged on the loan, original balance of the loan, and the volume of loans originated) between the first quarters straddling bankruptcy reform (Q1 2005 to Q1 2006) and the same quarters one year after reform (Q1 2006 to Q1 2007).[109] Table 7.4 reports the raw means for the three periods.[110] Credit expands the year after the law changes (2006–2007), but the growth is much more muted than in the period spanning bankruptcy reform. For example, between Q1 2006 and Q1 2007, the mean maximum FICO score decreased one point; noticeably less than the five-point decrease after BAPCPA. Similarly,

Table 7.4 Raw Means of Outcomes of Interest in the First Quarters of 2005, 2006, and 2007

	Q1 2005	Q1 2006	Q1 2007
	Mean	Mean	Mean
Maximum FICO score	720	715	714
Margin (%)	4.2	4.6	5.1
Original balance ($)	8,614	10,015	10,147
Loans originated	4,960	15,318	19,658

loan volumes increased 128 percent between Q1 2007 and Q1 2006, but this is not the astounding 309 percent increase we observe between Q1 2005 and Q1 2006. Continuing the puzzling trend, margins increased 50 basis points between the first quarter of 2006 and the first quarter of 2007.

If securitization were a principal driver of the expansion of credit we observe between before and after bankruptcy reform, we would expect similar effects in the cost and availability of credit between the bankruptcy reform period (2005–2006) as well as the period after (2006–2007). That is not what the data show: the changes in borrower composition and the spike in loan volumes are quite pronounced in the period around bankruptcy reform, while not nearly as much in the same period one year later.

Figure 7.7 depicts securitizations outstanding, which are necessarily cumulative. Figure 7.8 presents annual PSLABS issuances, which is a closer analogue to loan originations—closer but with one caveat. When comparing securitization issuances and loan originations, it is important to consider that PSLABS issuances necessarily lag originations. This is because it takes some time to package and securitize loans that are made during a particular time period. In addition, the typical securitization trust contains loans originated during multiple years as part of the risk spreading investors require. The "youngest" loans included in a portfolio of PSLABS were typically originated 3–6 months prior to the issuance of the securities.[111] Because of this lag, if the secondary market was the reason for the large expansion of credit we observe in the time period around bankruptcy reform (and not BAPCPA), we should observe an increase in securitizations in 2005 (or before) relative to later years. The expected increase should attenuate in 2006 and later

Figure 7.8 Issuances of Private Student Loan Asset Backed Securities Peaked in 2006 before Declining Dramatically during the Great Recession

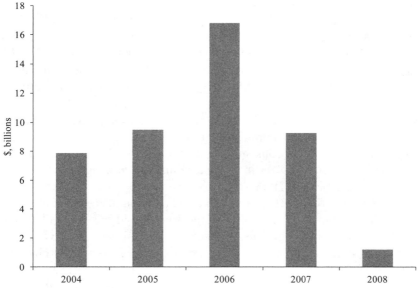

SOURCE: CFPB PSL report (see Note 112).

to account for the "cooling off" in credit expansion that we discussed above. We observe the opposite. As shown in Figure 7.8, securitization issuances spike in 2006, the year immediately *after* BAPCPA became effective.

Because of the lag in issuing securities, PSLABS packaged and offered to investors in 2006 were primarily made up of loans originated before bankruptcy reform. Regardless of when these loans were originated, however, when BAPCPA became effective on October 17, 2005, all private student loans became presumptively nondischargeable and thus more valuable to investors. It is thus not surprising to observe a spike in securitization issuances in 2006 as shown in Figure 7.8 and a corresponding faster increase in PSLABS outstanding between 2005 and 2006, as shown in Figure 7.7. The expected recovery of PSLs was higher now that they (effectively) could not be discharged in bankruptcy. This likely increased the demand for PSL securities from the secondary market but only after BAPCPA was enacted.[113] This latter increased demand, however, could not be the cause of what we observe during the 2005–2006 period.

Demand for PSLABS was progressively increasing well before BAPCPA was enacted. It is likely responsible for expansion of the PSL market.[114] However, a steady expansion of PSLABS from 2003–2007 and a spike in PSLABS issuances in 2006 (which necessarily included few loans originated post-BAPCPA) are inconsistent with a hypothesis that the sudden expansion of credit we observe between Q1 2005 and Q1 2006 (around bankruptcy reform) was caused by securitization. Instead, what we know about securitization volumes in the period during this time is more consistent with a story that bankruptcy reform further stoked the fires of the secondary market, leading to the peak in PSLABS issuances in 2006.

If securitization does not explain the expansion of credit we observe, then what accounts for the puzzling increase in margins? One plausible explanation is that the increased prices are driven by lender advertising. We've reported evidence that the composition of borrowers changed after BAPCPA: in other words, credit expanded to borrowers who would not have received loans before the law changed. The data also show that borrowers who would have received loans before BAPCPA obtained loans in increasing numbers after the law change.

There is reason to think that advertising might have been well targeted to the relevant population. Advertisements for PSLs could have come through regular channels (such as television, direct mail, and the Internet). Lenders could have also targeted students directly. During this period, the lenders in our study were part of FFELP and were federal as well as private student loans. If a student had applied for a FFELP loan from a lender, they would have some information about both the appetite and credit profile of the student, not to mention their contact information. Armed with this knowledge, the lender could reach out directly to students and promote their PSL product. This focused advertisement would lead to increased student demand for PSLs, which would have driven up the cost of the loans. There is anecdotal evidence of a growth in direct-to-consumer marketing during this time period and continuing for a few years.

We need much more information than we have available to test this theory. Ideally, we would have some data on advertising trends over time. We would also really want to have data on how margins were changing before 2005. It seems plausible that lenders began trying to fan demand as a result of securitization before BAPCPA. In that case, BAPCPA may have further increased marketing efforts. The increase in margins that we observe may be part of a broader trend that continues in the period one year after bankruptcy reform; potentially a lagging result of the increase in advertisement the previous year. Regrettably, the data available do not allow us to corroborate these suppositions.

As a final note, we briefly discuss the potential welfare effects of bankruptcy reform vis-à-vis PSLs. Our data do not allow us to draw conclusions about whether the expansion of credit was welfare-enhancing. Robert Lawless and others have noted that a rapid expansion of credit is usually correlated with increased bankruptcy filings.[115] Comparing PSLs to loans issued by nonprofit institutions, the CFPB found that "more careful underwriting ([by nonprofits] relative to [PSL] lenders) reduced default rates."[116] It is worth remembering, however, that in terms of less-than-prime borrowers, the credit expansion we observe was modest: the effect on the average credit score was the same as applying for multiple credit cards within a short period.

Arguably, however, an expansion of credit is precisely what supporters of the special treatment for PSLs intended. As then Representative Lindsey Graham (R-SC) stated during the 1999 debates arguing for the passage of the law:

> There is a growing industry in the private sector. There is a $1.25 billion loan volume for where private lenders who will loan money to students for their college expenses as the federally guaranteed program does not in every occasion meet the needs of the student, and we are trying to give the private lender the same protection under bankruptcy that the federally guaranteed loan program has and nonprofit organizations have. We are trying to make sure they are [sic] available loans, loans are available to students to meet their financial needs, and this would have a beneficial effect, make sure that the loan volume necessary to take care of college expenses are available for students . . . [117]

The congressional record is bare of any other explanations for the purpose of the special treatment of PSLs. John Pottow has theorized that nondischargeability can be justified "as an attempt to make private loans 'cheaper' for students" and to create a "a robust private lending market . . . a bountiful capital supply available for loans."[118]

A bountiful capital supply was indeed available for loans immediately after BAPCPA, although the capital supply disappeared almost as quickly as it had appeared. After growing 20 percent per year between 2005 and 2007, PSL originations in our sample peaked at $10.1 billion and dropped to pre-2005 levels in 2010–2011.[119] Of course, other intervening factors likely played a role here, the Great Recession and credit crunch in particular. Nonetheless, it is important to note that a law's purported positive effects (increasing availability of credit) may be short lived, while its potential negative ones (nondischargeability in bankruptcy) continue on.

The increase in the risk premium lenders charge for a loan, on the other hand, does not seem welfare enhancing to borrowers. A 35-basis-point increase in the price of a $10,000 15-year loan can translate to an added cost to the borrower of almost $25 per year or $365 over the life of the loan.[120] This increase becomes more significant when one considers that the lenders in the sample made an additional 10,358 loans in the postperiod. If we take our $25 per year increase as an average for all loans, this would mean that BAPCPA may have cost student borrowers an additional $382,950 per year in the first quarter of 2006.[121]

CONCLUSION

The 2005 amendments to the Bankruptcy Code were a watershed moment almost a decade in the making. Proponents of bankruptcy reform blamed rapidly rising bankruptcy filings on strategic consumers using the Bankruptcy Code to escape their debts. They argued that reform was necessary to prevent strategic borrower behavior and reduce the cost of consumer credit. Opponents of the proposed bankruptcy reforms pointed to the dearth of data supporting the strategic consumer story and instead cited behavioral experiments establishing consumers' less-than-perfect rationality and empirical evidence that the majority of bankruptcy filers had very low income and few assets. Opponents predicted that there would be no discernible change in the cost of consumer credit or loan volumes. In this chapter, we developed and tested theoretical models predicting the effects of the part of the law change on PSLs granted to students at four-year undergraduate institutions.[122] Using a unique data set of PSL originations before and after the law change, we tested those predictions using OLS regression, Blinder-Oaxaca, matching, and DD methods.

Some of our findings are unsurprising: the law change caused a moderate expansion of credit for less creditworthy borrowers, although the average borrower credit score decreased only slightly in practical terms. Loan volumes also tripled; we attribute 60 percent of that increase to the law change. Contrary to our hypotheses, however, we find that the overall cost of private student loans at four-year undergraduate institutions increased by an average of 35 basis points as a result of the law change. We posit that the larger cost may have been driven by increased demand for PSLs from students as a result of lender advertising. We speculate that the increased marketing may have started before BAPCPA.

Our analysis so far suggests that this is a story about distributions—that is, that certain students may have seen an increase in the cost of their loans and others might have seen a decrease. In future work, we intend to investigate the variation in credit quality and margins to see whether the effect of BAPCPA was different across types of schools (e.g., higher versus lower prestige); types of borrowers (e.g., prime versus subprime); or types of loans (e.g., those marketed through the school versus those marketed directly to the consumer).[123] We expect that this will give us a more complete picture of the effects of BAPCPA.[124]

Notes

This chapter conforms generally to the Bluebook legal style of citation. For the latest edition, see *The Bluebook: A Uniform System of Citation*, 19th ed. (Cambridge, MA: Harvard Law Review Association, 2010).

1. Bankruptcy Abuse Prevention and Consumer Protection Act of 2005 (BAPCPA), Pub.L. 109–8, 119 Stat. 23 (2005).
2. In 1999 and 2000, the House and Senate passed bills that were vetoed by President Clinton. *Clinton vetoes bankruptcy bill*, Associated Press, Dec. 20, 2000, *available at* http://lubbockonline.com/stories/121900/upd_075-5725.shtml; 145 Cong. Rec. H2655-02 (daily ed. May 5, 1999) (statement of Rep. Conyers).

3. For more information on the history and motivation of BAPCPA, *see* Susan Block-Lieb & Edward J. Janger, *The Myth of the Rational Borrower: Rationality, Behavioralism, and the Misguided "Reform" of Bankruptcy Law*, 84 TEX. L. REV. 1481, 1483 (2006).

4. *Id.* at 1562.

5. *See, e.g.,* Section 439A of the Higher Education Act, codified at 20 U.S.C. 1087-3 (1976); 11 U.S.C. 523(a)(8) (1979) (Pub.L. 96-56, § 3 (1979)); 11 U.S.C. 523(a) (8) (1990) (see Pub.L. 101-647, § 3621(1) (1990)); 11 U.S.C. 523(a)(8) (1998) (see Pub.L. 105-244, § 971(a) (1998)).

6. The first policy prescribes that similarly situated creditors not receive an advantage over others—sometimes termed "equity is equality"—for our purposes, unsecured creditors are all asked to share the loss equally. The second policy prescribes that the debtor should exit bankruptcy unshackled from the debts that were weighing down her economic productivity, or in bankruptcy parlance, that the debtor receive a "fresh start," or a discharge of her debts. *See, e.g.,* Rafael I. Pardo & Michelle R. Lacey, *Undue Hardship in the Bankruptcy Courts: An Empirical Assessment of the Discharge of Educational Debt*, 74 UNIV. OF CIN. L. REV. 405, 413-419 (2005) [hereinafter Pardo & Lacey (2005)]; National Bankruptcy Review Commission, BANKRUPTCY: THE NEXT TWENTY YEARS 179 (1997), *available at* http://govinfo .library.unt.edu/nbrc/report/07consum.pdf.

7. An Act to establish a uniform system of bankruptcy in the United States, 30 Stat. 544 Section 17 (July 1, 1898). Exceptions to discharge have also been added for various kinds of fraud or false representations or violations of the law. *See, e.g.,* 11 U.S.C. §§ 523(a)(2), (a)(4), (a)(6), (a)(9), (a)(11), (a)(12), (a)(13) & (a)(19). Many are also concerned with excepting taxes or duties owed to a state or federal entity. *See, e.g.,* 11 U.S.C. §§ 523(a)(1), (a)(7), (a)(11), (a)(12), (a)(14), (a)(14A), (a) (17), (a)(18) & (a)(19). The stated reason for the change here was the possibility for fraud and strategic filing by debtors seeking to start their postgraduation career without any student loans.

8. 11 U.S.C. §§ 523(a)(5), (a)(15). 108 Cong. Rec. H156 (2004) (statement of Rep. Cantor). Senator Sessions also stated that the bill would "also provide[ ] tremendous benefits for women and children." 109 Cong. Rec. S1915 (2005) (statement of Sen. Sessions).

9. *What are the main differences between federal student loans and private student loans?* CONSUMER FIN. PROT. BUREAU (July 26, 2013), http://www.consumer-finance.gov/askcfpb/545/what-are-main-differences-between-federal-student-loans-and-private-student-loans.html.

10. In our sample, 80 percent of student borrowers in Q1 2005 applied with a coborrower. That proportion had risen slightly to 82 percent in Q1 2006. Federal loans have no cosigners, but Federal PLUS Loans are available to parents of undergraduates who qualify for federal loans.

11. See Appendix Figure 1 at page 96 of the CFPB PSL REPORT for a graphical representation of the various indices used to calculate PSL interest rates from 2004– 2012. Most federal loans are fixed rate. CONSUMER FIN. PROT. BUREAU, PRIVATE STU-

DENT LOANS 96 (2012), http://files.consumerfinance.gov/f/201207_cfpb_Reports_Private-Student-Loans.pdf [hereinafter CFPB PSL REPORT].

12. *Id.* at 12. By comparison, rates for federal student loans that did not require cosigners in 2011 were either 4.5 percent or 6.8 percent fixed, depending on the type of loan. A 4.5 percent fixed rate was available for undergraduate students taking out a subsidized Stafford Loan; 6.8 percent was available for undergraduate unsubsidized Stafford Loans and for graduate student subsidized and unsubsidized Stafford Loans. FinAid, Historical Interest Rates, http://www.finaid.org/loans/historicalrates.phtml. The federal loan program has had multiple instances where loans were offered as variable rates but has always had a cap of 8.25 percent APR for Stafford Loans and 9 percent for PLUS Loans. *Id.*

13. Federally insured Stafford Loans issued by banks were also securitized during this time period. CFPB report at 17-18. For an explanation of asset-backed securitization, see CFPB report at 104.

14. There was no "consumer rebate."

15. Rohit Chopra, *Student Debt Swells, Federal Loans Now Top a Trillion*, CONSUMER FIN. PROT. BUREAU (July 17, 2013), http://www.consumerfinance.gov/newsroom/student-debt-swells-federal-loans-now-top-a-trillion.

16. *Income-Based Plan | Federal Student Aid*, FED. STUDENT AID, http://studentaid.ed.gov/repay-loans/understand/plans/income-based (accessed Apr. 11, 2014).

17. For a full list, see *Forgiveness, Cancellation, and Discharge | Federal Student Aid*, FED. STUDENT AID, http://studentaid.ed.gov/repay-loans/forgiveness-cancellation#death-discharge (accessed Apr. 11, 2014).

18. *Id.* at 10.

19. Department of Education, Default Rates: Cohort Default Rates 2005-09, http://ifap.ed.gov/eannouncements/010512DefaultRates20052009.html.

20. CFPB PSL REPORT, *supra* note 11, at 64-65.

21. *Id.* at 64.

22. *Id.*

23. *See* Dodd-Frank Wall Street Reform and Consumer Protection Act § 1035, Pub. L. 111-203 (2010).

24. Pardo & Lacey, *supra* n. 6, at 427; *see id.* at note 112 and 113 for citations to illustrative cases.

25. The GAO found that despite a general default rate on educational loans of 18 percent, less than 0.75 percent of all education loans were discharged in bankruptcy. H.R. Rep. No. 95-595, at 132 (1977), reprinted in 1978 U.S.C.C.A.N. 5963, 6094. The GAO also found that the majority of students were not filing for bankruptcy immediately upon graduation. The average time between when a student obtained a loan and when they filed for bankruptcy in the GAO sample was 41 months. *Id.* at 6103-04. In addition, lucrative careers were not significantly represented among those who sought to discharge their student loans. While 72 percent of the individuals who discharged student loans in the GAO sample were employed, the top occupations were teacher (10 percent), clerk (8 percent), salesman (6 percent), housewife (5 percent), and student (4.5 percent). *Id.* Also, the individuals seeking

the protection of the bankruptcy laws were not particularly well off. The average earnings for the individuals studied for the year prior to filing for bankruptcy were $5,361 in 1977 dollars ($20,787.42 today). *Id.* at 6105.

26. 11 U.S.C. § 523(a)(8) (2005).

27. The design of bankruptcy protections for student loans has clear welfare implications: in 2011, Felicia Ionescu modeled the effect of alternative bankruptcy regimes for federal student loans under uncertainty about college completion and future earnings, and concluded that nondischargeability benefits high ability, low income students, and that welfare effects differ by bankruptcy regime. Felicia Ionescu. *Risky Human Capital and Alternative Bankruptcy Regimes for Student Loans*, 5 J. HUMAN CAPITAL 153 (2011).

28. H.R. Rep. No. 95-595, at 154-55 (1977), reprinted in 1978 U.S.C.C.A.N. 5963, 6115-16 (section 439A, effective September 30, 1977). Representative Edwards advised that "[i]f the exception to discharge is to be enacted, we must provide for a more definite standard that will not encourage forum shopping." *Id.* That, unfortunately, did not happen.

29. *See* Higher Education Amendments of 1976, Pub. L. 94-482 § 439, 90 Stat. 2081 (Oct. 12, 1976)(section 439A, effective September 30, 1977); 11 U.S.C. § 523(a) (8) (1979) (Pub.L. 96-56, § 3 (1979)); 11 U.S.C. 523(a)(8) (1990) (see Pub.L. 101-647, § 3621(1) (1990)); 11 U.S.C. 523(a)(8) (1998) (see Pub.L. 105-244, § 971(a) (1998)); 11 U.S.C. 523(a)(8) (2005) (see Pub.L. 109-8, § 220 (2005)). For an empirical account of undue hardship determinations made by bankruptcy courts arguing that the legal outcomes in the determination of undue hardship can be best explained by "differing judicial perceptions of how the same standard applies to similarly situated debtors," see Pardo & Lacey (2005), *supra* note 6, at 486.

30. Brunner v. N. Y. State Higher Educ. Servcs. Corp., 831 F. 2d 395 (2d Cir. 1987). This is a three-part test; the debtor is required to meet all parts:

> (1) That the debtor cannot maintain, based on current income and expenses, a "minimal" standard of living for herself and her dependents if forced to repay the loans; (2) that additional circumstances exist indicating that this state of affairs is likely to persist for a significant portion of the repayment period of the student loans; and (3) that the debtor had made good faith efforts to repay the loan.

> *Id.* at 396. At least one court has referred to the standard as the "certainty of hopelessness." Daniel A. Austin, *Student Loan Debt in Bankruptcy: An Empirical Assessment* at 5 (May 27, 2014)(forthcoming Suffolk U. L. R.), *available at* http://papers.ssrn.com/sol3/papers.cfm?abstract_id=2442312 (quoting In re Roberson, 999 F. 2d 1132 (7th Cir. 1993)). Note, however, that recently some courts seem to be relaxing the standard. *Id.*

31. *See* FED. R. BANKR. PROC. 7001; Jason Iuliano, *An Empirical Assessment of Student Loan Discharges and the Undue Hardship Standard*, 86 AM. BANKR. L. J. 495, 496 (2012).

32. United Student Aid Funds v. Espinosa, 559 U.S. 260 (2010).

33. In other words, the loans continue to accrue interest and fees while the individual

is in bankruptcy and she is still liable for all that the contract obligates her to pay even after she receives her bankruptcy discharge.

34. Iuliano, *supra* note 31, at 504-05.

35. *Id.* Using a different sampling protocol drawing from cases between 2005 and 2013 in 10 judicial districts, Daniel Austin estimates that less than 0.33 percent of individuals with student loans seek to discharge them in bankruptcy. *See* Austin, *supra* n. 30, at 5.

36. Pardo and Lacey's 2005 study offered the very first empirical evidence of outcomes in undue hardship cases. The study suffered from serious limitations, since it was based on published judicial opinions, rare and nonrandom events in themselves, and was composed of only cases that went to trial and produced a published opinion. Not all trials produce a published opinion and not all attempts to discharge student debt go to trial. Pardo & Lacey (2005), *supra* note 6. Their 2009 study examined a data set of 115 student-loan discharge proceedings—for both private and federal loans—that were filed between 2002 and 2006 in the Western District of Washington. Rafael I. Pardo and Michelle R. Lacey, *The Real Student Loan Scandal: Undue Hardship Discharge Litigation*, 83 Am. Bankr. L. J. 179, 200 (2009) [hereinafter Pardo & Lacey (2009)].

37. *See* Iuliano, *supra* note 31, 509 (mean age 49 and median 48.5); Pardo & Lacey (2005), *supra* note 6, at 442-43 (mean 41.5, median 41); Pardo & Lacey (2009), *supra* note 36, at 204 (mean: 45; median not reported).

38. Iuliano, *supra* note 31, at 508 (68 percent unmarried, 46 percent had dependents); Pardo & Lacey (2005), *supra* note 6, at 445-47 (62 percent unmarried, 56 percent had dependents); Pardo & Lacey (2009), *supra* note 36, at 204 (80 percent unmarried, 38 percent had dependents).

39. *See* Iuliano, *supra* note 31, at 508 (60 percent of discharge seekers were employed versus 81 percent of the overall bankruptcy population); Pardo & Lacey (2009), *supra* note 36, at 204 (58 percent were employed).

40. Iuliano, *supra* note 31, at 511.

41. Pardo & Lacey (2005), *supra* note 6, at 474 (mean: $47,137); Iuliano, *supra* note 31, at 510 (mean: $80,746). *See also* Pardo & Lacey (2009), *supra* note 36, at 207 (mean: $76,139).

42. Iuliano, *supra* note 6, at 518 (52 percent); Pardo & Lacey (2009), *supra* note 36, at 204 (55 percent).

43. Pardo & Lacey (2005), *supra* note 6, at 477.

44. Pardo & Lacey (2009), *supra* note 36, at 184.

45. Iuliano, *supra* note 31, at 505. Most of those discharges came about as a result of a settlement with a student loan creditor (56 cases or 69 percent of all debtors who obtained relief). Only in 22 percent of cases in which a debtor obtained a partial discharge or more did the bankruptcy judge make a determination that the debtors satisfied the undue hardship standard. *Id.* at 512.

46. Pardo & Lacey (2005), *supra* note 6.

47. *Id.* at 433.

48. Pardo & Lacey (2009), *supra* n. 36, at 185.

49. Mark Krantowitz, FinAid.org, Impact of the Bankruptcy Exception for Private

STUDENT LOANS ON PRIVATE STUDENT LOAN AVAILABILITY (Aug. 14, 2007), http://www.finaid.org/educators/20070814pslFICOdistribution.pdf.
50. *Id.* at 2.
51. Krantowitz's data came from PSLs included in the prospectuses of asset backed securitizations (student loan asset backed securities, or SLABs for short) done between 2002 and 2007. Krantowitz, *supra* note 49 at 1. One issue with Krantowitz's analysis is that one of the SLABs examined included loans that may have been nondischargeable before BAPCPA because of the involvement of a nonprofit entity. In the case of one of the SLABs examined in the report, First Marblehead, the loans were guaranteed by The Education Resources Institute, or TERI, a national nonprofit. *Id.* at 5. It is not entirely unclear that these loans would have been nondischargeable prior to BAPCPA, *id.*, but the uncertainty can also cloud the results
52. *Id.* at 4.
53. *Id.*
54. *Id.* at 5. The report noted that the prospectuses for the SLABs examined did not disclose any change in underwriting criteria for loans originated after BAPCPA. *Id.*
55. Block-Lieb & Janger, *supra* note 3, at 1511-14. *See also* Marquette Nat'l Bank of Minneapolis v. First of Omaha Service Corp., 439 U.S. 299 (1978).
56. *Id.* at 1484 (citing 151 CONG. REC. S1813, S 1842 (daily ed. Mar. 1, 2005) (statement of Sen. Hatch insisting that there is a "bankruptcy tax" of "$400-a-year on every household in the country," which could amount to a "mortgage or a rent payment" for many families).
57. *Id.*
58. *Id.* citing Posting of Richard Posner to Becker-Posner Blog, http://www.becker-posner-blog.com (Mar. 27, 2005, 02:20 PM) ("If bankruptcy is more costly, there will be less of it.").
59. In other words, r can be thought of as the present discounted value of the flow of payments made by a borrower who follows the repayment schedule. Therefore, for a given loan term and conditions, a higher value of r implies a higher interest rate for borrowers.
60. This includes partially paid loans for which the remaining outstanding balance is sent to collections.
61. "To model decision-making under uncertainty, almost all game theory uses the theories of von Neumann and Morgenstern (1944) and of Savage (1972). That is, if the consequence function is stochastic and known to the decision-maker . . . then the decisionmaker is assumed to behave as if he maximizes the expected value of a [utility] function . . ." Martin Osborne and Ariel Rubinstein. *A Course in Game Theory 5* (1994).
62. We would expect BAPCPA to diminish the opportunity for strategic default, even if there was rampant strategic behavior pre-BAPCPA.
63. Note that neither the shift in demand nor supply need be parallel. Consider the case where $\hat{v}(z,r) = v(kz,r)$ where k is a constant. Then $\frac{dz}{dk}$ is a function of r, so shifts

do not have to be parallel. It follows from Equation 7.3 that shifts in supply also do not have to be parallel.

64. Joseph E. Stiglitz and Andrew Weiss. *Credit Rationing in Markets with Imperfect Information*, 71 AM. ECON. REV. 393 (1981).

65. This assumption is based on our informal understandings of the market. More research is needed.

66. A number of scholars have argued that the Stiglitz-Weiss model is no longer applicable in a world of sophisticated credit scoring models, and "big data" number crunching lenders can differentiate between good and bad risks and thus can price products according to risk. Risk-based pricing is very much alive in the context of PSLs and can be seen in our data. *See* Block-Lieb & Janger, *supra* note 3 and Kathleen C. Engel and Patricia A. McCoy, *A Tale of Three Markets: The Law and Economics of Predatory Lending*, 80 TEXAS L. REV. 1255 (2002).The rise of the securitization market has also been cited as a reason why credit rationing may no longer occur as in the Stiglitz-Weiss model, given that there is more capital available to lenders. *See generally* Engel and McCoy. In any event, the Stiglitz-Weiss model predictions are very similar to the competition model above. The primary difference is that the Stiglitz-Weiss model predicts that loan pricing (lender margins) should remain the same for originations after the law change.

67. Block-Lieb & Janger, *supra* note 3.

68. Students may be unaware of the law change or what it means for their private student loans or they may suffer from a number of other behavioral biases other than present bias, such as optimism bias or probability neglect. Cass Sunstein, *Probability Neglect: Emotions, Worst Cases, and Law*, 112 YALE L. J. 61 (2002).

69. Block-Lieb & Janger, *supra* note 3 at 1562.

70. We consider the Block-Lieb hypothesis to be a distinct model even though it can be described as a subset of the CP model.

71. CFPB PSL REPORT, *supra* note 11.

72. *Id.* at 7. "The participating lenders included: RBS Citizens N.A., Discover Financial Services, The First Marblehead Corporation, JPMorgan Chase Bank, N.A., PNC Bank, N.A., Sallie Mae, Inc., SunTrust Banks, Inc., U.S. Bank National Association, and Wells Fargo Bank, N.A.." *Id.* at 109.

73. Most of the PSLs in the data set had variable interest rates that varied according to an index, such as LIBOR or the Prime Rate. The "margin" on those loans is the premium "added to the current index value to determine the total interest rate for the loan. The margin is set at the time of origination and varies based on the credit worthiness of a borrower. This variation in margin value is one way that a creditor might establish 'risk-based' pricing." *Id.* at 108.

74. Details of this merge are described *id.* at 93-95.

75. *The Integrated Postsecondary Education Data System – About IPEDS*, INSTITUTE OF EDUCATION SCIENCES, http://nces.ed.gov/ipeds/about/ (accessed Apr. 11, 2014).

76. *Id.*

77. *Postsecondary Education Participants System (PEPS) homepage*, FED. STUDENT AID, http://www2.ed.gov/offices/OSFAP/PEPS/index.html (accessed Apr. 11, 2014).

78. "Title IV" refers to the part of the Higher Education Act of 1965 that covers the administration of federal financial aid programs. *Title IV Program Volume Reports | Federal Student Aid*, FED. STUDENT AID, http://studentaid.ed.gov/about/data-center/student/title-iv (accessed Apr. 11, 2014). The Federal Family Education Loan Program (FFELP) was in effect from 1965–2010 and was a public-private partnership whereby private lenders would originate federal loans. It was eliminated in 2010 when it was projected it would save $68 billion over 11 years. Tracey D. Samuelson, *Student Loan Reform: What Will It Mean For Students?* CHRISTIAN SCI. MONITOR (Mar. 30, 2010), *available at* http://www.csmonitor.com/Business/2010/0330/Student-loan-reform-What-will-it-mean-for-students.

79. We do this because changes in the rules for federal loans might lead to changes in the demand for federal student loans or PSLs not due to BAPCPA and it would be impossible to disentangle them. UNITED STATES DEPARTMENT OF EDUCATION. Dear Colleague Letter (Apr. 27, 2006), http://ifap.ed.gov/dpcletters/attachments/GEN0605.pdf (accessed June 6, 2014).

80. ASSOCIATED PRESS, *supra* note 2.

81. Editorial, *Banks Win, You Lose,* Wilmington Star-News, Mar. 10, 2005, at 8A. *But see* Michele Heller, *Bankruptcy Bill Backers Not Quite Ready to Party*, AMERICAN BANKER, Apr. 1, 2005.

82. Bankruptcy Abuse Prevention and Consumer Protection Act of 2005 (BAPCPA), Pub.L. 109–8, 119 Stat. 23 (2005).

83. To the extent that lenders made changes to their underwriting criteria in anticipation of the law taking effect, the effects that we report should be interpreted as smaller than the true effect.

84. While the lender data also contain information about the initial interest rate disclosed to the borrower, the salient measure to lenders is their returns from the loan net of their cost of funding, which is more closely described by the margin over the index, since the index is likely chosen to correspond to the index of the source of funding.

85. Discussions with industry participants suggest that private student loans over the 2005–2011 period were underwritten based on the highest credit score among borrowers and coborrowers.

86. The constant is subsumed in X_i.

87. *See* Alan S. Blinder, *Wage Discrimination: Reduced Form and Structural Estimates*, 8 J. HUMAN RESOURCES 436 (1973); Ronald Oaxaca, *Wage Differentials in Urban Labor Markets*, 14 INT'L ECON. REV. 693 (1973).

88. This group is an analogue to the minority group in the Blinder-Oaxaca decomposition.

89. Ronald Oaxaca & Michael Ransom, *Identification in Detailed Wage Decompositions,* 81 REV. ECON. & STATISTICS 154 (1999).

90. Paul Rosenbaum & Daniel Rubin, *The Central Role of the Propensity Score in Observational Studies for Causal Effects*, 70 BIOMETRIKA 41 (1983).

91. *Id.*

92. Support is defined in the statistical sense; the common support is the set of covariate values that are in the distribution of covariate variables of both the treated and control group.

93. *See Trends in Student Aid,* 2013. *College Board.* http://trends.collegeboard.org/ sites/default/files/student-aid-2013-full-report.pdf (accessed June 3, 2014).

94. *See Title IV Program Volume Reports*: *Federal Student Aid*, FED. STUDENT AID, http://studentaid.ed.gov/about/data-center/student/title-iv (accessed Apr. 11, 2014).

95. For example, during the sample period the annual Stafford Loan limits were $2,625 for dependent freshmen, $3,500 for dependent sophomores, and $5,500 for upperclassmen. PLUS Loans were limited to cost of attendance minus the expected family contribution. Borrowers qualify for subsidized Stafford Loans based on financial need.

96. See Appendix 7A for additional detail.

97. *See generally* Steve Pischke, Lecture Notes on Measurement Error (Spring 2007), http://econ.lse.ac.uk/staff/spischke/ec524/Merr_new.pdf (accessed July 27, 2014).

98. School fixed effect is simply a dummy variable for each school. Sample sizes may increase between specifications 2 and 3 because the school fixed effect is from the lender data sample, whereas the school type is from the merge with the PEPs data, and tuition and fees are imputed from the merge with IPEDS.

99. This is obtained from subtracting 100 percent from the 274.3 percent marginal effect.

100. As above, we attribute the change to a change in underwriting standards for a given type of students, to the effect due to coefficients in a Blinder-Oaxaca decomposition.

101. This corresponds to a coefficient on postperiod of 1.233. A back-of-the-envelope calculation yields that 92 percent of the threefold increase in PSL origination volume in the first quarter of 2006 can be explained by the law change.

102. It is also important to note that we do not observe changes in school aid.

103. Parent PLUS loans in this period were fixed at 4.17 percent in the 2004–2005 academic year and 6.10 percent in the 2005–2006 academic year for credit-worthy parents, whereas PSLs offered were typically variable rate loans and had initial rates of as much as 19 percent for the riskiest borrowers. *See Interest Rates on the Federal PLUS Loan*, PARENTPLUSLOAN.COM, http://www.parentplusloan.com/ plus-loans/plus-loan-interest-rate.php (accessed June 9, 2014).

104. At the same time, PSL asset-backed securities (PSLABS) also increase two-fold, going from just under $8 billion to over $16 billion dollars between 2005 and 2006. CFPB PLS REPORT, *supra* note 34, at 18.

105. H_0 predicted that none of the outcomes of interest would change, but we found that they all did.

106. Non-GSA Mortgage-related ABS issuances peaked in 2003 at over $3.2 billion. That peak was followed by a drop to $2.3 billion in 2004 and slight recovery to $2.7 billion in 2005. *US Mortgage-Related Securities Issuance and Outstanding (xls)*, SECURITIES INDUSTRY AND FINANCIAL MARKETS ASSOCIATION (SIFMA) (June 3, 2014), http://www.sifma.org/research/statistics.aspx (accessed June 11, 2014). GSA backed securities also peaked in 2003 at 2.8 billion. *US Agency Mortgage Securities Issuance and Outstanding (xls)*, SECURITIES INDUSTRY AND FINANCIAL MARKETS ASSOCIATION (SIFMA) (June 3, 2014), http://www.sifma.org/research/ statistics.aspx (accessed June 11, 2014).

107. One possible indication of this is the low percentage of PSLs that are ever involved in a bankruptcy. While we only have data for 2005 onwards, in 2005 less than 0.4 percent of all outstanding loans were in bankruptcy. CFPB PSL Report, *supra* note 11, at 64.

108. *US ABS Issuance and Outstanding (xls)*, Securities Industry and Financial Markets Association (SIFMA) (June 3, 2014), http://www.sifma.org/research/statistics.aspx (accessed June 11, 2014).

109. We are not aware of any significant legal changes between Q1 2006 and Q1 2007 that would affect our sample. In particular, federal loan interest rates and amount caps remained the same during this time period.

110. Ideally, we'd also like to look at the period before 2005, but unfortunately, we do not have that data.

111. *See, e.g.,* SLC Student Loan Trust 2005-3 at S-19, The Student Loan Corporation (Dec. 1, 2005), *available at* https://www.navient.com/assets/about/investors/debtasset/SLC-Loan-Trusts/2005-3/20054.pdf (6 months) (accessed June 11, 2014); SLM Student Loan Trust 2003-14 at S-43, Sallie Mae Servicing (Nov. 6, 2003), *available at* https://www.navient.com/assets/about/investors/debtasset/SLM-Loan-Trusts/01-05/2003-14/200314.pdf (3 months) (accessed June 11, 2014).

112. CFPB PSL Report, *supra* note 11, at 18. Unfortunately, we do not have data before 2004.

113. *See* Andrea Murad and Jeffrey Prackup, *Private Student Loan ABS Tutorial*, Fitch Ratings 2 ("The Bankruptcy Abuse Prevention and Consumer Protection Act of 2005 codifies this treatment by broadly defining an education loan under the bankruptcy code to include all education loans made to borrowers or to parents of borrowers attending Title IV eligible institutions. This treatment aids lenders in collecting on private loans and results in higher recoveries relative to other unsecured consumer loans."), *available at* http://www.ihep.org/assets/files/gcfp-files/Private_Student_Loan_ABS_Tutorial.pdf (accessed June 12, 2014).

114. We cannot isolate all possible causal factors and run our analyses in a vacuum, but to the extent policymakers cannot pass laws in a vacuum either, it is valuable to understand the effect of the law.

115. *See* Bob Lawless, *One More Time, with Feelings*, CreditSlips (Aug. 22, 2011), http://www.creditslips.org/creditslips/2011/08/one-more-time-with-feeling.html; Block-Lieb & Janger, *supra* note 3.

116. CFPB PSL Report, *supra* note 11, at 30. The CFPB also found that default rate for nonprofit institution loans were "approximately half of their for-profit market counterparts." *Id.*

117. 145 Cong. Rec., *supra* note 2. (statement of Rep. Graham).

118. In other words,

> [i]f an otherwise dischargeable unsecured debt is rendered nondischargeable by the law, then the bankruptcy-state scenario regarding that debt becomes worse for the debtor (it does not go away) and better for the lender (it does not go away). In a world of competitive, zero-profit lend-

ing markets, this increased payoff for the lender must be translated ex ante into an improved cost of capital for the borrower.

Furthermore, we might also expect, in "a robust private lending market . . . [to find] a bountiful capital supply available for loans." John A. E. Pottow, *The Nondischargeability of Student Loans in Personal Bankruptcy Proceedings: The Search for a Theory*, 44 Can. Bus. L. J. 245, 262 (2006).

119. CFPB PSL Report, *supra* note 11, at 17.
120. Assuming the loan would have been at 8 percent but instead was at 8.3 percent.
121. This calculation is incredibly simplified, but it was computed by multiplying the $25/year additional cost by the number of PSLs originated in Q1 2006 (15,318).
122. We consider the Block-Lieb hypothesis to be a distinct model even though it can be described as a subset of the CP model.
123. We intend to apply techniques that take the distribution of borrower characteristics into account, including quantile regression, the DiNardo, Fortin, Lemieux decomposition. John DiNardo, et al., *Labor Market Institutions and the Distribution of Wages, 1973–1992: A Semiparametric Approach*, 64 Econometrica 1001 (1996).
124. There is another avenue of further research. This chapter focuses on undergraduates at four-year institutions. Given the diversity of educational options available, such as two-year schools, certificate programs, and postgraduate education of various kinds, another extension of this work would be to consider the effects of BAPCPA on loans in these other educational markets.

Appendix 7A

Tables

Table 7A.1 Loan-Level OLS Analysis, Q1 2005 and Q1 2006

	(1)	(2)	(3)	(4)	(5)
Maximum FICO score					
Post	−5.825***	−5.890***	−5.262***		
	(0.0811)	(0.0752)	(0.679)		
N	19,759	19,759	20,170		
R^2	0.013	0.083	0.192		
Margin					
Post	0.0046***	0.0046***	0.0042***	0.0036***	0.0033***
	(4.5e-05)	(4.5e-05)	(0.00022)	(0.00022)	(0.00022)
N	19,759	19,759	20,170	20,170	20,170
R^2	0.042	0.042	0.200	0.327	0.389
Original balance					
Post	1,326***	1,325***	1,268***	1,198***	1,189***
	(16.68)	(16.88)	(104.7)	(104.1)	(103.6)
N	19,759	19,759	20,170	20,170	20,170
R^2	0.0159	0.0161	0.181	0.186	0.187
Controls					
Tuition and fees	X	X			
Year in school	X	X	X	X	X
School type	X	X			
Has a coborrower		X		X	X
Maximum FICO score				X	
Spline of maximum FICO score					X
School fixed effects			X	X	X

NOTE: *p < 0.10; **p < 0.05; ***p < 0.01. Standard errors in parentheses. Each cell corresponds to a separate regression. Restricted to four-year undergraduates in the first quarters of 2005 and 2006. Spline of FICO scores in 20-point intervals.

SOURCE: Authors' calculations using CFPB private student loan data, IPEDS, and PEPS.

Table 7A.2 Loan-Level Oaxaca-Blinder Decompositions, Q1 2005 and Q1 2006

	(1)	(2)	(3)	(4)	(5)
			Panel A: Max FICO		
Before BAPCPA	720.4***	720.4***	720.3***		
	(0.654)	(0.654)	(0.706)		
After BAPCPA	715.0***	715.0***	715.0***		
	(0.388)	(0.388)	(0.402)		
Difference	5.439***	5.439***	5.377***		
	(0.761)	(0.761)	(0.812)		
Endowments	−0.329***	−0.398*	−0.939		
	(0.0941)	(0.219)	(1.200)		
Coefficients	5.967***	6.018***	1.058		
	(0.761)	(0.726)	(4.741)		
Interactions	−0.199*	−0.181	5.257		
	(0.113)	(0.117)	(4.840)		
			Panel B: Original balance		
Before BAPCPA	11,171***	11,171***	11,221	11,221	11,221***
	(42.67)	(42.67)	(0)	(0)	(42.15)
After BAPCPA	11,183***	11,183***	11,288	11,288	11,288***
	(37.65)	(37.65)	(0)	(0)	(37.05)
Difference	−12.11	−12.11	−66.82	−66.82	−66.82
	(56.90)	(56.91)	(0)	(0)	(56.12)
Endowments	−18.66*	−13.41	−399.4	−255.1	−116.2***
	(10.53)	(10.85)	(0)	(0)	(10.06)
Coefficients	−7.194	−11.60	112.4	174.2	32.94
	(56.12)	(56.07)	(0)	(0)	(56.32)
Interactions	13.75***	12.91***	220.2	14.03	16.39
	(4.836)	(4.902)	(0)	(0)	(11.01)
			Panel C: Margins		
Before BAPCPA	0.0436***	0.0436***	0.0436	0.0436	0.0436***
	(6.40e−05)	(6.40e−05)	(0)	(0)	(6.32e−05)
After BAPCPA	0.0469***	0.0469***	0.0470	0.0470	0.0470***
	(5.31e−05)	(5.31e−05)	(0)	(0)	(5.26e−05)
Difference	−0.00335***	−0.00335***	−0.00347	−0.00347	−0.00347***
	(8.31e−05)	(8.31e−05)	(0)	(0)	(8.22e−05)
Endowments	−8.05e−06	−1.41e−05	−0.000660	−0.00127	−0.00110***
	(1.12e−05)	(1.16e−05)	(0)	(0)	(4.47e−05)

Table 7A.2 (continued)

	(1)	(2)	(3)	(4)	(5)
	Panel C: Margins (continued)				
Coefficients	−0.00336***	−0.00336***	−0.00289	−0.00247	−0.00256***
	(8.24e−05)	(8.24e−05)	(0)	(0)	(7.32e−05)
Interactions	2.49e−05***	2.48e−05***	8.36e−05	0.000276	0.000194***
	(7.18e−06)	(7.28e−06)	(0)	(0)	(1.96e−05)
Controls					
Tuition and fees	x	x			
Year in school	x	x	x	x	x
School type	x	x			
Has a coborrower		x		x	x
Maximum FICO score				x	
Spline of maximum FICO score					x
School fixed effects			x	x	x

NOTE: *p < 0.10; **p < 0.05; ***p < 0.01. Standard errors in parentheses. Restricted to four-year undergraduates in the first quarters of 2005 and 2006. Spline of FICO scores in 20-year intervals. Tuition and fees calculated based on IPEDS data and student's reported state of residence.

SOURCE: Authors' calculations using CFPB private student loan data, IPEDS, and PEPS.

Table 7A.3 Loan-Level Propensity Score Matching, Q1 2005 and Q1 2006

	(1)	(2)	(3)	(4)	(5)
	Panel A: Maximum FICO score				
Unmatched	−5.439	−5.439	−5.189		
	(0.777)***	(0.777)***	(0.784)***		
Average treatment	−4.971	−3.458	−4.225		
on the treated	(1.585)***	(1.402)***	(1.376)***		
	Panel B: Margin				
Unmatched	0.004	0.004	0.004	0.004	0.004
	(0.000)***	(0.000)***	(0.000)***	(0.000)***	(0.000)***
Average treatment	0.003	0.004	0.004	0.004	0.003
on the treated	(0.001)***	(0.000)***	(0.000)***	(0.000)***	(0.000)***
	Panel C: Original balance				
Unmatched	1371.186	1371.1853	1352.15	1352.147	1352.147
	(125.50)***	(125.50)***	(127.05)***	(127.05)***	(127.05)***
Average treatment	1272.251	1120.066	1425.717	1303.748	1157.226
on the treated	(240.41)***	(213.86)***	(214.30)***	(168.91)***	(170.74)***
Number of observations					
Untreated	4,828	4,828	4,838	4,838	4,838
Treated	14,931	14,931	13,634	13,634	13,634
Controls					
Tuition and fees	x	x			
Year in school	x	x	x	x	x
School type	x	x			
Has a coborrower		x		x	x
Maximum FICO score				x	
Spline of maximum FICO score					x
School fixed effects			x	x	x

NOTE: *p < 0.10; **p < 0.05; ***p < 0.01. Standard errors in parentheses. Restricted to four-year undergraduates in the first quarters of 2005 and 2006. Spline of FICO scores in 20-point intervals. Propensity scores calculated using probit regression. Nearest neighbor matching with replacement. Tuition and fees calculated based on IPEDS data and student's reported state of residence.

SOURCE: Authors' calculations using CFPB private student loan data, IPEDS, and PEPS.

Table 7A.4 Private Student Loan Volumes at the School Level, Q1 2005 and Q1 2006

	(1)	(2)	(3)	(4)	(5)	(6)
	Panel A: OLS					
Post	0.546***	0.472***	0.472***	0.820***	1.008***	1.009***
	(0.169)	(0.174)	(0.174)	(0.108)	(0.0829)	(0.0811)
	1.726	*1.603*	*1.603*	*2.270*	*2.740*	*2.743*
	Panel B: Oaxaca decomposition					
Difference	0.541***	0.436**	0.590***	0.744***	0.590***	0.590***
	(0.178)	(0.182)	(0.165)	(0.222)	(0.183)	(0.180)
	1.718	*1.547*	*1.804*	*2.104*	*1.804*	*1.804*
Difference due to endowments	−0.00419	0.00179	−0.135	−0.0761	−0.292**	−0.289**
	(0.0484)	(0.0489)	(0.113)	(0.180)	(0.138)	(0.136)
	0.996	*1.002*	*0.835*	*0.927*	*0.747*	*0.749*
Difference due to coefficients	0.546***	0.492***	0.873***	0.974***	1.069***	1.072***
	(0.170)	(0.184)	(0.103)	(0.154)	(0.0777)	(0.0748)
	1.726	*1.636*	*2.394*	*2.649*	*2.912*	*2.921*
Difference due to interactions	0.000748	−0.0581	−0.148*	−0.153	−0.187**	−0.193**
	(0.00896)	(0.0857)	(0.0825)	(0.144)	(0.0757)	(0.0769)
	0.999	*0.944*	*0.862*	*0.858*	*0.829*	*0.824*
	Panel C: Propensity score matching					
Average treatment on the treated	0.993***	1.016***	1.146***	1.141***	1.148***	1.148***
	(0.0408)	(0.0412)	(0.0413)	(0.0410)	(0.0412)	(0.0413)
	2.699	*2.762*	*3.146*	*3.130*	*3.152*	*3.152*
Controls						
Tuition and fees	x	x	x	x	x	x
Graduation rate		x	x	x	x	x
Carnegie classification			x	x	x	x
ln(full-time equivalent students)				x	x	x
HBCU, HSI					x	
% black, % Hispanic						x

NOTE: *p < 0.10; **p < 0.05; ***p < 0.01. Standard errors in parentheses. Marginal effects in italics. Restricted to four-year undergraduates in the first quarters of 2005 and 2006. Marginal effects calculated by exponentiating estimated coefficients. Outcome is natural log of PSL borrowers in the lender data.

SOURCE: Authors' calculations using CFPB private student loan data, IPEDS, PEPS, and Title IV Program Volume Reports.

Table 7A.5 Difference-in-Difference Estimates of the Effects of BAPCPA on Loan Volumes and Original Balances, Q1 2005 and Q1 2006

Outcome	Control group				
	(1)	(2)	(3)	(4)	(5)
	Stafford subsidized loans	Stafford unsubsidized loans	All Stafford Loans	PLUS Loans	All federal loans
Loan volumes					
ln(originations)	0.512***	0.459***	0.491***	0.450***	0.487***
	(0.0210)	(0.0215)	(0.0210)	(0.0231)	(0.0207)
	1.669	*1.582*	*1.634*	*1.568*	*1.627*
ln(borrowers)	0.491***	0.438***	0.471***	0.434***	0.467***
	(0.0208)	(0.0214)	(0.0209)	(0.0231)	(0.0206)
	1.634	*1.550*	*1.602*	*1.543*	*1.595*
Average loan size					
Original balance	641.6***	647.5***	624.5***	−120.7*	542.9***
	(163.5)	(159.9)	(161.2)	(68.55)	(143.1)
ln(original balance)	0.0544***	0.0451***	0.0450***	-0.0143*	0.0330***
	(0.0153)	(0.0151)	(0.0148)	(0.00843)	(0.0117)
	1.056	*1.570*	*1.046*	*0.986*	*1.034*

NOTE: $*p < 0.10$; $**p < 0.05$; $***p < 0.01$. Standard errors in parentheses. Marginal effects in italics. Restricted to four-year undergraduates in the first quarters of 2005 and 2006. Marginal effects calculated by exponentiated estimated coefficients. Note that program effects on loan size may be biased downward.

SOURCE: Authors' calculations using CFPB private student loan data, IPEDS, PEPS, and Title IV Program Volume Reports.

Appendix 7B

Bias in Difference-in-Differences Estimates

Suppose that the outcome equation for federal loans is determined by the following equation and that y_i^* is bounded above by y^{max}

$$y_i^* = f(x_i) + \varepsilon_i$$

$$y_i = \begin{cases} \tilde{y} \text{ if } y_i^* \geq \tilde{y} \\ y_i^* \text{ otherwise} \end{cases}$$

Then the observed mean first difference, $\left(\overline{y_f^{post}} - \overline{y_f^{pre}}\right)$, can be written as a function of the uncensored loan amount, b_i^* function, and the maximum loan amount allowable.

$$\overline{y_f^{*,post}} - \overline{y_f^{*,pre}} = \left(\overline{y_f^{post}} - \overline{y_f^{pre}}\right) + \frac{1}{y^{max} - \tilde{y}} \int_{\tilde{y}}^{y^{max}} (y_f^{post} - y_f^{pre}) ds$$

So when we take difference-in-differences when the outcome for private loans is not censored (i.e., $b_i = b_i^*$), the estimate $\hat{\delta}$ of program effect δ is biased downwards.

$$\hat{\delta} = \left(\overline{y_p^{*,post}} - \overline{y_p^{*,pre}}\right) - \left(\overline{y_f^{*,post}} - \overline{y_f^{*,pre}}\right)$$

$$= \left(\overline{y_p^{post}} - \overline{y_p^{pre}}\right) - \left[\left(\overline{y_f^{post}} - \overline{y_f^{pre}}\right) + \frac{1}{y^{max} - \tilde{y}} \int_{\tilde{y}}^{y^{max}} (y_f^{post} - y_f^{pre}) ds\right]$$

$$= \delta - \frac{1}{y^{max} - \tilde{y}} \int_{\tilde{y}}^{y^{max}} (y_f^{post} - y_f^{pre}) ds$$

We do not observe $y_f^* \geq \tilde{y}$, so we cannot estimate the magnitude of the bias.

Appendix 7C

Stiglitz-Weiss Analysis

This appendix contains the relevant theorems, notation, and equations from Stiglitz and Weiss's 1981 paper. For ease of discussion, we retain Stiglitz and Weiss's numbering.

Each project, indexed by θ, is assumed to have a probability distribution of gross return R. The distribution of returns is denoted $F(R,\theta)$ and the density of returns is denoted $f(R,\theta)$. Higher values of θ correspond to higher levels of risk in the sense of mean-preserving spreads, i.e., for $\theta_1 > \theta_2$

$$\int_0^\infty Rf(R,\theta_1)dR = \int_0^\infty Rf(R,\theta_2)dR$$

then for $y \geq 0$,

$$\int_0^y Rf(R,\theta_1)dR \geq \int_0^y Rf(R,\theta_2)dR$$

An individual who borrows amount B at interest rate $\hat{r}$ repays his loan if $R > B(1 + \hat{r})$. Note that this is a simplification from the Stiglitz-Weiss model as there is no term for collateral, since student loans are unsecured. The return to the creditor or bank is denoted $\rho(R, \hat{r}) = \min(R, B(1 + \hat{r}))$. Upper bars denote means.

Theorem 1: For a given interest rate $\hat{r}$, there is a critical value $\hat{\theta}$ such that a firm borrows from the bank if and only if $\theta > \hat{\theta}$.

Theorem 3: The expected return on a loan to a bank is a decreasing function of the riskiness of the loan to the bank.

Theorem 5: Whenever $\rho(\hat{r})$ has an interior mode, there exists supply functions of funds such that competitive equilibrium entails credit rationing.

Corollary 1: As the supply of funds increases, the excess demand for funds decreases, but the interest rate charged remains unchanged, so long as there is any credit rationing.

Equation (7.5): (Zero-profit condition)

$$\Pi(\hat{r},\hat{\theta}) = \int_0^\infty \max[R - (\hat{r} + 1)B; 0]dF(R,\hat{\theta}) = 0$$

Private student loan borrowers are analogous to the firms in the model: projects, or school-major choices, with different mean returns can be distinguished from each other—to the lender returns to education for individuals in the same major at the same school are drawn from the same distribution.[1] Private student loan borrowers with the same expected mean return differ from each other in their risk parameter, which Stiglitz-Weiss denote θ, where risk is increasing in θ. In the analysis below, we consider credit score a proxy for $-\theta$, since risk is decreasing in credit score. The BAPCPA reforms that effectively made most loans nondischargeable in bankruptcy decrease the risk associated with any given loan, which effectively increases the expected return to the creditor, as described in Stiglitz and Weiss's Theorem 3.[2]

Given the Stiglitz-Weiss model and the theories described in the paper, our hypotheses for the effect of the change to the bankruptcy laws making private student loans presumptively nondischargeable can be stated as follows:

- *H1—Loan pricing (that is, lender margins) should remain the same for originations after the law change.* Since the profitability of a given loan increases for creditors, following Theorem 3 the supply of credit should increase.[3] Assuming an interior mode for the return to the creditor of lending at a given interest rate, Theorem 5 implies that credit rationing will still exist. Given these conditions, Corollary 1 states that "as the supply of funds increases, the excess demand for funds decreases, but the interest rate charged remains unchanged, so long as there is credit rationing."[4]

- *H2—Lenders should be willing to lend to borrowers with lower credit quality than they were willing to lend before the law change.* This is essentially a decrease in the critical value $\hat{\theta}$, which Theorem 1 states that an individual will borrow from the creditor if and only if the borrower's value of θ exceeds $\hat{\theta}$.[5]

- *H3—Overall loan volumes should increase.* This follows from the argument presented for H1.

Appendix Notes

1. One can think of a choice of major at a particular school as an investment with uncertain returns. For example, a freshman liberal arts student might know the distribution of returns of liberal arts majors from his school but does not know what his particular return will be ex ante.
2. *See* Stiglitz and Weiss *supra* note 64.
3. Theorems refer to theorems in Stiglitz and Weiss's paper.
4. *Id.* at 398.
5. Consider Stiglitz and Weiss's Equation (5). *Id.*

8
Default and Repayment among Baccalaureate Degree Earners

Lance J. Lochner
University of Western Ontario

Alexander Monge-Naranjo
Federal Reserve Bank of St. Louis and
Washington University in St. Louis

A growing number of college students in the United States borrow thousands of dollars from public and private lenders to finance their higher education, and an increasing portion of them have been defaulting on their obligations. Over the past decade, the total number of Stafford Loan borrowers has nearly doubled to 10.4 million recipients in 2011–2012. In recent years, undergraduates have borrowed more than $70 billion annually in federal student loans. More ominously, student loan default rates have risen continuously since 2005 after falling for more than a decade. Three-year cohort default rates stand at 13.4 percent for students entering repayment in 2009. Among students from private for-profit institutions, three-year default rates exceed 20 percent.[1] Against this backdrop, there is growing concern that many students are borrowing too much, especially in the wake of the Great Recession. These developments have led to renewed interest in the design of federal student loan programs, including a reevaluation of student borrowing limits, interest rates, and income-contingent repayment schemes. Unfortunately, much of this discussion is occurring amid scant systematic evidence on the determinants of student loan repayment and default, especially for recent cohorts.

Dynarski (1994), Flint (1997), and Volkwein et al. (1998) study the determinants of student loan default using nationally representative data from the 1987 National Postsecondary Student Aid Study that surveyed borrowers leaving school in the late 1970s and 1980s. Other empirical studies have generally examined default behavior at specific institutions or in individual states in the United States.[2] Gross et al. (2009) provide a review of this literature and conclude that factors such as race, socioeconomic background, educational attainment, type of postsecondary institution, student debt levels, and postschool earnings are important determinants of default. Minorities, students from low-income families, and college dropouts all tend to have higher default rates, as do students attending two-year and for-profit private institutions. Default is also more likely for those with high debt levels and low postschool earnings.

We go beyond previous analyses of default to consider other important measures of student loan repayment and nonpayment that are likely to be of greater interest to potential lenders (public or private). Most lenders are concerned about the expected return on their investments, although government lenders may have other objectives. While default is a key factor affecting the expected returns on student loans, other factors can also be important. For example, government student loans offer opportunities for loan deferment or forbearance, which temporarily suspend payments.[3] The timing of default and deferment/forbearance can also influence returns to lenders. From the lender's point of view, it matters if a borrower defaults (without reentering repayment) immediately after leaving school or after five years of standard payments. The discounted value of payments from the former is much lower than from the latter. Similarly, the discounted present value of payments is much lower for borrowers who defer payments for extended periods of time than for those who do not. These simple examples suggest that the credit-worthiness of different types of borrowers (based on their background or their schooling choices) depends on the expected payment streams and not simply whether they had ever entered default or are currently in default at some arbitrary survey date.

Unfortunately, an analysis of expected returns across different types of borrowers is impossible given current data sources, since it requires data on potential determinants of repayment and access to full repayment histories. As far as we know, these data are not available. In this chapter, we use data from the Baccalaureate and Beyond Longitudinal Studies (B&B) to analyze a number of different repayment and nonpayment measures that provide useful information about expected returns on student loans. As discussed further in the following section, the B&B follows a random sample of 1992–1993 U.S. college graduates for 10 years and contains rich information about the individual and family background of respondents, choice of college major and institution, student borrowing levels, postschool earnings, and loan repayment status (including outstanding balances) 5 and 10 years after graduation. We use the student loan records to compute five different measures related to repayment and nonpayment of student loans 10 years after graduation: 1) the fraction of initial student debt still outstanding; 2) an indicator for default status; 3) an indicator for nonpayment status (includes default, deferment, and forbearance); 4) the fraction of initial debt that is in default; and 5) the fraction of initial debt that is in nonpayment. We then study the determinants of all of these repayment/nonpayment measures, focusing on the roles of individual and family background factors, college major, postsecondary institution characteristics, student debt levels, and postschool earnings. We find that many of the factors identified in earlier studies are important for our more recent sample of borrowers; however, the importance of some factors depends on the measure of repayment or nonpayment under consideration. We highlight a number of general lessons and open questions arising from our results in the concluding section.

DATA: THE BACCALAUREATE AND BEYOND LONGITUDINAL STUDY

We use the B&B to analyze patterns in student loan repayment and default for college graduates up to 10 years after graduating. The B&B was initially drawn as a subsample from the 1993 National Postsecondary Student Aid Study, a nationally representative random sample of all postsecondary students in the United States.[4] More specifically, the B&B has followed the roughly 16,000 respondents who received baccalaureate degrees in the 1992–1993 academic year through 2003. The B&B uses data from three basic sources: 1) survey data in 1993, 1994, 1997, and 2003; 2) institutional records on college costs and financial aid; and 3) snapshots from student loan administrative records in 1998 and 2003. With extensive information about family background and demographic characteristics, student achievement as measured by SAT/ ACT scores, college-related outcomes (e.g., undergraduate major, institution attended, graduate school attendance, and postgraduate degrees), labor market outcomes every few years, and student loan balances and repayment status 5 and 10 years after graduation, the B&B offers a unique opportunity for studying student loan repayment and default behavior in the United States.

The B&B sample is relatively homogeneous in its educational attainment: all students have at least a BA/BS degree. The lack of college dropouts and students with less than four-year degrees is unfortunate, since previous research shows that repayment problems are most common among these individuals.[5] Still, we find that many students who graduated from college in 1992–1993 have experienced repayment problems.

To focus on a typical American college student, we exclude noncitizens, the disabled, and individuals receiving their BA/BS at age 30 or older (less than 14 percent received their BA/BS at later ages). Because new graduates who then attend graduate school are eligible for automatic loan deferments when they are enrolled, they will have spent less time in repayment. This directly reduces their opportunities for both repayment and default within any given time frame, making it difficult to compare their repayment/default outcomes with those of students who have not participated in postgraduate studies. Our main analysis, therefore, excludes respondents who attended 12 or more months of graduate school as of 1997, received any postgraduate degrees by 2003, or were enrolled in school in 2003.[6] Altogether, this leaves 4,300 U.S. citizens who received baccalaureate degrees in 1992–1993 but participated in little schooling thereafter. Roughly half of these graduates report that they borrowed money for their undergraduate schooling as of 2003. Our analysis of repayment and default focuses on these 2,180 borrowers.

The B&B contains standard demographic characteristics such as gender and race/ethnicity (Asian, black, Hispanic, white). We also use measures of maternal education, categorizing students based on whether their mothers never attended college, attended but did not receive a BA/ BS, or completed their BA/BS. Dependency status (for financial aid purposes) is also available for students, along with parental income in 1991 for those who are dependents. The B&B also contains data on student SAT and ACT scores. We categorize individuals into quartiles based on their SAT scores if they are available. If an individual did not report an SAT score, we use the corresponding ACT quartile.[7] The data also include information about the major course of undergraduate study and the type of institution from which individuals graduated (public, private nonprofit, private for-profit, historically black college/ university). We use the undergraduate institution from which individuals graduate to include a measure of the selectivity of the institution as determined by Barron's 1992 Admissions Competitiveness Index. We consider the following three competitiveness categories: 1) most competitive and highly competitive, 2) very competitive and competitive, and 3) all others. Sample averages for all of these variables are reported for our sample of borrowers and nonborrowers, as well as borrowers only, in Table 8A.1.

Our main focus is on student borrowing, repayment, and default measured 10 years after graduation. As noted earlier, roughly half of our sample borrowed funds for their undergraduate studies. Among those who borrowed, the average amount of undergraduate loans was $9,300. On average, another $600 was borrowed for graduate studies. The latter amount is small, since our sample restrictions ensure that students in our sample spent very little (or no) time in graduate school. Ten years after graduation, borrowers still owed, on average, $2,600 on their undergraduate loans. Two-thirds had repaid their undergraduate loans in full.

Table 8.1 reports repayment status for borrowers as of 1998 and 2003. In both years, 92 percent were repaying their loans or had already fully repaid their loans. The fraction of borrowers receiving a deferment or forbearance declined from 3.8 percent in 1998 to 2.5 percent in 2003, while the share of borrowers in default rose from 4.2 percent to 5.8 percent over this period.[8] These figures suggest that deferment and forbearance are important forms of nonpayment with a diminishing role over time: They make up nearly half of all nonpayments five years after school, falling to slightly less than one-third five years later.

Table 8.2 shows transition rates for these repayment states from 1998 to 2003. The rows in the table list the probabilities of being in repayment (including those who fully repaid), receiving a deferment or forbearance, or being in default 10 years after school (in 2003) conditional on each of those repayment states five years earlier in 1998.

**Table 8.1 Repayment Status for Undergraduate Borrowers 5 and 10
                Years after Graduation**

Status	1998	2003
Fully repaid	0.269	0.639
	(0.013)	(0.013)
Repaying or fully paid	0.920	0.917
	(0.008)	(0.007)
Deferment or forbearance	0.038	0.025
	(0.006)	(0.004)
Default	0.042	0.058
	(0.006)	(0.005)

NOTE: Estimates are based on the B&B sample of borrowers. Standard errors are in
  parentheses.
SOURCE: Authors' calculations.

Ninety-four percent of borrowers in repayment (including those who
had fully repaid) in 1998 were also making their payments or had
fully repaid their loans by 2003. Four percent of borrowers who were
in repayment (or fully repaid) in 1998 were in default five years later.
Only 75 percent of borrowers in deferment/forbearance in 1998 were in
repayment (or fully repaid) five years later, while 16.5 percent were still
in deferment/forbearance and 8.5 percent were in default. Among those
in default in 1998, 54 percent had returned to repayment (or had fully

Table 8.2 Repayment Status Transition Probabilities

	Repayment status in 2003		
Repayment status in 1998	Repaying/ fully paid	Deferment/ forbearance	Default
Repaying or fully paid	0.939	0.020	0.040
	(0.006)	(0.004)	(0.005)
Deferment or forbearance	0.749	0.165	0.085
	(0.063)	(0.057)	(0.032)
Default	0.544	0.038	0.418
	(0.070)	(0.020)	(0.068)

NOTE: The table shows the probability of each status in 2003 conditional on the status
  in 1998. Estimates based on the B&B sample of borrowers. Standard errors are in
  parentheses.
SOURCE: Authors' calculations.

repaid) five years later, while 42 percent remained in default. Although there is considerable persistence in these repayment states, many borrowers who were not making payments five years after school (i.e., in deferment/forbearance or default) were making payments (or had fully repaid their loans) five years later. Not surprisingly, deferment/forbearance is the least persistent state, since it is designed to temporarily help borrowers in need. Indeed, borrowers cannot typically receive a deferment or forbearance indefinitely. In the end, most borrowers who receive this form of assistance return to repayment; however, one in six end up defaulting.

Finally, the B&B asked respondents about their earnings in the 1997 and 2003 surveys; we also use these data. The 1997 survey asked respondents about their annual salaries for the jobs they were working during April of that year, while the 2003 survey asked respondents about their total income from work earned in 2002. Based on these questions, respondents in our sample (borrowers and nonborrowers alike) reported average earnings of roughly $30,000 in 1997 and $50,000 in 2002.

DETERMINANTS OF STUDENT BORROWING AND REPAYMENT

In this section, we study the determinants of undergraduate borrowing and repayment behavior measured in 2003, roughly 10 years after graduation. Since the standard repayment plan for Stafford Loans is based on a 10-year repayment period, students who were always in good standing and making the standard payment should have paid down most, if not all, of their loans. As we show, many did not. In addition to studying the fraction of debt students repaid within the first 10 years after school, we also examine the traditional metric used to study student loan repayment behavior: default.[9] We then extend this metric to include borrowers in deferment or forbearance and report on the fraction of undergraduate debts remaining for borrowers who have defaulted or are in nonpayment more generally.

We begin with an analysis of average postschool earnings, undergraduate borrowing, and repayment/nonpayment rates by student characteristics. We then explore differences in these outcomes based on the types of institutions from which students graduated. Finally, we use standard multivariate regression methods to examine the importance of individual/family and institutional factors, along with college major, student borrowing, and postschool earnings levels in determining student loan repayment, default, and other measures of nonpayment. This enables us to identify which factors are most important while simultaneously controlling for other potentially important factors.

Differences by Borrower Characteristics

Table 8.3 characterizes the postschool labor market outcomes, undergraduate borrowing, and repayment outcomes across different types of students defined by gender, race/ethnicity, SAT/ACT quartiles, and maternal education. Because we are primarily interested in repayment/nonpayment, this table focuses on our sample of borrowers only. Before discussing repayment, we briefly comment on differences in earnings and undergraduate borrowing across groups as reported in columns (2) and (3).

Column (2) reveals a large difference in earnings (including incomes of zero for the nonemployed) between men and women, while differences by race/ethnicity, student aptitude, and family background are more modest. Male college graduates earn about 70 percent more than female graduates 10 years after finishing school. Blacks earn about 15 percent less than whites, while Asians earn about 15 percent more. Hispanics had earnings similar to whites in our sample of borrowers. Earnings increase over SAT/ACT quartiles 1–3; however, earnings for the top quartile are very similar to those in the second quartile (nearly 20 percent less than the third quartile). This seemingly perverse pattern at the top is largely due to our sample selection criteria, which exclude those who attended 12 or more months of graduate school (by 1997) or received a graduate degree. This restriction disproportionately affects the top aptitude quartile, and removing it yields very similar average income levels for the top two quartiles (see Table 8A.2). Differences in earnings based on maternal education are relatively modest, although those with mothers who received a BA/BS degree earned almost $9,000 more than those whose mothers did not attend college.

Column (3) in Table 8.3 reveals very small differences in average undergraduate loan amounts compared across gender and SAT/

ACT quartiles. Differences by race/ethnicity and maternal background are more pronounced, though still modest. In considering race/ethnicity, Hispanics borrowed the least, at $8,100, while whites borrowed the most, at about $1,300 more. Students whose mothers finished college borrowed nearly $1,200 more than students whose mothers never attended college. These two patterns suggest that whites and borrowers from higher socioeconomic families are attending more expensive institutions, on average.

The remaining columns in Table 8.3 focus on repayment and nonpayment of student loans. Column (4) shows the average fraction of undergraduate loan amounts still outstanding in 2003. This provides a useful measure of returns to lenders within the first 10 years. As noted earlier, borrowers who make standard payments every month should owe very little (or nothing) on their undergraduate loans by this time. A high value here indicates low payment levels or periods of nonpayment. As the first row in Table 8.3 shows, of the $9,300 initially borrowed, students still owed 19 percent, on average, 10 years later. Column (5) reports the fraction of borrowers in default, while column (6) reports a broader measure of nonpayment that includes borrowers in deferment, forbearance, or default. In our sample, 5.8 percent of all borrowers were in default 10 years after finishing college, while 8.3 percent were not making payments for various reasons (i.e., deferment, forbearance, or default). Finally, columns (7) and (8) report the average share of undergraduate loan amounts currently in default or currently not being repaid because of deferment, forbearance, or default.[10] If borrowers in default or nonpayment 10 years after leaving school are very unlikely to return to good standing, these figures suggest that the expected loan loss rate (for a typical borrower) faced by lenders is around 2.8 percent (based on defaults), or as high as 5.2 percent (based on any nonpayment). These amounts are notably lower than default/nonpayment rates themselves (columns [5] and [6]) because many defaulters (nonpayers) repay some of their student debts before entering default (nonpayment).

Now, consider differences in repayment and nonpayment patterns by gender as reported in Table 8.3. Consistent with significantly lower postschool earnings, women owe more on their loans than men 10 years after finishing college (22 percent vs. 15 percent) and have higher rates of nonpayment (9.5 percent versus 6.7 percent). The fraction of debt in nonpayment was also 2.5 times higher for women than for men. Yet,

Table 8.3 Average Earnings, Undergraduate Borrowing, and Repayment/Nonpayment Measures in 2003 by Individual Characteristics

	(1)	(2)	(3)	(4)	(5)	(6)	(7)	(8)
Characteristic	N	Earnings ($000s)	Total undergrad loan amount ($000s)	Share of undergrad debt still owed	Fraction in default	Fraction not paying	Default × share of debt still owed	Not paying × share of debt still owed
Full sample	2,120	49.629 (1.300)	9.336 (0.179)	0.188 (0.012)	0.058 (0.005)	0.083 (0.007)	0.028 (0.005)	0.052 (0.007)
Males	900	64.199 (2.426)	9.646 (0.304)	0.146 (0.014)	0.057 (0.008)	0.067 (0.008)	0.019 (0.005)	0.028 (0.006)
Females	1,210	37.705 (1.097)	9.091 (0.212)	0.221 (0.018)	0.059 (0.008)	0.095 (0.010)	0.034 (0.008)	0.071 (0.013)
Asians	50	58.085 (3.975)	8.706 (1.039)	0.236 (0.075)	0.112 (0.043)	0.130 (0.047)	0.020 (0.013)	0.026 (0.015)
Blacks	150	42.123 (2.513)	9.165 (0.522)	0.506 (0.064)	0.132 (0.029)	0.180 (0.032)	0.156 (0.057)	0.208 (0.060)
Hispanics	130	47.235 (3.115)	8.127 (0.786)	0.216 (0.054)	0.113 (0.038)	0.134 (0.041)	0.031 (0.011)	0.048 (0.020)
Whites	1,780	49.965 (1.483)	9.441 (0.197)	0.158 (0.012)	0.047 (0.005)	0.070 (0.007)	0.017 (0.003)	0.040 (0.007)
SAT/ACT Q1	510	41.641 (1.641)	9.466 (0.460)	0.236 (0.025)	0.061 (0.010)	0.097 (0.014)	0.032 (0.008)	0.059 (0.011)
SAT/ACT Q2	500	50.197 (2.164)	9.153 (0.319)	0.141 (0.015)	0.048 (0.010)	0.054 (0.010)	0.022 (0.007)	0.025 (0.007)
SAT/ACT Q3	480	60.087 (3.914)	9.673 (0.371)	0.175 (0.031)	0.047 (0.009)	0.076 (0.014)	0.010 (0.004)	0.026 (0.007)

SAT/ACT Q4	370	50.540	9.131	0.151	0.061	0.084	0.027	0.052
		(2.508)	(0.378)	(0.022)	(0.012)	(0.014)	(0.009)	(0.014)
Mother no	920	48.168	8.911	0.223	0.060	0.088	0.027	0.058
college		(1.726)	(0.240)	(0.021)	(0.008)	(0.011)	(0.005)	(0.012)
Mother some	610	44.452	9.184	0.140	0.055	0.069	0.028	0.039
college		(1.960)	(0.297)	(0.014)	(0.010)	(0.011)	(0.008)	(0.009)
Mother BA+	580	56.838	10.161	0.180	0.058	0.089	0.028	0.055
		(3.177)	(0.416)	(0.021)	(0.010)	(0.014)	(0.013)	(0.016)

NOTE: The table shows sample means based on the B&B sample of borrowers. Standard errors are in parentheses.
SOURCE: Authors' calculations.

these differences are not apparent when comparing default rates, which are nearly identical for men and women. Even with similar default rates, women have defaulted on 80 percent more debt than men. These figures highlight the value of considering alternative measures of repayment and nonpayment beyond traditionally used default rates. Despite very similar default rates between male and female student borrowers, lenders can expect faster payments and a higher recovery rate from male students.

Differences in repayment behavior are much more pronounced by race/ethnicity than by gender, with particularly stark differences between blacks and whites. On average, black borrowers still owe 51 percent of their student loans 10 years after college, while white borrowers owe only 16 percent. Hispanics and Asians owe 22 percent and 24 percent, respectively. Black borrowers have defaulted on 16 percent of their undergraduate debt and are in nonpayment on 21 percent. By contrast, the next highest rates of nonpayment are for Hispanics, who have defaulted on only 3.1 percent of their debt and are in nonpayment on 4.8 percent. Given these dramatic differences, it is interesting to note that default rates are quite similar for all three minority groups (13 percent for blacks, 11 percent for Hispanics and Asians), while they are much lower for whites (less than 5 percent). There are larger differences between blacks and the other minority groups for nonpayment rates that include deferment and forbearance (18 percent for blacks versus 13 percent for Hispanics and Asians). Once again, important differences in repayment and expected loan losses by lenders are obscured by focusing exclusively on default rates. It is also worth noting that the racial/ethnic differences in repayment/nonpayment outcomes are unlikely to be driven by differences in borrowing or postschool earnings, which are quite modest. We explore this issue further below.

The share of undergraduate debt remaining 10 years after graduation is highest for students with the lowest SAT/ACT scores (24 percent for the lowest quartile, and 14–18 percent for all other quartiles). All default and nonpayment outcomes show an interesting U-shaped pattern in achievement that is roughly consistent with the inverted U-shaped pattern for earnings. Default and nonpayment rates are as high as 6 percent and 10 percent, respectively, for the lowest SAT/ACT group; they then fall to around 5 percent for the second and third quartiles before returning to higher levels for the top ability group. A similar, though weaker, pattern is evident for the share of debt in default or nonpayment. Unlike the relationship for earnings, the surprising non-monotonic relationship between achievement and default/nonpayment is not a consequence of our sample restriction that excludes those with graduate degrees or 12 or more months of graduate school. A similar pattern arises even when we do not impose this restriction. Indeed, the fraction of debts in default or nonpayment is actually highest for the top SAT/ACT quartile in the unrestricted sample (see Table 8A.2).

The last three rows in Table 8.3 show that socioeconomic status, as measured by maternal education, is only weakly and statistically insignificantly related to default and nonpayment.[11]

By contrast, the fraction of debt repaid after 10 years is significantly higher for borrowers whose mothers attended college. Students with stronger socioeconomic backgrounds appear to reduce their loan balances more quickly; however, they do not appear to be any less likely to enter default, deferment, or forbearance.

Differences by Institutional Characteristics

We next explore differences in borrowing and repayment/nonpayment patterns, categorizing individuals based on the type of institution from which they graduated. Table 8.4 shows differences by institutional control (public, private not-for-profit, and private for-profit), and by college selectivity as determined by Barron's. Given the high nonpayment rates for black college graduates reported in Table 8.3, we also examine outcomes for blacks graduating from historically black colleges and universities (HBCU) versus those from traditional non-HBCU institutions. Table 8.4, like Table 8.3, is based on our sample of borrowers.

There is considerable interest today in the high default rates at private for-profit institutions. There is also concern about the high debt levels associated with attendance at private institutions more generally. The first few rows of Table 8.4 offer more detailed evidence on these issues from 1992–1993 graduates 10 years after school. Postschool earnings are quite similar across graduates from public and private for-profit and nonprofit institutions; however, student debt levels are highest for graduates of nonprofit institutions ($11,200), followed by for-profit institutions ($9,700) and public institutions ($8,400). Unfortunately, the sample size for for-profit institutions is quite small (33), making it dif-

Table 8.4 Average Earnings, Undergraduate Borrowing, and Repayment/Nonpayment Measures in 2003 by Type of Institution Attended

	(1)	(2)	(3)	(4)	(5)	(6)	(7)	(8)
Institution type	N	Earnings ($000s)	Total undergrad. loan amount ($000s)	Share of undergrad. debt still owed	Fraction in default	Fraction not paying	Default × share of debt still owed	Not paying × share of debt still owed
Public	1,350	49.458 (1.630)	8.407 (0.224)	0.174 (0.015)	0.056 (0.006)	0.076 (0.008)	0.025 (0.004)	0.047 (0.009)
Private nonprofit	720	49.827 (2.268)	11.207 (0.297)	0.213 (0.021)	0.054 (0.009)	0.086 (0.012)	0.032 (0.012)	0.061 (0.014)
Private for-profit	30	51.434 (7.896)	9.738 (1.263)	0.199 (0.073)	0.182 (0.091)	0.264 (0.108)	0.059 (0.042)	0.087 (0.047)
Most competitive	150	61.583 (4.663)	11.453 (0.650)	0.202 (0.034)	0.043 (0.016)	0.087 (0.022)	0.009 (0.005)	0.043 (0.014)
Competitive	1,300	49.990 (1.558)	9.471 (0.235)	0.168 (0.013)	0.054 (0.007)	0.075 (0.008)	0.026 (0.005)	0.041 (0.006)
Noncompetitive	620	46.041 (2.696)	8.668 (0.308)	0.230 (0.026)	0.065 (0.011)	0.096 (0.015)	0.034 (0.012)	0.076 (0.021)
Black, not HBCU	100	44.421 (3.088)	10.085 (0.667)	0.448 (0.054)	0.170 (0.042)	0.223 (0.045)	0.157 (0.045)	0.203 (0.048)
Black, HBCU	50	38.850 (4.075)	7.855 (0.837)	0.589 (0.132)	0.078 (0.033)	0.119 (0.041)	0.155 (0.124)	0.215 (0.129)

NOTE: The table shows sample means based on the B&B sample of borrowers. Standard errors are in parentheses.
SOURCE: Authors' calculations.

ficult to draw strong conclusions about borrowing and repayment/non-payment rates for this group; note the large standard errors across the table for this institution type. On average, the fraction of debt still owed is slightly lower for public school graduates, but the differences across institution types are statistically insignificant. Default and nonpayment rates are very similar for public school graduates and nonprofit graduates, but they are three to four times higher (18 percent and 26 percent, respectively) for for-profit graduates. Unfortunately, because of small sample sizes, we cannot statistically distinguish across the groups. The extremely high default/nonpayment rates for for-profit graduates do not appear to translate into much higher shares of debt in default/nonpayment as observed in the last two columns.

Our next set of results compares students based on Barron's rankings of institutional selectivity. Earnings and debt levels are both notably higher among students from the most competitive institutions. Differences in repayment, default, and nonpayment measures across school selectivity are quite modest and generally not statistically significant. As might be expected, default and nonpayment rates are generally lowest for graduates of the most competitive institutions; however, they do not have the lowest share of debt still owed. In general, these differences are not statistically significant. There is little evidence to suggest that institutional selectivity is a particularly important determinant of repayment and nonpayment; however, we examine below whether important differences are confounded by other systematic differences in the characteristics and choices of individuals attending these institutions.

Finally, the bottom of Table 8.4 compares the outcomes for blacks attending HBCU and non-HBCU institutions. Small sample sizes are a problem here, as with for-profit institutions, yet a few patterns are worth noting. While earnings of HBCU graduates are similar to those of black graduates from non-HBCUs, HBCU graduates leave school with significantly lower debt. The most notable differences between HBCU and non-HBCU graduates, however, are for default and nonpayment. Blacks from HBCUs have default (nonpayment) rates of 8 percent (12 percent) compared with roughly twice those rates for non-HBCU graduates. Despite these sizable differences, the fraction of debt in default or nonpayment is remarkably similar (16 percent and 20–21 percent, respectively).

A Multivariate Analysis of Student Loan Repayment

As Tables 8.3 and 8.4 show, many important dimensions of heterogeneity across college graduates may affect repayment behavior. Therefore, it is important to simultaneously account for all of these factors before drawing strong conclusions about which are most important and why. We use standard multivariate regression methods to do this. These methods can be helpful in sorting out questions such as the following: Are default rates so high among blacks because they attend different types of schools than whites? Or because their SAT/ACT scores are lower? Or because their mothers are less educated? Do differences in repayment or nonpayment across institution types simply reflect the students they attract?

Before exploring repayment and nonpayment outcomes, we begin by examining which factors determine how much a student borrows (based on our full sample of borrowers and nonborrowers). Table 8.5 shows the ordinary least squares (OLS) regression estimates for total undergraduate loan amounts (in thousands of dollars) as a function of individual characteristics, college major, institutional characteristics, and state fixed effects based on the institutions from which students graduated.[12] Column (1) includes only demographic characteristics: gender, race/ethnicity, SAT/ACT quartile, maternal education, dependency status (for financial aid purposes), and parental income (in thousands of dollars) interacted with dependency status.[13] This specification is useful for measuring the full impact of these individual/family characteristics on borrowing (and repayment/nonpayment outcomes examined in subsequent tables) and incorporates any effects coming through choice of major or institution of attendance. Column (2) controls for the same background characteristics, as well as college major (all other majors not specifically listed reflect the omitted category), while column (3) includes controls for background characteristics and institution characteristics (e.g., type of control and Barron's selectivity). Column (4) includes all three types of variables: background, college major, and institutional characteristics. Comparing estimated effects of background characteristics across columns (1) versus (2) through (4) is informative about the extent to which individual characteristics affect borrowing through the choice of college major or institution. Column (5) adds state fixed effects to the specification in column (4), accounting for any unobserved differences in policies, educational institutions, and labor markets that vary across states. Similar specifications are used to study repayment, default, and more general measures of nonpayment below.

Several individual and family characteristics are important determinants of borrowing. Black students borrow significantly more than all other racial/ethnic groups. Columns (1) and (2) suggest that black graduates borrow nearly $2,000 more than whites. Accounting for choice of major, this difference grows even larger, suggesting that blacks tend to choose majors that are not typically associated with extensive borrowing. We also estimate higher levels of borrowing for students with better SAT/ACT scores. Comparing columns (1) and (4) suggests that much of this difference is explained by choice of major and institution: Higher-scoring students are inclined to attend schools and to choose majors associated with greater borrowing. Table 8.3 shows that students whose mothers have college education tend to borrow more. Regression results in Table 8.5 show that the opposite is true once we account for other personal differences, especially race, achievement, and parental income. Accounting for these other factors, students whose mothers received their BA/BS borrow roughly $1,500 less than those whose mothers did not attend college. The estimates also suggest that a $10,000 increase in parental earnings is associated with about $250 less in borrowing. We find no evidence to suggest that differences in borrowing by maternal education or parental income are due to differential choices regarding major and institution.

Some majors appear to be associated with greater borrowing—engineering, health-related majors, history, and especially biology—though not necessarily with high-paying professions. Institutional characteristics also appear to be important determinants of borrowing. Students graduating from private (for-profit or nonprofit) institutions tend to borrow about $3,000 more than those attending public institutions, all else equal. Black students attending HBCUs tend to borrow $1,500–$2,000 less than blacks attending other institutions. Less-competitive institutions are associated with about $600–$700 less in borrowing, although these differences are not statistically significant at the 0.05 level.

Altogether, many factors affect undergraduate borrowing; however, differences across individuals, college majors, and institutions are generally modest. Tables 8.6–8.10 show the extent to which these same

Table 8.5 Explaining Total Undergraduate Student Loan Amounts

Variable	(1)	(2)	(3)	(4)	(5)
Male	0.086	0.046	0.192	0.139	0.096
	(0.211)	(0.222)	(0.208)	(0.218)	(0.215)
Black	1.875**	1.843**	2.559**	2.460**	2.803**
	(0.486)	(0.486)	(0.559)	(0.557)	(0.549)
Hispanic	0.670	0.744	0.695	0.733	1.561**
	(0.523)	(0.521)	(0.520)	(0.518)	(0.551)
Asian	−0.626	−0.767	−0.499	−0.673	−0.079
	(0.609)	(0.609)	(0.600)	(0.600)	(0.616)
SAT/ACT Q2	0.254	0.110	0.215	0.089	0.139
	(0.282)	(0.282)	(0.278)	(0.278)	(0.273)
SAT/ACT Q3	0.723**	0.545	0.588**	0.413	0.348
	(0.293)	(0.296)	(0.291)	(0.294)	(0.290)
SAT/ACT Q4	1.076**	0.749**	0.639**	0.312	0.195
	(0.318)	(0.325)	(0.322)	(0.328)	(0.324)
Mother some college	−0.641**	−0.608**	−0.625**	−0.580**	−0.310
	(0.263)	(0.262)	(0.259)	(0.257)	(0.254)
Mother BA+	−1.447**	−1.402**	−1.607**	−1.525**	−1.445**
	(0.247)	(0.246)	(0.244)	(0.243)	(0.240)
Dependent	−0.131	−0.041	−0.376	−0.291	−0.643**
	(0.270)	(0.269)	(0.266)	(0.265)	(0.265)
Parental income	−0.025**	−0.025**	−0.026**	−0.026**	−0.023**
× dependent	(0.002)	(0.002)	(0.002)	(0.002)	(0.002)
Business		0.004		−0.075	−0.184
		(0.374)		(0.368)	(0.360)
Education		0.436		0.306	0.215
		(0.375)		(0.368)	(0.363)
Engineering		1.263**		1.445**	1.228**
		(0.467)		(0.460)	(0.453)
Health		1.904**		1.953**	1.755**
		(0.459)		(0.451)	(0.447)
Public affairs		−0.402		−0.588	−0.893
		(0.603)		(0.592)	(0.584)
Biology		3.189**		2.897**	2.951**
		(0.532)		(0.527)	(0.523)

Table 8.5 (continued)

Variable	(1)	(2)	(3)	(4)	(5)
Math/science		0.318		0.321	0.447
		(0.488)		(0.482)	(0.476)
Social science		0.453		0.340	0.112
		(0.407)		(0.400)	(0.395)
History		1.618**		1.008	1.195
		(0.797)		(0.779)	(0.767)
Humanities		0.440		0.013	−0.031
		(0.408)		(0.403)	(0.396)
Psychology		−0.072		0.122	0.330
		(0.609)		(0.596)	(0.588)
Private for-profit			2.798**	3.049**	3.036**
			(1.045)	(1.039)	(1.023)
Private nonprofit			3.075**	3.089**	2.656**
			(0.226)	(0.225)	(0.235)
HBCU			−2.128**	−1.945**	−1.552
			(0.909)	(0.907)	(0.906)
Competitive			−0.657	−0.565	−0.675
			(0.385)	(0.384)	(0.397)
Noncompetitive			−0.651	−0.567	−0.720
			(0.427)	(0.426)	(0.440)
State fixed effects	No	No	No	No	Yes
N	3,750	3,750	3,700	3,690	3,690
R^2	0.062	0.077	0.113	0.128	0.183

NOTE: *p < 0.10; **p < 0.05; ***p < 0.01. Estimates based on the sample of B&B borrowers and nonborrowers. Standard errors are in parentheses.
SOURCE: Authors' calculations.

factors affect repayment and nonpayment behavior for our sample of borrowers only. All of these tables have the same structure, which is very similar to that of Table 8.5. Indeed, the specifications in columns (1)–(4) are the same as in Table 8.5. These specifications are informative about the importance of characteristics and choices known ex ante (i.e., when lenders decide how much to lend to students). It is also useful to consider the extent to which ex post borrowing and earnings levels affect repayment/nonpayment outcomes conditional on these other factors, as well as the extent to which background, college major, and institutional characteristics affect repayment/nonpayment through borrowing and earnings levels. To explore these issues, column (5) adds measures of earnings in 1997, earnings in 2002, and the total amount borrowed for undergraduate schooling (all in $000s) to the background, college major, and institutional characteristics of column (4). Column (6) also includes state fixed effects.

In Table 8.6, we consider the share of undergraduate debt still owed 10 years after graduation. These OLS regressions produce a number of interesting results. First, column (1) shows that, conditional on other background characteristics, the share of debt owed by men was almost 5 percentage points less than the share owed by women. About one-quarter of this difference is explained by choice of college major (see column [2]) and another half by differences in postschool earnings (see column [5] and recall that initial borrowing amounts were the same for men and women as shown in Table 8.5). Most strikingly, the share of debt still owed was 22–27 percentage points higher for blacks than for whites. While this gap is smaller than the unconditional gap in Table 8.3, it is still statistically and economically quite significant. Comparing columns (1)–(5) suggests that very little of this gap is explained by choice of major, institution, loan amounts, or postschool earnings. Hispanics owe a slightly larger share of their debt than do whites; however, half of the effect disappears when accounting for state fixed effects. Accounting for other individual characteristics eliminates the raw differences by SAT/ACT scores in the fraction of debt still owed. We also observe no differences by dependency status or parental income. Students whose mothers graduated or obtained postgraduate degrees owe 4–7 percentage points less as a fraction of their initial loan when compared with students whose mothers never attended college.

Engineering majors reduce their loans more within the first 10 years after graduating, owing 10 percentage points less as a share of their initial loan (compared with "other" majors). Column (5) in Table 8.6 suggests that this is not explained by differences in borrowing or post-school earnings.

Accounting for earnings and borrowing levels (and state fixed effects), social science and humanities majors appear to owe about 8 percentage points more (than "other" majors) as a share of their original loan amounts. Institutional characteristics do not play an important role in determining repayment rates after accounting for loan amounts and postschool earnings.

As might be expected, both earnings and loan levels are important determinants of the share of debt repaid. Students with higher earnings in 1997 had repaid a greater fraction of their debt (roughly 1.2 percentage points for every $10,000 in earnings), while those with higher student debt levels had repaid a lower fraction (roughly 1.3 percentage points for every additional $1,000 in debt). It is also worth noting that the R-squared values (reported at the bottom of the table) suggest that debt levels and postschool earnings account for about 7 percent of the variation in the share of debt owed, as much as individual background characteristics, college major, and institutional characteristics combined (compare columns [4] and [5]).

We now turn to measures of nonpayment. Tables 8.7 and 8.8 show average marginal effects from probit specifications for default and our broader measure of nonpayment that also includes deferment/forbearance. There is considerable agreement for both of these outcomes, so we discuss them together. Both blacks and Asians have significantly higher default and nonpayment rates than whites (differences are about 6–9 percentage points), with slightly greater differences observed for the broader measure of nonpayment.[14] Default/nonpayment rates are quite similar for whites and Hispanics. The estimated effects of race/ethnicity are similar across all specifications, suggesting that racial and ethnic differences in default and nonpayment rates are not driven by differences in choice of major or institution, student debt levels, or even postschool earnings realizations. Parental income for dependent students reduces default and nonpayment, but the effects are small in magnitude (e.g., an additional $10,000 in income lowers the probability of default by less than 0.01) and drop by half when accounting for borrowing and postschool income levels. Before accounting for loan amounts and postschool income (column [4]), we see that business majors are significantly less likely to experience default/nonpayment, while history and math/science majors are more likely to experience these problems. Perhaps surprisingly, the estimated effects of college major are not much different after accounting for student borrowing and postschool earnings (compare columns [4] and [5]). None of the institutional characteristics appear to influence default/nonpayment once individual background characteristics are accounted for. Finally,

Table 8.6 Explaining Fraction of Undergraduate Student Debt Still Owed 10 Years after Graduation

Variable	(1)	(2)	(3)	(4)	(5)	(6)
Male	-0.0467**	-0.0341	-0.0471**	-0.0344	-0.0170	-0.0194
	(0.0168)	(0.0177)	(0.0169)	(0.0178)	(0.0189)	(0.0190)
Black	0.2710**	0.2720**	0.2560**	0.2510**	0.2440**	0.2160**
	(0.0329)	(0.0332)	(0.0391)	(0.0393)	(0.0390)	(0.0396)
Hispanic	0.0610	0.0602	0.0681	0.0669	0.0675	0.0347
	(0.0358)	(0.0360)	(0.0366)	(0.0367)	(0.0369)	(0.0411)
Asian	0.0697	0.0621	0.0659	0.0598	0.0616	0.1070
	(0.0547)	(0.0546)	(0.0555)	(0.0554)	(0.0594)	(0.0615)
SAT/ACT Q2	-0.0000	0.0013	0.0017	0.0032	0.0088	0.0056
	(0.0225)	(0.0225)	(0.0228)	(0.0228)	(0.0236)	(0.0236)
SAT/ACT Q3	0.0046	0.0112	0.0056	0.0129	0.0179	0.0235
	(0.0233)	(0.0238)	(0.0238)	(0.0242)	(0.0249)	(0.0252)
SAT/ACT Q4	0.0143	0.0187	0.0093	0.0146	0.0228	0.0289
	(0.0252)	(0.0260)	(0.0259)	(0.0266)	(0.0272)	(0.0276)
Mother some college	-0.0556**	-0.0573**	-0.0557**	-0.0573**	-0.0449**	-0.0467**
	(0.0197)	(0.0197)	(0.0199)	(0.0199)	(0.0204)	(0.0205)
Mother BA+	-0.0596**	-0.0659**	-0.0655**	-0.0724**	-0.0550**	-0.0616**
	(0.0201)	(0.0202)	(0.0204)	(0.0205)	(0.0210)	(0.0213)
Dependent	-0.0073	-0.0079	-0.0129	-0.0132	-0.0190	-0.0094
	(0.0221)	(0.0223)	(0.0224)	(0.0226)	(0.0230)	(0.0237)
Parental income × dependent	0.0002	0.0002	0.0002	0.0001	0.0004	0.0004
	(0.0003)	(0.0003)	(0.0003)	(0.0003)	(0.0003)	(0.0003)

257

	(1)	(2)	(3)	(4)
Business	-0.0475 (0.0314)	-0.0488 (0.0317)	-0.0199 (0.0321)	-0.0200 (0.0320)
Education	-0.0333 (0.0304)	-0.0356 (0.0306)	-0.0437 (0.0317)	-0.0411 (0.0320)
Engineering	-0.1040** (0.0359)	-0.1090** (0.0365)	-0.0856** (0.0375)	-0.0896** (0.0378)
Health	-0.0127 (0.0363)	-0.0167 (0.0365)	-0.0040 (0.0376)	-0.0073 (0.0380)
Public affairs	-0.0368 (0.0504)	-0.0404 (0.0507)	-0.0165 (0.0507)	0.0022 (0.0509)
Biology	0.0052 (0.0402)	0.0036 (0.0407)	-0.0225 (0.0407)	-0.0502 (0.0420)
Math/science	-0.0259 (0.0380)	-0.0254 (0.0387)	-0.0189 (0.0403)	-0.0589 (0.0409)
Social science	0.0390 (0.0336)	0.0397 (0.0340)	0.0577 (0.0345)	0.0783** (0.0351)
History	0.0216 (0.0606)	0.0119 (0.0607)	0.0186 (0.0604)	0.0236 (0.0610)
Humanities	0.0559 (0.0336)	0.0600 (0.0342)	0.0742** (0.0352)	0.0826** (0.0353)
Psychology	0.0482 (0.0484)	0.0494 (0.0486)	0.0666 (0.0512)	0.0610 (0.0514)
Private for-profit	-0.0411 (0.0781)	-0.0491 (0.0780)	-0.0832 (0.0888)	-0.0656 (0.0890)

(continued)

Table 8.6 (continued)

Variable	(1)	(2)	(3)	(4)	(5)	(6)
Private nonprofit			0.0520**	0.0474**	−0.0000	0.0044
			(0.0178)	(0.0178)	(0.0187)	(0.0197)
HBCU			0.0416	0.0611	0.0488	0.0409
			(0.0649)	(0.0653)	(0.0665)	(0.0686)
Competitive			−0.0115	−0.0090	0.0111	−0.0126
			(0.0320)	(0.0322)	(0.0327)	(0.0344)
Noncompetitive			−0.0046	−0.0003	0.0203	−0.0118
			(0.0350)	(0.0353)	(0.0359)	(0.0378)
1997 earnings					−0.0012**	−0.0011**
($000s)					(0.0005)	(0.0005)
2002 earnings					−0.0004	−0.0004
($000s)					(0.0003)	(0.0003)
UG loan amount					0.0130**	0.0133**
($000s)					(0.0012)	(0.0012)
State fixed effects	No	No	No	No	No	Yes
N	1,850	1,850	1,820	1,820	1,610	1,610
R^2	0.0507	0.0653	0.0562	0.0717	0.1410	0.1910

NOTE: *$p < 0.10$; **$p < 0.05$; ***$p < 0.01$. The table shows coefficient estimates based on OLS regressions for the fraction of student loan debt still owed in 2003. Standard errors are in parentheses.

SOURCE: Authors' calculations.

we observe sizable and statistically significant effects of student borrowing levels and postschool earnings. An extra $10,000 in earnings in 2002 is associated with a roughly 0.8 (1.2) percentage-point drop in the probability of default (nonpayment), while an additional $1,000 in student loans increases the likelihood of default (nonpayment) by 0.3 (0.4) percentage points.

Finally, we consider the extent to which these factors affect the share of undergraduate debt on which borrowers have defaulted or are not currently paying (10 years after graduating). Tables 8.9 and 8.10 show results from OLS regressions for these two dependent variables. Here, we find that compared with whites, blacks default on 11–13 percent more of their debt and are in nonpayment on about 13–16 percent more of their debt. Despite similarly high default and nonpayment rates for Asians and blacks (Tables 8.7 and 8.8), Asians neither default on nor are in nonpayment on a larger fraction of their debts relative to whites and Hispanics. These findings suggest that blacks enter nonpayment relatively early in the repayment process, while Asians enter relatively late after much of their debt has been repaid. The effects of race/ethnicity on the share of debts in default/nonpayment are not driven by major, institution choices, differences in debt levels, or postschool earnings. The final two rows of Table 8.10 suggest that after accounting for earnings and borrowing differences, students from the top SAT/ACT quartile are in nonpayment on a greater fraction of their undergraduate debt (about 4 percentage points more) than all other achievement groups. Other individual/family characteristics have little impact on the fraction of debt in default/nonpayment. Choice of college major also appears to have only minor (and generally statistically insignificant at the 0.05 level) effects on the share of debt in default/nonpayment; however, the estimates in the final two columns suggest that health majors default on a significantly smaller fraction, while humanities majors are in nonpayment on a significantly higher fraction. Institutional control and college selectivity are unrelated to the share of debts in default/nonpayment; however, black borrowers attending HBCUs appear to stop paying and default on a significantly lower fraction of their debt than otherwise similar black borrowers who attend non-HBCUs. As with the probability of default and nonpayment, higher earnings reduce the share of debt on which individuals default or stop paying, while higher debt levels increase the share. Contrary to the case with default and nonpayment,

Table 8.7 Explaining Default 10 Years after Graduation

Variable	(1)	(2)	(3)	(4)	(5)	(6)
Male	−0.0023	−0.0058	−0.0058	−0.0089	−0.0001	0.0005
	(0.0118)	(0.0124)	(0.0119)	(0.0125)	(0.0137)	(0.0137)
Black	0.0733**	0.0687**	0.0804**	0.0732**	0.0665**	0.0554**
	(0.0190)	(0.0189)	(0.0219)	(0.0217)	(0.0223)	(0.0222)
Hispanic	0.0194	0.0184	0.0216	0.0191	0.0317	0.0267
	(0.0232)	(0.0232)	(0.0232)	(0.0232)	(0.0232)	(0.0233)
Asian	0.0709**	0.0704**	0.0750**	0.0745**	0.0734**	0.0718**
	(0.0293)	(0.0292)	(0.0295)	(0.0292)	(0.0323)	(0.0326)
SAT/ACT Q2	−0.0040	−0.0125	−0.0071	−0.0163	−0.0071	−0.0087
	(0.0157)	(0.0157)	(0.0159)	(0.0159)	(0.0165)	(0.0165)
SAT/ACT Q3	−0.0079	−0.0146	−0.0074	−0.0133	−0.0175	−0.0150
	(0.0167)	(0.0169)	(0.0169)	(0.0169)	(0.0180)	(0.0179)
SAT/ACT Q4	0.0185	0.0052	0.0206	0.0073	0.0056	0.0061
	(0.0171)	(0.0175)	(0.0173)	(0.0176)	(0.0184)	(0.0184)
Mother some college	0.0104	0.0119	0.0126	0.0143	0.0177	0.0225
	(0.0139)	(0.0138)	(0.0139)	(0.0138)	(0.0142)	(0.0142)
Mother BA+	0.0182	0.0149	0.0180	0.0139	0.0064	0.0029
	(0.0140)	(0.0138)	(0.0142)	(0.0141)	(0.0151)	(0.0151)
Dependent	−0.0040	−0.0132	−0.0012	−0.0122	−0.0152	−0.0170
	(0.0182)	(0.0185)	(0.0184)	(0.0186)	(0.0191)	(0.0191)
Parental income × dependent	−0.0010**	−0.0008**	−0.0010**	−0.0008**	−0.0005	−0.0004
	(0.0004)	(0.0004)	(0.0004)	(0.0004)	(0.0004)	(0.0004)

	(1)	(2)	(3)	(4)
Business	−0.0765**	−0.0748**	−0.0831**	−0.0810**
	(0.0281)	(0.0279)	(0.0310)	(0.0310)
Education	−0.0239	−0.0240	−0.0321	−0.0256
	(0.0212)	(0.0210)	(0.0213)	(0.0212)
Engineering	−0.0224	−0.0369	−0.0226	−0.0177
	(0.0257)	(0.0275)	(0.0291)	(0.0289)
Health	−0.0183	−0.0254	−0.0376	−0.0475
	(0.0250)	(0.0253)	(0.0267)	(0.0268)
Public affairs	−0.0127	−0.0137	−0.0168	−0.0171
	(0.0339)	(0.0336)	(0.0328)	(0.0328)
Biology	0.0125	0.0140	0.0062	0.0089
	(0.0249)	(0.0249)	(0.0246)	(0.0245)
Math/science	0.0451**	0.0478**	0.0380	0.0329
	(0.0225)	(0.0225)	(0.0240)	(0.0241)
Social science	−0.0310	−0.0288	−0.0321	−0.0221
	(0.0242)	(0.0240)	(0.0244)	(0.0241)
History	0.0681**	0.0678**	0.0491	0.0501
	(0.0329)	(0.0325)	(0.0329)	(0.0329)
Humanities	−0.0010	−0.0008	−0.0031	0.0008
	(0.0225)	(0.0224)	(0.0228)	(0.0226)
Psychology	0.0001	−0.0016	−0.0673	−0.0657
	(0.0318)	(0.0315)	(0.0430)	(0.0435)
Private for-profit	−0.0110	−0.0156		
	(0.0590)	(0.0607)		

(continued)

Table 8.7 (continued)

Variable	(1)	(2)	(3)	(4)	(5)	(6)
Private nonprofit			0.0085	0.0069	-0.0088	-0.0056
			(0.0125)	(0.0124)	(0.0131)	(0.0133)
HBCU			-0.0331	-0.0281	-0.0099	-0.0049
			(0.0373)	(0.0373)	(0.0371)	(0.0376)
Competitive			0.0158	0.0145	0.0138	0.0117
			(0.0240)	(0.0234)	(0.0251)	(0.0249)
Noncompetitive			0.0167	0.0164	0.0274	0.0181
			(0.0259)	(0.0254)	(0.0268)	(0.0269)
1997 earnings ($000s)					-0.0003	-0.0001
					(0.0004)	(0.0004)
2002 earnings ($000s)					-0.0008**	-0.0008**
					(0.0003)	(0.0003)
UG loan amount ($000s)					0.0027**	0.0028**
					(0.0008)	(0.0008)
Division fixed effects	No	No	No	No	No	Yes
N	1,870	1,870	1,840	1,840	1,610	1,610
Log likelihood	-436.7	-421.4	-426.4	-410.0	-337.9	-328.0

NOTE: *p < 0.10; **p < 0.05; ***p < 0.01. The table shows average marginal effects based on probit specifications for default in 2003.
Standard errors are in parentheses.
SOURCE: Authors' calculations.

earnings in 1997 (a few years after graduation) rather than in 2003 are most important here. This finding is not surprising because most individuals enter default/nonpayment in the first few years after graduation. An extra $10,000 in 1997 earnings reduces the fraction of debt in nonpayment by about 0.4 percentage points, while an additional $1,000 in undergraduate debt reduces this fraction by just over 0.3 percentage points.

SUMMARY OF FINDINGS

Given the large number of specifications we consider for each outcome, it is useful to briefly summarize our findings. Table 8.11 shows the estimates for all five repayment/nonpayment outcomes based on our most general specification (column [6] of Tables 8.6–8.10). To further focus on the factors that matter, only variables that are statistically significant for at least one outcome are included.

Among the individual and family background characteristics, only race is consistently important for all measures of repayment/nonpayment. Ten years after graduation, black borrowers owe 22 percent more on their loans, are 6 (9) percentage points more likely to be in default (nonpayment), have defaulted on 11 percent more loans, and are in nonpayment on roughly 16 percent more of their undergraduate debt compared with white borrowers. These striking differences are largely unaffected by controls for choice of college major, institution, or even student debt levels and postschool earnings. By contrast, the repayment and nonpayment patterns of Hispanics are very similar to those of whites. Asians show high default/nonpayment rates (similar to blacks), but their shares of debt still owed or debt in default/nonpayment are not significantly different from those of whites. This suggests that many Asians who enter default/nonpayment do so after repaying much of their student loan debt. Maternal college attendance is associated with a greater share of debt repaid after 10 years, while dependency status and parental income are largely unimportant for repayment/nonpayment after controlling for other factors.

The B&B data suggest some variation in repayment/nonpayment across college major choices; however, which majors are most "success-

Table 8.8 Explaining Nonpayment (Default, Deferment, or Forbearance) 10 Years after Graduation

Variable	(1)	(2)	(3)	(4)	(5)	(6)
Male	−0.0170	−0.0197	−0.0212	−0.0235	−0.0049	−0.0027
	(0.0139)	(0.0145)	(0.0140)	(0.0146)	(0.0155)	(0.0155)
Black	0.0900**	0.0855**	0.0999**	0.0906**	0.0905**	0.0853**
	(0.0224)	(0.0224)	(0.0259)	(0.0257)	(0.0246)	(0.0247)
Hispanic	0.0070	0.0045	0.0108	0.0070	0.0269	0.0286
	(0.0281)	(0.0281)	(0.0282)	(0.0282)	(0.0266)	(0.0269)
Asian	0.0790**	0.0768**	0.0826**	0.0810**	0.0885**	0.0888**
	(0.0364)	(0.0362)	(0.0368)	(0.0364)	(0.0372)	(0.0377)
SAT/ACT Q2	−0.0178	−0.0249	−0.0210	−0.0287	−0.0257	−0.0265
	(0.0184)	(0.0183)	(0.0187)	(0.0186)	(0.0187)	(0.0187)
SAT/ACT Q3	−0.0150	−0.0189	−0.0157	−0.0188	−0.0191	−0.0182
	(0.0194)	(0.0195)	(0.0196)	(0.0197)	(0.0197)	(0.0197)
SAT/ACT Q4	0.0268	0.0114	0.0257	0.0106	0.0081	0.0062
	(0.0196)	(0.0202)	(0.0200)	(0.0205)	(0.0203)	(0.0202)
Mother some college	−0.0025	−0.0009	−0.0004	0.0017	0.0008	0.0076
	(0.0160)	(0.0160)	(0.0161)	(0.0160)	(0.0159)	(0.0159)
Mother BA+	0.0014	−0.0036	−0.0006	−0.0069	−0.0055	−0.0068
	(0.0164)	(0.0163)	(0.0167)	(0.0166)	(0.0167)	(0.0168)
Dependent	0.0324	0.0256	0.0340	0.0251	0.0126	0.0112
	(0.0210)	(0.0212)	(0.0211)	(0.0213)	(0.0210)	(0.0210)
Parental income × dependent	−0.0014**	−0.0013**	−0.0015**	−0.0013**	−0.0008	−0.0007
	(0.0004)	(0.0004)	(0.0004)	(0.0004)	(0.0004)	(0.0004)

	(1)	(2)	(3)	(4)
Business	−0.0709**	−0.0702**	−0.0522	−0.0507
	(0.0292)	(0.0293)	(0.0294)	(0.0294)
Education	−0.0411	−0.0415	−0.0478	−0.0421
	(0.0254)	(0.0253)	(0.0252)	(0.0252)
Engineering	−0.0315	−0.0480	−0.0262	−0.0211
	(0.0310)	(0.0329)	(0.0349)	(0.0348)
Health	−0.0040	−0.0113	−0.0120	−0.0195
	(0.0285)	(0.0288)	(0.0286)	(0.0287)
Public affairs	−0.0159	−0.0167	−0.0019	−0.0050
	(0.0398)	(0.0397)	(0.0367)	(0.0367)
Biology	0.0073	0.0060	−0.0004	−0.0014
	(0.0304)	(0.0305)	(0.0292)	(0.0293)
Math/science	0.0555**	0.0587**	0.0538	0.0480
	(0.0272)	(0.0273)	(0.0281)	(0.0283)
Social science	−0.0302	−0.0282	−0.0252	−0.0136
	(0.0280)	(0.0279)	(0.0275)	(0.0273)
History	0.0868**	0.0847**	0.0653	0.0658
	(0.0402)	(0.0400)	(0.0382)	(0.0383)
Humanities	0.0141	0.0139	0.0184	0.0231
	(0.0258)	(0.0258)	(0.0254)	(0.0252)
Psychology	0.0416	0.0404	0.0097	0.0120
	(0.0344)	(0.0344)	(0.0363)	(0.0365)
Private for-profit	0.0116	0.0154		
	(0.0620)	(0.0611)		

(continued)

Table 8.8 (continued)

Variable	(1)	(2)	(3)	(4)	(5)	(6)
Private nonprofit			0.0201	0.0167	−0.0036	−0.0000
			(0.0143)	(0.0142)	(0.0144)	(0.0146)
HBCU			−0.0465	−0.0322	−0.0438	−0.0399
			(0.0445)	(0.0442)	(0.0434)	(0.0443)
Competitive			−0.0100	−0.0129	0.0033	−0.0020
			(0.0255)	(0.0251)	(0.0265)	(0.0265)
Noncompetitive			−0.0071	−0.0094	0.0171	0.0043
			(0.0279)	(0.0277)	(0.0286)	(0.0289)
1997 earnings ($000s)					−0.0005	−0.0003
					(0.0005)	(0.0005)
2002 earnings ($000s)					−0.0012**	−0.0012**
					(0.0003)	(0.0003)
Undergrad. loan amount ($000s)					0.0040**	0.0040**
					(0.0009)	(0.0008)
Division fixed effects	No	No	No	No	No	Yes
N	1,870	1,870	1,840	1,840	1,610	1,610
Log likelihood	−555.1	−538.4	−543.4	−525.9	−404.7	−396.1

NOTE: *p < 0.10; **p < 0.05; ***p < 0.01. The table shows average marginal effects based on probit specifications for nonpayment in 2003. Standard errors are in parentheses.
SOURCE: Authors' calculations.

ful" in terms of repayment of debt depends on the measure. Engineering majors owe a significantly smaller share of their debts (than "other" majors) after 10 years, while social science and humanities majors owe a larger share. Humanities majors are also in nonpayment on the greatest share of debt. Default rates are lowest for business majors, whereas health majors default on the lowest fraction of their debts (these are the only significantly different coefficients). In most cases, differences in these repayment measures across majors are modest compared with differences between blacks and whites.

Differences in repayment/nonpayment across the type of institutional control or selectivity are always small and generally statistically insignificant for our sample of 1992–1993 graduates. Among black borrowers, those attending HBCUs tend to be in nonpayment on significantly less debt (roughly 12 percent less); however, other repayment/nonpayment measures show no statistically significant effects of an HBCU. Unfortunately, low sample sizes and correspondingly high standard errors limit the conclusions we can draw from our analysis of HBCUs.

Student debt and postschool income levels are both statistically significant determinants of all measures of repayment and nonpayment, although the estimated effects are modest (e.g., an extra $10,000 in 2002 earnings reduces the probability of nonpayment by 1.2 percentage points and $1,000 in additional student debt raises the probability of nonpayment by 0.4 percentage points). For measures related to the fraction of student debt outstanding, earnings a few years after school are more important than earnings 10 years later when we measure repayment/nonpayment. The opposite is true when considering simple default/nonpayment rates.

SOME GENERAL LESSONS AND CONCLUSIONS

To the extent that government and private lenders care about expected returns on student loans they distribute, we show that analyses of default rates at some arbitrary date offer an incomplete picture for several reasons. First, many borrowers who enter default eventually return to good standing. Second, borrowers enter default at differ-

Table 8.9 Explaining Fraction of Student Loan Debt in Default 10 Years after Graduation

Variable	(1)	(2)	(3)	(4)	(5)	(6)
Male	-0.0107	-0.0105	-0.0117	-0.0124	-0.0060	-0.0058
	(0.0083)	(0.0088)	(0.0084)	(0.0090)	(0.0010)	(0.0102)
Black	0.1060**	0.1050**	0.1300**	0.1290**	0.1160**	0.1080**
	(0.0163)	(0.0165)	(0.0195)	(0.0196)	(0.0205)	(0.0212)
Hispanic	0.0248	0.0249	0.0262	0.0257	0.0297	0.0164
	(0.0177)	(0.0178)	(0.0181)	(0.0182)	(0.0193)	(0.0219)
Asian	0.0069	0.0028	0.0077	0.0039	0.0042	0.0031
	(0.0273)	(0.0273)	(0.0278)	(0.0277)	(0.0315)	(0.0330)
SAT/ACT Q2	0.0069	0.0052	0.0038	0.0018	0.0060	0.0086
	(0.0111)	(0.0112)	(0.0113)	(0.0114)	(0.0125)	(0.0126)
SAT/ACT Q3	0.0026	0.0008	0.0025	0.0004	0.0033	0.0062
	(0.0116)	(0.0118)	(0.0118)	(0.0120)	(0.0132)	(0.0135)
SAT/ACT Q4	0.0213	0.0163	0.0215	0.0157	0.0192	0.0216
	(0.0124)	(0.0129)	(0.0128)	(0.0132)	(0.0142)	(0.0147)
Mother some college	-0.0016	-0.0026	-0.0014	-0.0024	0.0011	0.0009
	(0.0098)	(0.0098)	(0.0099)	(0.0100)	(0.0107)	(0.0110)
Mother BA+	-0.0156	-0.0186	-0.0143	-0.0176	-0.0152	-0.0185
	(0.0100)	(0.0100)	(0.0102)	(0.0102)	(0.0111)	(0.0114)
Dependent	-0.0081	-0.0130	-0.0064	-0.0116	-0.0111	-0.0118
	(0.0110)	(0.0111)	(0.0112)	(0.0113)	(0.0122)	(0.0127)
Parental income	-0.0002	-0.0002	-0.0002	-0.0002	-0.0001	-0.0001
× dependent	(0.0002)	(0.0002)	(0.0002)	(0.0002)	(0.0002)	(0.0002)

Business	-0.0333**		-0.0315**	-0.0266	-0.0235
	(0.0156)		(0.0158)	(0.0169)	(0.0171)
Education	-0.0229		-0.0213	-0.0317	-0.0323
	(0.0150)		(0.0152)	(0.0166)	(0.0171)
Engineering	-0.0328		-0.0297	-0.0210	-0.0159
	(0.0179)		(0.0182)	(0.0198)	(0.0202)
Health	-0.0291		-0.0337	-0.0394**	-0.0424**
	(0.0180)		(0.0181)	(0.0198)	(0.0203)
Public affairs	-0.0115		-0.00849	-0.00620	-0.00579
	(0.0251)		(0.0253)	(0.0268)	(0.0273)
Biology	-0.0155		-0.0147	-0.0214	-0.0199
	(0.0198)		(0.0202)	(0.0214)	(0.0224)
Math/science	0.0226		0.0283	0.0404	0.0375
	(0.0189)		(0.0193)	(0.0213)	(0.0219)
Social science	-0.0162		-0.0128	-0.0133	-0.0081
	(0.0166)		(0.0168)	(0.0182)	(0.0187)
History	0.0208		0.0235	0.0179	0.0103
	(0.0295)		(0.0297)	(0.0312)	(0.0320)
Humanities	0.0269		0.0301	0.0277	0.0305
	(0.0167)		(0.0170)	(0.0185)	(0.0188)
Psychology	-0.0212		-0.0232	-0.0367	-0.0397
	(0.0241)		(0.0242)	(0.0271)	(0.0276)
Private for-profit		-0.0208	-0.0272	-0.0420	-0.0310
		(0.0382)	(0.0381)	(0.0456)	(0.0463)

(continued)

Table 8.9 (continued)

Variable	(1)	(2)	(3)	(4)	(5)	(6)
Private nonprofit			−0.0038	−0.0057	−0.0200**	−0.0117
			(0.0089)	(0.0089)	(0.0098)	(0.0105)
HBCU			−0.0805**	−0.0803**	−0.0644	−0.0604
			(0.0322)	(0.0324)	(0.0349)	(0.0366)
Competitive			0.0187	0.0197	0.0214	0.0120
			(0.0160)	(0.0161)	(0.0173)	(0.0185)
Noncompetitive			0.0079	0.0098	0.0130	−0.0050
			(0.0174)	(0.0176)	(0.0190)	(0.0203)
1997 earnings ($000s)					−0.0006**	−0.0005
					(0.0003)	(0.0003)
2002 earnings ($000s)					−0.0001	−0.0001
					(0.0001)	(0.0001)
Undergrad. loan amount ($000s)					0.0026**	0.0029**
					(0.0006)	(0.0007)
State fixed effects	No	No	No	No	No	Yes
N	1,870	1,870	1,840	1,840	1,630	1,630
R^2	0.0302	0.0434	0.0341	0.0483	0.0634	0.0911

NOTE: *$p < 0.10$; **$p < 0.05$; ***$p < 0.01$. The table shows coefficient estimates based on OLS regressions for the fraction of student loan debt in default in 2003. Standard errors are in parentheses.
SOURCE: Authors' calculations.

ent times. Total discounted payments are much lower from borrowers who default (without reentering repayment) early relative to late in their repayment period. Third, other forms of nonpayment are also important, especially during early years. For example, deferment and forbearance are more common than default 5 years after entering repayment. Even if borrowers eventually repay their loans, pushing payments years into the future can be costly to lenders, especially if interest is forgiven.

Differences between default rates and other measures of nonpayment can be sizable. For example, our results suggest that modest black-white differences in default understate much larger differences in expected losses when measured by the fraction of initial debt still owed or in default after 10 years. The opposite is true comparing Asians and whites. Default and nonpayment rates are high for Asians 10 years into repayment, but the fraction of debt repaid within 10 years and the fraction in default are not statistically higher than corresponding rates for whites. Although blacks and Asians default at similar rates, blacks stop paying their loans early while Asians enter default relatively late.

Not surprisingly, borrowers are less likely to experience repayment problems when they have low debt levels or high postschool earnings. These effects are robust and important. As a ballpark figure for all repayment/nonpayment measures, an additional $1,000 in debt can be roughly offset by an additional $10,000 in income. For example, an additional $1,000 in student debt increases the share of debt in nonpayment by 0.3 percentage points, while an extra $10,000 in earnings 9 years after graduation reduces this share by 0.4 percentage points.

Given the importance of postschool earnings for repayment, it is natural to expect that differences in average earnings levels across demographic groups or college majors would translate into corresponding differences in repayment/nonpayment rates—but this is not always the case. Despite substantial differences in postschool earnings by race, gender, and academic aptitude, differences in student loan repayment/ nonpayment across these demographic characteristics are, at best, modest for all except race. And, while blacks have significantly higher nonpayment rates than whites, the gaps are not explained by differences in postschool earnings, nor are they explained by choice of major, type of institution, or student debt levels. Differences in postschool earnings (and debt) also explain less than half of the variation in repayment/nonpayment across college majors. We estimate little difference

Table 8.10 Explaining Fraction of Student Loan Debt in Nonpayment 10 Years after Graduation

Variable	(1)	(2)	(3)	(4)	(5)	(6)
Male	-0.0191	-0.0163	-0.0196	-0.0180	-0.0148	-0.0140
	(0.0132)	(0.0139)	(0.0134)	(0.0142)	(0.0137)	(0.0139)
Black	0.1340**	0.1350**	0.1590**	0.1560**	0.1590**	0.1580**
	(0.0259)	(0.0262)	(0.0311)	(0.0313)	(0.0282)	(0.0290)
Hispanic	0.0091	0.0111	0.0109	0.0121	0.0244	0.0214
	(0.0282)	(0.0283)	(0.0289)	(0.0290)	(0.0265)	(0.0300)
Asian	-0.0033	-0.0100	-0.0006	-0.0067	0.0033	0.0083
	(0.0434)	(0.0434)	(0.0443)	(0.0443)	(0.0432)	(0.0453)
SAT/ACT Q2	-0.0184	-0.0190	-0.0197	-0.0207	-0.0052	0.0017
	(0.0177)	(0.0178)	(0.0181)	(0.0181)	(0.0171)	(0.0173)
SAT/ACT Q3	-0.0177	-0.0178	-0.0161	-0.0169	0.0028	0.0023
	(0.0184)	(0.0188)	(0.0189)	(0.0192)	(0.0181)	(0.0185)
SAT/ACT Q4	0.0266	0.0206	0.0275	0.0204	0.0394**	0.0411**
	(0.0198)	(0.0205)	(0.0204)	(0.0211)	(0.0196)	(0.0202)
Mother some college	-0.0061	-0.0089	-0.0061	-0.0090	-0.0152	-0.0140
	(0.0156)	(0.0156)	(0.0158)	(0.0158)	(0.0148)	(0.0151)
Mother BA+	-0.0222	-0.0267	-0.0211	-0.0263	-0.0157	-0.0132
	(0.0159)	(0.0159)	(0.0162)	(0.0162)	(0.0152)	(0.0156)
Dependent	-0.0014	-0.0054	0.0001	-0.0041	0.0019	-0.0015
	(0.0174)	(0.0177)	(0.0178)	(0.0180)	(0.0167)	(0.0174)
Parental income × dependent	-0.0002	-0.0002	-0.0002	-0.0002	-0.0001	0.0000
	(0.0003)	(0.0003)	(0.0003)	(0.0003)	(0.0002)	(0.0002)

	(1)	(2)	(3)	(4)
Business	−0.0358	−0.0345	−0.0112	−0.0101
	(0.0248)	(0.0252)	(0.0232)	(0.0235)
Education	−0.0371	−0.0363	−0.0361	−0.0424
	(0.0239)	(0.0242)	(0.0228)	(0.0234)
Engineering	−0.0300	−0.0258	−0.0171	−0.0084
	(0.0284)	(0.0291)	(0.0272)	(0.0277)
Health	0.0150	0.0100	−0.0216	−0.0266
	(0.0286)	(0.0290)	(0.0272)	(0.0279)
Public affairs	0.0062	0.0066	0.0328	0.0233
	(0.0399)	(0.0404)	(0.0367)	(0.0374)
Biology	−0.0255	−0.0260	−0.0275	−0.0280
	(0.0315)	(0.0323)	(0.0294)	(0.0307)
Math/science	0.0099	0.0152	0.0413	0.0330
	(0.0301)	(0.0308)	(0.0292)	(0.0300)
Social science	−0.0098	−0.0056	0.0062	0.0078
	(0.0264)	(0.0269)	(0.0249)	(0.0256)
History	0.0444	0.0451	0.0486	0.0359
	(0.0470)	(0.0474)	(0.0429)	(0.0438)
Humanities	0.0678**	0.0724**	0.0853**	0.0809**
	(0.0266)	(0.0271)	(0.0254)	(0.0258)
Psychology	0.0058	0.0038	0.0110	−0.0002
	(0.0384)	(0.0387)	(0.0372)	(0.0378)
Private for-profit	−0.0337	−0.0420	−0.0733	−0.0590
	(0.0609)	(0.0609)	(0.0625)	(0.0635)

(continued)

Table 8.10 (continued)

Private nonprofit			0.0091	0.0064	−0.0140	−0.0006
			(0.0141)	(0.0142)	(0.0135)	(0.0145)
HBCU			−0.0864	−0.0758	−0.1270**	−0.1170**
			(0.0513)	(0.0517)	(0.0479)	(0.0501)
Competitive			0.0163	0.0167	0.0235	0.0106
			(0.0255)	(0.0257)	(0.0238)	(0.0253)
Noncompetitive			0.0197	0.0200	0.0193	−0.00482
			(0.0278)	(0.0281)	(0.0261)	(0.0278)
1997 earnings ($000s)					−0.0005	−0.0004
					(0.0004)	(0.0004)
2002 earnings ($000s)					−0.0004**	−0.0004**
					(0.0002)	(0.0002)
Undergrad. loan amount ($000s)					0.0033**	0.0034**
					(0.0009)	(0.0009)
State controls	No	No	No	No	No	Yes
N	1,870	1,870	1,840	1,840	1,630	1,630
R^2	0.0228	0.0355	0.0241	0.0368	0.0655	0.0960

NOTE: $*p < 0.10$; $**p < 0.05$; $***p < 0.01$. The table shows coefficient estimates based on OLS regressions for the fraction of student loan debt in default in 2003. Standard errors are in parentheses.
SOURCE: Authors' calculations.

in repayment/nonpayment across different types of institutions attended by students.

Our findings raise a number of important questions. First, what explains the poor repayment performance for black borrowers conditional on their postschool income, debt, and other demographic characteristics? Recent research by Lochner, Stinebrickner, and Suleymanoglu (2013) suggests that parental transfers are an important determinant of student loan repayment for Canadian borrowers with low postschool earnings. Given relatively low wealth levels among U.S. blacks (Barsky et al. 2002; Oliver and Shapiro 1997), it is likely that differences in parental support at least partially explain their high nonpayment rates. This issue certainly merits greater attention.

Second, what explains the large differences in national cohort rates by institution type (e.g., two- vs. four-year or public vs. private schools)? Official two-year cohort default rates for the 2010 cohort are more than twice as high at four-year for-profit schools as they are at four-year public or private not-for-profit schools (13.6 percent versus 6.0 percent and 5.1 percent, respectively). Yet, our results based on individual-level data suggest little difference in repayment patterns across institution types for college graduates. The discrepancy between our findings and official default rates can almost certainly be traced to much higher dropout rates at for-profit schools than at public or private not-for-profit schools (Deming, Goldin, and Katz 2012) and much higher default rates for dropouts (Gross et al. 2009). In this case, the default problem at private for-profit schools may simply be a symptom of an underlying dropout problem. More generally, it is important to remember that our repayment/nonpayment patterns are based on a sample of baccalaureate degree recipients, and that some of these relationships might differ for borrowers without a four-year degree.

Third, with so many important changes in the labor market and higher education sector over the past few decades, how different would things look for today's graduates? Recent evidence by Lochner, Stinebrickner, and Suleymanoglu (2013) suggests that the role of postschool income may have become more important for recent students, consistent with increased government attention to repayment enforcement. The increasing importance of college major as a determinant of earnings (Gemici and Wiswall 2011) suggests that greater differences in repayment across majors for more recent cohorts might also be expected, but

Table 8.11 Summary of Results from Specification (6) for All Repayment/Nonpayment Outcomes

Variable	Share of undergrad debt still owed	Fraction in default	Fraction not paying	Default × share of debt still owed	Not paying × share of debt still owed
Black	0.2160**	0.0554**	0.0853**	0.1080**	0.1580**
	(0.0396)	(0.0222)	(0.0247)	(0.0212)	(0.0290)
Asian	0.1070	0.0718**	0.0888**	0.0031	0.0083
	(0.0615)	(0.0326)	(0.0377)	(0.0330)	(0.0453)
SAT/ACT Q4	0.0289	0.0061	0.0062	0.0216	0.0411**
	(0.0276)	(0.0184)	(0.0202)	(0.0147)	(0.0202)
Mother some college	−0.0467**	0.0225	0.0076	0.0009	−0.0140
	(0.0205)	(0.0142)	(0.0159)	(0.0110)	(0.0151)
Mother BA+	−0.0616**	0.0029	−0.0068	−0.0185	−0.0132
	(0.0213)	(0.0151)	(0.0168)	(0.0114)	(0.0156)
Business	−0.0200	−0.0810**	−0.0507	−0.0235	−0.0101
	(0.0320)	(0.0310)	(0.0294)	(0.0171)	(0.0235)
Engineering	−0.0896**	−0.0177	−0.0211	−0.0159	−0.0084
	(0.0378)	(0.0289)	(0.0348)	(0.0202)	(0.0277)
Health	−0.0073	−0.0475	−0.0195	−0.0424**	−0.0266
	(0.0380)	(0.0268)	(0.0287)	(0.0203)	(0.0279)
Social science	0.0783**	−0.0221	−0.0136	−0.0081	0.0078
	(0.0351)	(0.0241)	(0.0273)	(0.0187)	(0.0256)
Humanities	0.0826**	0.0008	0.0231	0.0305	0.0809**
	(0.0353)	(0.0226)	(0.0252)	(0.0188)	(0.0258)

HBCU	0.0409	−0.0049	−0.0399	−0.0604	−0.1170**
	(0.0686)	(0.0376)	(0.0443)	(0.0366)	(0.0501)
1997 earnings ($000s)	−0.0011**	−0.0001	−0.0003	−0.0005	−0.0004
	(0.0005)	(0.0004)	(0.0005)	(0.0003)	(0.0004)
2003 earnings ($000s)	−0.0004	−0.0008**	−0.0012**	−0.0001	−0.0004**
	(0.0003)	(0.0003)	(0.0003)	(0.0001)	(0.0002)
Undergrad. loan amount	0.0133**	0.0028**	0.0039**	0.0029**	0.0034**
($000s)	(0.0012)	(0.0008)	(0.0008)	(0.0007)	(0.0009)

NOTE: **$p < 0.05$. The table shows estimated coefficients/average marginal effects from specification (6) of Tables 8.6–8.10 if the estimate is statistically significant for any repayment or nonpayment outcome. Standard errors are in parentheses.
SOURCE: Authors' calculations.

this is far from certain given the modest role of earnings differences in explaining variation in repayment/nonpayment by college major in our sample. It is even more difficult to predict how other results might change. Data on more recent cohorts are obviously needed to better inform current policy debates.

We conclude by arguing that future research and policy discussions of student loan repayment need to move beyond an exclusive focus on default rates. Other forms of nonpayment are common, and the actual timing of default matters as much as whether default occurs.

Notes

We thank Brian Greaney for his excellent research assistance and Brian Jacob and other participants at the Conference on Student Loans for their comments. We would also like to thank the Institute of Education and Sciences at the U.S Department of Education for providing us access to the data. The research results and conclusions are ours and do not necessarily reflect the views of the U.S. Department of Education. This paper has been screened to ensure that no confidential data are revealed. The views expressed are those of the individual authors and do not necessarily reflect official positions of the Federal Reserve Bank of St. Louis, the Federal Reserve System, or the Board of Governors.

1. See College Board (2012) for these and related statistics.
2. See Schwartz and Finnie (2002) and Lochner, Stinebrickner, and Suleymanoglu (2013) for empirical analyses of student loan repayment, delinquency, and default in Canada.
3. Expected returns on income-contingent lending programs, such as the new Pay As You Earn student loan repayment program in the United States, can lead to full or partial loan forgiveness for borrowers experiencing low income levels for extended periods. This clearly lowers the expected returns on the loans. Furthermore, the timing of payments can affect expected returns if lenders have discount rates that are different from the nominal interest rates charged on the loans.
4. All averages in the tables in the chapter use the B&B panel weights to account for the sampling scheme of the original National Postsecondary Student Aid Study survey and attrition in subsequent surveys.
5. See Gross et al. (2009) for a survey of the literature on student loan default.
6. To understand the implications of these restrictions, we performed an analogous analysis without imposing the restrictions on months of postgraduate study and degrees. In regressions using this broader sample (analogous to those used in Tables 8.5–8.10), we also included indicator variables for the following graduate degrees: master's level, professional degree, and doctoral degree. These results are qualitatively similar to those reported in the text, with a few exceptions specifically noted below.

7. These quartiles are based on the test score distributions for the full population rather than our restricted sample.

8. Our repayment measures are based on individual loan records from the National Student Loan Data System, accessed in both 1998 and 2003. Loan status (for both dates) is determined from the most recent available status date at the time records were accessed. Our measures of default include borrowers who had defaulted or had expunged their student debt through bankruptcy. Since borrowers may have more than one loan in the system, we cycle through all government student loans in a borrower's records and set the default indicator to one if any of the loans are determined to be in default (or expunged through bankruptcy). Similarly, if any loans are in deferment or forbearance, we set the indicator for deferment/forbearance equal to one.

9. Default is defined as 270 days (9 months) of missed payments (excluding borrowers in formal programs designed to reduce payment, such as deferment or forbearance).

10. Columns (7) and (8) report the sample averages for the shares of unpaid undergraduate loans multiplied by the default and nonpayment indicators, respectively.

11. Throughout the chapter, we refer to results as statistically significant based on a 0.05 significance level.

12. Tobit estimates generally yield similar conclusions about which variables are important and their relative magnitudes/signs.

13. Unfortunately, parental income is unknown for students classified as independent.

14. When we do not exclude borrowers with longer periods of postgraduate studies or graduate degrees from our sample, Asians have default/nonpayment rates similar to those of whites and Hispanics.

Appendix 8A

Supplemental Tables

Table 8A.1 Sample Means for Full Sample and Borrowers Only

Characteristic	Full sample	Borrowers only
Male	0.442	0.444
	(0.013)	(0.010)
Asian	0.025	0.031
	(0.004)	(0.004)
Black	0.067	0.049
	(0.006)	(0.004)
Hispanic	0.060	0.043
	(0.007)	(0.004)
White	0.844	0.873
	(0.010)	(0.007)
Mother no college	0.442	0.369
	(0.013)	(0.009)
Mother some college	0.280	0.263
	(0.012)	(0.009)
Mother BA+	0.278	0.368
	(0.012)	(0.009)
Dependent	0.576	0.671
	(0.013)	(0.009)
Parental income	25.453	41.417
× dependent	(0.856)	(1.151)
SAT/ACT Q1	0.286	0.272
	(0.013)	(0.009)
SAT/ACT Q2	0.282	0.290
	(0.013)	(0.009)
SAT/ACT Q3	0.247	0.259
	(0.012)	(0.009)
SAT/ACT Q4	0.185	0.179
	(0.011)	(0.007)
Business	0.240	0.254
	(0.014)	(0.010)

(continued)

Table 8A.1 (continued)

Education	0.132	0.117
	(0.009)	(0.006)
Engineering	0.073	0.062
	(0.006)	(0.004)
Health	0.067	0.060
	(0.006)	(0.004)
Public affairs	0.038	0.038
	(0.005)	(0.004)
Biology	0.047	0.037
	(0.005)	(0.003)
Math/science	0.054	0.052
	(0.005)	(0.004)
Social science	0.082	0.090
	(0.006)	(0.005)
History	0.018	0.015
	(0.004)	(0.003)
Humanities	0.079	0.087
	(0.006)	(0.005)
Psychology	0.033	0.032
	(0.004)	(0.003)
Private for-profit	0.022	0.016
	(0.005)	(0.003)
Private nonprofit	0.322	0.283
	(0.013)	(0.009)
HBCU	0.029	0.020
	(0.005)	(0.003)
Most competitive	0.063	0.074
	(0.006)	(0.005)
Competitive	0.633	0.649
	(0.013)	(0.009)
Noncompetitive	0.304	0.278
	(0.013)	(0.009)

NOTE: Standard errors are in parentheses.
SOURCE: Authors' calculations.

Table 8A.2 Average Earnings, Undergraduate Borrowing, and Repayment/Nonpayment Measures in 2003 by Individual Characteristics (Sample without Graduate School Attendance/Degree Restrictions)

Characteristic	N	Earnings ($000s)	Total undergrad loan amt. ($000s)	Share of undergrad debt still owed	Fraction in default	Fraction not paying	Default × share of debt still owed	Not paying × share of debt still owed
Full sample	3,790	51.063	9.287	0.233	0.050	0.092	0.029	0.066
		(0.864)	(0.133)	(0.009)	(0.004)	(0.005)	(0.005)	(0.007)
Males	1,620	64.951	9.426	0.206	0.050	0.091	0.029	0.060
		(1.595)	(0.216)	(0.012)	(0.006)	(0.008)	(0.009)	(0.010)
Females	2,170	39.755	9.176	0.254	0.049	0.092	0.029	0.071
		(0.757)	(0.165)	(0.013)	(0.005)	(0.007)	(0.005)	(0.009)
Asians	120	62.395	8.856	0.286	0.050	0.071	0.009	0.033
		(3.150)	(0.604)	(0.063)	(0.020)	(0.023)	(0.006)	(0.017)
Blacks	260	44.910	9.464	0.523	0.098	0.207	0.110	0.243
		(1.861)	(0.394)	(0.045)	(0.019)	(0.026)	(0.036)	(0.044)
Hispanics	230	48.860	7.823	0.198	0.070	0.122	0.017	0.055
		(2.400)	(0.552)	(0.035)	(0.022)	(0.027)	(0.006)	(0.016)
Whites	3,150	51.032	9.356	0.210	0.045	0.082	0.025	0.055
		(0.988)	(0.147)	(0.009)	(0.004)	(0.006)	(0.005)	(0.007)
SAT/ACT Q1	820	42.424	9.565	0.261	0.057	0.107	0.025	0.073
		(1.211)	(0.354)	(0.023)	(0.008)	(0.011)	(0.005)	(0.010)
SAT/ACT Q2	900	49.344	9.129	0.229	0.041	0.067	0.015	0.041
		(1.447)	(0.238)	(0.016)	(0.007)	(0.009)	(0.004)	(0.008)

(continued)

Table 8A.2 (continued)

Characteristic	N	Earnings ($000s)	Total undergrad loan amt. ($000s)	Share of undergrad debt still owed	Fraction in default	Fraction not paying	Default × share of debt still owed	Not paying × share of debt still owed
SAT/ACT Q3	880	56.850	9.132	0.189	0.038	0.082	0.020	0.044
		(2.274)	(0.251)	(0.019)	(0.006)	(0.011)	(0.006)	(0.008)
SAT/ACT Q4	830	57.154	9.486	0.230	0.057	0.106	0.051	0.094
		(1.739)	(0.291)	(0.016)	(0.010)	(0.012)	(0.019)	(0.021)
Mother no college	1,490	50.677	8.732	0.243	0.055	0.089	0.023	0.058
		(1.254)	(0.181)	(0.016)	(0.006)	(0.008)	(0.004)	(0.009)
Mother some college	1,090	48.534	9.226	0.202	0.049	0.095	0.046	0.085
		(1.339)	(0.226)	(0.013)	(0.008)	(0.010)	(0.014)	(0.016)
Mother BA+	1,200	53.796	10.051	0.249	0.043	0.092	0.021	0.060
		(1.891)	(0.283)	(0.017)	(0.006)	(0.010)	(0.007)	(0.010)

NOTE: The table shows sample means based on sample of borrowers without restrictions on graduate school participation/degrees. Standard errors are in parentheses.
SOURCE: Authors' calculations.

References

Barsky, Robert, John Bound, Kerwin Kofi Charles, and Joseph P. Lupton. 2002. "Accounting for the Black-White Wealth Gap: A Nonparametric Approach." *Journal of the American Statistical Association* 97(459): 663–673.

College Board. 2012. *Trends in Student Aid, 2012.* New York: College Board.

Deming, David J., Claudia Goldin, and Lawrence F. Katz. 2012. "The For-Profit Postsecondary School Sector: Nimble Critters or Agile Predators?" *Journal of Economic Perspectives* 26(1): 139–164.

Dynarski, Mark. 1994. "Who Defaults on Student Loans? Findings from the National Postsecondary Student Aid Study." *Economics of Education Review* 13(1): 55–68.

Flint, Thomas A. 1997. "Predicting Student Loan Defaults." *Journal of Higher Education* 68(3): 322–354.

Gemici, Ahu, and Matthew Wiswall. 2011. "Evolution of Gender Differences in Post-Secondary Human Capital Investments: College Majors." IESP Working Paper No. 03-11. New York: Institute for Education and Social Policy, New York University.

Gross, Jacob P. K., Osman Cekic, Don Hossler, and Nick Hillman. 2009. "What Matters in Student Loan Default: A Review of the Research Literature." *Journal of Student Financial Aid* 39(1): 19–29.

Lochner, Lance, Todd Stinebrickner, and Utku Suleymanoglu. 2013. "The Importance of Financial Resources for Student Loan Repayment." CIBC Working Paper No. 2013-7. Ontario, Canada: Western Social Science.

Oliver, Melvin L., and Thomas M. Shapiro. 1997. *Black Wealth/White Wealth: A New Perspective on Racial Inequality.* New York: Routledge.

Schwartz, S., and Ross Finnie. 2002. "Student Loans in Canada: An Analysis of Borrowing and Repayment." *Economics of Education Review* 21(5): 497–512.

Volkwein, J. Fredericks, Bruce P. Szelest, Alberto F. Cabrera, and Michelle R. Napierski-Prancl. 1998. "Factors Associated with Student Loan Default among Different Racial and Ethnic Groups." *Journal of Higher Education* 69(2): 206–237.

9

The Effects of Student Loans on Long-Term Household Financial Stability

Dora Gicheva
University of North Carolina at Greensboro

Jeffrey Thompson
Federal Reserve Board of Governors

Student debt has been growing at a pace considerably faster than inflation, but so have the costs of and returns to postsecondary education. For full-time undergraduate students in four-year colleges and universities, the average cost, in 2012 dollars, of published tuition, fees, room and board net of grant aid and tax benefits has increased from $7,620 to $11,630 for public institutions and from $17,470 to $22,830 for private nonprofit institutions between the 1992–1993 and 2011–2012 academic years (College Board 2012a). Since many students use loans to supplement grant aid, it is not surprising that the average inflation-adjusted amount of federal loans per full-time-equivalent (FTE) undergraduate student has increased by over $3,000 (in 2012 dollars) during the same period (College Board 2012b). Combined with an increase from 9 million to 14 million FTE undergraduate students and growth in graduate enrollment and costs, these trends have amounted to remarkable growth in aggregate student borrowing, even without accounting for the private loan industry and the private for-profit education sector. At the same time, there is evidence that the return to college and graduate degrees has been increasing as well during the same period, although it is more difficult to quantify the increase because college and high school graduates may have different inherent abilities regardless of educational attainment (Willis and Rosen 1979). Using March Current Population Survey (CPS) data, Avery and Turner (2012) estimate that the discounted value of the difference in mean earnings of college graduates and high school graduates, accounting for tuition payments and a four-year delay in labor market entry, has increased by more than $100,000 in 2009 dollars over the period above. It is difficult to disentangle all of these concurrent trends and to determine based on aggregate statistics alone whether the current debt levels are excessively high or still below the efficient level.

By examining how student borrowers fare financially after graduation, we attempt to further the existing knowledge of the costs associated with education debt and the manageability of the typical debt burden. We compare the financial stability of individuals who have borrowed for education to similar individuals who have not. We show unintended consequences of student debt of which borrowers and policymakers should be mindful: impaired access to financial markets after graduation and implied financial hardship for many borrowers. Our results, however, should be interpreted with caution because the optimal level of student debt and its repercussions vary considerably with individual ability, family background, and other characteristics. Furthermore, it is difficult to define a counterfactual outcome for a student borrower because this type of debt may have a pronounced positive impact on one's lifetime earnings stream or occupational attainment.

We explore further the manageability of student debt for individuals who do not complete a bachelor's degree, for whom the net benefit of education loans is expected to be considerably lower without the boost in earnings associated with a college degree. Wei and Horn (2013) compare two cohorts of respondents from the Beginning Postsecondary Survey 1995–1996 and 2003–2004 six years postcollege entry. They show a steady noncompletion rate but a pronounced increase in the student debt-to-income ratio of individuals in the sample without a degree, from 24 to 35 percent, as well as a substantial fraction of noncompleters with debt exceeding annual income. Our study provides more information about the financial hardship faced by this segment of borrowers.

We show that, keeping education constant, more student debt is associated with a higher probability of being credit constrained and a greater likelihood of declaring bankruptcy. We find evidence that homeownership rates may also be affected by education loans. Controlling for earnings tends to strengthen these relationships, which is consistent with omitted variable bias combined with positive return to student loans. The relationship between education debt and financial status appears to be related to current economic conditions: it weakens when we control for aggregate economic conditions and consumer bankruptcy rates. Households that hold student debt and include a non-completer tend to be more credit constrained.

Student loans have undisputed value. Many high school graduates are otherwise unable to borrow against future income and would not enroll in college or persist until graduation, owing to credit constraints. Although there is no consensus in the literature about the fraction of high school graduates who face credit constraints when making education decisions, researchers are generally in agreement that the importance of these constraints has been increasing since the 1980s.[1] There is further evidence that some students borrow less than the optimal amount and substitute work hours for loans, which can affect academic performance and the probability of dropping out (e.g., Berkner, He, and Cataldi 2002; Stinebrickner and Stinebrickner 2003).

The other side of the coin is overborrowing, which can be defined as borrowing above the efficient amount or beyond what constitutes a manageable level of debt given the obtained education. Inefficiently high borrowing can occur when students overestimate the expected returns to education or underestimate the probability of dropping out.[2] Lack of full information combined with the high risk inherent in education investments can lead to financial hardship for many borrowers. Hansen and Rhodes (1988) attempt to quantify the manageable education debt level and find that in the early 1980s in California, only about 4 or 5 percent of college seniors held potentially unmanageable student debt, assuming earnings roughly equal to the average starting salary for a college graduate at the time ($20,000). The debt levels in their sample are subject to considerably less variation than what we currently observe; only 2 percent of the students they analyze accumulated more than $16,000 in debt. Baum and Schwartz (2006) expand the analysis and point out that the manageable loan repayment to income ratio increases with household income and varies by family structure, location, and other demographic characteristics. The median debt level at the time of their study, $20,000, is manageable for a single individual whose income is at least $30,000. However, student loans may be one area where focusing on outliers is no less important than analyzing trends around the median. According to the Federal Reserve Bank of

New York Consumer Credit Panel/Equifax data, while 55.5 percent of borrowers owed $10,000 or less at the end of 2005, 17.7 percent had a balance of $25,000 or more, with 3 percent owing above $75,000 (Lee 2013). It is of course likely that many borrowers from the right tail of the debt distribution are also found in the right tail of the income distribution, for example, individuals who borrowed large amounts to complete professional degree programs with large expected returns.

Our chapter adds to the existing literature that examines implications of student debt beyond increased educational attainment. Previous studies have analyzed the relationship between school loans and the decision to attend graduate school (Fox 1992; Schapiro, O'Malley, and Litten 1991; Weiler 1994), the choice of specialty by medical school graduates (e.g., Bazzoli 1985; Colquitt et al. 1996; Hauer et al. 2008; and Woodworth, Chang, and Helmer 2000, among others), law school graduates' choice to enter public sector law (Field 2009; Kornhauser and Revesz 1995) and other postgraduation career decisions (Minnicozzi 2005; Rothstein and Rouse 2011). These studies are conducted in fairly specialized settings or focus on the graduates of one specific institution. Analyses of more inclusive groups of graduates tend to be more descriptive than causal and ignore the endogeneity of student loans and a wide range of omitted variables (e.g., Chiteji 2007; Choy and Carroll 2000). Our goal is to study a more nationally representative sample of households who accrued education debt at different points in time. To at least partially account for the complex relationship between student loans, education, career outcomes, and income, we instrument for the amount borrowed and show results conditional on a rich set of covariates associated with higher labor market earnings. The study extends Gicheva (2013), where a similar instrumental variable approach is used and student debt is linked to lower probability of marriage, and Bricker and Thompson (2013), who find correlation between previously accumulated student debt and the likelihood of experiencing financial distress during the recession of 2009.

CONCEPTUAL FRAMEWORK

Suppose that household i's earnings (in their natural logarithm form) are given by

$$Y_i = f(S_i) + \varepsilon_i,$$

where S is a measure of the respondent and spouse or partner's educational attainment that incorporates all productive components of schooling, such as education quality and highest degree attained. The additional component ε_i accounts for all other random and nonrandom factors that affect earnings. The function $f(s)$ is strictly increasing, which assumes positive returns to education. Educational attainment is a function of the amount of accumulated student debt L:

$$S_i = g(L_i).$$

The sign of $g'(L_i)$ depends on the counterfactual to a dollar of student loans. Under a fixed payment schedule, borrowers make a payment that constitutes a constant fraction of their total debt each period, mL, with m between zero and one. Household i's earnings net of the loan payment are thus $(Y_i - mL_i)$.

Financial distress is experienced when net income falls below a certain threshold, c. The probability P_D of experiencing financial distress is

$$P_D = \Pr\,[\varepsilon_i < c - f(S_i) + mL_i].$$

This probability increases with the amount borrowed L as long as

$$\frac{\mathrm{d}(c - f(S) + mL)}{\mathrm{d}L} = -f'(S)g'(L) + m > 0.$$

Scenario 1: The counterfactual of a dollar of student loans is a dollar in grant aid or a dollar decrease in the tuition price charged by institutions of higher education. Then $g'(L) = 0$, and

$$\frac{d(c - f(S) + mL)}{dL} = m;$$

the probability of experiencing financial distress increases with student loans.

Scenario 2: Student debt is associated with increased educational attainment, so that $g'(L) \geq 0$. Then

$$\frac{d(c - f(S) + mL)}{dL} = -f'(S)g'(L) + m,$$

which may be positive or negative. Holding constant S_i, however,

$$\frac{d(c - f(S) + mL)}{dL}\bigg|_{S=\bar{S}} = m \geq -f'(S)g'(L) + m.$$

The relationship between financial distress and student loans is stronger and positive when we condition on educational attainment.[3]

For individuals who obtain some postsecondary education but do not complete a degree, let

$$S_i = \tilde{g}(L_i),$$

with $0 \leq \tilde{g}'(L_i) \leq g'(L_i)$: educational attainment does not increase as much with the amount borrowed as it does for individuals who attain a degree. Then under Scenario 1, the relationship between financial distress and student borrowing would be similar for completers and noncompleters, but under Scenario 2, the probability of financial distress increases faster with student loans for noncompleters. The difference between the two groups should narrow once we condition on the available human capital measures. We explore these relationships empirically in the rest of the chapter.

EMPIRICAL METHODOLOGY

Specification

We estimate linear probability models in which the dependent variable is a binary measure of household financial stability. The observed relationship between student debt and the outcomes of interest is likely to be confounded by unobserved heterogeneity, even when all available human capital and occupation controls are included. By their nature, student loans are correlated with the type of education obtained and with academic success (Stinebrickner and Stinebrickner 2003)—variables we do not observe—which may in turn affect factors such as job stability, starting wages, and career wage growth, as well as other correlates of financial status. To help us avoid some of these issues, we use an instrument for the amount of accumulated student debt that exploits time variations in the size of the federal and private student loan programs.

Our instrument is based on the observed upward trend in student borrowing since the 1970s, when the federal student loan program was in its early stages. The growth in the aggregate level of education debt can be attributed in part to policy changes that should be exogenous to households' financial stability. There have been multiple reauthorizations of the Higher Education Act (HEA) of 1965 that have impacted the amount and types of financial aid available to postsecondary students. The 1992 reauthorization has had the strongest impact on federal loans. The amendment introduced unsubsidized Stafford Loans, increased the annual and aggregate limits for subsidized Stafford Loans, substantially increased the annual and eliminated aggregate PLUS Loan limits, and extended federal loan eligibility to more students from middle- and high-income families. As a result, the total amount of federal student loans, in 2011 dollars, increased from $23 billion to $35.5 billion between the 1992–1993 and 1994–1995 academic years. The share of all federal student aid composed of federal loans increased from 61 to 73 percent over the same period (College Board 2012b). The introduction of non-federal loans in the mid-1990s also played a major role in the growth of aggregate student borrowing. Private debt peaked in 2006–2007, when the total amount of newly borrowed funds accounted for 26 percent of all student borrowing and experienced a sharp decline after 2008. It is more difficult to measure changes in the take-up rate for student loans, but it has likely increased along with the mean and median debt level among borrowers. The College Board (2012b) reports that the number of borrowers under the Stafford Loan program increased from 4.4 million in 1995–1996 to 10.3 million in 2010–2011. Increasing costs of higher education are potentially part of the explanation, as well as policy changes that increase the appeal of loans for certain groups of the population, such as allowing parents to defer repayment on PLUS Loans until six months after the student has left school, changing interest rates, or transitioning toward an online-based FAFSA application.

The instrument we use is constructed as the average amount borrowed per FTE student (including nonborrowers) in constant 2011 dollars, as reported by the College Board (2012b) in the year when a respondent was 17 years old (this is referred to as the cohort year in the rest of the chapter).[4] High school graduates who made their borrowing decisions in years that loans were more widely available and commonly used among one's peers are more likely to borrow or take on larger debt. Our instrument accounts for changes in the take-up of student loans as well as changes in eligibility, so we are able to exploit variations in both. This instrument is used in Gicheva (2013) to examine the impact of student debt on the rate of transitioning into first marriage. Figure 9.1 shows the values used in the estimation, which combine federal and private loans. Policy-induced changes, such as the increase in federal borrowing after the 1992 reauthorization of the HEA or the upsurge in private loans in the early and mid-2000s, are reflected by the trends depicted in Figure 9.1, where in addition to a steady upward trend we observe more pronounced jumps in the expected years.

Since the variation in the instrument is only across cohorts, and the variable exhibits a persistent trend, it is possible that our estimation strategy may pick up similar trends in the outcome variables that are attributable to other factors unrelated to student borrowing. Figure 9.2 plots homeowner rates for two age groups (25–29 and 45–49), the annual unemployment rate for one age group (25–29) and the nonbusiness bankruptcy rate per household in years when respondents were surveyed. The bankruptcy rate fluctuates between less than 1 percent in 1995 and 2007 and 1.3 or 1.4 percent in 1998, 2001, 2004, and 2010. While 40 percent or fewer of younger households own their home, this

Figure 9.1 Average Education Loans per Full-Time Equivalent Student (2011 $)

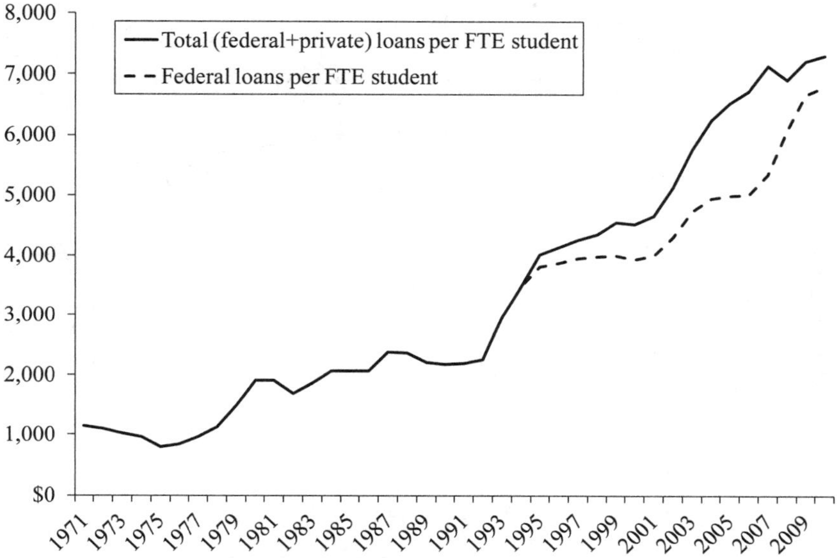

SOURCE: College Board (2012b).

fraction is over 70 percent for the older age group. Homeownership rates increase for 25–29-year-olds between 1995 and 2007, with the most pronounced increase in the late 1990s, and drop between 2007 and 2010. The decline starts earlier for older individuals, and the preceding increase is not as pronounced. Other age groups (not plotted in Figure 9.2) are subject to comparable fluctuations. The unemployment rate fluctuates between 4.7 and 6.1 percent in the first five sampling years and increases sharply in 2010 to 10.9 percent. Overall, the trends in these data do not mirror the sustained upward movement exhibited by student loans, but we nonetheless include the aggregate bankruptcy rate, along with the homeownership rate by five-year age group as controls in the estimation. There may also be spurious correlation in the data between student debt and economic conditions, such as unemployment due to recessions happening for unrelated reasons at the time when education borrowing was on the rise. To account for this we also control for the survey-year unemployment rate specific to the age group (in five-year

Figure 9.2 Aggregate Trends in Homeownership, Bankruptcy, and Unemployment

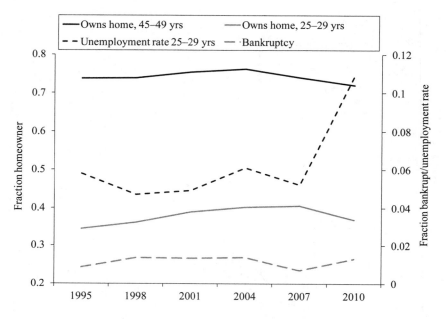

NOTE: The bankruptcy rate is the annual number of nonbusiness bankruptcy filings from the American Bankruptcy Institute divided by total number of U.S. households from the U.S. census.

SOURCE: Data on household homeownership rates are from the U.S. census. The unemployment rate is reported by the Bureau of Labor Statistics using CPS data.

intervals) of the respondent and spouse or partner. All standard errors in the regressions are clustered by year of birth, and all regressions use the standard Survey of Consumer Finances (SCF) weights.

Survey of Consumer Finances Data

We use data from the six waves of the SCF conducted between 1995 and 2010. Several features of the survey make it appropriate for addressing the questions of interest and implementing our empirical approach. The survey collects very detailed information about households' financial assets and liabilities, including full student borrowing histories. This allows us to observe the long-term impact of education-related debt, as many borrowers are interviewed 10 years or more after incurring their debt. The fact that the SCF is a triennial cross-sectional survey lets us observe the financial status of households with student loans during years characterized by differing economic conditions.

As a survey of household finances and wealth, the SCF includes some assets that are broadly shared across the population (bank savings accounts), as well as some that are held more narrowly and are concentrated in the tails of the distribution (direct ownership of bonds). To support estimates of a variety of financial characteristics as well as the overall distribution of wealth, the survey employs a dual-frame sample design.

A national area-probability (AP) sample provides good coverage of widely spread characteristics. The AP sample selects household units with equal probability from primary sampling units that are selected through a multistage selection procedure, which includes stratification by a variety of characteristics, and selection proportional to their population. Because of the concentration of assets and nonrandom survey response by wealth, the SCF also employs a list sample that is developed from statistical records derived from tax returns under an agreement with Statistics of Income.[5] (See Kennickell [2000] for additional details on the SCF list sample.) This list sample consists of households with a high probability of having high net worth.[6]

The SCF joins the observations from the AP and list sample through weighting.[7] The weighting design adjusts each sample separately, using all the useful information that can be brought to bear in creating post-strata. The final weights are adjusted so that the combined sample is nationally representative of the population and assets. These weights are used in all regressions.

The SCF measure of student loans combines all debt accumulated by household members, so we are implicitly making the assumption that a dollar of student loans has the same impact on household financial hardship regardless of whether the debt was incurred by the household head, the head's spouse, or someone else.[8] In our estimation we account for the likely situation in which parents accumulate education loans to finance their children's education by using information on children's ages and the time when the debt was incurred. An additional limitation of the SCF information about student loans is that the year of loan origination is replaced by the year of consolidation for loans that were consolidated.

We focus on three distinct measures of financial hardship: 1) being denied credit, 2) not paying bills on time, and 3) filing bankruptcy in the 10-year period prior to the interview date. We also construct an indicator for homeownership as an additional measure of a household's financial stability.

We restrict the sample to respondents who were born in 1954 or later (or, in cases when a spouse or partner is present, the average year of birth is 1954 or higher), because earlier cohorts completed high school before the federal student loan program took off in the 1970s. We also drop observations with age lower than 29. Most schooling should be completed by this age, and in addition, the age restriction eliminates individuals who were too young to incur consumer debt at the beginning of the 10-year interval covered by the bankruptcy indicator. Furthermore, the excluded age groups tend to have relatively low home-ownership rates.[9] Other covariates that we include in the regressions include demographic characteristics of the survey respondent (gender, race, and a quadratic in age) and indicators for the highest completed education level, presence of college-age children in the primary economic unit (PEU), and disability status.

Summary statistics of these variables, for respondents in the cohorts for 1971 and after in the 1995–2010 surveys, are included in Table 9.1. The different dependent variables we consider in the next section of the chapter are listed at the top. More than one-third—36.5 percent—of households indicate that they were either denied credit, granted less credit than they had applied for initially, or did not apply at all because they feared rejection in the previous five years. Jappelli (1990) and Duca and Rosenthal (1993) find that the SCF questions about credit applications and outcomes provide a useful indicator of households that are credit constrained. Jappelli (1990) finds that the families who believed they would be turned down looked and behaved like the families that had applied for and been denied credit.

Nearly 9 percent of households experienced a spell of late payment (60 days or more) while paying bills at some point in the last five years. Just over 8 percent of households have had a bankruptcy in the last 10 years, and slightly more than 6 in 10 households report owning their

Table 9.1 Summary Statistics

Variable	Mean	Min	Max
Denied credit (or did not apply because feared rejection)	0.365 (0.481)	0	1
Late payment (60 days or more) in last five years	0.085 (0.279)	0	1
Bankrupt in last 10 years	0.083 (0.275)	0	1
Homeowner	0.610 (0.488)	0	1
Female	0.542 (0.498)	0	1
College degree	0.199 (0.399)	0	1
Master's degree	0.062 (0.241)	0	1
Doctorate	0.013 (0.112)	0	1
White	0.684 (0.465)	0	1
Black	0.140 (0.347)	0	1
Hispanic	0.112 (0.315)	0	1
Age	40.564 (7.318)	29	70
Any college-aged kids in primary economic unit (18–24)	0.112 (0.315)	0	1
Disabled (either respondent or spouse/ partner)	0.065 (0.247)	0	1
County per-capita income ("relative" divided by national average)	1.0 (0.3)	0.5	3.0
County unemployment rate	6.031 (2.696)	1.1	16.4
Ln(normal income)	10.967 (0.953)	0	19.536
Ln(predicted wage)	10.493 (1.597	−0.693	13.933

NOTE: Weighted summary statistics for the 1995–2010 SCF samples. $N = 12,413$. Standard deviations in parentheses.

SOURCE: Authors' calculations using SCF data. County per-capita income and the county unemployment rate are derived from Bureau of Economic Analysis data.

primary residence, but as Figure 9.2 suggests, the rate varies considerably with age.

Slightly more than half of the respondents are female (54 percent). Twenty percent report a bachelor's degree as the highest degree earned, with 6 percent reporting a master's, and only 1 percent claiming a PhD. Nearly 70 percent of the sample is white, 14 percent African American, and 11 percent Hispanic, with the remainder identifying as either Asian or "other." The average age of survey respondents is 40.6. Eleven percent of households live with a college-aged (18–24) person (other than the spouse). In 1 of every 15 households either the respondent or the spouse identifies themselves as having a work-related disability.[10]

Annual average county-level unemployment rate and per-capita personal income figures from the Bureau of Economic Analysis are merged into the SCF for each survey year. Unemployment averages 6 percent and ranges from 1.1 to 16.4 percent. In addition to controlling for unemployment at the county level, we include the survey year age-specific unemployment rate reported by the Bureau of Labor Statistics using CPS data. Since economic conditions at the time of graduating college have been found to have lasting impact on the return to schooling (Kahn 2010) and on the decision to continue one's education (Johnson 2013), we also control for the cohort year unemployment rate for 24–29-year-olds in the United States. This variable ranges from 4.1 to 10.7 percent for observations in our sample. County per-capita personal income, relative to the national average, ranges from 0.5 (half the national average) to 3.0. We also use "predicted wage income," which is calculated using the internal SCF data using occupation, human capital, and demographic controls and CPS data.[11] Predicted earnings average nearly $52,000 and range from $0 to $1.1 million.[12]

Figure 9.2 suggests that the outcome variables we consider vary on an aggregate level with each installment of the SCF and with respondents' ages. To account for this we also include in the estimation the survey-year household bankruptcy rate in the United States. We construct this rate as the number of nonbusiness bankruptcy filings reported by the American Bankruptcy Institute (n.d.) divided by the U.S. Census estimate of the total number of households in the United States. Since the bankruptcy outcome we consider is retrospective, we calculate the average bankruptcy rate in the survey year and preceding four years to use in the estimation. The homeownership rates we use are based on

CPS/Housing Vacancy Survey housing inventory estimates (U.S. Census Bureau n.d.). In the models that estimate the effect of student loans on the probability of owning a home, we control for the age-specific homeowner rate in the survey year.

Nearly one in five households has some student loan debt, with the average loan (among debt holders) equal to $32,000. The questions in the SCF on student loans reflect loans with an outstanding balance for any member of the PEU. Over the period we are studying in this chapter, the share of households with educational loans and the size of the average loan rose. Table 9.2 shows trends in the share of households in the age group we study with any student loan debt and the average outstanding balance among those with loans. The share of households with student loans rose from 16 percent in 1995 to 24 percent in 2010. The average loan balance rose from nearly $19,000 to more than $37,000 (adjusted for inflation using U.S. CPI-U and expressed in 2010 dollars).

Table 9.2 Student Loans in the SCF

	Share of PEU with any student loan debt (%)	Average borrowing ($000s) among those with debt
1995	16.1	18.9
1998	15.1	22.1
2001	14.8	37.8
2004	16.7	29.5
2007	19.1	34.3
2010	24.1	37.6

SOURCE: Authors' calculations using SCF data.

RESULTS

Student Debt and Financial Stability among All Households

We begin our analysis by focusing on one outcome: bankruptcy. Our estimates for the relationship between student debt and the likelihood of filing for bankruptcy over a 10-year period are presented in Table 9.3, along with the coefficients on other covariates.

Column (1) of Table 9.3 shows the first-stage estimation results from a model that includes the full set of controls. The excluded instrument is highly significant and has the expected positive sign and an F statistic of 25.3. A dollar increase in the aggregate annual amount borrowed per FTE student in the cohort year defined in the previous section corresponds on average to a $2.53 increase in the total amount borrowed by the individual and other members of the PEU. More education is naturally associated with higher debt, and so is the presence of college-age children in the household. Higher predicted earnings are also correlated with more education debt, consistent with a positive expected return to student loans. The coefficient on the age-specific unemployment rate is positive and highly significant.

In order to explore the mechanism through which student loans are related to long-term financial distress, we report three sets of second-stage results. The model in column (2) is most parsimonious, using only student debt, indicators for female, African American, and Hispanic, and a quadratic in age as explanatory variables, but we still instrument for the amount borrowed. Debt has a strong positive impact on the probability of filing for bankruptcy, with $1,000 in loans increasing the likelihood by 0.8 percentage points. Based on the argument made earlier in the "Conceptual Framework" section, adding controls for educational attainment and other measures of human capital should strengthen the relationship when the counterfactual of student loans is lower educational attainment, which is indeed what we observe in column (3). This specification includes indicators for undergraduate and graduate degree attainment, the natural logarithm of predicted earnings and normal household income, disability status and presence of college-aged children in the PEU, as well as the county unemployment rate and county per-capita income as controls for economic conditions. The coefficient on student loans increases to 0.01. This result highlights the importance of including a rich set of human capital covariates in any model that examines the implications of student debt.

In the full model in column (4) we add more controls for the economic conditions affecting households in the sample. In particular, we include the age-specific unemployment rate at the time of the survey, the unemployment rate among 24–29-year-olds in the cohort year, and the five-year bankruptcy rate. The latter has a very strong, positive, and highly significant effect, with a 0.1 percentage point increase in the

Table 9.3 Full-Sample Estimation Results for the Probability of Bankruptcy

	(1) First stage (full model)	(2)	(3)	(4)
Amount borrowed		0.00793***	0.00956***	0.00644**
		(4.037)	(3.674)	(2.089)
Average loans per FTE	0.00253***			
	(4.655)			
College degree	3.273***		−0.113***	−0.103***
	(3.749)		(−10.06)	(−8.109)
Master's degree	8.418***		−0.162***	−0.137***
	(5.005)		(−6.266)	(−4.369)
Doctorate	15.51**		−0.288***	−0.239***
	(2.676)		(−5.489)	(−4.375)
College-aged kids in household	2.329***		−0.0139	−0.00756
	(3.722)		(−0.744)	(−0.433)
Disabled	0.372		0.0487***	0.0488***
	(0.625)		(3.442)	(3.471)
County relative per-capita income	0.307		−0.0607***	−0.0527***
	(0.430)		(−3.679)	(−3.519)
County unemployment rate	0.0208		-0.00325	0.000557
	(0.148)		(−1.669)	(0.274)
Ln(normal income)	0.989		−0.0208**	−0.0189***
	(1.482)		(−2.702)	(−2.978)
Ln(predicted earnings)	0.719***		0.00437*	0.00612**
	(4.906)		(1.815)	(2.661)
Age-specific unemployment rate	0.831***			0.00705
	(4.203)			(1.218)
Cohort unemployment rate aged 24–29	−1.055			0.0104
	(−0.669)			(0.486)
Five-year bankruptcy rate	155.9			17.86***
	(0.944)			(4.689)
Constant	−5.308	−0.740***	−0.494***	−0.624***
	(−0.517)	(−6.158)	(−3.866)	(−5.144)

NOTE: *significant at the 0.10 level; **significant at the 0.05 level; ***significant at the 0.01 level. The dependent variable is an indicator for bankruptcy during the previous 10 years. Robust t-statistics in parentheses. All specifications include controls for female, black, Hispanic, age, and age squared.

SOURCE: Authors' calculations using data from the SCF, the Bureau of Economic Analysis (county income and unemployment rate), the Bureau of Labor Statistics using CPS data (cohort-specific unemployment rates), and the American Bankruptcy Institute (bankruptcy rate).

aggregate bankruptcy rate increasing the 10-year probability of observing bankruptcy in our sample by 1.8 percentage points. The coefficient on the amount of student loans decreases but remains positive and significant (0.006).

The results from the full model in Table 9.3 are summarized in column (1) of Table 9.4, which also shows the estimation results for the other three outcomes of interest. All specifications in Table 9.4 include the full set of controls, and in the homeownership model we also hold constant the survey year homeowner rate by five-year age group. The coefficient on the amount borrowed for education has the "anticipated" sign when we consider the probability of being denied credit (column [2]) or owning a home (column [4]). While the coefficient in column (1) is positive and the same in magnitude as the one in the bankruptcy specification, it is not statistically different from zero (t-statistic of 1.3). On the other hand, $10,000 more in student loans decreases the probability of owning a home by 9 percentage points; this estimate is significant at the 10 percent level. The coefficient in the late payment specification (column [3]) is negative, close to zero in absolute value, and not statistically significant.

Overall, the results from the specifications in Table 9.4 are suggestive of a potentially causal relationship between outstanding student

Table 9.4 Full-Sample Estimation Results, All Outcomes

	(1)	(2)	(3)	(4)
			Late	
Dependent variable	Bankrupt	Denied credit	payments	Homeowner
Amount borrowed	0.00644**	0.00643	−0.00274	−0.00899*
	(2.089)	(1.322)	(−1.105)	(−1.726)
Five-year	17.86***	−0.283	4.696	3.733
bankruptcy rate	(4.689)	(−0.0699)	(1.653)	(0.744)
Age-specific				−0.0232
homeowner rate				(−0.595)

NOTE: *significant at the 0.10 level; **significant at the 0.05 level; ***significant at the 0.01 level. Robust t-statistics in parentheses. All specifications include the controls from the full model in Table 9.3.

SOURCE: Authors' calculations using data from the SCF, the Bureau of Economic Analysis (county income and unemployment rate), the Bureau of Labor Statistics using CPS data (cohort-specific unemployment rates), the American Bankruptcy Institute (bankruptcy rate), and the U.S. Census (homeownership).

loan balances and household financial distress, but the findings are not particularly strong and tend to be noisy. The coefficients on the education variables in Table 9.3 also indicate that since higher attainment levels are negatively related to various financial distress measures, we might be able to get a clearer picture of the long-term impacts of student loans by contrasting completers and noncompleters. As discussed in the "Conceptual Framework" section, we expect the relationship between student loans and financial distress to be more pronounced for individuals who attend college without attaining a degree. The next section of results includes a series of specifications in which we contrast the impact of outstanding student loan debt on financial distress measures for college completers and noncompleters.

Results by College Completion Status

We focus on college attendance because it is by far the most common level of postsecondary education in the data and among the U.S. population, and because the consequences of holding student debt and not completing an undergraduate degree are an important policy concern. As shown earlier in Table 9.1, college as the highest degree attained is much more common than graduate degrees. The more detailed college attendance and completion statistics in Table 9.5 show that only one quarter as many respondents (and spouses) report graduate school as the highest level of school attended as college. The rate of completion is also much higher among those who attend graduate school; only 1 in 10 graduate school attending respondents or spouses fail to complete.[13] Because there are relatively few graduate school attendees and

Table 9.5 Sample Distribution of College and Beyond College Attendance and Degree Completion

	Respondent		Spouse	
	Noncompleter	Completer	Noncompleter	Completer
Highest level of attendance				
College	2,060	3,365	1,306	2,856
Graduate school	205	1,862	140	1,171

SOURCE: Authors' calculations using SCF data.

even fewer noncompleters, the next step of our analysis focuses only on cases with college as the highest level of attendance.

Table 9.6 contains the key coefficient of interest, the one on student loans, for a similar instrumental variable specification for each of the dependent variables, as shown in Table 9.4, using several different sample selections to contrast completers and noncompleters among college attenders. The specifications include indicators for female, black, and Hispanic, a quadratic in age, county relative per-capita income, the county unemployment rate, the cohort unemployment rate for age 24–29, the five-year bankruptcy rate, and the age-specific homeowner rate in the case of the homeowner specifications. We estimate each model both with and without the predicted wage variable. Earlier we posit that holding constant the portion of earnings that varies with the amount and quality of schooling would magnify the coefficient on student loans more for completers than for noncompleters when education loans are not directly replaceable by grant aid. The odd-numbered columns in Table 9.6 contain results for the specifications without predicted earnings, while the results in the even-numbered columns account for this measure of schooling and occupation.

Because the SCF student loan questions pertain to any outstanding loans for any member of the PEU, it is possible that the debt will actually be for currently (or recently) attending children and not have meaningful relationship with the college completion status of the respondent or spouse/partner. To isolate households where the loans are for the respondent and/or spouse/partner, we further restrict the sample of "noncompleters" to exclude households with both college-aged kids (18–24) in the home and with any of the student loans taken out within the past three years.

We consider three subsamples of college attenders. Results for the broadest subsample, including all PEUs where either the respondent or the spouse has college as the highest level attended, are contained in Panel A. Panel B includes results for a second subsample, which includes cases where either the respondent or the spouse has college as the highest level of school attended, while the other member of the couple reports some lower level of attendance. The final subsample is restricted to households where both the respondent and the spouse/partner (if there is one present) have college as the highest level of school attended (Panel C).

The consistent result across each of the three subsamples of college attenders is that the magnitude of the impact of outstanding student loan balances is much greater among noncompleters than among those who obtain a college degree. The coefficient on student loans is almost always greater in absolute value in the noncompleter specifications. In addition, adding the predicted wage to the models tends to decrease the difference between the two groups.

Among households where either the respondent or the spouse/partner (possibly both) failed to complete college, $1,000 in outstanding education loans raises the probability of bankruptcy by 1.2 percentage points (Panel A, columns [5] and [6]) and lowers the probability of owning a home by 1.4 percentage points (column [4]). The student debt coefficients for the other outcomes have the anticipated sign but are not significant at standard levels. Among college completers, only the coefficient for late payments is statistically significant at the 10 percent level, though the magnitude of the student loan debt measure is slightly lower than it is for noncompleters.

In the households where the sole college attender did not receive a degree, $1,000 in outstanding college debt raises the probability of experiencing bankruptcy in the last 10 years by almost four percentage points. That level of outstanding loans decreases the probability of owning a home by 5.6 percentage points. The effects of debt are much smaller, and largely not significant, among households where the sole college attender completed his or her degree. The coefficient for late payments, while borderline insignificant, is positive and larger than that for noncompleters, where the point estimate is negative.

Among households in which both the respondent and spouse/partner attended college and at least one person failed to complete, $1,000 in outstanding student loan debt raises the probability of having late payments by two percentage points and decreases the probability of owning a home by three percentage points. There is only one outcome where the coefficient on outstanding student loans is statistically significant among completers when we condition on the CPS earnings variable (late payments). In each case, however, the magnitudes on these coefficients are much smaller among completers, ranging from one-fifth to one-half as large as the effects among noncompleters.

Table 9.6 Coefficients on Amount Borrowed by Dependent Variable and Completion Status for College Attenders (Any College Attended)

	(1)	(2)	(3)	(4)	(5)	(6)	(7)	(8)	N
	Denied credit		Late payments		Bankruptcy		Homeowner		
Panel A									
At least one college attender among respondent (R) and spouse/partner (SP)									
At least one attender fails to complete	0.00685 (0.966)	0.00842 (1.111)	0.00559 (1.021)	0.00689 (1.175)	0.0124** (2.424)	0.0124** (2.324)	−0.00637 (−1.016)	−0.0138** (−2.182)	4,047
All attenders complete	0.00229 (0.808)	0.00874 (1.051)	0.00184 (1.443)	0.00400* (1.854)	0.000823 (0.913)	0.00168 (1.132)	−0.00144 (−0.558)	−0.00671 (−1.640)	2,921
Panel B									
Only one college attender among respondent and spouse/partner									
Attender fails to complete	0.0167 (0.467)	0.0220 (0.575)	−0.00876 (−0.449)	−0.00816 (−0.400)	0.0396* (1.976)	0.0387* (1.883)	−0.0399* (−1.694)	−0.0562* (−1.917)	1,604
Attender completes	0.00280 (0.355)	0.00279 (0.338)	0.00686 (1.584)	0.00756 (1.665)	−0.00106 (−0.358)	−0.00118 (−0.399)	0.0126 (1.406)	0.00909 (1.118)	1,758

Panel C

Respondent and spouse/partner both attend college								
At least one attender fails to complete	0.00571	0.00830	0.0125	0.0201*	0.00665	0.00578	−0.0113	−0.0296**
	(1.084)	(1.102)	(1.549)	(1.804)	(0.648)	(0.445)	(−1.117)	(−2.180)
								1,058
Both attenders complete	0.00170	0.00414	0.00235*	0.00386**	0.00192	0.00244	−0.00226	−0.00574
	(0.721)	(1.210)	(1.764)	(2.069)	(1.480)	(1.534)	(−0.775)	(−1.591)
								1,276
Control for Ln(predicted earnings)	No	Yes	No	Yes	No	Yes	No	Yes

NOTE: *significant at the 0.10 level; **significant at the 0.05 level; ***significant at the 0.01 level. Robust t-statistics in parentheses. All specifications include the controls for female, black, Hispanic, a quadratic in age, county relative per-capita income, the county unemployment rate, the cohort unemployment rate for aged 24–29, the five-year bankruptcy rate, and the age-specific homeowner rate (columns [7] and [8]).

SOURCE: Authors' calculations using data from the SCF, the Bureau of Economic Analysis (county income and unemployment rate), the Bureau of Labor Statistics using CPS data (cohort-specific unemployment rates), the American Bankruptcy Institute (bankruptcy rate), and the U.S. Census (homeownership).

DISCUSSION

Our results indicate that holding student debt is likely associated with decreased financial stability, particularly for individuals who accumulate debt but do not complete a bachelor's degree. Several related mechanisms can lead to the observed relationship between student loans and financial distress. Further work is needed to provide more information about the specific issues caused by education debt. Debt repayment has a direct impact on disposable income, which can place financial strain on households when combined with liquidity constraints that prevent graduates from borrowing against future income. Brown and Caldwell (2013) show a recent trend in the Federal Reserve Bank of New York Consumer Credit Panel of 25- and 30-year-old student borrowers having lower credit scores on average than the scores of similarly aged nonborrowers. This comparison, however, does not account for correlates of income, financial stability, and good credit rating that are linked to student debt, such as educational attainment and occupation. Homeownership can be affected through a higher consumer debt-to-income ratio, which mortgage lenders take into account, or the ability to save enough for a down payment. Even if student debt does not play a role in the rate at which graduates transition into homeownership, it can affect the value of the homes they purchase or the resources that are devoted to other consumption categories.

Changing aggregate labor market conditions may indirectly lead us to observe a relationship between education loans and financial hardship if the ongoing steady increase in student borrowing has coincided with continued decline in the returns to postsecondary education. Under this scenario, it would not be the case that loans per se cause financial hardship. Households that obtained schooling in more recent years would fare worse financially, owing to the lower returns to their education, but such households are also more likely to hold debt because of exogenous increases in aggregate borrowing. However, trends from the March CPS suggest increasing, not decreasing, high school–college wage differential (see, for example, Avery and Turner [2012] and Day and Newburger [2002]).

Given the high uncertainty in the ex post return to a college or advanced degree, the observed levels of student borrowing may be ex ante efficient, but the households that are the "lottery losers" are observed experiencing financial distress. Student debt generally cannot be discharged in personal bankruptcy, and therefore borrowers who experience bad income shocks after graduation are unable to use a major component of the safety net available to holders of other types of debt. Borrowers who leave school without completing a degree have been identified as a group that is particularly susceptible to being burdened by student debt, and we present evidence that confirms this. The currently existing insurance mechanism that is built into the federal loan program includes such options as income-contingent and income-based repayment plans and deferment options, but private student loans come with little borrower protection. Our results may indicate the need for more borrower protection, although we draw no conclusions about the potential for moral hazard issues with which such policies may be associated.

Notes

The analysis and conclusions set forth are those of the authors and do not indicate concurrence by other members of the research staff or the Board of Governors. The authors would like to thank Jesse Rothstein and other participants at the Upjohn/EPI/Spencer Conference on Student Loans for their helpful comments.

1. See Lochner and Monge-Naranjo (2012) for an overview of the literature.
2. For example, Avery and Kane (2004) observe this trend among Boston high school students coming from both low-income and more affluent families. Avery and Turner (2012) show that in the Beginning Postsecondary Survey 2004:2009, 38 percent of dependent students entering college in 2003 who expect to attain a BA degree have not earned any postsecondary degree by 2009; 51 percent of these students end up with student loans, with the average borrower holding $14,500 in student debt. According to analysis of the same data presented by the College Board (2012b), 5 percent of students who borrowed $75,000 or more and 10 percent of students who borrowed between $50,000 and $75,000 left school without a degree by 2009.
3. As researchers, we observe an imperfect measure of schooling S_i and occupation. In our empirical analysis it is used to construct a predicted wage income variable that is based on Current Population Survey (CPS) respondents' earnings.
4. Since in our data student loans are measured at the household level in our data, for respondents with a spouse or partner we use the mean of the two ages.
5. See Wilson and Smith (1983) and Internal Revenue Service (1992) for a description of the Statistics of Income file. The file used for each survey largely contains

data from tax returns filed for the tax year two years before the survey takes place. See Kennickell (1998) for a detailed description of the selection of the 1998 list sample.

6. For reasons related to cost control on the survey, the geographic distribution of the list sample is constrained to that of the area-probability sample.

7. The evolution of the SCF weighting design is summarized in Kennickell (2000), with additional background by Kennickell and Woodburn (1992).

8. In this chapter we use the term *household* for simplicity. The SCF actually uses a concept of primary economic unit (PEU), which includes family members living together in the housing unit who are financially dependent on the respondent. Family here includes unmarried partners and their children. Residents of the household who do not usually live in the residence or who are economically independent of the survey respondent are not considered to be part of the PEU, and any student loans they may hold are not included in the SCF.

9. See, for example, U.S. Census Bureau (2013).

10. The disability status is not necessarily caused by work but is identified by the respondent in a battery of questions about employment status.

11. As described in the 2010 SCF documentation:

> For each occupation group, regressions were run separately for males and females of the log of annualized wages on a constant, a spline on age [AGE, MAX(0, AGE-35), MAX(0, AGE-55))], a dummy variable for part-time employment (1 = working fewer than 20 hours per week), a dummy variable for self-employment (1 = self-employed), a dummy for race (1 = Hispanic or nonwhite), and dummy variables for years of education (1 = 12 years of education, some college or an associate's degree, bachelor's degree, higher degree than bachelor's degree). If there were too few people in a CPS three-digit occupation group, either the SCF case was matched to a neighboring occupation group, or the match was made at the level of the two-digit occupation code. Some of the model coefficients may be identically zero where there are too few cases in the appropriate cells in the CPS data to identify these coefficients; for example, a coefficient for the (36,55) element of the age spline may be identically zero if there are no CPS cases in that age group for the given occupation.

12. Before taking the natural log of predicted earnings, which is the variable included in the regressions below, we add $0.50 to all observations reporting zero predicted earnings. Predicted earnings are not adjusted for inflation.

13. Attendance and completion in the SCF are constructed from two variables. The attendance variable asks (separate for respondent and spouse) the highest level of school attended, including four possible responses for college (one, two, three, or four years of college) and only one for any level of graduate school attended. Among those with any college attendance, both respondent and spouse are asked the degree completed with 10 options, including associate's, bachelor's, master's, and a variety other advanced degrees.

References

American Bankruptcy Institute. n.d. "Annual Business and Non-business Filings by Year, 1980–2012." Alexandria, VA: American Bankruptcy Institute.

Avery, Christopher, and Thomas J. Kane. 2004. "Student Perceptions of College Opportunities. The Boston COACH Program." In *College Choices: The Economics of Where to Go, When to Go, and How to Pay For It*, Caroline M. Hoxby, ed. Chicago, IL: University of Chicago Press, pp. 355–394.

Avery, Christopher, and Sarah Turner. 2012. "Student Loans: Do College Students Borrow Too Much—Or Not Enough?" *Journal of Economic Perspectives* 26(1): 165–192.

Baum, Sandy, and Saul Schwartz. 2006. *How Much Debt Is Too Much? Defining Benchmarks for Manageable Student Debt*. New York and Berkeley, CA: College Board and The Project on Student Debt.

Bazzoli, Gloria. 1985. "Does Educational Indebtedness Affect Physician Specialty Choice?" *Journal of Health Economics* 4(1): 1–19.

Berkner, Lutz, Shirley He, and Emily Forest Cataldi. 2002. *Descriptive Summary of 1995-96 Beginning Postsecondary Students: Six Years Later*. Statistical Analysis Report No. 2003-151. Washington, DC: National Center for Education Statistics.

Bricker, Jesse, and Jeffrey Thompson. 2013. "Does Education Loan Debt Influence Household Financial Distress? An Initial Assessment Using the 2007-09 SCF Panel." Photocopy; available from the authors.

Brown, Meta, and Sydnee Caldwell. 2013. "Young Student Loan Borrowers Retreat from Housing and Auto Markets." *Liberty Street Economics* (blog), April 17, Federal Reserve Bank of New York. http://libertystreeteconomics .newyorkfed.org/2013/04/young-student-loan-borrowers-retreat-from -housing-and-auto-markets.html (accessed April 23, 2014).

Chiteji, Ngina S. 2007. "To Have and to Hold: An Analysis of Young Adult Debt." In *The Price of Independence: The Economics of Early Adulthood*, Sheldon Danziger and Cecilia E. Rouse, eds. New York: Russell Sage Foundation, pp. 231–258.

Choy, Susan P., and C. Dennis Carroll. 2000. "Debt Burden Four Years after College." Washington, DC: National Center for Education Statistics.

College Board. 2012a. *Trends in College Pricing, 2012*. New York: College Board.

———. 2012b. *Trends in Student Aid, 2012*. New York: College Board.

Colquitt W., M. Zeh, C. Killian, and J. Cultice. 1996. "Effect of Debt on U.S. Medical School Graduates' Preferences for Family Medicine, General Internal Medicine, and General Pediatrics." *Academic Medicine* 71(4): 399–411.

Day, Jennifer Cheeseman, and Eric Newburger. 2002. "The Big Payoff: Educational Attainment and Synthetic Estimates of Work-Life Earnings." Current Population Reports, July, P23-210. Washington, DC: U.S. Census Bureau.

Duca, John V., and Stuart S. Rosenthal. 1993. "Borrowing Constraints, Household Debt, and Racial Discrimination in Loan Markets." *Journal of Financial Intermediation* 3(1): 77–103.

Field, Erica. 2009. "Educational Debt Burden and Career Choice: Evidence from a Financial Aid Experiment at NYU Law School." *American Economic Journal: Applied Economics* 1(1): 1–21.

Fox, Marc. 1992. "Student Debt and Enrollment in Graduate and Professional School." *Applied Economics* 24(7): 669–677.

Gicheva, Dora. 2013. "In Debt and Alone? Examining the Causal Link between Student Loans and Marriage." Working paper. Greensboro, NC: University of North Carolina.

Hansen, W. L., and M. Rhodes. 1988. "Student Debt Crisis: Are Students Incurring Excessive Debt?" *Economics of Education Review* 7(1): 101–112.

Hauer, Karen, Steven Durning, Walter Kernan, Mark Fagan, Matthew Mintz, Patricia O'Sullivan, Michael Battistone, Thomas DeFer, Michael Elnicki, Heather Harrell, Shalini Reddy, Christy Boscardin, and Mark Schwartz. 2008. "Factors Associated with Medical Students' Career Choices Regarding Internal Medicine." *Journal of the American Medical Association* 300(10): 1154–1164.

Internal Revenue Service. 1992. Individual Income Tax Returns. 1990 Internal Revenue Service. Washington, DC: Internal Revenue Service.

Jappelli, Tulio. 1990. "Who Is Credit-Constrained in the U.S. Economy?" *Quarterly Journal of Economics* 105(1): 219–234.

Johnson, Matthew T. 2013. "The Impact of Business Cycle Fluctuations on Graduate School Enrollment." *Economics of Education Review* 34(C): 122–134.

Kahn, Lisa B. 2010. "The Long-Term Labor Market Consequences of Graduating from College in a Bad Economy." *Labour Economics* 17(2): 303–316.

Kennickell, A. B. 1998. "List Sample Design for the 1998 Survey of Consumer Finances," Federal Reserve Board Working Paper. Washington, DC: Board of Governors of the Federal Reserve System.

_____. 2000. "Wealth Measurement in the Survey of Consumer Finances: Methodology and Directions for Future Research." Federal Reserve Board Working Paper. Washington, DC: Board of Governors of the Federal Reserve System.

Kennickell, A. B., and R. L. Woodburn. 1992. "Estimation of Household Net Worth Using Model-Based and Design-Based Weights: Evidence from the

1989 Survey of Consumer Finances." Federal Reserve Board Working Paper. Washington, DC: Board of Governors of the Federal Reserve System.

Kornhauser, L. A., and R. L. Revesz. 1995. "Legal Education and Entry into the Legal Profession: The Role of Race, Gender, and Educational Debt." *New York University Law Review* 70(4): 829–945.

Lee, Donghoon. 2013. "Household Debt and Credit: Student Debt." Federal Reserve Bank of New York, February 28. http://www.newyorkfed.org/newsevents/mediaadvisory/2013/Lee022813.pdf (accessed April 23, 2014).

Lochner, Lance, and Alexander Monge-Naranjo. 2012. "Credit Constraints in Education." *Annual Review of Economics* 4(1): 225–256.

Minnicozzi, Alexandra. 2005. "The Short Term Effect of Educational Debt on Job Decisions." *Economics of Education Review* 24(4): 417–430.

Rothstein, Jesse, and Cecilia Rouse. 2011. "Constrained after College: Student Loans and Early-Career Occupational Choice." *Journal of Public Economics* 95(1-2): 149–163.

Schapiro, Morton, Michael O'Malley, and Larry Litten. 1991. "Progression to Graduate School from the 'Elite' Colleges and Universities." *Economics of Education Review* 10(3): 227–244.

Stinebrickner, Ralph, and Todd R. Stinebrickner. 2003. "Working during School and Academic Performance." *Journal of Labor Economics* 21(2): 449–472.

U.S. Census Bureau. n.d. "Table 15. Annual Estimates of the Housing Inventory by Age of Householder and Family Status: 1982 to Present." Washington, DC: U.S. Census Bureau. http://www.census.gov/housing/hvs/data/histtabs.html, Table 15 (accessed January 31, 2014).

———. 2013. "Homeownership Rates by Age of Householder and Household Type: 1990–2010." Table 992. *Statistical Abstract of the United States, 2012.* Washington, DC: U.S. Census Bureau. https://www.census.gov/compendia/statab/2012/tables/12s0992.pdf (accessed April 29, 2014).

Wei, Christina Chang, and Laura Horn. 2013. "Federal Student Loan Debt Burden of Noncompleters." *Stats in Brief.* NCES 2013-155. Washington, DC: National Center for Education Statistics.

Weiler, William. 1994. "Expectations, Undergraduate Debt and the Decision to Attend Graduate School: A Simultaneous Model of Student Choice." *Economics of Education Review* 13(1): 29–41.

Willis, Robert J., and Sherwin Rosen. 1979. "Education and Self-Selection," *Journal of Political Economy* 87(5): S7–36.

Wilson, O. H., and William J. Smith, Jr. 1983. "Access to Tax Records for Statistical Purposes." In *Proceedings of the Section on Survey Research Methods.* Alexandria, VA: American Statistical Association, pp. 595–601.

Woodworth, P., F. Chang, and S. Helmer. 2000. "Debt and Other Influences on Career Choices among Surgical and Primary Care Residents in a Community-Based Hospital System." *American Journal of Surgery* 180(6): 570–575.

10
Making Sense of Loan Aversion

Evidence from Wisconsin

Sara Goldrick-Rab
University of Wisconsin–Madison

Robert Kelchen
Seton Hall University

In 2012 total student loan debt in the United States reached an all-time high of $966 billion, with one-third of that debt held by 15 million people under age 30 (Lee 2013). Student loans are now the primary means through which American families finance postsecondary education. With the costs of attendance higher than ever, and grant aid often available only for the financially needy or exceptionally talented, nearly two-thirds of all undergraduates receive at least some government-backed credit to cover those costs. That credit is comparatively accessible, requiring a lengthy application but no credit history, and students and families can borrow a sizable amount of money. Yet not all students and families borrow, even when declining to borrow means that they are hard-pressed to afford college, and there is little evidence to help account for that apparent aversion. Thus, while there is widespread concern about the amount of borrowing and "overborrowing," high rates of delinquency and default in some sectors of the market, and debate about whether the resulting debt-income ratio is appropriate, deepening our understanding of the initial borrowing decision itself remains an important task.

Since college attainment is tightly linked to families' ability to pay for college (e.g., Bailey and Dynarski 2011), substantial inequalities arise from students' need to borrow and their decisions about how to respond to that need. Two groups of students on opposite ends of the income spectrum often find themselves able to avoid borrowing. The first group is exceptionally wealthy, possessing the financial strength to cover college costs without credit, while the second group is exceptionally poor (and often quite talented), thus receiving sufficient grant aid to cover costs without need for credit. Most students and families fall into the great grey middle in between. These people have demonstrable financial need (as calculated by formulaic federal needs analysis), meaning that there is a gap between their available resources and the costs of college attendance. They are nearly always offered loans, but a sizable fraction decline to take them.[1] This is especially common among students from lower-income families; national data suggest that as many as 45 percent of the neediest undergraduates do not take up loans, even though this leaves them short of the resources required to cover their costs of attendance (Cunningham and Santiago 2008).[2]

Declining loans that could help meet the costs of college attendance is typically referred to as loan aversion and according to some economists constitutes bizarre behavior (Cadena and Keys 2013). But aversion is a frequently used but poorly understood term, since it is unclear whether these students are actually averse to loans (implying a belief about borrowing), have a lack of information about them, or are not offered them at all (The Institute for College Access and Success [TICAS] 2007). In addition, since data on loan aversion typically come from student surveys, it is difficult to know whether stated attitudes translate into action. Finally, there is little systematic information about demographic differences in loan aversion and to what they may be attributed.

This generally weak knowledge base means that it is unclear whether and what kind of intervention is required and/or appropriate to *encourage* borrowing among (some) students to increase their chances of degree completion. In addition, more research is needed to determine the processes underlying the decision to forgo student loans, and in particular whether that decision constitutes loan aversion.

With these challenges in mind, this chapter contributes to the study of loan aversion by drawing on a comprehensive set of information about a focal group of students: Pell Grant recipients. The relatively low graduation rate of Pell recipients is a national concern and the focus of numerous initiatives such as the "Reimagining Aid Design and Delivery" project funded by the Bill and Melinda Gates Foundation. Since the purchasing power of the Pell Grant is at its lowest point in history (covering just 30 percent of the costs of a public four-year university on average), even low-income students have to cover as much as $12,000 of college costs on their own (Goldrick-Rab 2013). Why do some low-income students accept loans to cover this need while others do not?

We begin by triangulating evidence from both surveys and administrative records to get a handle on how differences in the *measurement* of loan-taking decisions might affect conclusions. We next examine differences in those decisions among more than 600 first- time undergraduates receiving the Pell Grant across 10 of Wisconsin's public universities. In particular, we attend to demographic variation suggested by prior literature, including disparities based on race/ethnicity, parental education, and immigrant status. We also consider the role played by the institutional contexts where students attend college by examining the associations between loan decisions and university characteristics. After replicating some key borrowing disparities noted in earlier studies, we test several explanations for these differences. Specifically, we consider the moderating effects on loan decisions according to families' financial resources; perceived returns to education; financial knowledge; attitudes, beliefs, and dispositions; work behaviors; and social capital. Finally, we examine the evidence regarding the association between loan taking and educational outcomes.

Overall, our findings strongly suggest that the manner in which loan decisions are measured have serious implications about the prevalence and antecedents of so-called loan aversion. Some analyses indicate that the decision to decline loans may be a strategy undertaken by students with strong family commitments and those living in contexts where the use of credit for consumption is normalized. We conclude with a discussion of future areas for research and intervention, noting that there are still many unknowns regarding the consequences of loan taking, both on average and for different groups of students. This chapter suggests that loan aversion may not be something to overcome, but that it may in fact benefit some students, perhaps while hampering the college attainment of others.

TRENDS IN COLLEGE FINANCING AND LOAN TAKING

The United States has never had a free system of public higher education; instead, political goals of equitable opportunity are pursued through a complex price-discounting strategy known as financial aid. To induce students from low-income families to choose college, government, philanthropy, and educational institutions collaboratively frame college enrollment as an affordable decision for all qualified students. Families and students are encouraged to embrace the financial aid system's workings, norms, and values, which include the contention that higher education yields private and public returns, and individuals should therefore feel comfortable taking on debt to invest in their human capital development (Baum and Schwartz 2012; Leslie and Brinkman 1987; Manski and Wise 1983; McPherson and Schapiro 1991). Institutions of higher education are then left to determine the value of their services and set their own prices. The return to individual investments is expressed in terms of increased earnings observed at some time in the future, but it requires significant near-term sacrifice (Carnevale, Rose, and Cheah 2011). Concomitantly, because of the social benefits accrued to an educated populace, the government asserts its authority to help ensure that low-income citizens can pursue higher education through vouchers (such as Pell Grants) and government-managed loan systems (Advisory Committee on Student Financial Assistance 2012).

The availability and use of federal loans has changed radically over time. Prior to the 1992 reauthorization of the Higher Education Act, federal loans consisted almost entirely of subsidized loans targeting needy families. Total federal loan volume was around $22 billion (in 2011 dollars) in 1991–1992. Over the course of the next year, that number grew by almost 50 percent with the introduction of unsubsidized loans, which at the time constituted 9 percent of all student loan dollars across all sources. The growth of unsubsidized loans was dramatic, swelling from about $10 billion (in 2011 dollars) in 1995–1996 to more than $20 billion in 2005–2006, and to almost $50 billion in 2011–2012. Those increases correspond to real declines in family income associated with the recession and increasing college costs, including at public colleges and universities. Growth in subsidized loans was slower, since they are means-tested and less available (Baum and Payea 2012).

Currently, dependent undergraduate students can borrow up to $5,500 in Stafford Loans (including a maximum of $3,500 in subsidized loans) in their first year of study, and up to $6,500 (including up to $4,500 in subsidized loans) in their second year. The limit for the third year and beyond is $7,500 (including up to $5,500 in subsidized loans). Average total borrowing per full-time equivalent undergraduate student rose by 45 percent, from $3,677 (in 2011 dollars) to $5,335 between 2001–2002 and 2006–2007, and by another 4 percent to $5,540, in 2011–2012 (Baum and Payea 2012).

With declining family resources and higher costs of attendance, students today by and large cannot forgo loans and instead turn to work to fill the financial holes. The average unmet financial need of Pell recipients is about $12,000 at four-year colleges and universities; a student must work, at federal minimum wage, almost 35 hours a week, 52 weeks a year, to cover those costs, which research suggests is nearly impossible if the student hopes to complete college on time (Goldrick-Rab 2013). Moreover, while many students have an "expected family contribution," (EFC) which suggests that the family should be able to pay for college, some families are unable or unwilling to do so, and thus students borrow unsubsidized loans to cover that EFC. It is therefore unsurprising that over the last decade, the total number of federal Stafford Loan borrowers increased by 95 percent, from 5.4 million in 2001–2002 to 10.4 million in 2011–2012 (Baum and Payea 2012). This means that the percentage of undergraduates holding loans grew from 23 to 35 percent over that 10-year period. Moreover, the percentage of undergraduates borrowing both subsidized and unsubsidized federal loans grew from 9 percent in 2001–2002 to 25 percent in 2011–2012 (College Board 2012).

Borrowing is more common among students at public universities and less so among students attending public two-year colleges. The percentage of students borrowing to attend public universities has remained steady at around 55 percent since 1999, but the average amount borrowed among bachelor's degree recipients has grown from just over $20,000 to nearly $25,000. In addition, borrowing grew more rapidly from 2005–2006 to 2010–2011 than it had during the preceding five years. Debt per borrower grew at an average annual rate of 2.1 percent beyond inflation, and average debt per graduate grew at an average annual rate of 2.7 percent (Baum and Payea 2012).

Students from low-income families are far more likely to borrow for college. An analysis of bachelor's degree recipients graduating from public universities in 2007–2008 found that 68 percent of students from families earning less than $30,000 per year had an average cumulative debt load of $16,500, while just 40 percent of students from families earning $120,000 or more annually held any debt, with an average amount of $14,500 (Baum and Payea 2012). The resulting disparity in debt-to-income ratio is substantial—low-income families hold debt amounting to about 70 percent of their income, while wealthier families have debt amounting to around 10 percent of income (a rate deemed manageable by the financial industry).[3]

Evidence from several waves of the National Postsecondary Student Aid Study (NPSAS) suggests that between 40 and 50 percent of students borrowing subsidized Stafford Loans took the maximum allowable amount over the past two decades, even after two increases in the maximum. More than one in four students borrowing the maximum amount of federal loans in the 2007–2008 academic year also took out a private loan or a federal PLUS loan (Wei and Skomsvold 2011). This suggests that more students are borrowing close to the limits and that loan caps may contribute to the mistaken appearance of loan aversion. There is some evidence that loan limits may hinder the ability of a small number of students to complete college; for example, recent work by Johnson (2013) found that a simulated $5,000 increase in student loan limits would increase bachelor's degree attainment rates by 0.7 percentage points. Thus, even in the face of growing concern about the overall amount of borrowing, there is some reason to think that in the current context, students from low-income families might face greater odds of college success if they were willing or able to borrow more.

A DESCRIPTIVE PORTRAIT OF LOAN AVERSION

The body of research on loan aversion is mainly descriptive, with a few multivariate studies and laboratory experiments included. These provide a broad sense of the characteristics of students who decline loans, and some targeted tests of whether that apparent aversion can be overcome through intervention.

The NPSAS of 2003–2004 can be used to form a portrait of loan-averse students.[4] An examination of this data by Cunningham and Santiago (2008) confirms that students who decline to borrow have less unmet need—simply put, they do not need to borrow. In addition, among students with a significant amount of unmet need ($2,000 or more), loan aversion is more common among students from low-income families, those who attend part time, and students attending public four-year (rather than private four-year) institutions. Loan aversion is less common among black students compared to white students, and it is more common among Asian and Hispanic students compared to white students.

After comparing these results to data from the 1992–1993 NPSAS, Cunningham and Santiago (2008) note that racial/ethnic differences in borrowing seem to be a new phenomenon, emerging with the growth of students borrowing associated with the use of unsubsidized loans. This raises additional questions about whether the use of subsidized and unsubsidized loans differs by race/ethnicity as well.[5] It is worth noting that research evidence has clearly established racial/ethnic variation in rates of loan default, with black students at the greatest risk of defaulting on their loans (Gross et al. 2009), even as the loans may be more effective in increasing completion rates (Jackson and Reynolds 2013).

Smaller qualitative studies identify similar patterns. For example, Burdman (2005) conducts interviews with students, counselors, outreach professionals, and financial aid administrators that suggest that aversion to loans may reduce opportunities for a subset of low-income and minority students, particularly low-income, first-generation, and Mexican-American students. She finds that students whose parents had less education appeared more likely to work full time and avoid borrowing than students whose parents have college or graduate degrees. Among full-time students, those whose parents did not finish high school were more than twice as likely as those whose parents had graduate degrees to work full time instead of borrowing. Among full-time dependent students, low-income students were less likely to borrow than other students, and when they did borrow, they took smaller loans. But debt aversion, she suggested, may also affect the initial choice of whether and where to attend college—before students have the opportunity to actually receive a loan offer and reject it.

However, other evidence suggests that students may be mislabeled as loan averse when they are actually amenable to borrowing. For example, Eckel et al. (2007) study educational finance preferences using an experiment in which real money was distributed (e.g., the choices were not hypothetical). The sample was drawn from across Canada and included 900 students aged 18–55 who were recruited for participation in the exercise. Based on the results, the authors conclude that debt aversion plays little or no role in the demand for postsecondary education finance in the form of a loan. Students with experience carrying and managing debt are more willing than others to take on additional debt to finance postsecondary education. But presenting students with only loan options for postsecondary education is unlikely to negatively impact investment in postsecondary education, as long as care is taken that the price of the loans is not too high. Johnson and Montmarquette (2011) elicit similar findings in another Canadian study with a sample of low-income and rural students. They find a greater willingness to pay for college with loans among rural respondents, and no systematic loan aversion. Finally, in a third Canadian study, Palameta and Voyer (2010) find that roughly 5–20 percent of their overall sample of low-income high school students was loan averse, depending on the price of the offered grant. In their experimental study, as the price of attending college increased, a higher percentage of students were inclined to choose a stand alone grant but not a grant/loan combination. The results show that overall some underrepresented groups are slightly but significantly more likely to make loan-averse decisions. Of course, it is unclear if the Canadian context and student body is sufficiently similar to the United States to extrapolate these findings.

EXPLANATIONS FOR LOAN AVERSION: THEORY AND EVIDENCE

Loan aversion is often described as common, unfortunate, and not easily overcome, but these depictions are typically based on conjecture rather than evidence. Reports on loan aversion, such as those issued by The Project on Student Debt and the Institute on Higher Education Policy (e.g., Burdman 2005; TICAS 2007; Cunningham and Santiago

2008) tend to point to two explanations for declining loans while possessing unmet financial need: a preference for using alternative sources of financing (e.g., savings or work earnings), or cultural/ethnic perspectives that discourage borrowing. Practitioners suggest that aversion may be growing in response to the Great Recession and news about rising default rates in some sectors. But there are many more theoretical explanations for why students and families may choose to decline to accept the loans offered to them. In this section we adapt a model of understanding the use and effects of financial aid initially described in Goldrick-Rab, Harris, and Trostel (2009).

First, families may vary in their *financial strength*, and this could—in a manner consistent with rational choice theory—lead them to decline loans. Families that can afford the net price of attendance, either because they have sufficient wealth or receive sufficient grant aid, may reject loans offered to them.[6] Again, this is a heterogeneous group—both the wealthiest and poorest families, those with the highest and lowest incomes, the highest and lowest EFCs, and who are facing the highest and lowest net prices are the most likely to borrow. But among students from low-income families, rational choice theory would lead to the expectation that loan aversion is more common among families with greater incomes, a higher EFC, or a lower net price. On the other hand, families with more debt may also be loan averse.

Another explanation for loan aversion points to the problem of *informational asymmetries*. Many policymakers, practitioners, and researchers highlight a large body of economic theory and evidence suggesting that college is an excellent investment for most low-income students, even as loan balances increase (Avery and Turner 2012; Baum and Schwartz 2012). On average, each additional year of education generates a payoff in the labor market, and the lifetime returns to degrees are substantial, even for groups marginalized by race, class, or ethnicity. Even during the recent deep recession, college graduates fared better than high school graduates (Carnevale, Rose, and Cheah 2011). Informational barriers are typically given as the reason why many students and families insist that the costs of attendance are too high and unaffordable (Hoxby and Avery 2012; Hoxby and Turner 2013). At least one U.S. experiment indicates that providing more information can moderately reduce that perception (Hoxby and Turner 2013). However, an experiment in the Netherlands suggests the opposite, finding that students who receive additional information on the terms of loans do not adjust their loan-taking behaviors over time (Booij, Leuven, and Oosterbeek 2012).

Research by McKinney, Roberts, and Shefman (2013) indicates that many community college financial aid counselors believe that their low-income students do not understand the long-term implications of taking out student loans. Similarly, some researchers contend that college attainment would increase if students had a "payback calculator" in hand when assessing the value of taking on another year of college and its accompanying debt (Haveman n.d.). In particular, if students could compare the value of a government-subsidized loan to the opportunity costs of working, they would choose to borrow (Baum and Schwartz 2012). However, these payback calculators are usually designed to inform the initial attendance decision instead of whether to persist in college and have not been subjected to rigorous experimental testing.

Moreover, at least two studies question whether borrowing for college is inherently rational, noting that students who decline loans may be seeking to avoid temptation or trouble. Dowd (2008) posits that students with stronger senses of self (e.g., internal locus of control and self-control) and correspondingly higher educational expectations ought to behave more like econometricians when making decisions—presumably *increasing* their likelihood of borrowing for college. However, Dowd is unable to empirically test this hypothesis. Instead, Cadena and Keys (2013) indirectly test the hypothesis that loan aversion is driven by self-control. They use two waves of federal NPSAS data by comparing the rates of loan rejection among students who are living on and off campus and are eligible for the maximum amount of subsidized loans. They report that their findings "support a self-control explanation . . . students are rejecting the loans, in part, to avoid the temptation to over-spend out of borrowed money" (p. 1118).

It may also be the case that the decision to decline loans is related to students' sense of why they are enrolled and what they aim to achieve, and particularly to variation in their expected returns. Evidence suggests that students repeatedly revise and rethink their rationales for pursuing college degrees, practically on a daily basis, as they proceed through college (Armstrong and Hamilton 2013; Clydesdale 2007; Deil-Amen and Goldrick-Rab 2009; Manski and Wise 1983). Students who are academically prepared for college may perceive borrowing as less risky, perhaps because pursuing college incurs fewer psychic costs. To be clear, while this idea expands on theories of college as a "great experiment" (Manski and Wise 1983), it is too simplistic to suggest that when college feels worthwhile, students will decide to take on loans, as other contexts can also offset or mediate these decisions. For example, some research indicates that the longer a student is enrolled in college, the less likely she or he is to be risk averse (Davies and Lea 1995). The increase in a student's debt load seems to precede a change in their feelings toward debt—in other words the more debt accrued, the greater the tolerance for debt.

One key attribute of many theories of loan aversion, particularly those drawn from economics, is that they are methodologically individualistic in their approach, assuming that students make borrowing decisions independently. But there is a growing body of research suggesting differential responsiveness to financing options according to the setting and context in which decisions are made (Armstrong and Hamilton 2013; Dowd 2008; Goldrick-Rab, Harris, and Trostel 2009; Hossler, Schmit, and Vesper 1999; McDonough 1997; Paulsen and St. John 1997; Perna 2006, 2008; St. John, Paulsen, and Carter 2005; Tinto 1993). Individuals can make decisions in the context of their familial needs or their community needs, and the role played by those other actors is more important than what is assumed by "preferences" in economic models, since the influence of those contexts can be reciprocal. For example, loan decisions may be both shaped by and contribute to the social and cultural capital students obtain from their relationships (Goldrick-Rab, Harris, and Trostel 2009; McDonough and Calderone 2006; Paulsen and St. John 1997).

More broadly, a student's willingness to borrow may be moderated by university institutional culture—specifically, how university administrators, faculty, staff, and students explicitly and implicitly add (or reduce) college costs by demanding more (or less) from students in order for them to fully engage in college life. Indeed, borrowing behaviors vary substantially by institution and how much time students spend in college. At schools like most of those in this study—public universities—56 percent of students who spent a year or less enrolled without completing a degree borrowed, compared to 63 percent of those who stayed up to two years (Baum and Payea 2012). While such institutional differences in loan taking are well documented, explanations for those differences are not always articulated (Cunningham and Santiago 2008; Gross et al. 2009).

In *Paying for the Party*, Armstrong and Hamilton (2013) document the impacts of what Jacob, McCall, and Stange (2013) term the "country-clubification" of state universities. Responding to the demands of many wealthy and out-of-state students for the college experiences that preserve and enhance their existing social advantages, these public institutions are increasingly spending limited resources to create opportunities and settings for elitist socialization. High-income students respond positively to higher sticker prices, seeking out colleges and universities that cost *more*, while low-income students prefer institutions that cost less (Hoxby and Avery 2012). The expenses associated with higher sticker prices crowd out other spending, and the resulting climate has the potential to alienate working-class students for whom college is meant to be a route out of poverty, not a visit to elite cultures. They cannot participate without taking on loans, and even with the loans, they often still cannot afford full participation.

On the other hand, loan aversion may be related to the familial environments in which students were raised. This would be consistent with evidence on risk aversion. For example, Hryshko, Luengo-Prado, and Sørensen (2011) provide evidence from the Panel Study of Income Dynamics (PSID), measuring risk aversion based on a set of survey questions probing respondents' willingness to accept jobs with various combinations of income probabilities. Risk aversion is inferred from the answers to these questions, and the composite risk-aversion measure is regressed on a variety of background variables. The authors find that the best demographic predictors of risk aversion are age, gender, and parental education, as well as whether they lived with both parents when they were younger. They find that males and children of more educated parents are less risk averse. While they do not find that income is a predictor of risk aversion, this is partly because parents' education and income are correlated; they do find a simple (negative) correlation with risk aversion as expected.

Absent sufficient social capital to help them understand student loans in particular, students may seek attitude-behavior consistency by either refusing loans because they also refuse credit cards, or reframing student debt as different from other forms of debt so as to justify accepting it. For example, Davies and Lea (1995) describe students who are averse to taking on debt but maintain consistency between that attitude and their behavior (loan taking in college) by not recognizing student loans as like credit card debt. The way debt is framed may therefore be important to whether or not students accept it. In a laboratory experiment conducted with financial aid recipients in Chile, Colombia, and Mexico, Caetano, Palacios, and Patrinos (2011) conclude that debt aversion—widely detected in their sample—is due to labeling effects. Specifically, labeling a contract as a "loan" decreased its probability of being selected over a financially equivalent "contract" by more than 8 percent. The authors also find that students are willing to pay a premium of about 4 percent of the financed value to avoid a contract labeled as debt. They conclude that debt aversion exists and may potentially distort investments.

Another possibility is that students' orientations toward loans are related to their familial beliefs, particularly their time horizon or future time perspective, a measure of the extent to which individuals focus on the future rather than the present or past. This time horizon is typically measured using a discount rate, which reflects the weight that individuals place on events in the future compared to those of today. Individuals with a future orientation, which is considered a hallmark of "modern" American life, tend to have lower discount rates as they place relatively more weight on the future and a longer time horizon. Meanwhile, a present orientation, with a higher discount rate and a shorter time horizon, is labeled traditional, and in a sense, "backward."

Economists theorize that students who have a long time horizon— those who give considerable weight in their thinking to their long-term well-being—are more likely to make investments with long-term payoffs, including investing in retirement savings and borrowing for school. There are clear socioeconomic differences in time horizons. For example, Lawrence (1991) shows that higher socioeconomic adults (those who tend to be white and who have higher incomes) have longer time horizons. Specifically, these adults evidently "discount" or reduce the value of future costs and benefits at a rate of 12 percent per year, whereas economically disadvantaged adults discount the future at a rate of 19 percent per year, compared to the 8–9 percent yield of long-term Treasury notes during that time frame. Put differently, the time horizon of economically disadvantaged people is less than two-thirds as long as economically advantaged people. Similarly, a study conducted in

Canada examines loan aversion among students from a range of family income backgrounds, using a set of lab experiments. The authors find that loan aversion was more common for low-income students because they had a greater tendency to discount future rewards (Palameta and Voyer 2010).

However, it is also possible that a shorter time horizon is linked to variation in expected returns to college, particularly due to the estimated chances of completing degrees and finding employment after graduation. For example, Latino students interviewed in focus groups in one study expressed an aversion to loans because they must be repaid even if degrees are not completed. They also said they would prefer to make their college choices based on their current economic situations and what they can afford while managing their family and personal responsibilities. "They would rather 'pay as they go,' and they believe they can get a quality education wherever they enroll, as long as they are motivated" (Cunningham and Santiago 2008, p. 18). This may be related to the disproportionate number of Latino (and Asian) students from immigrant families, which tend to operate in unbanked cash economies (Teranishi 2010). Very different results were obtained from a sample studied at one California university (Brint and Rotondi 2008), where the authors report that students no longer think of loans as a burden to be avoided or discharged quickly, but rather as a means of freedom, which opens up (rather than limits) behavioral options. The increased availability of loan repayment options—such as income-based repayment, income-contingent repayment, and pay-as-you-earn—has the potential to reduce the risk of borrowing for college, but these programs are only utilized by a small percentage of eligible students. Only one-tenth of the 15 million students with Federal Direct Loans are enrolled in these income-based options (Chopra 2013).

A low future time perspective, or a past orientation, appears unresponsive to changes in information possessed by the individual. For example, in a study of retirement savings, Jacobs-Lawshen and Hershey (2005) find that increasing the knowledge of financial planning among those with a past orientation induced no increase in their rates of retirement savings. They conclude, "When it comes to savings, it is difficult to overcome a short time horizon. Failing to look to the future ensures a minimal impact of risk tolerance on saving, almost irrespective of how much one knows about financial planning" (p. 339). A critical question is whether saving for retirement should be thought of as comparable to borrowing for college, given the long-term payoffs, and whether or not borrowing for college is a "failure" in the same way that not saving for retirement is said to be. Additionally, a study by Norvilitis and Mendes-Da-Silva (2013) provides some indication that students with a stronger sense of delayed gratification (a future orientation) have lower levels debt.

Another aspect of students' preferences, which may be grounded in the beliefs of their families, relates to their work orientation. More than 75 percent of undergraduates work, but according to some studies, working during college (especially over long hours), has been linked to lower rates of degree completion (King 2002; Pascarella and Terenzini 2005). Other studies, however, find the opposite (Bozick 2007; Staff and Mortimer 2007; Stinebrickner and Stinebrickner 2003). A posited advantage of loans, therefore, has been the ability to alleviate the need to work (or work so much). But a work orientation may go beyond a preference, especially when one considers the value that some individuals place on working, or what some sociologists refer to as the "centrality" of work. Put simply, people have many reasons for working, some of which are not plainly economic. For example, ethnographic evidence indicates that some students elect to work in order to honor their family or culture, or because they have always worked (Mortimer 2003; Weis 1985). If work is central to the lives of students, serving to connect them to others and bring meaning to their lives, then it may well not be replaced with loans (Feldman and Doerpinghaus 1992; Lobel 1991).

It may also be the case that students vary in the social capital they can draw on to understand and make sense of loans. One of the primary difficulties with current financial aid policy is that it is poorly understood by nearly all of its constituents (Goldrick-Rab and Roksa 2008). Most people do not know what opportunities for aid exist, how to access the various programs, and what one can expect to receive. Low-income parents and students are less likely to receive high-quality information about financial aid opportunities, and as a result are less likely to file a federal application for student aid (FAFSA) or apply to more expensive colleges (which may, in fact, offer them a better financial aid package) (Long 2008). Upper-income students receive information about college from a variety of sources, while low-income students rely on their high school counselors, largely because their parents and siblings did not attend college (Cabrera and La Nasa 2000). As a result, students from poor families who would likely qualify for all or nearly all of the aid required to finance college fail to even apply, since they have limited access to information about how to apply for aid, little assistance in filling out the extraordinarily complex application, and substantial (and warranted) fears that college is unaffordable. Students from low-income families who are insufficiently educated as to the variation in quality among college financing strategies, and frustrated by the time-consuming nature of the application process, unwittingly take on high-interest private loans, credit cards, or off-campus employment without complete knowledge of the consequences (Cabrera and La Nasa 2000). Thus, the amount of social capital held, as embodied in, for example, assistance with the FAFSA, may explain disparities in loan aversion.

RESEARCH QUESTIONS AND HYPOTHESES

Drawing on this wide array of prior economic and sociological theory and evidence, we conceive of the choices involved in accepting or rejecting student loans as involving both individual-level and family or community decisions. We ask the following five research questions:

1) How does the way loan aversion is measured affect the assessment of which students are loan averse?

2) What are the key demographic disparities in loan aversion among students from low-income families?

3) Which of the following factors appears to moderate those observed disparities in loan aversion: family financial strength; perceived returns to degree; financial knowledge; attitudes, beliefs, and dispositions; work behaviors; and social capital?

4) How is the assessment of these moderators affected by measurement of loan aversion?

5) How is loan aversion related to postsecondary outcomes?

METHODOLOGY

Using survey and administrative records for a sample of Pell Grant recipients participating in the Wisconsin Scholars Longitudinal Study (WSLS), we examine the incidence and correlates of loan-taking behaviors among low-income students—all of whom have unmet financial need—and consider a range of potential explanations for observed variation in these.[7] To examine the reasons for loan aversion, we focus on a relatively young sample of first-time, full-time undergraduates attending two-year and four-year colleges in one state's public higher education system. In addition, after exploring institutional differences in loan taking, we use college fixed effects to control for any institutional differences and focus on student-level differences.

Setting

This study takes place in Wisconsin, where more than 80 percent of undergraduates are enrolled in the public University of Wisconsin (UW) System and Wisconsin Technical College System. As in many states, over the past decade state appropriations per full-time equivalent student have declined (State Higher Education Executive Officers 2013). As a result, the costs of attendance continue to rise, and demonstrated need unmet through financial grant aid is swelling. For example, in 2010–2011, the average family contribution to college costs in the UW System was $4,686, the average amount of need-based aid was $7,303, and the average amount of unmet financial need was $5,236— up from $1,951 in 2002–2003 (Wisconsin Higher Educational Aids Board 2012).

Wisconsin is also typical when it comes to key indicators of college access and success. The on-time college-going rate among high school graduates is 61 percent (the national average is 62 percent), the average ACT composite test score is 22 (the national average is 21), 52 percent of undergraduates file applications for financial aid (compared to 50 percent nationally), the first-to-second-year retention rate at universities is 77 percent (76 percent nationally), and the six-year graduation rate for bachelor's students is 58 percent (56 percent nationally) (Goldrick-Rab and Harris 2010).

Data

Data for this study come from multiple sources, and all details of each measure are provided in Table 10.1. We utilize two measures of loan aversion. The first is based on a question administered in a survey conducted during the students' first semester of college, in fall 2008. As part of a much longer survey about college plans and finances, students were asked: "Suppose you could take out a loan up to $10,000 with a 7 percent interest rate. How much money would you take?" Students could choose from the following five choices: $0, $1,000, $2,500, $5,000, and $10,000. In fall 2008, the interest rate on subsidized student loans was 6.0 percent, and for unsubsidized student loans the rate was 6.8 percent.[8] We did not tell the students this information in the survey, and the overall responses and level of financial aid knowledge suggested in the study provide little reason to think that they were aware the degree to which the rate we inquired about was slightly higher than the current unsubsidized rate and a point higher than the subsidized rate. At the time data were collected, income-based repayment was not available.[9] We code students who said they would take *none* of the loan they were offered as loan averse.

In addition, we used information from students' financial aid packages, also obtained in fall 2008, which indicated whether students were offered loans, how much they were offered and of what type (subsidized or unsubsidized), and the amount accepted. This is an uncommon approach, as few data sets include loan offered, usually only recording the loans accepted.[10] We code a student as loan averse if she refused all loans offered in that term.[11] We also include a substantial number of demographic characteristics and measures of moderating concepts drawn from both survey and administrative data. All details on these are found in Table 10.1.

Sample

The overall WSLS sample includes 3,000 students. For this chapter, we focus on a subsample that includes the 684 students attending 10 of the state's 13 public universities and the 13 public two-year colleges for whom we observe both the key survey and administrative measures of loan aversion described above. The sample is 58 percent female and

74 percent non-Hispanic white, and almost 80 percent of the students lack a parent with a bachelor's degree. About 4 percent of the students are first-generation immigrants, 10 percent are second-generation, and 9 percent speak a language other than English in their homes. On average, in their first year of college these Pell recipients faced a net price of more than $8,000 after taking all grant aid into account. Most of them had a substantial amount of unmet financial need, as defined by the cost of attendance less all grant aid. On average, unmet need was $7,700. More specifically, over 85 percent had unmet need exceeding $3,500 (the maximum subsidized Stafford Loan for first-year students), and 72 percent had unmet need of greater than the $5,500 that first-year students may borrow in subsidized and unsubsidized loans.

Almost 17 percent of these students grew up in poverty, and almost one-third qualify for a zero expected family contribution, meaning that their families are not expected to pay anything toward their postsecondary education. About 12 percent of students reported providing financial support to their families when attending school, with more than one-third feeling a sense of financial obligation to their families, and 25 percent drawing no monetary support from their families. They held very little credit card debt—just about $150 on average. Fifty-eight percent of students in the sample did not even have a credit card.

In terms of academic preparation, students had an ACT score of just over 21, the statewide average, and nearly three quarters had strong high school preparation for college, but only about half said it was extremely likely that they would complete a bachelor's degree, and one in five said they were having trouble with college. On average, they expected to enter a career paying just over $60,000 per year. Slightly more than 60 percent of students answered at least 12 of 15 questions regarding financial knowledge correctly, and just under half said they were competent at managing their money.

This sample of Pell Grant recipients exhibits a long time horizon and overwhelming willingness to sacrifice today's needs for their future potential. Very few indicate a general averse to all forms of debt. About 95 percent evidenced an internal locus of control, and 75 percent said that debt was not a normative part of today's lifestyle or that taking out loans was a good thing to help you enjoy life. The vast majority worked while in high school, and about half worked while in college as well, an average of eight hours per week.

Table 10.1 Description of Measures, Sources, and Coding

Concept/measure	Source	Question wording (survey)	Response categories	Coding
Loan aversion				
Aversion A	Baseline survey, Fall 2008	Suppose you could take out a loan up to $10,000 with a 7 percent interest rate. How much money would you take?	$0, $1,000, $2,500, $5,000, and $10,000	Loan averse = $0
Aversion B	Financial aid package, Fall 2008			Loan averse = accepted $0 of loan offered, conditional on offer
Demographics				
Gender	Baseline survey, Fall 2008	What is your gender?	Female, male	Female = 1
Race/ethnicity	Baseline survey, Fall 2008	What is your race/ethnicity?	Non-Hispanic White, African-American, Latino, Southeast Asian, Native American	If multiple categories were checked, the underrepresented group = 1
Parental education	Baseline survey, Fall 2008	What is the highest level of education completed by either parent?	Grade 1–8, some high school, GED, high school graduate, some college/technical degree/associate's, bachelor's degree, master's degree or above	First-generation student = no parent with more than high school degree
Immigrant status	Baseline survey, Fall 2008	Were you/your mother/your father born in the United States?	Yes/no	1st gen = student born outside U.S.; 2nd gen = either parent born outside U.S.
Primary language	Baseline survey, Fall 2008	What language is spoken most often inside your family's home?	English, Spanish, Hmong, Chinese, other	Other than English = 1

Variable	Source	Question	Response	Coding
Institutional cost				
Net price	Financial aid package, Fall 2008			Difference between institutional cost of attendance and all grant aid awarded to student
Family financial strength				
Childhood poverty	Survey, Fall 2009	"When I was growing up there wasn't enough to eat at home." "When I was growing up I had to wear secondhand clothes."	Indicate if true	If either answer is yes, poverty = 1
Expected family contribution	Financial aid package, Fall 2008			Computed using 2008 FAFSA and federal formula; both continuous measure and flag for $0 EFC (lowest) included
Financial reciprocity	Baseline survey, Fall 2008	"Since starting college, have you regularly given any family or friends (not including spouses) more than $50 per month? Do not include loans."	Yes/no	Coded 1 = yes
Financial obligation to family	Baseline survey, Fall 2008	"I feel obligated to support my family financially."	5-point Likert scale indicating agreement/disagreement	1 = Somewhat or strongly agree
No financial help from family	Baseline survey, Fall 2008	"In the past year…my family provided money for my education."	5-point Likert scale indicating agreement/disagreement	1 = Not at all
Credit card debt	Baseline survey, Fall 2008	"How much do you owe on all of your credit cards combined?"	<$100; $100–499; $500–999; $1,000–4,999; $5,000 or more	

(continued)

Table 10.1 (continued)

Concept/measure	Source	Question wording (survey)	Response categories	Coding
Perceived returns to degree				
Likely to complete degree	Baseline survey, Fall 2008	"How likely are each of the following scenarios; you will get a bachelor's degree"	5-point Likert scale indicating agreement/disagreement	1 = Extremely likely
ACT score	ACT record data			
Strong high school coursework	Financial aid package, Fall 2008	Presence or absence of "Academic Competitiveness Grant"	ACG was a federal grant indicating the student had completed rigorous high school coursework, based on an analysis of transcripts	1 = ACG present
Course difficulty	Baseline survey, Fall 2008	"Classes are more difficult than I expected."	5-point Likert scale indicating agreement/disagreement	1 = Somewhat or strongly agree
Expected monetary returns to degree	Baseline survey, Fall 2008	"For the career you most plan to have, how much money do you expect to make in a year?"	Fill in blank	Logged earnings
Financial knowledge				
Overall knowledge	Baseline survey, Fall 2008	"What is the difference between a grant and a loan?" "Which statement best describes the difference between a subsidized and unsubsidized loan?" And two series of questions about financial aid criteria and credit scores	15 Items testing general financial literacy and specific financial aid knowledge (see notes for more)	Coded 0–15, also high = 12+

Perceived competence with money	Baseline survey, Fall 2008	"How well do you think you handle managing money?"	5-point Likert scale	1 = Very or extremely well
Attitudes, beliefs, dispositions				
Time horizon	Baseline survey, Fall 2008	"If you were guaranteed you would receive the money, which of the following options would you select right now?"	$75 right now; $100 in 3 months; $250 in one year; $500 in 3 years	Coded as four binary variables ($75 right now omitted)
Willingness to sacrifice	Baseline survey, Fall 2008	"I am willing to sacrifice today so that my life will be better tomorrow."	5-point Likert scale indicating agreement/disagreement	1 = Somewhat or strongly agree
Generalized debt aversion	Baseline survey, Fall 2008	"Is it ever okay to borrow money?"	Yes/no	1 = Yes
Self-control	Baseline survey, Fall 2008	"Being in debt is part of today's lifestyle." "Taking out a loan is a good thing because it allows you to enjoy life."	5-point Likert scale indicating agreement/disagreement	1 = Somewhat or strongly disagree with either statement
Internal locus of control	Baseline survey, Fall 2008	"I am responsible for what happens to me."	5-point Likert scale indicating agreement/disagreement	1 = Somewhat or strongly agree
Work behaviors				
Worked in high school	Baseline survey, Fall 2008	"When you were a high school senior how many hours, on average, did you work each week?"	Open-ended	Coded 1= if any hours recorded
Currently working	Baseline survey, Fall 2008	"Have you been working since you started college?"	Yes/no	Coded 1 = yes

(continued)

Table 10.1 (continued)

Concept/measure	Source	Question wording (survey)	Response categories	Coding
Number of hours working	Baseline survey, Fall 2008	"In the last seven days how many hours did you spend working on-campus? Working off-campus?"	Open-ended	Total number of hours recorded
Social capital				
FAFSA assistance-person	Baseline survey, Fall 2008	"Who helped you fill out your financial aid application? Check all that apply."	Parent, sibling, spouse, guidance counselor, friend, someone else, no one (filled it out myself)	No help; family (parent, sibling spouse); other (friend, guidance counselor, someone else)
FAFSA assistance-level of education	Baseline survey, Fall 2008	"Did the person who helped you earn a college degree?"	Yes/no	Coded 1 = yes
Confident help is available	Baseline survey, Fall 2008	"How confident are you that, if faced with financial problems, you could get help from other people rather than dropping out of school?"	5-point Likert scale	1 = Very or extremely confident
Academic outcomes				
Enrollment	National student clearinghouse records and college transcripts by term			

Credits earned	College transcripts by term
On 4-year degree track	College transcripts by term
Semesters enrolled	
Cumulative GPA	College transcript

| Completed 90 credits within 3 years | |
| Total number of terms enrolled | |

NOTE: The data set includes a measure of religious preference and a measure of work centrality but both lack sufficient variation for inclusion. Measures of financial knowledge include A) In your opinion what is the difference between a grant and a loan? (i) Grant comes from Federal government, loans come from Wisconsin; (ii) A grant doesn't have to be paid back; a loan has to be paid back; (iii) A grant has to be paid back but no interest is charged, a loan must be paid back and interest is charged. B) Which of the following describes the biggest difference between subsidized and unsubsidized Stafford Loans? (i) A subsidized loan does not charge interest, an unsubsidized loan charges interest, (ii) a subsidized loan is paid for by parents, an unsubsidized loan is paid off by students, (iii) a subsidized loan costs students more than an unsubsidized loan, (iv) a subsidized loan does not charge interest until the student leaves college, an unsubsidized loan begins to charge interest as soon as the student receives the loan. C) Agree/disagree: A government loan is a kind of financial aid. D) Agree/disagree: The money students earn while working in college is used to calculate how much aid they get. E) Agree/disagree: If a student earns more than a certain amount from working, their financial aid might be reduced. F) Agree/disagree: Students receive the same amount of financial aid for every year they are in school. G) Agree/disagree: Students will receive the same amount of financial aid if they switch schools. H) Agree/disagree: Students who take time off from school will get the same amount of financial aid if/when they return. I) Which of the following factors are used to calculate credit scores? Check all that apply: number of jobs held, amount of existing debt, gender, whether payments were made on time, types of credit used, race/ethnicity, recent applications for credits cards or other loans.

It is worth noting that Avery and Turner (2012) hypothesize that the FAFSA is one of the greatest deterrents to loan taking, but in this sample we observe a substantial group of needy students who complete the FAFSA and still decline all loans. Most students in the sample (87 percent) got assistance from a family member when completing the FAFSA for college, with about 42 percent getting assistance from a college-educated person. But only about one-third reported being confident that they could obtain financial help if in trouble so as to avoid leaving college. Overall, about 70 percent of these students remained enrolled at their initial institution a year after they first began.

Table 10.2 also compares the characteristics of this sample to the characteristics of all students in the WSLS attending those same universities and colleges. There are some notable differences between the analytic sample and the overall WSLS sample, with the analytic sample being less racially diverse and by some measures more economically advantaged. These are important considerations when thinking about the generalizability of the results.

Analysis

We use blocked probit regressions with marginal effects to examine potential explanations for why students decline loans—we do this first using the administrative measure (Table 10.6) and then the survey measure (Table 10.7). We also use probit regression to examine the association between loan aversion and college performance and retention.

BORROWING BEHAVIORS AMONG PELL GRANT RECIPIENTS

Next, we describe the findings regarding the measurement of loan aversion, the characteristics of loan-averse students, and the characteristics of institutions where loan-averse students are more or less prevalent.

Table 10.2 Descriptive Statistics by Sample Inclusion

Characteristic	Not in sample	Analytic sample difference
Female (%)	54.6	4.2
		(2.7)
Race/ethnicity (%)		
Non-Hispanic white	69.4	5.1*
		(2.8)
Latino	7.3	−1.8
		(1.5)
Hmong (Southeast Asian)	10.0	−2.4
		(1.8)
Native American	4.3	−1.3
		(1.2)
Black	6.8	0.8
		(1.5)
Parental education < bachelor's degree (%)	78.6	0.9
		(2.5)
Immigrant status		
First-generation (%)	6.9	−2.4*
		(1.4)
Second-generation (%)	12.0	−2.5
		(2.0)
English not first language (%)	12.4	−3.4*
		(1.9)
Institutional cost		
Net price ($)	6,199	1,596***
		(322)
Family financial strength		
Childhood poverty (%)	9.3	6.8***
		(1.8)
Expected family contribution ($)	1,447	280***
		(107)
Zero EFC (%)	35.0	−7.6***
		(2.5)
Financial reciprocity (%)	12.6	−1.4
		(2.0)
Financial obligation to family (%)	34.5	−1.3
		(3.0)

(continued)

Table 10.2 (continued)

Characteristic	Not in sample	Analytic sample difference
No financial help from family (%)	20.0	5.7**
		(2.6)
Credit card debt ($)	107	54*
		(29)
Perceived returns to degree		
Likely to complete bachelor's degree (%)	51.6	1.5
		(3.2)
ACT score	21.5	0.2
		(0.4)
Strong high school coursework (%)	71.9	5.6
		(4.0)
College difficulty (%)	20.5	12.8
		(2.4)
Expected monetary returns to degree ($)	60,362	438
		(3,725)
Financial knowledge		
Overall knowledge	11.8	0.2
		(0.1)
High financial knowledge (%)	59.5	3.8
		(3.1)
Perceived financial competence (%)	42.8	1.7
		(3.1)
Attitudes, beliefs, and dispositions		
Time horizon (%)		
$75 right now	22.5	−2.4
		(2.6)
$100 in three months	16.2	−0.4
		(2.4)
$250 in one year	16.1	0.4
		(2.3)
$500 in three years	45.2	2.4
		(3.2)
Willing to sacrifice (%)	76.1	7.8***
		(2.6)

Table 10.2 (continued)

Characteristic	Not in sample	Analytic sample difference
Generalized debt aversion (%)	5.9	−0.1
		(1.4)
Self-control (%)	79.7	−3.5
		(2.6)
Internal locus of control (%)	94.5	2.8**
		(1.3)
Work behaviors		
Worked in high school (%)	83.8	3.0
		(2.2)
Currently working (%)	53.2	−0.2
		(3.2)
Current number of hours working	8.6	−1.0
		(0.8)
Social capital		
FAFSA assistance—type of person (%)		
No help—filled out alone	9.0	3.4*
		(1.9)
Family	87.0	−3.0
		(2.2)
Other person	14.3	−4.0*
		(2.1)
FAFSA assistance from college-educated person (%)	42.3	0.2
		(3.1)
Confident help is available (%)	34.5	3.3
		(3.0)
Retention at initial college in year 2 (%)	69.5	2.8
		(2.5)
Maximum sample size	880	684

NOTE: *p < 0.10; **p < 0.05; ***p < 0.01. Standard errors are in parentheses. Loan aversion categories were defined in the following ways: 1) Administrative: If a student accepted none of his/her loan offer (if offered any). 2) Survey: If responded he/she would not take any money at a 7 percent interest rate. The sample includes students at included UW System campuses only.
SOURCE: Sources for each measure are listed in Table 10.1.

Measurement

As noted earlier, most research on loan aversion has been conducted using either in-depth interviews or surveys. Measuring loan aversion in this way inherently relies on student self-reports of attitudes and/or behaviors and does not capture their actual behaviors. For this reason, we begin with a simple analysis triangulating how these two sources of data align when it comes to classifying students as loan averse. In total, 48 percent of the sample is loan averse according to either the survey or the administrative measures. The survey measure classifies 401 of students as loan averse, while the administrative measure applies that label to just 128 students. As Table 10.3 indicates, we find that the correlation between the survey and administrative measures is weak ($r = 0.21$) and aligned for only 64 percent of the sample, with 52 percent agreement that a student is *not* loan averse, and 12 percent agreement that the student *is* loan averse. Fully 29 percent of the sample would be classified as loan averse using the survey measure, even though in practice they accepted loans. In addition, 7 percent of students who said they would *not* borrow loans according to the survey *did* accept loans according to the administrative data. While these differences could be explained by other factors (for example, students might report not *wanting* to take loans but do it anyway), and therefore this evidence is not sufficient to record these as "misclassifications," the apparent disconnect is worthy of further investigation.

It is possible that some students who expressed loan aversion on the survey may have done so because they had already accepted loans and did not (or could not) want to borrow more. Nearly 72 percent of students whom according to the survey might be loan averse do appear

Table 10.3 Relationship between Survey and Administrative Data Measures of Loan Aversion

	Administrative data (%)	
Survey data	Borrower	Loan averse
Borrower	52	7
Loan averse	29	12

NOTE: Total sample size = 684; percentaged according to that total $R = 0.213$.
SOURCE: Survey data are from the fall WSLS, and administrative data are from the University of Wisconsin system.

to be in this category, suggesting that loan aversion using survey data may be overstated. On the other hand, the survey classified about 7 percent of students as willing to accept loans, even though the administrative data indicate that they refused the loans they were offered. This may be because students regretted the decision to refuse loans and were expressing on the survey a wish to take them, or because on the survey the students meant they would take them, but not right now or not under the conditions in which they were offered.

Given the indication of apparently substantial measurement error present when loan aversion is measured using survey data, we take additional steps in the next analyses to consider which students may be mislabeled as loan averse when only survey data are used.

Student-Level Differences in Borrowing

Table 10.4 displays the differences in characteristics between loan-averse students and borrowers using both the administrative data measure of loan aversion and the survey measure of loan aversion. The overall trends in student characteristics are consistent with most prior research. We find that Southeast Asian students (predominately Hmong in this sample) are greatly overrepresented among loan-averse students, while African Americans are substantially overrepresented among loan takers. Both first- and second-generation immigrants and students for whom English is not spoken at home are far more likely to be loan averse. In this sample of students from low-income families, where almost 80 percent of students do not have at least one parent with a bachelor's degree, more parental education seems to lead to less loan aversion. Students facing higher net prices were also less likely to be loan averse.

Notably, students from families with less financial strength are more often loan averse. This is also more common among students who grew up in poverty or have lower expected family contributions, and among those who report that their families do not provide monetary support for their college education and yet feel obligated to financially support their family while in college.

We hypothesized that students who perceive stronger returns to their degrees would be more likely to borrow for college, but we find limited support for this assertion. Overall, it seems that students with

Table 10.4 Descriptive Statistics by Borrowing Behavior

Characteristic	Admin. sample		Survey sample		Test for measurement difference (p-value)
	Borrowers	Loan averse difference	Borrowers	Loan averse difference	
Demographics					
Female (%)	57.8	5.6	59.8	−2.4	0.167
		(5.2)		(4.1)	
Race/ethnicity (%)					
Non-Hispanic White	76.4	−10.9**	74.9	−0.9	0.051
		(4.8)		(3.5)	
Latino	5.1	2.5	5.8	−0.7	0.262
		(2.6)		(1.8)	
Hmong (Southeast Asian)	5.3	13.5***	5.2	5.9***	0.032
		(3.7)		(2.2)	
Native American	2.9	0.6	2.8	0.6	0.992
		(2.0)		(1.4)	
Black	8.4	−4.8***	9.0	−3.5*	0.622
		(1.8)		(2.0)	
Parental education < bachelor's degree (%)	79.9	−2.4	80.8	−3.4	0.858
		(4.4)		(3.3)	
Immigrant status					
First-generation (%)	3.2	7.3***	2.2	5.4***	0.468
		(2.8)		(1.7)	

Second-generation (%)	8.1	8.0** (3.7)	8.6	2.2 (2.4)	0.115
English not first language (%)	6.2	16.2*** (4.0)	6.5	5.9** (2.4)	0.008
Institutional cost					
Net price ($)	8,027	−1,322*** (385)	8,391	−1,428*** (290)	0.808
Family financial strength					
Childhood poverty (%)	15.3	4.5 (4.1)	15.0	2.6 (3.0)	0.654
Expected family contribution ($)	1499	−396*** (137)	1475	−109 (113)	0.062
Zero EFC (%)	27.6	6.3 (4.9)	27.3	3.5 (3.8)	0.614
Financial reciprocity (%)	10.8	2.4 (3.4)	11.3	−0.2 (2.6)	0.486
Financial obligation to family (%)	31.3	11.1** (5.2)	29.8	8.4** (4.0)	0.638
No financial help from family (%)	23.7	11.2** (5.0)	25.6	0.3 (3.7)	0.043
Credit card debt ($)	157	24 (69)	220	−139*** (41)	0.066

(continued)

Table 10.4 (continued)

Characteristic	Admin. sample		Survey sample		Test for measurement difference (p-value)
	Borrowers	Loan averse difference	Borrowers	Loan averse difference	
Perceived returns to degree					
Likely to complete bachelor's degree (%)	53.5	−1.9	53.2	−0.2	0.774
		(5.3)		(4.1)	
ACT score	21.8	−0.7	21.5	0.5	0.014
		(0.4)		(0.3)	
Strong high school coursework (%)	78.9	−8.1*	75.9	3.8	0.020
		(4.6)		(3.4)	
College difficulty (%)	34.1	−4.1	37.7	−10.4***	0.253
		(4.8)		(3.8)	
Expected monetary returns to degree ($)	61,510	−4228	60,844	−108	0.487
		(4,306)		(4,442)	
Financial knowledge					
Overall knowledge	12.0	−0.2	12.0	0.0	0.280
		(0.2)		(0.2)	
Above average financial knowledge (%)	63.2	0.8	62.1	3.0	0.702
		(5.2)		(4.0)	
Perceived financial competence (%)	44.1	1.7	41.8	6.3	0.436
		(5.3)		(4.1)	

Attitudes, beliefs, and dispositions				
Time horizon (%)				
$75 right now	20.8	−3.7 (3.9)	22.1	−4.7 (3.2)	0.830
$100 in three months	16.5	−3.7 (3.3)	16.4	−1.4 (3.0)	0.581
$250 in one year	16.8	−1.7 (3.9)	18.5	−4.8 (3.0)	0.405
$500 in three years	46.0	9.1* (5.2)	43.0	11.0*** (4.1)	0.747
Willing to sacrifice (%)	84.1	−1.2 (3.9)	84.3	−0.9 (3.1)	0.945
Generalized debt aversion (%)	5.4	2.7 (2.7)	5.7	0.3 (1.9)	0.440
Self-control (%)	74.8	8.1** (4.0)	70.7	13.2*** (3.4)	0.262
Internal locus of control (%)	97.5	−0.9 (1.8)	97.0	0.9 (1.3)	0.414
Work behaviors				
Worked in high school (%)	87.0	−1.0 (3.4)	88.1	−3.0 (2.8)	0.621
Currently working (%)	50.8	13.1** (5.3)	50.1	6.9* (4.2)	0.303
Current number of hours working	6.9	3.9*** (1.2)	7.2	0.9 (0.8)	0.014

(continued)

Table 10.4 (continued)

Characteristic	Admin. sample		Survey sample		Test for measurement difference (p-value)
	Borrowers	Loan averse difference	Borrowers	Loan averse difference	
Social capital					
FAFSA assistance—type of person (%)					
No help—filled out alone	12.7	−1.6 (3.4)	11.9	1.3 (2.8)	0.493
Family	84.6	−3.5 (4.0)	84.9	−2.1 (3.0)	0.767
Other person	8.7	9.4** (3.9)	10.4	−0.2 (2.4)	0.018
FAFSA assistance from college-educated person (%)	42.0	2.8 (5.2)	40.0	6.0 (4.1)	0.587
Confident help is available (%)	38.1	−1.8 (5.1)	32.8	12.0*** (4.0)	0.016
Retention at initial college in year 2 (%)	76.2	0.6 (4.4)	72.1	10.2*** (3.4)	0.055
Sample size	556	128	401	283	

NOTE: *p < 0.10; **p < 0.05; ***p < 0.01. Standard errors are in parentheses. Difference = difference in means between borrowers and loan-averse students. Loan aversion categories were defined in the following ways: Administrative: If a student accepted none of his/her loan offer (if offered any). Survey: If responded he/she would not take any money at a 7 percent interest rate. The sample includes UW System administrative consenters with both survey and administrative data on loan aversion.

SOURCE: Sources for each measure are listed in Table 10.1.

stronger academic preparation and greater expected earnings are more likely to borrow. However, unexpectedly, students who find college more difficult are also more likely to borrow.

Perhaps most remarkable given current policy efforts, we find no statistically significant evidence that financial knowledge is related to borrowing behaviors among these low-income students. There is some indication that students who perceived themselves as financially competent were more loan averse, but the finding is sensitive to how loan aversion is measured and cannot be said to differ from zero. Thus, it does not appear that increasing the financial education of these students would alter their borrowing behavior.

Also contrary to prior studies, we find that in this sample of Pell Grant recipients, loan aversion is associated with a longer time horizon. The vast majority of students (about 84 percent) reported a willingness to sacrifice today for tomorrow, and while this did not differ for loan-averse students, those who were averse to loans were far more likely to choose to receive $500 in three years rather than a smaller amount of money sooner. It seems these students may forgo the short-term need for resources for what they perceive as a better deal in the future (having less debt). This is consistent with the finding that students with self-control are also overrepresented among loan-averse students.

Loan aversion appears to be offset by the decision to work during college. While not statistically significant, results indicate that students who worked in high school are more likely to borrow, while those working in college are less likely to borrow.

Finally, there is some evidence that the form of social capital held by students relates to their loan aversion. Students who believe they can get financial help if they need it are less likely to borrow, as are students who got help from someone other than a family member when applying for college. In other words, they may have additional supports that either help them perceive that loans are unnecessary or are inadvisable.

The measure used to define loan aversion generally does not seem to affect the description of who is loan averse and who is a borrower, with a few exceptions. First, and most importantly, if students are classified as loan averse using the survey data, then non-Hispanic white students are equally represented among loan takers and nontakers. However, if loan aversion is measured with administrative data, non-Hispanic white students are substantially overrepresented among loan takers. Also, the degree of loan aversion is much larger among Southeast Asian students when measured using administrative records compared to surveys. It is also possible that the survey and administrative measures may capture somewhat different aspects of loan aversion—for example, students may be more likely to decline loans in their first semester of college because they can gain support from their families while still expressing a desire to avoid taking on additional loans.

While the differences are not statistically significant, the trends regarding gender point in opposite directions using different data sources. Relying on the survey measure, women are more loan averse than men, but relying on the administrative measure, men are more averse than women.

The measurement of loan aversion has implications for some of these differences. For example, when aversion is assessed using the survey measure, it appears that borrowing is unrelated to whether a student is non-Hispanic white, has a lower expected family contribution, the family does not contribute to their education, or the number of hours they are working. However, if the administrative data is used to measure loan aversion, we find that non-Hispanic white students are more likely to borrow, as are students with higher EFCs, while students whose families do not support them and who work longer hours are more loan averse. The strength of the relationships between student characteristics and loan aversion also vary widely according to how aversion is measured.

Institutional Level

Financial aid administrators at the colleges and universities initiate the process of borrowing for students, and students' decisions are made in the context of their campus affordability climates (Goldrick-Rab and Kendall 2013). For this reason, we next explore how loan-taking behaviors varied according to the specific college or university students attended. Table 10.5 reveals that the percentage of loan-averse students varies substantially across these Wisconsin institutions, ranging from just 7.8 percent at the most selective institution (University B) to 38.8 percent at the two-year branch campuses.[12] These differences correlate with the academic abilities of students (the correlation between ACT score and loan aversion is around $r = -0.72$). But they do not align

Table 10.5 Distribution of Borrowing Behavior (Measured Using Administrative Data) by Campus and Selectivity

Campus	Loan averse (%)	ACT 25	ACT 75	Net price ($)	% Pell	Graduation rate	Default rate	Retention rate	% minority
UW colleges	38.8	18	23	4,566	24	20	8.5	82.0	9.1
Four-year	15.7								
Most selective									
University A	8.3	23	26	6,266	17	69	2.2	83.9	6.8
University B	7.8	26	30	6,246	12	81	1.4	93.8	12.8
Total	8.0								
Somewhat selective									
University C	11.9	20	24	6,779	21	51	3.5	75.8	7.4
University D	9.1	20	25	6,225	25	56	4.5	74.0	5.0
University E	16.7	20	24	6,418	22	55	4.2	74.9	5.9
University F	9.8	21	25	6,474	25	61	3.8	78.4	5.8
University G	10.0	20	24	4,657	38	41	9.2	71.6	7.0
University H	10.9	20	24	5,506	20	56	4.5	78.0	9.5
Total	11.1								
Least selective									
University I	18.7	19	24	8,578	23	43	5.7	73.3	17.0
University J	35.9	18	23	7,940	32	27	10.4	64.3	22.8
Total	24.5								

NOTE: All students in this analysis were offered a loan. Selectivity categories are based on retention rates and ACT scores. All institutional characteristics are from the 2008–2009 academic year, except student loan default rates, which are for the FY 2009 cohort. The net price listed is for the lowest-income students ($0–$30,000 per year family income). Student loan default rates listed here are over a three-year period. Institutions are not named consistent with the WSLS data agreement.

SOURCE: University of Wisconsin System campus aid officers (loan offers and acceptances); IPEDS (percent Pell, ACT, grad rate, and net price); U.S. Department of Education (default rate); UW System Fact Book (retention rate and percent minority).

with the institution's sticker price and available financial aid—many other institutions have similar net prices but different rates of loan aversion. It is also worth noting the range of students rejecting *part* of their loans—this is again most uncommon at selective institutions, but it is most common among three of the somewhat selective universities, and this is not easily explained by examining the characteristics of those institutions.

Focusing on the 10 universities, the highest rates of loan aversion are evident at the least selective schools, where students have the lowest ACT scores and graduation rates, face the highest net prices and highest default rates, and where the proportion of students on campus from racial/ethnic minority backgrounds and/or receiving the Pell Grant are among the highest. The lowest rates of loan aversion are found at the most selective institutions enrolling the smallest fraction of Pell recipients on their campuses, and where default rates are exceptionally low and graduation rates are exceptionally high. This suggests the possibility that either the institutional context in which students make their decisions about loans may contribute to their decisions, and/or these variations reflect strong sorting processes of borrowers across schools. Again, this merits future investigation.

EXPLAINING LOAN AVERSION

We now examine whether the observed differences in loan aversion discussed above persist when taking multiple differences among students into account. We also consider whether the observed demographic differences in loan aversion can be explained by the hypothesized moderating factors described earlier. Finally, we consider the variation in explanatory power of these factors, depending on how loan aversion is measured.

Multivariate Analyses

Net of a wide range of individual characteristics and controlling for the institution attended, the analysis of loan aversion measured using survey data reveals that black students are far more likely than non-Hispanic white students to borrow, and second-generation immigrants are much more likely than native students to borrow as well (see Table 10.6). Loan-averse students do not view debt as part of today's lifestyle and are unwilling to borrow to pay for a nicer lifestyle now. At the same time, they are also more likely to have been assisted by a college-educated person when completing the FAFSA, and to feel that they can find financial help if they need it in order to avoid having to drop out of college. Unexpectedly, students who find college *more* difficult are more likely to borrow—and this is after taking into account differences in their academic preparation and work behaviors. It may be that students who find college more difficult are more realistic and/or aware of their academic challenges, and thus are borrowing loans to free themselves to focus on school.

This same analysis also suggests that black and non-Hispanic white students vary in how they view debt (termed "self control" in the tables), and once that variation is accounted for, black students are more likely than non-Hispanic white students to borrow.[13] This relationship is strengthened after additional differences in work behavior and social capital are leveled. Similarly, second-generation immigrant students appear more likely than native students to view college as difficult, and once that difference is ameliorated, differences in immigrant status in loan taking appear more prominent. It is notable that first-generation immigrants appear somewhat more loan averse than native students, while second-generation immigrants are far less loan averse.

In sharp contrast, the same analyses using administrative data to measure loan aversion fail to identify any statistically significant relationships between these theoretically important factors and loan aversion (see Table 10.7). Using the exact same sample of students but measuring aversion as declining a loan offered, none of the observed disparities in borrowing behavior (such as those indicated in the administrative data panel of Table 10.3) persist net of other factors. This may be attributable to the much smaller number of students classified as loan averse using the administrative measure, which requires students to decline loans in a specific term (the same term in which the survey was fielded). If the estimates were more precise and the observed coefficients held, we might observe some similar patterns to the survey results but with much smaller disparities.

Table 10.6 Predicting Loan Aversion Using Student Characteristics: Survey Data
Dependent variable: Declined to accept any money in hypothetical loans

Measure	Model 1	Model 2	Model 3	Model 4	Model 5	Model 6
Female	0.002	0.010	0.008	0.006	-0.004	0.001
	(0.050)	(0.050)	(0.050)	(0.050)	(0.050)	(0.050)
Latino	-0.009	-0.020	-0.038	-0.065	-0.077	-0.072
	(0.106)	(0.103)	(0.101)	(0.098)	(0.095)	(0.096)
Hmong (Southeast Asian)	0.097	0.127	0.186	0.098	0.094	0.130
	(0.167)	(0.175)	(0.179)	(0.177)	(0.180)	(0.182)
Native American	-0.006	0.029	0.016	0.057	0.064	0.100
	(0.148)	(0.157)	(0.155)	(0.154)	(0.159)	(0.164)
Black	-0.137*	-0.139*	-0.176**	-0.176**	-0.186**	-0.183**
	(0.077)	(0.082)	(0.079)	(0.075)	(0.076)	(0.072)
Parental education < bachelor's degree	-0.085	-0.091	-0.079	-0.077	-0.075	-0.031
	(0.060)	(0.062)	(0.062)	(0.063)	(0.063)	(0.065)
First-generation immigrant	0.241	0.244	0.233	0.119	0.133	0.145
	(0.167)	(0.179)	(0.186)	(0.178)	(0.180)	(0.179)
Second-generation immigrant	-0.120	-0.147	-0.153	-0.173**	-0.169**	-0.161*
	(0.101)	(0.098)	(0.093)	(0.084)	(0.086)	(0.085)
English not first language	-0.006	0.045	0.021	0.177	0.167	0.164
	(0.156)	(0.164)	(0.160)	(0.174)	(0.175)	(0.176)
Net price ($000s)	-0.034	-0.037	-0.038	-0.037	-0.038	-0.037
	(0.025)	(0.028)	(0.038)	(0.042)	(0.041)	(0.044)

Childhood poverty	−0.020	−0.027	−0.034	−0.052	−0.043
	(0.067)	(0.066)	(0.064)	(0.064)	(0.063)
EFC ($000s)	0.018	0.017	0.017	0.021	0.015
	(0.030)	(0.030)	(0.030)	(0.033)	(0.029)
Zero EFC	0.063	0.079	0.048	0.052	0.060
	(0.076)	(0.075)	(0.076)	(0.078)	(0.076)
Financial reciprocity	−0.020	−0.021	−0.046	−0.074	−0.040
	(0.083)	(0.08)	(0.076)	(0.075)	(0.078)
Financial obligation to family	0.047	0.070	0.078	0.076	0.081
	(0.056)	(0.056)	(0.056)	(0.056)	(0.057)
No financial help from family	−0.035	−0.039	−0.044	−0.039	0.001
	(0.058)	(0.056)	(0.054)	(0.055)	(0.061)
Credit card debt ($000s)	−0.173	−0.148	−0.153	−0.156	−0.160
	(0.153)	(0.165)	(0.190)	(0.189)	(0.209)
Extremely likely to complete BA	0.005	0.001	−0.011	−0.010	−0.036
	(0.050)	(0.050)	(0.050)	(0.050)	(0.050)
ACT score	—	0.007	0.007	0.006	0.006
	—	(0.014)	(0.015)	(0.014)	(0.014)
Strong high school coursework (%)	—	−0.109	−0.099	−0.099	−0.106
	—	(0.076)	(0.077)	(0.078)	(0.076)
College difficulty	—	−0.150***	−0.157***	−0.155***	−0.158***
	—	(0.051)	(0.050)	(0.051)	(0.051)
Expected earnings from college (log $)	—	−0.050	−0.049	−0.042	−0.038
	—	(0.065)	(0.068)	(0.063)	(0.063)

(continued)

Table 10.6 (continued)

Measure	Model 1	Model 2	Model 3	Model 4	Model 5	Model 6
Financial knowledge (0–15)	—	—	−0.001	0.003	0.003	0.006
			(0.024)	(0.024)	(0.024)	(0.025)
Above avg financial knowledge	—	—	−0.046	−0.071	−0.077	−0.088
			(0.090)	(0.090)	(0.092)	(0.092)
Perceived financial competence	—	—	0.062	0.040	0.040	0.039
			(0.051)	(0.050)	(0.051)	(0.050)
Time horizon: $100 in 3 months	—	—	—	0.045	0.040	0.021
				(0.085)	(0.086)	(0.085)
Time horizon: $250 in 1 year	—	—	—	−0.077	−0.077	−0.093
				(0.072)	(0.074)	(0.070)
Time horizon: $500 in 3 years	—	—	—	0.069	0.070	0.044
				(0.069)	(0.070)	(0.070)
Willing to sacrifice today for tomorrow	—	—	—	−0.001	−0.012	0.005
				(0.077)	(0.080)	(0.077)
Generalized debt aversion	—	—	—	0.139	0.138	0.182
				(0.125)	(0.126)	(0.127)
Self-control	—	—	—	0.146***	0.135**	0.132**
				(0.052)	(0.053)	(0.054)
Internal locus of control	—	—	—	−0.030	−0.002	−0.038
				(0.183)	(0.177)	(0.184)
Worked in high school	—	—	—	—	−0.028	−0.027
				—	(0.067)	(0.069)

Currently working	—	—	—	—	0.097 (0.073)	0.084 (0.073)
Number of hours currently working	—	—	—	—	0.000 (0.004)	0.001 (0.004)
Family helped on FAFSA	—	—	—	—	—	0.002 (0.071)
Other person helped on FAFSA	—	—	—	—	—	−0.114* (0.069)
FAFSA help from college-educated person	—	—	—	—	—	0.095* (0.052)
Could get financial help if needed	—	—	—	—	—	0.106* (0.056)
F-value	2.58	2.27	2.40	2.20	2.06	2.01
Sample size	472	472	472	472	472	472

NOTE: *$p < 0.10$; **$p < 0.05$; ***$p < 0.01$. A missing data flag for childhood poverty is included in the model but not reported (not significant). The regression also controls for college fixed effects. All students in this analysis were offered a loan. Standard errors are in parentheses. The coefficients are the result of a probit model with marginal effects.

SOURCE: Sources for each measure are listed in Table 10.1.

Table 10.7 Predicting Loan Aversion Using Student Characteristics: Administrative Data

Dependent variable: Declined to accept any loans, if offered.

Measure	Model 1	Model 2	Model 3	Model 4	Model 5	Model 6
Female	0.011	0.012	0.012	0.007	0.009	0.006
	(0.012)	(0.013)	(0.012)	(0.008)	(0.010)	(0.007)
Latino	0.007	0.013	0.009	0.008	0.005	0.004
	(0.018)	(0.025)	(0.022)	(0.017)	(0.015)	(0.010)
Hmong (Southeast Asian)	0.035	0.077	0.081	0.084	0.083	0.064
	(0.052)	(0.090)	(0.094)	(0.096)	(0.100)	(0.078)
Native American	0.006	0.015	0.020	0.015	0.028	0.014
	(0.020)	(0.034)	(0.037)	(0.030)	(0.045)	(0.026)
Black	−0.010	−0.014	−0.014	−0.010	−0.010	−0.007
	(0.010)	(0.013)	(0.012)	(0.009)	(0.010)	(0.007)
Parental education < bachelor's degree	−0.010	−0.011	−0.011	−0.007	−0.007	−0.007
	(0.013)	(0.016)	(0.015)	(0.011)	(0.012)	(0.010)
First-generation immigrant	0.016	0.011	0.014	0.011	0.013	0.011
	(0.030)	(0.027)	(0.028)	(0.023)	(0.027)	(0.021)
Second-generation immigrant	−0.000	−0.005	−0.004	−0.007	−0.005	−0.004
	(0.012)	(0.011)	(0.011)	(0.008)	(0.008)	(0.006)
English not first language	0.002	0.001	0.003	0.008	0.004	0.003
	(0.014)	(0.016)	(0.017)	(0.018)	(0.014)	(0.011)
Net price ($000s)	−0.003	−0.001	−0.001	−0.001	−0.001	−0.001
	(0.014)	(0.008)	(0.009)	(0.006)	(0.009)	(0.007)
Childhood poverty	—	−0.007	−0.006	−0.003	−0.006	−0.004

	(1)	(2)	(3)	(4)	(5)
EFC ($000s)	—	-0.007 (0.008)	-0.007 (0.008)	-0.006 (0.006)	-0.006 (0.007)	-0.008 (0.005)
Zero EFC	—	-0.004 (0.042)	-0.003 (0.054)	-0.004 (0.051)	-0.004 (0.050)	-0.002 (0.041)
Financial reciprocity	—	0.006 (0.010)	0.009 (0.009)	0.007 (0.007)	0.003 (0.007)	0.004 (0.005)
Financial obligation to family	—	0.004 (0.012)	0.004 (0.013)	0.003 (0.010)	0.003 (0.008)	0.003 (0.008)
No financial help from family	—	0.007 (0.008)	0.005 (0.007)	0.003 (0.005)	0.003 (0.006)	0.007 (0.005)
Credit card debt ($000s)	—	-0.001 (0.011)	0.001 (0.009)	0.001 (0.006)	0.001 (0.007)	0.001 (0.009)
Extremely likely to complete BA	—	0.015 (0.007)	0.015 (0.008)	0.012 (0.010)	0.012 (0.005)	0.008 (0.009)
ACT score	—	—	0.001 (0.014)	0.000 (0.011)	0.000 (0.011)	0.000 (0.008)
Strong high school coursework (%)	—	—	-0.002 (0.007)	-0.004 (0.003)	-0.005 (0.003)	-0.005 (0.002)
College difficulty	—	—	-0.006 (0.009)	-0.004 (0.008)	-0.005 (0.010)	-0.003 (0.008)
Expected earnings from college (log $)	—	—	-0.015 (0.105)	-0.012 (0.091)	-0.010 (0.085)	-0.008 (0.065)
Financial knowledge (0–15)	—	—	-0.004	-0.003	-0.004	-0.002

(continued)

Table 10.7 (continued)

Measure	Model 1	Model 2	Model 3	Model 4	Model 5	Model 6
Above average financial knowledge	—	—	0.011 (0.030)	0.007 (0.023)	0.010 (0.030)	0.007 (0.019)
Perceived financial competence	—	—	0.002 (0.013)	0.000 (0.009)	0.001 (0.011)	-0.000 (0.008)
Time horizon: $100 in 3 months	—	—	—	0.004 (0.005)	0.007 (0.005)	0.005 (0.004)
Time horizon: $250 in 1 year	—	—	—	0.021 (0.011)	0.025 (0.013)	0.019 (0.010)
Time horizon: $500 in 3 years	—	—	—	0.018 (0.024)	0.018 (0.027)	0.013 (0.022)
Willing to sacrifice today for tomorrow	—	—	—	0.007 (0.018)	0.006 (0.018)	0.004 (0.014)
Generalized debt aversion	—	—	—	-0.002 (0.007)	-0.002 (0.007)	-0.001 (0.006)
Self-control	—	—	—	0.003 (0.008)	0.003 (0.008)	0.002 (0.007)
Internal locus of control	—	—	—	0.007 (0.009)	0.005 (0.010)	0.004 (0.007)
Worked in high school	—	—	—	— (—)	0.001 (0.005)	0.002 (0.004)

365

	(1)	(2)	(3)	(4)	(5)	(6)
Currently working	—	—	—	—	−0.009	−0.008
					(0.010)	(0.009)
Number of hours currently working	—	—	—	—	0.001	0.001
					(0.007)	(0.005)
Family helped on FAFSA	—	—	—	—	—	0.003
						(0.005)
Other person helped on FAFSA	—	—	—	—	—	−0.003
						(0.005)
FAFSA help from college-educated person	—	—	—	—	—	−0.001
						(0.004)
Could get financial help if needed	—	—	—	—	—	0.007
						(0.008)
F-value	3.33	2.65	2.80	2.46	2.22	2.00
Sample size	472	472	472	472	472	472

NOTE: *p < 0.10; **p < 0.05; ***p < 0.01. A missing data flag for childhood poverty is included in the model, but not reported (not significant). The regression also controls for college fixed effects. All students in this analysis were offered a loan. Standard errors are in parentheses. The coefficients are the result of a probit model with marginal effects.
SOURCE: Sources for each measure are listed in Table 10.1.

LOAN AVERSION AND EDUCATIONAL OUTCOMES

There are many mechanisms through which aversion to borrowing could affect educational outcomes, which could include both positive and negative pathways. For example, loan aversion may mean that students work harder and invest more energy in school to finish faster. Or it may mean that students must attend school part-time in order to afford college (Cunningham and Santiago 2008). The most important issue, however, is that selection into loan aversion is likely to bias the estimates of impacts. In other words, if loan-averse students are more often from families with less overall financial stability, this may overstate the negative impact of aversion for educational outcomes. In the present analysis we are not able to adequately remove potential biases resulting from unobserved characteristics of both students and their schools, which correlate both with loan aversion and the chances of college persistence. Thus, our results are best thought of as correlational.

The way in which loan aversion is measured has implications for whether or not it is associated with retention to the second year of college. As Table 10.8 indicates, if aversion is measured using survey data, we find that loan-averse students are 10 percentage points *more likely* to persist in college to their second year, whereas using the administrative data we observe no relationship whatsoever. But, net of other observable characteristics, borrowers outperform loan-averse students, enrolling for more semesters, earning more credits, and higher grade point averages. The results based on the administrative data indicate that borrowers had somewhat weaker outcomes than loan-averse students with regard to enrollment each term and earned a slightly lower cumulative grade point average (see Table 10.8).

DISCUSSION

Many of our descriptive findings echo those produced by Cunningham and Santiago's (2008) analysis of the 2003–2004 NPSAS data, confirming racial/ethnic variation in loan aversion, for example.[14] This sample exhibits less loan aversion overall, probably because the stu-

Table 10.8 Academic Outcomes by Borrowing

	Administrative data measure			Survey measure		
		Regressions			Regressions	
Measure	Loan averse	Unadjusted	Covariate-adjusted	Loan averse	Unadjusted	Covariate-adjusted
Enrollment by term						
Spring 2009	95.7	−0.5	−0.2	94.4	3.4**	4.2**
		(2.1)	(3.1)		(1.5)	(2.0)
Fall 2009	82.4	0.2	−4.8	78.1	10.5***	8.9***
		(3.9)	(3.9)		(2.9)	(3.1)
Spring 2010	76.2	1.4	−1.8	73.5	9.0***	6.9**
		(4.5)	(4.8)		(3.4)	(3.5)
Fall 2010	70.9	0.2	−3.2	66.9	10.2***	9.3**
		(4.8)	(5.8)		(3.7)	(4.1)
Spring 2011	70.6	−2.5	−8.3	65.4	7.8**	5.1
		(4.8)	(6.2)		(3.8)	(4.4)
Credits earned	64.8	2.0	−1.8	63.7	6.3***	4.6**
		(2.9)	(3.1)		(2.2)	(2.1)
On 4-year track (90 credits)	18.3	5.3	2.5	22.8	−0.2	−2.2
		(4.2)	(5.2)		(3.5)	(3.8)
Semesters enrolled	4.96	−0.07	−0.18	4.78	0.41***	0.31**
		(0.17)	(0.19)		(0.13)	(0.12)
Cumulative GPA	2.58	−0.05	−0.22***	2.42	0.26***	0.23***
		(0.08)	(0.08)		(0.07)	(0.06)
Sample size	128	684	678	401	684	678

NOTE: *p < 0.10; **p < 0.05; ***p < 0.01. All students in this analysis were offered a loan. Standard errors are in parentheses. OLS is used for continuous outcomes, while a probit model with marginal effects is used for binary outcomes. Covariate-adjusted estimates include race, gender, parental education, age, EFC, total grants accepted, and campus fixed effects.
SOURCE: University of Wisconsin System.

dents all received grant aid *and* attended college full time initially, factors that the authors found were associated with lower rates of loan aversion. However, our data and methods allowed us to dig deeper into both the accuracy of the assessment of loan aversion and the meaning of it. In particular, the additional examination of variation in borrowing behaviors according to immigration status and language spoken at home highlights some additional reasons to attend to variation in borrowing behaviors. The fastest growing segments of the undergraduate populations, especially at public two-year colleges, appear more disinclined to borrow.

Our analysis is consistent with recent research suggesting that declining student loans may not be irrational, but rather reflect students' and their families' tastes for commitment and preference for making do without debt (Cadena and Keys 2013). Students who borrow may not share these preferences or may find them outweighed by other needs, and they are more likely to find themselves having difficulty in college. We find complementary evidence from in-depth interviews conducted for the same study with a focal sample of 50 WSLS participants interviewed repeatedly over a five-year period. One student refused to borrow, putting great emphasis on his selection of a roommate who would support his choices to maximize his time spent working, minimize the time spent on leisure, live frugally, and focus on school. Another student was far less focused, trying to attend to every relationship in her life at the same time, prioritizing school, family, boyfriend, and work to the detriment of her physical and mental health, which ultimately drove her to take on loans shortly before dropping out of school.

Perhaps the greatest lesson from this study, however, is that the measurement of loan aversion affects conclusions about which students refuse to borrow and why. Most studies of loan aversion rely on student surveys, which this chapter suggests may overstate the prevalence of antiborrowing attitudes. This could mean that loan aversion is less common than previously estimated. On the other hand, it is also possible that the apparent disconnect between students' preferences and their actions does not reveal an inconsistency but rather points to constrained choices. It may be that students are borrowing when they prefer not to, which could contribute to negative outcomes of borrowing down the road. An increasing debt burden held by individuals who strongly preferred not to have debt could also have public policy implications.

It is possible that these debt holders will push for a policy solution that helps reduce the burden immediately after leaving college. Research by Ozymy (2012) suggests that lower-income college students are more likely to contact their elected officials regarding student loans than higher-income students, and self-interest is the likely reason. This could result in accelerating the shift in policy toward income-based repayment options from fixed repayment options.

Limitations

While this study has several strengths, including the use of multiple forms of data to measure loan aversion, detailed information on students' attitudes and behaviors, and the ability to connect loan aversion to educational outcomes, it also suffers some significant limitations. First and most importantly, the sample is constrained to a fraction of all Wisconsin Pell recipients, who likely differ in key ways from the national population of such students. Second, it is difficult to ascertain whether observed measurement differences in loan aversion are attributable to the difference between stated preferences and actual behavior, timing, or something else. Third, the analyses are relatively small in size, limiting statistical power.

Implications and Future Research

There is a critical question looming large and unanswered in this analysis, essential for how readers think about next steps: Is loan aversion a concern? Some will readily answer yes, thinking that deciding not to borrow means that students will be worse off in the long run if borrowing would have increased their chances of degree completion compared to the alternatives. Loan-averse students, in other words, may have a reduced risk of being burdened with unmanageable debt, while also increasing their chances of college dropout and reducing their expected lifetime earnings.

On the other hand, there are additional opportunity costs that accrue to some students, including those who are most often loan averse. The typical calculation for assessing whether debt is manageable and optimal compared to the returns to college relies on a comparison to a student's future earnings. Debt to future earnings ratios are most often the focus of calculations regarding the appropriateness of loans. However, not only do students from low-income families face more constrained labor markets and employment discrimination than other students, thus lowering their projected future earnings, but they also come from families with more existing debt and greater financial need—meaning that a portion of their future earnings are often already committed to their families, as a form of familial debt (Burton 2007). Thus it may be more appropriate to focus on debt to household ratio when assessing the rationality of loan aversion, and include a student's natal family (and even extended kin network) in that household calculation.

Today, nearly one in five households has student debt—double the share of two decades earlier—with an average balance of more than $26,000. While higher education advocates are right to point out that college is a good investment, and the price of a new sedan is comparable, they miss a critical point: poor families owe 24 percent of their household income to student debt, compared to 7 percent or less for families making more than $60,000 a year (Fry 2012). While the *amount* of debt may be relatively similar across levels of family income, its meaning is quite different. With such a differential impact on poor families, loan aversion may be a smart decision. The relevant lack of aversion, in other words, could also be viewed as problematic.

In the future, researchers should think about ways to increase the precision of how we measure loan-taking decisions (using both surveys and administrative data) so that it becomes possible to intervene to facilitate student decisions consistent with their own preferences and intentions. It would also be useful to conduct detailed mixed-method ethnographic studies of students and low-income families to examine how decisions about loan taking affect the degree to which higher education helps to increase their social mobility or perpetuates their economic struggles.

Notes

The Bill and Melinda Gates Foundation, Great Lakes Higher Education Guaranty Corporation, Institute for Research on Poverty, Spencer Foundation, William T. Grant Foundation, Wisconsin Center for the Advancement of Postsecondary Education, and an anonymous donor provided funding for this study, conducted in partnership with the Fund for Wisconsin Scholars, the Higher Educational Aids Board, the University of Wisconsin System, and the Wisconsin Technical College System. The authors thank Allie Gardner and Kaja Rebane for their help and support. All mistakes reside with the authors. Contact the lead author at srab@education.wisc.edu with questions and comments.

1. A small fraction of students attend colleges that do not participate in the Title IV financial aid program (these are mainly for-profit institutions), or colleges that decline to offer loans (most often community colleges and/or minority serving institutions).
2. Estimates vary; one recent study suggests that overall about one in six students at public and private four-year colleges and universities declines the entirety of the subsidized loans offered to them (Cadena and Keys 2013).
3. While some argue that the relevant ratio is debt-to-postgraduation income, it is important to recognize that among low-income families, money is often shared— that is, children continue to contribute to their families postgraduation and receive little financial assistance in return—and students more often reside in areas with fewer employment opportunities and lower wages.
4. The latest NPSAS was just released but is unavailable at the time of this writing because of the government shutdown.
5. Samples in this chapter are too small to examine differential patterns according to loan subsidization.
6. Net price is the difference between the institution's cost of attendance (the sticker price, including tuition, fees, room and board, and all other estimated costs) and all grant aid students receive. The net price thus includes the family's expected contribution (officially calculated by a federal formula) and all funds they are left to earn or borrow to pay for college.
7. The lead author directs the Wisconsin Scholars Longitudinal Study (WSLS), and more details about the study can be found at www.finaidstudy.org and in Goldrick-Rab et al. (2012). All data included in this analysis were collected over a five-year period by the WSLS research team.
8. Interest rates on unsubsidized Stafford Loans have been fixed at 6.8 percent from 2006–07 to 2012–13. The interest rate on subsidized Stafford Loans declined from 6.8 to 6.0 percent for loans issued in 2008–09, 5.6 percent in 2009–10, 4.5 percent in 2010–11, and 3.4 percent in 2011–12 and 2012–13. It remains 3.4 percent for the 2012–13 academic year. Beginning July 1, 2013, all interest rates are tied to the 10-year Treasury note.

9. Subsidized and unsubsidized Stafford Loans carry different repayment protections. Today, under Income-Based Repayment, the government will pay the interest for up to three years for borrowers whose incomes are too low to cover interest payments on their subsidized loans, but this is not the case for unsubsidized Stafford Loans.

10. We thank Dr. Stephen DesJardins for noting in his published papers that requesting loan offers when obtaining financial aid data is essential to exploring financial aid packages and their impacts.

11. We also considered defining a student as loan averse if s/he declined at least half of all of the loans offered. The correlation between the two measures was weaker (0.16), which is unsurprising, since the survey measure required rejection of all loans offered. We also considered categorizing a student as loan averse if s/he declined all unsubsidized loans, since the interest rate in the survey question was more consistent with these. The correlation between the survey and administrative measures this way was 0.28, suggesting that at least some students thought of the survey question as regarding that type of loan. However, we have a much smaller sample of those students compared to all students offered any loans, and declining subsidized loans is a behavior worth examining, so we focus on that larger sample here.

12. Consistent with the WSLS data agreement, universities are not named here.

13. In analyses not shown, we also find that students from three of the poorest areas in the state—Milwaukee, Kenosha, and Racine—are more loan averse.

14. Cunningham and Santiago (2008) found more aversion among Chinese and Vietnamese students, while we identified substantial aversion among Hmong students.

References

Advisory Committee on Student Financial Assistance. 2012. *Pathways to Success: Integrating Learning with Life and Work to Increase National College Completion.* Washington, DC: Advisory Committee on Student Financial Assistance.

Armstrong, Elizabeth A., and Laura T. Hamilton. 2013. *Paying for the Party: How College Maintains Inequality.* Cambridge, MA: Harvard University Press.

Avery, Christopher, and Sarah Turner. 2012. "Student Loans: Do College Students Borrow Too Much—Or Not Enough?" *Journal of Economic Perspectives* 26(1): 165–192.

Bailey, Martha J., and Susan M. Dynarski. 2011. "Inequality in Postsecondary Education." In *Whither Opportunity?* Greg J. Duncan and Richard J. Murnane, eds. New York: Russell Sage Foundation, pp. 117–132.

Baum, Sandy, and Saul Schwartz. 2012. "Is College Affordable? In Search of a Meaningful Definition." Issue brief. Washington, DC: Institute for Higher Education Policy.

Booij, Adam S., Edwin Leuven, and Hessel Oosterbeek. 2012. "The Role of Information in the Take-Up of Student Loans." *Economics of Education Review* 31(1): 33–44.

Bozick, Robert. 2007. "Making It through the First Year of College: The Role of Students' Economic Resources, Employment, and Living Arrangements." *Sociology of Education* 80(3): 261–285.

Brint, Steven, and Matthew Baron Rotondi. 2008. "Student Debt, the College Experience, and Transitions to Adulthood." Paper presented at the Annual Meeting of the American Sociological Association, held in Boston, July 31–August 4.

Burdman, Pamela. 2005. "The Student Debt Dilemma: Debt Aversion as a Barrier to College Access." Occasional Paper No. 13.05. Berkeley, CA: Center for Studies in Higher Education, University of California, Berkeley.

Burton, Linda. 2007. "Childhood Adultification in Economically Disadvantaged Families: A Conceptual Model." *Family Relations* 56: 329–345.

Cabrera, Alberto F., and Steven M. La Nasa. 2000. *Understanding the College Choice of Disadvantaged Students.* San Francisco, CA: Jossey-Bass Publishers.

Cadena, Brian C., and Benjamin J. Keys. 2013. "Can Self-Control Explain Avoiding Free Money? Evidence from Interest-Free Student Loans." *Review of Economics and Statistics* 95(4): 1117–1129.

Caetano, Gregorio, Miguel Palacios, and Harry Anthony Patrinos. 2011. *Measuring Aversion to Debt: An Experiment among Student Loan Candidates.* Working Paper No. 5737. Washington, DC: World Bank.

Carnevale, Andrew P., Stephen J. Rose, and Ban Cheah. 2011. *The College Payoff: Education, Occupations, Lifetime Earnings.* Washington, DC: Georgetown University Center on Education and the Workforce.

Chopra, Rohit. 2013. "A Closer Look at the Trillion." Washington, DC: Consumer Financial Protection Bureau. http://www.consumerfinance.gov/blog/a-closer-look-at-the-trillion/ (accessed October 2, 2013).

Clydesdale, Tim. 2007. *The First Year Out: Understanding American Teens after High School.* Chicago, IL: University of Chicago Press.

College Board. 2012. *Trends in Student Aid, 2012.* New York: College Board.

Cunningham, Alisa F., and Deborah A. Santiago. 2008. *Student Aversion to Borrowing: Who Borrows and Who Doesn't.* Washington, DC: Institute for Higher Education Policy.

Davies, Emma, and Stephen E. G. Lea. 1995. "Student Attitudes to Student Debt." *Journal of Economic Psychology* 16(4): 663–679.

Deil-Amen, Regina, and Sara Goldrick-Rab. 2009. *Institutional Transfer and the Management of Risk in Higher Education.* Madison, WI: Wisconsin Center for the Advancement of Postsecondary Education.

Dowd, Alicia C. 2008. "Dynamic Interactions and Intersubjectivity: Challenges to Causal Modeling in Studies of College Student Debt." *Review of Educational Research* 78(2): 232–259.

Eckel, Catherine C., Cathleen A. Johnson, Claude Montmarquette, and Christian Rojas. 2007. "Debt Aversion and the Demand for Loans for Postsecondary Education." *Public Finance Review* 35(2): 233–262.

Feldman, Daniel C., and Helen I. Doerpinghaus. 1992. "Patterns of Part-Time Employment." *Journal of Vocational Behavior* 41(3): 282–294.

Fry, Richard. 2012. "A Record One-in-Five Households Now Owe Student Loan Debt." Washington, DC: Pew Research Center's Social & Demographic Trends.

Goldrick-Rab, Sara. 2013. Testimony on College Affordability Prepared for the Senate Health, Education, Labor and Pensions Committee, in hearing on "The Challenge of College Affordability: The Student Lens." April 16.

Goldrick-Rab, Sara, and Douglas N. Harris. 2010. *Higher Education in Wisconsin: A 21st Century Status Report.* Madison, WI: Wisconsin Covenant Foundation.

Goldrick-Rab, Sara, Douglas N. Harris, Robert Kelchen, and James Benson. 2012. *Need-Based Financial Aid and College Persistence: Experimental Evidence from Wisconsin.* Madison, WI: Institute for Research on Poverty.

Goldrick-Rab, Sara, Douglas N. Harris, and Philip A. Trostel. 2009. "Why Financial Aid Matters (or Does Not) for College Success: Toward a New Interdisciplinary Perspective." In *Higher Education: Handbook of Theory and Research*, Vol. 24, John C. Smart, ed. New York: Springer, pp. 1–45.

Goldrick-Rab, Sara, and Nancy Kendall. 2013. *Constructing Affordability: How Institutional and Relational Contexts Affect Retention of Undergraduates from Low-Income Families.* Madison, WI: University of Wisconsin, Madison.

Goldrick-Rab, Sara, and Josipa Roksa. 2008. *A Federal Agenda for Promoting Student Success and Degree Completion.* Washington, DC: Center for American Progress.

Gross, Jacob P. K., Osman Cekic, Don Hossler, and Nick Hillman. 2009. "What Matters in Student Loan Default: A Review of the Research Literature." *Journal of Student Financial Aid* 39(1): 19–29.

Haveman, Robert. n.d. "Payback calculator." http://payback.wisc.edu/ (accessed March 27, 2014).

Hossler, Don, Jack Schmit, and Nick Vesper. 1999. *Going to College. How*

Social, Economic, and Educational Factors Influence the Decisions Students Make. Baltimore, MD: Johns Hopkins University Press.

Hoxby, Caroline M., and Christopher Avery. 2012. "The Missing 'One-Offs': The Hidden Supply of High-Achieving, Low-Income Students." NBER Working Paper No. 18586. Cambridge, MA: National Bureau of Economic Research.

Hoxby, Caroline, and Sarah Turner. 2013. "Expanding College Opportunities for Low-Income, High-Achieving Students." Discussion Paper No. 12-014. Stanford, CA: Stanford Institute for Economic Policy Research.

Hryshko, Dmytro, Maria Jose. Luengo-Prado, and Brent E. Sørensen. 2011. "Childhood Determinants of Risk Aversion: The Long Shadow of Compulsory Education." *Quantitative Economics* 2(1): 37–72.

Institute for College Access and Success. 2007. *Green Light & Red Tape: Improving Access to Financial Aid at California's Community Colleges.* Washington, DC: The Institute for College Access and Success.

Jackson, Brandon A., and John R. Reynolds. 2013. "The Price of Opportunity: Race, Student Loan Debt, and College Achievement." *Sociological Inquiry* 83(3): 335–368.

Jacob, Brian, Brian McCall, and Kevin M. Stange. 2013. "College as Country Club: Do Colleges Cater to Students' Preferences for Consumption?" NBER Working Paper No. 18745. Cambridge, MA: National Bureau of Economic Research.

Jacobs-Lawson, Joy M., and Douglas A. Hershey. 2005. "Influence of Future Time Perspective, Financial Knowledge, and Financial Risk Tolerance on Retirement Saving Behaviors." *Financial Services Review* 14(4): 331–344.

Johnson, Cathleen, and Claude Montmarquette. 2011. "Loan Aversion among Canadian High School Students." No. 2011s-67. Montreal: CIRANO.

Johnson, Matthew T. 2013. "Borrowing Constraints, College Enrollment, and Delayed Entry." *Journal of Labor Economics* 31(4): 669–725.

King, Jacqueline. 2002. *Crucial Choices: How Students' Financial Decisions Affect Their Academic Success.* Washington, DC: American Council on Education.

Lawrence, Emily C. 1991. "Poverty and the Rate of Time Preference: Evidence from Panel Data." *Journal of Political Economy* 99: 54–77.

Lee, Donghoon. 2013. "Household Debt and Credit: Student Debt." New York: Federal Reserve Bank of New York. http://www.newyorkfed.org/news events/mediaadvisory/2013/Lee022813.pdf (accessed October 1, 2013).

Leslie, Larry L., and Paul T. Brinkman. 1987. "Student Price Response in Higher Education: The Student Demand Studies." *Journal of Higher Education* 58(2): 181–204.

Lobel, Sharon Alisa. 1991. "Allocation of Investment in Work and Family Roles: Alternative Theories and Implications for Research." *Academy of Management Review* 16(3): 507–521.

Long, Bridget Terry. 2008. "What Is Known about the Impact of Financial Aid? Implications for Policy." NCPR working paper. New York: Teachers College, Colombia University.

Manski, Charles F., and David A. Wise. 1983. *College Choice in America.* Cambridge, MA: Harvard University Press.

McDonough, Patricia M. 1997. *Choosing Colleges: How Social Class and Schools Structure Opportunity.* Albany, NY: State University of New York Press.

McDonough, Patricia M., and Shannon Calderone. 2006. "The Meaning of Money: Perceptual Differences between College Counselors and Low-Income Families about College Costs and Financial Aid." *American Behavioral Scientist* 49(12): 1703–1718.

McKinney, Lyle, Toya Roberts, and Pamelyn Shefman. 2013. "Perspectives and Experiences of Financial Aid Counselors on Community College Students Who Borrow." *Journal of Student Financial Aid* 43(1): Article 2.

McPherson, Michael S., and Morten Owen Schapiro. 1991. "Does Student Aid Affect College Enrollment? New Evidence on a Persistent Controversy." *American Economic Review* 81(1): 309–318.

Mortimer, Jeylan T. 2003. *Working and Growing Up in America.* Cambridge, MA: Harvard University Press.

Norvilitis, Jill M., and Wesley Mendes-Da-Silva. 2013. "Attitudes toward Credit and Finances among College Students in Brazil and the United States." *Journal of Business Theory and Practice* 1(1): 132–151.

Ozymy, Joshua. 2012. "The Poverty of Participation: Self-Interest, Student Loans, and Student Activism." *Political Behavior* 34(1): 103–116.

Palameta, Boris, and Jean Pierre Voyer. 2010. *Willingness to Pay for Post-Secondary Education among Under-Represented Groups.* Toronto: Higher Education Quality Council of Ontario.

Pascarella, Ernest T., and Patrick T. Terenzini. 2005. *How College Affects Students: Findings and Insights from Twenty Years of Research. Vol. 2, A Third Decade of Research.* San Francisco, CA: Jossey-Bass.

Paulsen, Michael B., and Edward P. St. John. 1997. "The Financial Nexus between College Choice and Persistence." In *Researching Student Aid: Creating an Action Agenda*, R. A. Voorhees, ed. San Francisco, CA: Jossey-Bass, pp. 65–82.

Perna, Laura W. 2006. "Understanding the Relationship between Information about College Prices and Financial Aid and Students' College-Related Behaviors." *American Behavioral Scientist* 49(12): 1620–1635.

————. 2008. "Understanding High School Students' Willingness to Borrow to Pay College Prices." *Research in Higher Education* 49(7): 589–606.

Staff, J., and J. T. Mortimer. 2007. "Education and Work Strategies from Adolescence to Early Adulthood: Consequences for Educational Attainment." *Social Forces* 85: 1169–1194.

State Higher Education Executive Officers. 2013. *State Higher Education Finance: FY 2012*. Boulder, CO: State Higher Education Executive Officers.

St. John, Edward P., Michael B. Paulsen, and Deborah Faye Carter. 2005. "Diversity, College Costs, and Postsecondary Opportunity: An Examination of the Financial Nexus between College Choice and Persistence for African Americans and Whites." *Journal of Higher Education* 76(5): 545–569.

Stinebrickner, Todd, and Ralph Stinebrickner. 2003. "Understanding Educational Outcomes of Students from Low-Income Families: Evidence from a Liberal Arts College with a Full Tuition Subsidy Program." *Journal of Human Resources* 38(3): 591–617.

Teranishi, Robert T. 2010. *Asians in the Ivory Tower: Dilemmas of Racial Inequality in American Higher Education*. Multicultural Education Series. New York: Teachers College Press.

Tinto, Vincent. 1993. *Leaving College: Rethinking the Causes and Cures of Student Attrition*. 2nd ed. Chicago, IL: University of Chicago Press.

Wei, Christina Chang, and Paul Skomsvold. 2011. *Borrowing at the Maximum: Undergraduate Stafford Loan Borrowers in 2007–08*. Report No. 2012-161. Washington, DC: National Center for Education Statistics.

Weis, Lois. 1985. *Between Two Worlds: Black Students in an Urban Community College*. Boston, MA: Routledge Kegan & Paul.

Wisconsin Higher Educational Aids Board. 2012. *Wisconsin State Student Financial Aid Data for 2010–11*. http://www.heab.state.wi.us/docs/board/1112/rep1214.pdf (accessed March 27, 2014).

11
Federal Student Loan Policy

Improving Loan Design, Repayment, and Consumer Protections

Lauren Asher
Debbie Cochrane
Pauline Abernathy
Diane Cheng
Joseph Mais
Jessica Thompson
The Institute for College Access and Success

The need for higher education and training has never been as important to individuals and our economy as it is today, yet its affordability is seriously in question. College costs have skyrocketed, as family incomes and state funding for public higher education have declined, leading millions to take on student debt, drop out, or struggle to keep up with classes while working many hours per week to pay the bills. Even after recent significant increases, the maximum Pell Grant today covers the smallest share of the cost of attending a public college since the start of the program 40 years ago. It should be no surprise that the gaps in college enrollment, persistence, and graduation between students from high- and low-income families have widened over the last 30 years, threatening both the American Dream and our nation's economic competitiveness.

Although these gaps cannot be closed with financial aid policy alone, research shows that it can increase enrollment and completion. This chapter focuses specifically on student loan policy at the federal level and offers a number of recommendations to reduce complexity, improve targeting, contain debt burdens, and encourage completion and wise borrowing. These recommendations are part of a comprehensive package of reforms to federal student aid, detailed in our 2013 white paper, *Aligning the Means and the Ends: How to Improve Federal Student Aid and Increase College Access and Success* (The Institute for College Access and Success [TICAS] 2013). Unless otherwise noted, the information in this chapter is drawn from that paper.

BACKGROUND

As context for our recommendations, we provide some brief background information about federal and private student loans.

Federal Student Loans

The current federal student loan program is too complex, its benefits are poorly targeted, and its terms are too arbitrary. Much of the complexity is a holdover from when banks received subsidies to make Stafford Loans with terms set and guaranteed by the government. The resulting rules shielded banks—but not borrowers or taxpayers—from risk. Now that these federal loans are made directly and more cost-effectively by the U.S. Department of Education, the entire student loan system can and should be streamlined and improved.

From the myriad types and terms of different loans to the repayment process, it can be hard to figure out how federal student loans work. Consider, for example, the main source of undergraduate loans since July 2010: the Direct Stafford Loan program. There are "subsidized" and "unsubsidized" Stafford Loans, each with different eligibility criteria and treatment of interest during school and periods of deferment and with separate caps on how much a student can borrow each year and cumulatively. The vast majority (82 percent) of undergraduates with subsidized loans also have unsubsidized loans, so some of their loans accrue interest while they are in school and some do not.[1]

Subsidized loans currently provide students with valuable benefits, including a low fixed interest rate and no interest accrual while they are in school.[2] However, these benefits are not well targeted, as high-income students may qualify just because they attend a high-cost college, and most students with subsidized loans also have unsubsidized loans.

All Stafford Loans offer flexible repayment plans, as well as loan deferments and forbearances, yet more than one in eight student loan borrowers is defaulting within three years of entering repayment.[3] The consequences of defaulting on a federal loan can follow borrowers for the rest of their lives, ruining their credit, making it difficult to buy a car or rent an apartment, and limiting their job prospects. They may also face garnished wages, seized income tax refunds, and diminished Social Security checks.

Private Loans

Private educational loans are a much riskier way to pay for college than federal student loans. Most private loans have variable, uncapped interest rates and require a cosigner (U.S. Consumer Financial Protection Bureau and U.S. Department of Education 2012). No more a form of financial aid than a credit card, private loans typically have interest rates that, regardless of whether they are fixed or variable, are highest for those who can least afford them. Private loans lack the basic consumer protections and flexible repayment options of federal student loans, such as unemployment deferment, income-driven repayment, and loan forgiveness programs.

RECOMMENDATIONS

Reform is clearly and urgently needed. Our loan recommendations aim to better support access and success while containing costs and risks for both students and taxpayers. To achieve those goals, we propose simplifying the loan program, improving the targeting of benefits, containing debt burdens, and encouraging wise borrowing. Our recommendations include the following:

- Provide a single undergraduate student loan with no fees, a low in-school interest rate, and a fixed rate in repayment that is never much higher than the rate on loans being offered to current students.
- Streamline and improve federal loan repayment options.

- Improve the timing, content, and effectiveness of student loan counseling.
- Reduce the number of student loan defaults.
- Reform the student loan collections process.
- Strengthen consumer protections for private loan borrowers.

One Simple, Affordable Undergraduate Loan Program

We propose replacing the current Stafford Loans with one simple, affordable undergraduate loan. Our recommended changes are designed to simplify the loan program, ensure that loans both appear and are affordable for borrowers, and better align the cost of the loan for the student with the costs for the government. There is no way to perfectly balance all three of these goals. However, what we propose is an important step forward on each front, focused on making federal student loans a more effective tool for ensuring access and supporting success while containing risk for both the student and the taxpayer.

Specifically, we recommend that there be only one federal loan for undergraduate students, in place of the subsidized and unsubsidized Stafford Loans available today. A single loan will be much easier for borrowers to understand and monitor, and for schools and the Department of Education to administer. This loan—which we refer to in this chapter as the One Loan—has an interest rate that is lower while the student is in school and higher by a set margin, but capped, when the borrower enters repayment. The interest rates are tied to the government's cost of borrowing and designed to help offset the cost of the loan program, rather than being arbitrarily set by Congress.[4] The features of One Loans are described in the sections below.

Fixed interest rates and no fees

Fixed rates are important to provide certainty, predictability, and reassurance to students, many of whom have never borrowed before and may not fully understand the consequences of variable rates. The recent mortgage crisis demonstrated all too clearly that millions of Americans with mortgages did not understand the risks of variable rates, with terrible consequences for both them and our nation's economy. Fixed interest rates also further distinguish One Loans, which are a form of financial aid, from other financial products such as credit cards and private loans. As mentioned earlier, interest rates on private loans are usually variable, like a credit card. The private loans that offer fixed rates will almost certainly have higher interest rates than One Loans for all borrowers except those who have, or whose cosigners have, pristine credit. At the height of the lending boom in 2007–2008, a majority of private student loan borrowers had not taken out as much as they could have in federal loans first, underscoring the need to clearly distinguish federal student loans from private loans (TICAS 2011a).

The One Loan's fixed rate is tied to the government's cost of lending in the year the loan is disbursed. For instance, the interest rate on all loans disbursed in a given school year might be set based on the interest rate on the one-year Treasury bill or 10-year Treasury note at the final auction preceding June 1 of that year. Students who take out One Loans each year that they are in school may end up having loans with different interest rates, depending on the market conditions each year. However, all the other terms of their One Loans would be the same.

There is no reason for the new loan to have fees, which are remnants of the bank-based guaranteed loan program and add unneeded complexity to the loan. The fixed interest rate will be set to cover the cost of One Loans without needing to add supplemental fees.

Low in-school interest rate

The in-school interest rate on One Loans is based on the government's actual cost of borrowing when the loans are made. The rate for new loans would take effect each year on July 1 and apply to all loans issued through June 30 of the following year. The in-school rate applies while the borrower is enrolled at least half-time and during a six-month grace period after she leaves school, similar to the usual timing of the interest subsidy on subsidized Stafford Loans. Having a lower interest rate when students are in school is intended to encourage them to stay enrolled and complete their education, knowing that their interest rate will rise if they stop out or drop out.[5] Lower in-school interest rates also help encourage the use of federal loans over private loans or other types of financing available to consumers with limited or no credit histories. Charging a low in-school rate, rather than charging no interest, while the student is enrolled is designed to both lower the cost of providing the loan and discourage students from dragging out their time in school.

Higher, but capped, out-of-school rate

The One Loan's out-of-school interest rate is set at the in-school rate when the loans were taken out, *plus* a fixed margin designed to cover the cost of the loan program, including the interest-rate insurance described below, loan forgiveness and discharge, and administrative costs. For example, imagine a One Loan with an in-school interest rate of 3 percent based on the government's cost of borrowing that year. If, for illustration purposes only, the repayment rate were set at the in-school rate plus two percentage points, it would have an out-of-school interest rate of 5 percent. The out-of-school rate, while higher than the in-school rate, must be low enough to ensure that federal loans are—and look like—financial aid in contrast to other types of financing such as private loans.

The out-of-school interest rate on the One Loan will be subject to a universal cap, like Stafford Loan interest rates; currently the undergraduate Stafford Loan interest rate is capped at 8.25 percent.[6] A universal cap protects consumers from extremely high rates in the economy and reinforces the differences between federal loans and commercial financial products. For example, if the universal cap were 7 percent, the in-school interest rate were 6 percent, and the repayment rate set at the in-school rate plus two percentage points, the loan would have an out-of-school interest rate of 7 percent because the cap would keep the rate from rising above 7 percent.

Interest-rate insurance

The One Loan has an important new feature: a form of insurance that prevents interest rates from ever being too much higher than the rate on loans being offered to current students. This feature addresses the major disadvantage of fixed rates for borrowers, without requiring refinancing or consolidation. To prevent borrowers from getting stuck with high fixed rates when market rates decline significantly, the interest rate on One Loans will reset to a lower fixed rate when interest rates in the economy drop substantially from when the loan was issued.

For example, the interest-rate insurance might prevent outstanding One Loans from having a rate that is more than two percentage points above the rate on loans being offered to current students. If a borrower had a One Loan with an out-of-school interest rate of 6.5 percent, and interest rates dropped so that the One Loans to current students had an out-of-school rate of 3.8 percent, the borrower's interest rate would automatically drop from 6.5 percent to 5.8 percent, so that the rate was no more than two percentage points above the current rate.

The interest rate on affected One Loans would not increase, even if rates in the economy do. This helps borrowers who go to school when interest rates are unusually high, while avoiding the uncertainty and risk of a variable rate for all borrowers. We believe this interest rate insurance, which has some similarities to existing financial instruments (e.g., swaptions) can be provided at a reasonable cost to both borrowers and taxpayers, and incorporated into the fixed margin in the out-of-school interest rate.[7] The cost of this feature will depend on the selected interest rate margin, universal cap, and the specifics of the insurance.

Interest-free deferments for Pell Grant recipients

In addition to the One Loan's low in-school rate, universal interest rate cap, and interest rate insurance, which apply to all borrowers, the One Loan provides additional protection to borrowers from low-income families. Pell Grant recipients who take out loans would be eligible for interest-free deferments during periods of unemployment and economic hardship, just as with subsidized Stafford Loans currently.[8]

Subsidized Stafford Loans do not accrue interest while the borrower is in school, during the six-month grace period, or when payments are deferred for certain reasons after the borrower leaves school, including periods of unemployment and the first three years in IBR or PAYE if income-driven payments are less than monthly interest.[9] However, as mentioned above, these valuable benefits are not well targeted for several reasons: high-income students may qualify for subsidized loans just because they attend a high-cost college; and the vast majority of students with subsidized loans also have unsubsidized loans, which accrue interest during these periods.

The One Loan better targets these valuable benefits to the borrowers who most need them, when they need them most. Borrowers who received Pell Grants, by definition, come from low- and moderate-income families and are therefore much less likely to have family members who can support them during periods of unemployment or low earnings. The loans will provide interest relief on all loans held by Pell

Grant recipients, rather than just some of their loans, when they are unemployed or their incomes are too low to cover their interest in an income-driven repayment plan.

Retain current loan limits

The loans will have the same aggregate loan limits as Stafford Loans: currently $31,000 for dependent undergraduates and $57,500 for independent undergraduates. Student loans have become a fact of life for more and more Americans, and there is widespread and understandable concern about high and pervasive debt levels. Federal loan limits provide a necessary signal to students and colleges about how much borrowing might be too much. The higher loan limits for independent students rightly recognize that these students have greater financial responsibilities and may need to borrow more to stay and succeed in school.[10]

Some have suggested raising the current loan limits, while others have suggested lowering them, but the data do not support either suggestion (TICAS 2012a,b). As mentioned earlier, average debt for 2011 graduates of public and nonprofit four-year colleges was well below the aggregate limits—the average including private loans was $26,600 for the two-thirds who borrowed, and one-third of graduates had no student debt (TICAS 2012c). The majority of undergraduates who borrow private education loans could have borrowed more in federal student loans before turning to the riskier private market (TICAS 2011a). Finally, colleges already have the authority to limit or deny loans for individual students on a case-by-case basis (TICAS 2012d).

The Department of Education should, however, analyze the potential effects of prorating federal student loans by attendance status. Unlike Pell Grants, federal loans are not prorated based on a student's attendance status. In other words, students enrolled half time receive a prorated portion of the Pell Grant that students enrolled full time receive, but may receive the same loan amount as a full-time student. Students who take out full loans but make only part-time progress may be at an increased risk of dropping out and defaulting. Students who attend college part time are less likely to complete a degree or certificate (U.S. Department of Education 2011), and failure to complete a degree or certificate is one of the strongest predictors of future default

(Nguyen 2011; Gross et al. 2009). They may also be at greater risk of exhausting their loan eligibility before completing their degree. Prorating loans would involve reducing student eligibility for federal loans at a time when college is getting harder to afford, but it is possible that it could help encourage students to enroll in more courses per term, thereby completing a degree and reducing their risk of default. Given both the risks and the potential benefits, such a change warrants careful analysis and consideration.

Streamline and Improve Federal Loan Repayment Options

We have identified several ways to simplify and improve federal loan repayment options to help borrowers manage their debt, and reduce the financial distress and defaults that undermine the goals of increased enrollment and completion. There is even more complexity on the repayment side of the federal loan process than on the borrowing side. The number of repayment options and the variation in eligibility requirements, costs, and benefits can be overwhelming, even for those working in the field. With so many choices and variables, comparisons can become unwieldy and confusing, and borrowers may be more likely to end up in plans that do not fit their needs or goals. However, having some well-designed choices, combined with timely and effective counseling, can help borrowers find a good fit for their own situation, stay in repayment, and avoid default.

Let borrowers make one loan payment for all their federal loans

To reduce complexity and make it easier to stay current on their loans, we recommend that borrowers be able to make a single payment that covers all of their federal loans. Currently, this can only be accomplished through a separate consolidation process, which is a significant bureaucratic hurdle for borrowers and has trade-offs that are not in every borrower's best interest.[11] Borrowers should not have to consolidate their loans just to avoid making multiple payments to multiple servicers on their federal student loans each month.

Base repayment plan eligibility on total federal loan debt

The "standard" repayment plan for unconsolidated federal loans is currently a 10-year plan. Borrowers are automatically enrolled in this plan if they do not actively choose a different one before their first payment (U.S. Department of Education 2013a). If borrowers owe more than $30,000, they may be able to choose an "extended" 25-year plan instead, but only if they owe that much within one loan program.[12] For example, if they owe $31,000 in the Federal Family Education Loan Program (FFELP) or $31,000 in Direct Loans, they may qualify for the extended plan. But if they owe $15,000 in Direct Loans and $16,000 in FFELP Loans, they do not qualify. In contrast, total federal student loan debt, along with the borrower's income, is used to determine eligibility for income-driven repayment plans, in which borrowers pay for up to 20 or 25 years.[13] Meanwhile, borrowers who combine their loans into a Direct Consolidation Loan have access to "standard" repayment plans that gradually increase from 10 to 30 years depending on the borrowers' total federal loan debt.[14] Any signal to borrowers about optimal repayment periods, if one were ever intended, gets lost in all this complexity, and what is optimal to one borrower may not be for another.

Instead, we recommend that all borrowers have access to repayment plans based on their *total* federal student loan debt, with incrementally longer repayment periods available to those with larger total debt. Making these repayment options consistent for all loans would greatly simplify the process for borrowers, especially when paired with improved loan counseling that helps them identify their priorities and see which plan is the best fit. Borrowers who want to reduce the overall cost of their debt by paying it down faster will be able to select shorter repayment plans and make prepayments without penalty, as they can now. Borrowers who want assurance that their monthly payments will remain affordable, given their income, will have access to a streamlined income-driven plan, as discussed in detail below. Additionally, borrowers who want all their payments to count toward Public Service Loan Forgiveness will always be able to choose a 10-year payment plan.[15]

Currently, as mentioned above, borrowers who do not select a repayment plan are automatically placed in a 10-year plan, making it the "default" plan. A 10-year plan has significant benefits for borrowers *if* they can afford the monthly payments, which are higher than the monthly payments in longer plans. Given the growth in student debt levels over the past generation, a 10-year plan may be increasingly unrealistic for many borrowers.[16] Automatically enrolling borrowers in this plan, regardless of their total debt levels, could be setting some borrowers up to fail.

Nevertheless, there are trade-offs between shorter and longer repayment plans. Longer repayment periods provide lower monthly payments but also cost borrowers more over the life of the loan. The best plan for one borrower may not be the best for another borrower. The decision of which repayment plan is most appropriate for any given borrower—whether made by the individual or by the Department of Education through the selection of a "default" or mandatory plan—is important and needs to be considered carefully. As we discuss later in the chapter, loan counseling should be improved to help borrowers decide which plan is best for them. The Department of Education should also carefully analyze data on borrowers' repayment plan choices and outcomes—including their ability to make payments and total amount paid—to determine whether a 10-year plan remains the best option for borrowers who do not actively select another plan. It should also consider the broader implications of changing the default repayment plans for borrowers, colleges, and taxpayers.

Give all borrowers access to a single, improved income-driven repayment plan

When Congress created the Income-Based Repayment plan (IBR) for federal loans in 2007, it was a major step forward for student loan borrowers.[17] TICAS, through its Project on Student Debt, developed the policy proposal that laid the groundwork for IBR (TICAS et al. 2006). We first consulted with stakeholders on all sides and conducted an in-depth analysis of debt burdens and repayment plans. This analysis found that protections and options for borrowers with high debt relative to their income were inadequate, inconsistent, and inaccessible (TICAS 2006). With America's higher education system increasingly reliant on student loans, and the consequences of default so severe and long-lasting, students were bearing too much of the risk to ensure access or support success. We developed a "Plan for Fair Loan Payments" that called for affordable payments based on income and family size, coverage of both Direct and FFELP Loans, and a light at the end of the tunnel with forgiveness after 20 years of income-driven payments. These goals were supported by thousands of students, higher education leaders, loan industry representatives, civil rights groups, Republicans and Democrats in Congress, and organizations representing parents, college counselors, and others.[18]

Thanks to the broad coalition that helped make the case for a solution, IBR became available to all federal loan borrowers in July 2009 (TICAS 2009). Despite the absence of much publicity or borrower outreach in the first few years of the program, more than 1.3 million borrowers were enrolled in IBR by the winter of 2012 (U.S. Department of Education 2013b). IBR caps monthly payments at a manageable share of income and forgives any principal or interest that remains after 25 years of payments. To qualify, borrowers must have a "partial financial hardship," defined as a debt-to-income ratio that makes a 10-year payment unaffordable. Required payments can be as low as $0 for borrowers with very low incomes, and payments rise incrementally with income. Payments are capped at the lower of the monthly payment under the standard 10-year plan, or 15 percent of "discretionary income," which is defined as adjusted gross income (AGI) minus 150 percent of poverty for the borrower's family size.[19]

In recent years, the number of repayment options similar to IBR has grown. In early 2010, Congress passed the president's proposal to expand IBR for future borrowers (White House 2010). Starting in July 2014, new borrowers will be able to qualify for a lower monthly payment and shorter forgiveness period than the current IBR program provides: 10 percent of discretionary income and 20 years, instead of 15 percent and 25 years. In the fall of 2010, President Obama announced a new Pay As You Earn plan to give an estimated 1.6 million current students and recent graduates access to the same lower payment cap and shorter forgiveness period, with the goal of offsetting the recession's effect on their job prospects and earnings (White House 2011 and TICAS 2012f). To qualify for Pay As You Earn, students must have borrowed their first loan after September 30, 2007, and received at least one federal loan disbursement after September 30, 2011. Pay As You Earn became available to eligible borrowers in December 2012 through regulatory additions to a preexisting program called Income-Contingent Repayment (ICR), which is only available for borrowers with Direct Loans.[20]

ICR, which is still available, provides less relief than IBR in most cases. Direct Loan borrowers in any of these repayment plans who *also* work for public or nonprofit employers may have their loans discharged after just 10 years of payments, through the Public Service Loan Forgiveness plan Congress created at the same time as IBR.[21]

We recommend consolidating the well-intentioned, but highly complex, mix of currently available income-driven plans—current IBR, IBR for new borrowers in 2014, Pay As You Earn, and ICR—into one new and improved income-driven plan. Borrowers would no longer have to figure out which plans they qualify for or which of their loans will be covered by which payment cap or forgiveness period. Those already enrolled in IBR, Pay As You Earn, and ICR would have the option of staying put or switching to the new plan. For the purposes of this chapter, we refer to the new plan as Pay As You Earn 2 (PAYE2).

To simplify, strengthen, and improve access to income-driven payments, PAYE2 will be available to all borrowers, regardless of their debt or income level, whether their loans are Direct or FFELP, or when they borrowed. This will make it much easier for borrowers who want the assurance of manageable payments to enroll whenever it makes sense for them, whether it is before they make their first payment, after they have hit a rough patch, or when they are concerned about what the future will bring. Rather than requiring borrowers to have a certain debt-to-income ratio to enroll, borrowers with higher incomes relative to their debt will simply make larger payments as determined by the plan's sliding scale. This is already the case for those whose incomes rise substantially after they entered an income-driven plan. If borrowers have access to even lower monthly payments in another plan, and that is more important to them than the assurance of income-driven payments, they need not enroll in PAYE2.

Enabling all borrowers to enroll in PAYE2 will likely require adjustments in some aspects of income-driven plan design, such as the treatment of accrued interest, when to capitalize interest and how much, and whether and how borrowers can exit and reenter PAYE2. Further study is needed to determine optimal approaches. These changes will affect the benefits and risks of widespread enrollment in PAYE2.

PAYE2 will ensure that payments never exceed 10 percent of income while better targeting benefits. In its current design, Pay As You Earn has undeniable benefits for low- and moderate-income borrowers, but it may also result in some high-income borrowers getting substantial forgiveness when they could well afford to pay more. PAYE2 includes two adjustments that better target benefits while assuring that monthly payments never exceed 10 percent of the borrower's income and avoiding arbitrary cliffs, in which borrowers in very similar situations get very different benefits.

1) Gradually phase out the "income exclusion" for higher-income borrowers. PAYE2, like IBR and Pay As You Earn, calculates monthly payments based on the borrower's "discretionary income"—AGI minus an "income exclusion"—to protect income needed to cover basic living expenses. Currently, in IBR and Pay As You Earn, the income exclusion is 150 percent of the poverty level for the borrower's household size. Based on this definition, a borrower with a family of four and an AGI of $40,000 has $34,575 protected for basic living expenses. The family therefore has a discretionary income of $5,425, or $452 per month, so payments set at 10 percent of discretionary income would be $45 per month.[22]

   However, as borrowers' incomes rise, it becomes increasingly unnecessary to shield a share of their earnings. Borrowers with very high incomes are able to devote a larger share of their total incomes to loan payments and still have sufficient funds left over to cover basic necessities, such as food and housing. As a result, PAYE2 gradually phases out the income exclusion for borrowers with AGIs between $100,000 and $250,000, so that borrowers with AGIs of $250,000 or more would have their monthly payments calculated as 10 percent of their total AGI. Borrowers with AGIs below $100,000 would not be affected, and monthly payments for all borrowers would never be greater than 10 percent of their total income. The AGI levels at which the phase-out begins and ends would be indexed to inflation to ensure fairness over time.

2) Cap all monthly payments at 10 percent of income.

   Currently, in IBR and Pay As You Earn, some borrowers can end up paying less than 10 percent of their income, owing to a certain cap on their monthly payments. This occurs if, after entering IBR or Pay As You Earn, the borrower's income rises high enough that he no longer has a "partial financial hardship" (i.e., his debt-to-income ratio has declined so much that a 10-year payment is now affordable). When this occurs, his payments are capped at the monthly amount he would have had to pay had he entered a 10-year standard repayment plan when he entered IBR. For some high-income borrowers, this cap will be lower than 10 percent of their incomes. Removing the current 10-year-payment cap and instead capping payments at 10 percent of income better targets income-driven repayment benefits to those who need them and prevents high-income borrowers from receiving substantial loan forgiveness when they could have afforded to pay more.[23]

Additionally, PAYE2 will provide forgiveness after 20 years of payments. As we have long recommended, any debt remaining after 20 years of income-driven payments should be discharged. This will make it easier for borrowers to see the light at the end of the tunnel, and let them focus on saving for retirement and their children's education before the next generation is in college. The changes to payment determinations described above better target the forgiveness available after 20 years because higher-income borrowers will be more likely to pay off their debts within that period.

Furthermore, we recommend making it easier for all borrowers in income-driven plans to keep their income information up to date. Regardless of how many income-driven plans there are, there is a need to further improve the process through which borrowers provide updated income information to their loan servicers. Currently, borrowers in income-driven plans must provide tax or other income information each year to avoid reverting to non-income-driven payments that may be much higher than they can afford. Recent improvements require that borrowers be notified before they have to submit information and make it easier for some borrowers to submit it to their servicer (U.S Department of Education 2012a). Additionally, in late 2012, the Department of Education launched a user-friendly tool that lets borrowers electronically transfer their own tax information from the Internal Revenue Service (IRS) into an online form, both to apply for income-driven plans and to update their income information (U.S. Department of Education 2012b). Unfortunately, this process is only available to borrowers who have filed an IRS 1040 form. Borrowers with incomes too low to owe federal income tax may not have a 1040 form to draw from, requiring them to go through extra steps to verify their incomes. As a result, borrowers with the greatest need for income-driven payments may have the hardest time continuing to qualify for them.

To simplify the process for all borrowers, the income verification process for PAYE2 should enable borrowers to draw on earnings data in their W-2 and 1099 forms. In addition, borrowers should be able to give the Department of Education advance permission to access their AGI and W-2 information for some period of time (e.g., five years), as they could until recently for IBR and ICR, to reduce the risk of inadvertently missing a deadline.

Finally, any forgiven loan balances should not be treated as taxable income. Borrowers currently enrolled in IBR, ICR, and Pay As You Earn, as well as those who would be enrolled in our proposed PAYE2 plan, can have their loan balances forgiven after 20 or 25 years (depending on the program) of qualifying payments. Treating discharged loans as taxable income creates a tax liability that most recipients will be unable to afford, discourages enrollment in income-driven repayment plans, and is inconsistent with the treatment of other discharged loans.[24]

Improve the Timing, Content, and Effectiveness of Student Loan Counseling

Federal law and regulations require entrance and exit counseling for any student who receives a federal loan.[25] Entrance counseling has the potential to help students optimize their borrowing and better understand the risks and benefits, and exit counseling has the potential to help students select an appropriate repayment plan and avoid default. However, the timing and content of required counseling must be improved to better help students borrow wisely, complete college without burdensome debt, and repay their loans. With common-sense modifications and more research on what works, loan counseling can more effectively inform crucial decisions about borrowing and repayment.

Loan counseling should be conducted when it is most likely to have an impact: *before* students commit to borrowing. Currently, entrance counseling can occur after the promissory note is signed, as long as the counseling comes before the first loan disbursement. This timing problem can and must be fixed. Also, whereas entrance counseling is only required when students first borrow, interim counseling should take place at key points when borrowers are likely to benefit, such as when they have borrowed over a certain amount or sought certification of a private loan.

To be more effective, loan counseling must be individualized based on the borrower's specific situation and needs; it should not just disclose general information and options. Entrance counseling could give students an estimate of their total debt burden if they borrow the amount they are seeking in each year they plan to be in school and also provide the resulting monthly and total payments under different plans. Exit counseling could ask students about their plans and preferences and point them toward specific repayment plans based on this information. For instance, if a student has borrowed a small amount and has secured a job with sufficient pay, the counseling might encourage her to select a 10-year fixed payment plan to minimize the total amount she will pay over the life of the loan. On the other hand, if the student has borrowed a large amount and is unsure how much she is likely to earn, the counseling might highlight income-driven repayment as a way to keep her payments affordable. Currently, counseling does not have to be tailored to the individual student's situation and can, for example, use average loan amounts rather than the amount the student has actually borrowed.

Entrance and interim loan counseling should include warnings about the risks of private loans and discourage students from considering them if they have not exhausted their federal loan options. Students need to understand the protections and benefits that come from federal loans, including set and predictable interest rates, flexible repayment plans, deferment options, and forgiveness programs, *before* they take out a private loan. To the extent possible, exit counseling should include any private loan debt so students can select a repayment plan for their federal loans based on an understanding of their total debt, including any private loans.

Finally, all loan counseling should be consumer tested and improved based on feedback, and ongoing analysis should be conducted of counseling's impact on student decisions. For instance, existing data systems could be used to assess the impact of variations in entrance, interim, and exit counseling on student enrollment, persistence, borrowing, repayment, and default rates. Such analysis could be used to continually improve the counseling to better support student success, prevent loan defaults and unwise or unnecessary borrowing, and reduce the burden of student debt by helping students choose appropriate repayment plans.

Strengthen Consumer Protections

We recommend strengthening consumer protections to support smart borrowing, to prevent default, and to reduce the financial distress of borrowers with federal and private loans.

Federal loan borrowers

As a form of financial aid, federal student loans provide many important consumer protections that are not required of private education loans or other types of financing. Examples include discharges under circumstances such as school fraud, school closure, severe and permanent disability, or death; income-driven repayment plans that help ensure affordable payments and a light at the end of the tunnel; deferments and forbearances that let borrowers temporarily suspend payments without becoming delinquent or paying additional fees; and an opportunity to reenter repayment after default. Such policies are supposed to prevent or reduce defaults, unfair treatment, and extreme financial distress for borrowers who used federal loans to help pay for their own or their child's education. Unfortunately, the federal loan system does not work as well as it should to protect borrowers in challenging circumstances. The recommendations presented in this section are aimed at reducing red tape for distressed, disabled, or defrauded federal loan borrowers and reducing and preventing defaults. While far from comprehensive, these recommendations touch on several important areas for improvement in ways that address the interests of both borrowers and taxpayers.

Respond to signs of financial distress in ways that can prevent default.

- *Ensure that borrowers receive key information about their repayment options not only before they make their first payment but also when their payment patterns indicate likely financial distress.* For example, in 2012, a dozen members of Congress urged the Secretary of Education to alert borrowers to the availability of IBR and related plans as soon as those borrowers have been delinquent, in forbearance, or in economic hardship or unemployment deferment for more than 60 days (U.S. House of Representatives 2012).[26] Despite efforts to make repayment more manageable, default rates have risen even among those who entered repayment after IBR became available (TICAS 2012e). Borrowers struggling to keep up with monthly payments clearly need this information and related counseling. Once distressed borrowers are aware of income-driven repayment and how it could help them, they might also benefit from information about extended repayment plans, deferments, forbearances, and conditions for cancellation.

- *Automatically enroll severely delinquent borrowers in an income-driven repayment plan.* It takes at least nine months of nonpayment to default on a federal student loan. The federal loan promissory note should require borrowers to give the Department of Education permission to access their IRS information if they miss at least six consecutive payments. Using their income and family size, the Department of Education could then determine what their income-driven payment would be.[27] If it were less than their current payment, the Department of Education would notify the borrower and, unless they chose another plan, automatically enroll the borrower in the income-driven plan. For borrowers with very low incomes, income-driven payments may be as little as $0, and income-driven payments will be lower than 10-year payments for most borrowers under financial strain. By enrolling them and engaging in follow-up contact and counseling, the Department of Education may be able to prevent otherwise very likely defaults and the associated costs for both borrowers and taxpayers. Notification and ease of use will be essential to this policy's effectiveness, as borrowers need to know that their payment has been lowered and how and why to update their income and family size at least annually.

Determine why most delinquent borrowers are not successfully contacted before they default. Data show that a significant number of borrowers who default were never successfully contacted by their lenders because their lenders did not have current contact information (U.S. Department of Education 2010). It will be very difficult to reduce default rates and help more borrowers enroll in affordable repayment plans if servicers and/or the Department of Education lack accurate, up-to-date contact information for federal loan borrowers or functional systems for reaching them. The Department of Education should conduct a study to determine the main causes of this serious problem, use the findings to identify needed changes, make any such changes that are within its authority, and recommend that Congress make additional changes if necessary.

Reconsider the use of private debt collectors for federal student loans. Currently, the federal student loans collections process is almost entirely in the hands of private debt collection agencies (U.S. Department of the Treasury 2009). These debt collectors are given the authority to act on behalf of the lender or guarantor in everything from rehabilitation of a defaulted loan to information about loan discharges to negotiating loan compromises. Because their contracts with the Department of Education provide bigger rewards for collecting larger dollar amounts, these debt collectors have a disincentive to inform borrowers of their rights or to set reasonable and affordable payment amounts based on the borrowers' financial circumstances, as required by law (Hechinger 2012). Given the commission structure and conflicts of interest, it is not surprising that the National Consumer Law Center has found a remarkable amount of deceptive, unfair, and illegal conduct by private collectors involving federal student loans (Loonin 2012). Recent news investigations have also documented such conduct and the underlying "boiler-room" business model (Hechinger 2012 and Martin 2012).

Collections should prioritize the interests of borrowers and taxpayers, not collection agencies. With the Department of Education spending more than $1.4 billion a year on commission-based contracts with private debt collectors, an examination of whether outsourcing is the most effective or appropriate approach is long overdue (Martin 2012). In 2009, the IRS conducted an extensive review of its private collections contracts and moved to bring the function in-house (IRS 2009). The Treasury Department is responsible for the collection of debt owed to the federal government but has delegated to the Education Department the authority to collect on defaulted student loans.[28] We recommend that the Treasury Department withdraw the delegation of its authority for a randomly selected number of defaulted loans for the purpose of studying whether taxpayers' and borrowers' interests would be better served by collecting all defaulted federal student loans by trained Treasury employees rather than by private debt collectors.

Rethink default penalties to ensure that distressed borrowers have a way out. While there should clearly be some penalties associated with defaulting on a federal student loan, they should not be designed to keep borrowers without financial means in default indefinitely, with already unmanageable debt just continuing to mount. For example, collection fees of up to 25 percent are currently added to what borrowers owe when they default, even if the actual costs of the collections activities are much less.[29] These fees go to the private collection agencies discussed above. If a borrower went into default because she could not afford her loan payments, high fees make it even less likely that she will ever be able to get out of default. Another policy that can trap borrowers in default is limiting them to only one chance at rehabilitation. It is worth considering whether borrowers who redefault should be allowed to rehabilitate their loans more than once after some period of successful payments.

Ensure that borrowers who are abused or defrauded by a college can get relief. The Department of Education should use its full authority to enforce the law that relieves borrowers of debt resulting from illegal or abusive school practices. The "false certification" provisions in law are designed to offer relief for harmed students as well as to discourage illegal, abusive school practices. The law provides for the discharge of loans falsely certified by institutions and for the Secretary to recover the loan amounts from the schools and their affiliates. While the statutory authority is broad, the Department of Education has interpreted these false certification provisions very narrowly, denying needed relief to borrowers who suffered harm at the hands of their school. Borrowers should be eligible for relief if, for example, a school improperly or falsely certifies students' satisfactory academic progress, enrolls students in career education programs that lack the programmatic accreditation necessary for employment in the occupation, enrolls students who do not speak English in programs taught only in English, or enrolls students with criminal records in programs that prepare them for employment in professions from which they are barred because of their criminal record.[30] The regulations must be revised so that borrowers can count on relief from debts resulting from a school's harmful actions when there is reasonable evidence that the harm took place.[31]

Private loan borrowers

As discussed earlier, private education loans are a much riskier way to pay for college than federal student loans. Whether private loan rates are variable or fixed, lower-income students often receive the worst rates and terms, and private loans do not have the important borrower protections and repayment options that come with federal loans. The following policy changes would help prevent students from unnecessarily taking out risky private loans, ensure that consumers have information they need to make wise borrowing decisions, and stop deceptive and predatory private lending practices.

Prevent unnecessary private loan borrowing by requiring school certification of private loans. The majority of undergraduates who borrow private education loans could have borrowed more in federal student loans before turning to the riskier private market (TICAS 2011a). Unfortunately, many students who borrow private loans—and the parents who cosign these loans—do not understand the difference between federal and private loans until it is too late (TICAS 2011c). Requiring private lenders to confirm a borrower's eligibility with his or her school before disbursing the loan ensures the student is eligible for that loan and the loan amount. It also gives the school a chance to help the student make an informed borrowing decision. Before the credit crunch, about a third of all private loans to undergraduates were made *without* such school certification (U.S. Consumer Financial Protection Bureau and U.S. Department of Education 2012). Currently, most lenders voluntarily ask schools to certify their private loans, but lenders are not required to do so, and changing credit conditions could once again create incentives to cut schools out of the loop. In addition, many schools do not take the opportunity to counsel students before certifying. Students, schools, and lenders, as well as the U.S. Consumer Financial Protection Bureau (CFPB) and the Department of Education, have all endorsed requiring "school certification" of private loans, including notifying the student of any remaining federal aid eligibility before the loan is certified.[32] The CFPB could require such certification for all private loans, and legislation introduced in 2013 (S. 113 and H.R. 3612) would do so as well (Durbin 2013; Polis 2013).

Treat private loans like other consumer debt in bankruptcy. Since 2005, it has been much more difficult to discharge private education loans than credit cards and other consumer debt in bankruptcy, often leaving even the most destitute borrowers with no way out. A joint report to Congress from the CFPB and Department of Education found that this change coincided with rapid growth in questionable lending practices, compounding the risk to student borrowers (CFPB and U.S. Department of Education 2012). It also found a lack of evidence to support industry claims that restricting bankruptcy rights improved loan prices or access to credit. House and Senate legislation (the *Fairness for Struggling Students Act of 2013* and the *Private Student Loan Bankruptcy Fairness Act of 2013*) would restore fair bankruptcy treatment to private loan borrowers and is supported by TICAS and a broad coalition representing students, consumers, and colleges.[33]

Enable private loan borrowers to refinance or modify their loans. Borrowers who face unmanageably high payments on their private loans do not have access to lower payments through IBR or other federal repayment plans, and private lenders are not required to provide the types of repayment options and borrower protections that are built into federal loans, such as unemployment deferments and forbearances without fees. Private loans typically have variable interest rates that are highest for the students and cosigners who can least afford them. Those who borrowed their loans at a high rate are often unable to refinance despite historically low interest rates in the economy, even if their current credit score would qualify them for a lower fixed or variable rate if they took out a loan today (CFPB 2012). Keeping borrowers locked into high rates and high payments poses risks not only to their ability to meet basic needs but also to retirement savings and homeownership, and to the broader economy as a result (Chopra 2012; CFPB 2012). We recommend that the CFPB and Congress develop standards for loan refinancing and/or modification to make private loan borrowers' debt more manageable.[34]

CONCLUSION

The American Dream envisions a nation where everyone can fully participate in our democracy, and our fates are determined by ability and accomplishment rather than circumstances of birth. Ensuring college access and increasing student success are crucial to achieving and preserving that dream and the economic opportunity and mobility on which it depends. College education is increasingly the primary path to stable employment, higher wages, retirement benefits, and health insurance, as well as a key predictor of civic participation, better health, and the next generation's odds of getting ahead—or at least not falling behind. An educated workforce is also essential to America's economic competitiveness; our nation needs more people to get quality training and education after high school than ever before. However, as college education has become more essential for all these reasons, income gaps in enrollment and completion have widened rather than narrowed.

To meet the broadly shared goal of greatly increasing the share of Americans with a college education, federal student aid policies, including those related to student loans, must be improved to better support access and success for lower-income students. When student financial aid works as it should, students who are willing to study hard can afford to go to college, which is what we mean by college access, and they can complete a meaningful degree or certificate without burdensome debt, which is what we mean by student success.

Notes

1. Calculations by TICAS on 2011–2012 data from the College Board (2012).
2. For more information about both subsidized and unsubsidized Stafford Loans, see http://studentaid.ed.gov/types/loans/subsidized-unsubsidized (accessed June 11, 2014).
3. For the most recent federal loan cohort default rates, see https://studentaid.ed.gov/about/data-center/student/default from the U.S. Department of Education (accessed June 11, 2014).
4. The Bipartisan Student Loan Certainty Act signed into law in the summer of 2013 ties interest rates for new Stafford and PLUS Loans to the 10-year Treasury note yield when the loan was issued, but the rates are still not based on the government's actual cost of lending and running the loan program.

5. This refers to the fact that interest rates for One Loans are lower when borrowers are in school, and higher when they enter repayment. If students discontinue their studies, whether temporarily (stop out) or permanently (drop out), they will no longer qualify for the lower in-school interest rate (though the in-school interest rate will still cover the six-month grace period after students leave school.)

6. Enacted in the summer of 2013, the Bipartisan Student Loan Certainty Act capped interest rates for undergraduate Stafford Loans at 8.25 percent, graduate Stafford Loans at 9.5 percent, and PLUS Loans at 10.5 percent.

7. For information on swaptions, see http://en.wikipedia.org/wiki/Swaption (accessed June 11, 2014).

8. For more information about existing deferments for federal student loans, see http://studentaid.ed.gov/repay-loans/deferment-forbearance (accessed June 11, 2014).

9. The grace period interest subsidy was temporarily eliminated for loans issued in 2012–2013 and 2013–2014.

10. For more information on independent students, see TICAS, Education Trust, and CLASP (2012).

11. For more information about federal loan consolidation, see http://studentaid.ed.gov/repay-loans/consolidation (accessed June 11, 2014).

12. For more information about the extended repayment plan, see http://studentaid.ed.gov/repay-loans/understand/plans/extended (accessed June 11, 2014).

13. All of the borrower's Direct and FFELP Loans count in determining eligibility for IBR and Pay As You Earn, with the exception of Parent PLUS and consolidation loans that repaid Parent PLUS Loans. For more information, see http://studentaid.ed.gov/repay-loans/understand/plans/income-based and http://studentaid.ed.gov/repay-loans/understand/plans/pay-as-you-earn (accessed June 11, 2014).

14. Depending on total educational indebtedness, a borrower with a Direct Consolidation Loan has access to a "standard" repayment period of 10, 12, 15, 20, 25, or 30 years in a non-income-based plan. For more information, see http://loanconsolidation.ed.gov/examples/repyperiod.html from the U.S. Department of Education (accessed June 11, 2014). The Direct Consolidation Loan program defines total debt for this purpose as total Direct Loan debt plus FFELP debt up to the same amount as the Direct Loan total. For more information about the definition, see http://1.usa.gov/WBrewl (accessed June 11, 2014).

15. For more information about the payments that qualify for Public Service Loan Forgiveness, which include 10-year payments and payments made in income-driven plans, see http://1.usa.gov/OjQu3p (accessed June 11, 2014).

16. For example, in 2008, 1 in 10 graduates from four-year colleges had at least $40,000 in student loans, up from just 3 percent in 1996 (using constant 2008 dollars) (TICAS 2010).

17. The IBR plan was created as part of the College Cost Reduction and Access Act of 2007.

18. For more information about the Plan for Fair Loan Payments and support for its goals, see "The Plan for Fair Loan Payments," The Project on Student Debt, http://bit.ly/VLVIbj (accessed June 11, 2014).

19. For more information about IBR, see http://studentaid.ed.gov/repay-loans/under stand/plans/income-based and http://IBRinfo.org (accessed June 11, 2014).
20. For more information about ICR, see http://studentaid.ed.gov/repay-loans/ understand/plans/income-contingent (accessed June 11, 2014).
21. For more information about Public Service Loan Forgiveness, see http://student aid.ed.gov/repay-loans/forgiveness-cancellation/charts/public-service and http:// www.ibrinfo.org/what.vp.html#pslf (accessed June 11, 2014).
22. Calculations by TICAS based on data from the U.S. Department of Health and Human Services (2012).
23. The Obama administration and others have also proposed eliminating the standard payment cap so that borrowers in income-driven repayment plans are always making payments based on their incomes. See, for example, U.S. Department of Education (2014) and HCM Strategists et al. (2014).
24. The Obama Administration and a bipartisan group of representatives have proposed preventing debt discharged under IDR plans from being considered taxable income. For more information, see U.S. Department of the Treasury (2014) and H.R. 2492 (2009).
25. For information on current loan counseling requirements, see the U.S. Department of Education (2012c). For information on the federal regulations regarding loan counseling, see 34 CFR 685.304, http://bit.ly/XtgttB (accessed June 11, 2014).
26. In the fall of 2013, the U.S. Department of Education reached out by e-mail to over 3 million federal student loan borrowers, including those carrying higher than average debt or showing signs of financial distress, to inform them about income-driven repayment options. See U.S. Department of Education (2013c).
27. Income would be adjusted gross income (AGI) or, if no tax form were available for the past two tax years, wages from W-2 forms. While the family size definition may not be identical to the U.S. Department of Education's definition, it is a proxy under these circumstances and could be amended by the borrower.
28. As specified in 31 U.S.C.§3711: "For purposes of this section, the Secretary of the Treasury may designate, and withdraw such designation of debt collection centers operated by other Federal agencies. The Secretary of the Treasury shall designate such centers on the basis of their performance in collecting delinquent claims owed to the Government."
29. For more information, see https://www.myeddebt.com/borrower/collectionCosts Navigate (accessed June 11, 2014).
30. For examples of teachers being pressured to manipulate grades in order to retain students, see Field (2011).
31. For more information, see comments on false certification in TICAS (2011b).
32. For more information, see the December 10, 2009, letter signed by 25 organizations in support of mandatory certification. See http://bit.ly/Y1qwUN (accessed June 11, 2014). Also see the May 7, 2010, letter signed by lenders and others urging inclusion of mandatory school certification in the Senate financial reform bill, referenced in Lederman (2010).
33. For more information, see the coalition letter to Senator Durbin in support of the Fairness for Struggling Students Act of 2013, available at http://projecton

studentdebt.org/pub_view.php?idx=872 (accessed June 11, 2014), and the coalition letter to Representative Cohen in support of the Private Student Loan Bankruptcy Fairness Act of 2013, available at http://projectonstudentdebt.org/pub_view .php?idx=871 (accessed June 11, 2014).

34. The Refinancing Education Funding to Invest for the Future Act was introduced in the summer of 2013 and endorsed by TICAS. For more information about the bill, see S. 1266 of the act and Brown (2013).

References

Brown, Sherrod. 2013. "Sen. Sherrod Brown Unveils Plan to Refinance Private Student Loans." Press release. http://1.usa.gov/1lijiuB (accessed June 11, 2014).

Chopra, Rohit. 2012. Testimony before the Senate Committee on Banking, Housing and Urban Affairs, Subcommittee on Financial Institutions and Consumer Protection, July 24. http://1.usa.gov/OsqctM (accessed June 11, 2014).

College Board. 2012. *Trends in Student Aid, 2012.* Table 6a. New York: College Board.

Durbin, Dick. 2013. "As Student Loan Debt Surpasses $1 Trillion, Senators Introduce Legislation to Address Crisis." Press release. http://1.usa.gov/ WxsVYM (accessed June 11, 2014).

The Fairness for Struggling Students Act of 2013 (S. 114). Introduced January 23, 2013. http://thomas.loc.gov/cgi-bin/query/z?c113:S.114 (accessed June 11, 2014).

Field, Kelly. 2011. "Faculty at For-Profit Colleges Allege Constant Pressure to Keep Students Enrolled." *The Chronicle of Higher Education*, May 11. http://chronicle.com/article/Pawns-in-the-For-Profit/127424/.

Gross, Jacob P. K., Osman Cekic, Don Hossler, and Nick Hillman. 2009. "What Matters in Student Loan Default: A Review of the Research Literature." *Journal of Student Financial Aid* 39(1): 19.

HCM Strategists, Institute for Higher Education Policy, National Association of Student Financial Aid Administrators, New America Foundation, and Young Invincibles. 2014. *Automatic for the Borrower: How Repayment Based on Income Can Reduce Loan Defaults and Manage Risk.* http://bit .ly/1fLBIOK (accessed June 11, 2014).

Hechinger, John. 2012. "Obama Relies on Debt Collectors Profiting from Student Loan Woe." *Bloomberg News*, March 25. http://www.bloomberg.com/ news/2012-03-26/obama-relies-on-debt-collectors-profiting-from-student -loan-woe.html (accessed June 11, 2014).

House Resolution (H.R.) 2492. 2009. "To amend the Internal Revenue Code of 1986 to exclude from gross income discharges of student loans the repayment of which is income contingent or income based." May 19. http://thomas .loc.gov/cgi-bin/bdquery/z?d111:H.R.2492 (accessed June 11, 2014).

Internal Revenue Service (IRS). 2009. "IRS Conducts Extensive Review, Decides Not to Renew Private Debt Collection Contracts: IRS Employees More Flexible, More Cost Effective." Press release. March 5. http://www.irs .gov/uac/IRS-Conducts-Extensive-Review-Decides-Not-to-Renew-Private -Debt-Collection-Contracts (accessed June 11, 2014).

Lederman, Doug. 2010. "Unlikely Bedfellows on Student Loans." *Inside Higher Ed*, May 11. http://www.insidehighered.com/news/2010/05/11/certify (accessed June 11, 2014).

Loonin, Deanne. 2012. "The Looming Student Debt Crisis: Providing Fairness for Struggling Students." Testimony before the U.S. Senate Judiciary Subcommittee on Administrative Oversight and the Courts, March 20. http:// bit.ly/1gmksQf (accessed June 11, 2014).

Martin, Andrew. 2012. "Debt Collectors Cashing In on Student Loans." *New York Times*, September 8. http://www.nytimes.com/2012/09/09/business/ once-a-student-now-dogged-by-collection-agencies.html (accessed June 11, 2014).

Nguyen, Mary. 2011. *Degreeless in Debt: What Happens to Borrowers Who Drop Out.* Washington, DC: Education Sector at American Institutes for Research. http://bit.ly/1p7zIHw (accessed June 11, 2014).

Polis, Jared. 2013. "Polis Introduces Legislation to Address Crisis of Rising Student Loan Debt." Press release. http://polis.house.gov/news/document single.aspx?DocumentID=362465 (accessed June 11, 2014).

Private Student Loan Bankruptcy Fairness Act of 2013 (H.R. 532). Introduced February 6, 2013. http://thomas.loc.gov/cgi-bin/query/z?c113:H.R.532 (accessed June 11, 2014).

The Institute for College Access and Success (TICAS). 2006. *Addressing Student Loan Repayment Burdens: Strengths and Weaknesses of the Current System.* Berkeley, CA: TICAS. http://ticas.org/pub_view.php?idx=103 (accessed June 11, 2014).

———. 2009. "New Federal Income-Based Repayment Plan Goes into Effect July 1." Press release. http://ticas.org/files/pub/July_1_IBR_Alert.pdf (accessed June 11, 2014).

———. 2010. *High Hopes, Big Debts.* Oakland, CA: TICAS. http://bit.ly/ YN6wZ5 (accessed June 11, 2014).

———. 2011a. *Private Loans: Facts and Trends.* Oakland, CA: TICAS. http:// projectstudentdebt.org/files/pub/private_loan_facts_trends.pdf (accessed June 11, 2014).

———. 2011b. Comments in response to Docket ID ED-2011-OPE-0003, the May 5, 2011 U.S. Department of Education Notice of Establishment of Negotiated Rulemaking Committees and Notice of Public Hearings. http://ticas.org/files/pub/TICASNegReg_Comments_5.20.2011.pdf   (accessed June 11, 2014).

———. 2011c. *Critical Choices: How Colleges Can Help Students and Families Make Better Decisions about Private Loans*. Oakland, CA: TICAS. http://projectonstudentdebt.org/pub_view.php?idx=766 (accessed June 11, 2014).

———. 2012a. *"Over-Borrowing" Not the Problem at For-Profit Colleges*. Oakland, CA: TICAS. http://bit.ly/Xo5KTh (accessed June 11, 2014).

———. 2012b. *Data Show No Evidence of "Over-Borrowing" at Community Colleges*. Oakland, CA: TICAS. http://bit.ly/WYyge7 (accessed June 11, 2014).

———. 2012c. *Student Debt and the Class of 2011*. Washington, DC: TICAS. http://projectonstudentdebt.org/files/pub/classof2011.pdf   (accessed June 11, 2014).

———. 2012d. *Making Loans Work: How Community Colleges Support Responsible Student Borrowing*. Oakland, CA: TICAS. http://projectonstudentdebt.org/files/pub/Making_Loans_Work.pdf (accessed June 11, 2014).

———. 2012e. "Student Loan Default Rates Show Continued Borrower Distress: Income-Based Repayment Plan Could Help More Borrowers Avoid Default." Press release. Oakland, CA: TICAS. http://www.ticas.org/files/pub/Release_CDRs_092812.pdf (accessed June 11, 2014).

———. 2012f. "Pay As You Earn Now Available to Help New College Grads" (blog), December 20. http://views.ticas.org/?p=956 (accessed June 11, 2014).

———. 2013. "Aligning the Means and the Ends: How to Improve Federal Student Aid and Increase College Access and Success." White paper. Oakland, CA: TICAS. http://www.ticas.org/pub_view.php?idx=873 (accessed June 11, 2014).

TICAS, the Education Trust, and CLASP. 2012. "Independent Students Depend on Pell Grants for Access to College." Berkeley, CA, and Washington, DC: TICAS, the Education Trust, and CLASP. Washington, DC. http://bit.ly/R1p9tn (accessed June 11, 2014).

TICAS, Public Advocates, et al. 2006. "Petition for Rulemaking to Amend Title 34, Sections 682.210, 685.204, and 685.209 of the Code of Federal Regulations." The Project on Student Debt at TICAS, Berkeley, CA. http://projectonstudentdebt.org//files/File/Petition_to_ED_5.2.06.pdf   (accessed June 11, 2014).

U.S. Consumer Financial Protection Bureau (CFPB). 2012. *Annual Report of*

the CFPB Student Loan Ombudsman. Washington, DC: CFPB. http://files
.consumerfinance.gov/f/201210_cfpb_Student-Loan-Ombudsman-Annual
-Report.pdf (accessed June 11, 2014).

U.S. Consumer Financial Protection Bureau and U.S. Department of Education.
2012. *Private Student Loans: Report to the Senate Committee on Banking,
Housing, and Urban Affairs, the Senate Committee on Health, Education,
Labor, and Pensions, the House of Representatives Committee on Financial
Services, and the House of Representatives Committee on Education and
the Workforce*. Washington, DC: CFPB and U.S. Department of Education.
http://files.consumerfinance.gov/f/201207_cfpb_Reports_Private-Student
-Loans.pdf (accessed June 11, 2014).

U.S. Department of Education. 2010. *Delinquency and Default Prevention
Training*. Webinar transcript, p. 27. Washington, DC: U.S. Department of
Education. http://www2.ed.gov/offices/OSFAP/training/materials/default
transcript.pdf (accessed June 11, 2014).

———. 2011. *Six-Year Attainment, Persistence, Transfer, Retention, and With-
drawal Rates of Students Who Began Postsecondary Education in 2003–
04*. Washington, DC: U.S. Department of Education. http://nces.ed.gov/
pubs2011/2011152.pdf (accessed June 11, 2014).

———. 2012a. Federal Register Notice, Docket ID ED–2012–OPE–0010.
Final regulations on the Federal Perkins Loan Program, Federal Family
Education Loan Program, and William D. Ford Federal Direct Loan Program. http://www.gpo.gov/fdsys/pkg/FR-2012-11-01/pdf/2012-26348.pdf
(accessed June 11, 2014).

———. 2012b. "Loan Servicing Information—Availability of Pay As You
Earn Repayment Plan and Electronic IBR/Pay As You Earn/ICR Repayment Plan Request." Washington, DC: U.S. Department of Education.
http://ifap.ed.gov/eannouncements/122112LSIPayAsYouEarnPlanIBRn
ICR.html (accessed June 11, 2014).

———. 2012c. *2012-13 Federal Student Aid Handbook*. Vol. 2, Ch. 6. Washington, DC: U.S. Department of Education. http://ifap.ed.gov/ifap/byAward
Year.jsp?type=fsahandbook&awardyear=2012-2013 (accessed June 11,
2014).

———. 2013a. *Exit Counseling Guide for Federal Student Loan Borrowers*.
Washington, DC: U.S. Department of Education. www.direct.ed.gov/pubs/
exitcounselguide.pdf (accessed June 11, 2014).

———. 2013b. "New Student Loan Repayment Option to Help Recent Graduates." *Homeroom: The Official Blog of the U.S. Department of Education*.
January 2, U.S. Department of Education. http://www.ed.gov/blog/2013/01/
new-student-loan-repayment-option-to-help-recent-graduates (accessed June
11, 2014).

————. 2013c. "U.S. Department of Education Announces Additional Efforts to Inform Student Borrowers of Repayment Options." Press release. Washington, DC: U.S. Department of Education. http://1.usa.gov/OGOQys (accessed June 11, 2014).

————. 2014. *Student Loans Overview: Fiscal Year 2015 Budget Proposal.* Washington, DC: U.S. Department of Education. http://www2.ed.gov/about/overview/budget/budget15/justifications/s-loansoverview.pdf (accessed June 11, 2014).

U.S. Department of Health and Human Services. 2012. "2012 HHS Poverty Guidelines." Washington, DC: U.S. Department of Health and Human Services. http://aspe.hhs.gov/poverty/12poverty.shtml (accessed June 11, 2014).

U.S. Department of the Treasury. 2009. *Fiscal Year 2008 Report to the Congress: U.S. Government Receivables and Debt Collection Activities of Federal Agencies.* Washington, DC: U.S. Department of the Treasury. http://www.fms.treas.gov/news/reports/debt08.pdf (accessed June 11, 2014).

————. 2014. "General Explanations of the Administration's Fiscal Year 2015 Revenue Proposals." Washington, DC: U.S. Department of the Treasury, p. 149. http://www.treasury.gov/resource-center/tax-policy/Documents/General-Explanations-FY2015.pdf (accessed June 11, 2014).

U.S. House of Representatives. 2012. Letter from 12 members of Congress to Secretary of Education Arne Duncan. http://1.usa.gov/1j3MAJm (accessed June 11, 2014).

The White House. 2010. "Ensuring That Student Loans Are Affordable." http://1.usa.gov/d32TEd (accessed June 11, 2014). Washington, DC: The White House.

————. 2011. "We Can't Wait: Obama Administration to Lower Student Loan Payments for Millions of Borrowers." Press release, October 25. Washington, DC: The White House. http://1.usa.gov/t63akG (accessed June 11, 2014).

12

Loans for Educational Opportunity

Making Borrowing Work for Today's Students

Susan Dynarski
University of Michigan

Daniel Kreisman
Georgia State University

Susan Dynarski and Daniel Kreisman presented a paper that proposes a new system of federal student lending based on an income-based model of repayment in which payments will automatically rise and fall with a borrower's earnings, just as contributions to Social Security do. The paper was commissioned by The Hamilton Project, and while this volume provides only a synopsis of it, the full version can be accessed at The Hamilton Project's Web site, http://www.hamiltonproject.org/files/downloads_and_links/ THP_DynarskiDiscPaper_Final.pdf.

Borrowing for college has risen steadily for decades, and student-loan debt has mounted to $1 trillion, now surpassing credit cards as the third-largest form of consumer debt. With 7 million student loans in default and rising tuition prices, some are beginning to wonder if the costs associated with student borrowing are out of line with the value of attending college.

The evidence, however, suggests we have a repayment crisis, not a student debt crisis. Four facts support this interpretation. First, typical borrowers have only a moderate amount of debt: 69 percent of students in recent cohorts borrow $10,000 or less, and 98 percent borrow $50,000 or less. Second, the payoff to a college education is high over the student's lifetime. The typical holder of a bachelor's degree earns several hundred thousand dollars more than a high school graduate over a lifetime. Even those who start college but do not graduate experience lifetime gains of about $100,000. Third, although default rates have been rising, they are not driven by the small fraction of borrowers with

411

large loans. Rather, it is borrowers with typical levels of student debt who struggle with their payments, especially in the first few years after college. Fourth, default is highly correlated with the age of the borrower, with younger borrowers at far greater risk of default and delinquency.

Many individuals have difficulty repaying loans because, under the existing system of federal lending, workers typically repay their loans early in their careers, when their incomes are relatively low and variable. A college education, however, is an investment that pays off over many decades. The mismatch between the timing of the costs and benefits of education is especially salient among young borrowers, who are most likely to default. A few missed payments, as penalties and fees accrue, can lead to rapidly rising loan balances. The damaged credit records that result from a few missed student loan payments can block young people from borrowing for other purposes, such as for cars and homes. Thus, the current system can turn reasonable levels of debt into repayment burdens that make financial independence and stability more difficult to achieve. Moreover, the current system harms taxpayers because, when delinquency and default rates on loans are high, the lender also suffers.

As an alternative, we propose a single, straightforward, income-based repayment system called Loans for Educational Opportunity (LEO). The main idea of this proposal is that the repayment of loans would be automatic and simple, and that repayments would increase (and decline) with earnings. Employers would deduct contributions in the same way that they deduct payroll taxes. For example, the W-4 would be modified to include a checkbox that asks whether a worker has a LEO. Borrowers could also indicate a higher repayment amount than the one that would otherwise be automatically deducted by filing a W-4 that specifies additional withholding. Self-employment and multiple jobs would be handled the same way as Social Security and income taxes, with quarterly payments and an annual reconciliation in April to correct any over- or underpayment. Contributions would stop when the loan is repaid or after 25 years.

We highlight four key principles:

1) Contribution rates should rise with earnings. Our simulations show that setting rates at 3 percent of earnings up to $10,000, 7 percent between $10,001 and $25,000, and 10 percent above $25,001 would result in the typical loan being paid off in 10–15

years. A flat contribution rate of 6–9 percent of earnings would achieve similar results but would lead to higher payments (as a share of earnings) for many borrowers.

2) Interest rates should hold the taxpayers harmless. The federal government should seek neither to make nor to lose money from student loans. Student loans correct a capital market failure: the private sector will not provide loans that are secured only by a borrower's future earnings. Interest rates should cover the costs of borrowing, credit risk from unpaid loans, and administrative overhead, and should adjust annually over the life of the loan and not be nominally capped.

3) Eliminate in-school interest subsidies. The subsidized Stafford Loan, which is limited to students with sufficient financial need, does not begin to charge interest until the students are out of school. This is expensive for the government and has little bearing on either college attendance or persistence because it does not put any money into the hands of students. Deferring interest accrual while students attend school serves only to shorten the repayment period for those who receive it and benefits borrowers with higher incomes more than those with lower incomes.

4) Allow existing borrowers to join the new system. Certain borrowers under the old federal loan system will have the opportunity to convert their loans to the new system. Only federal, undergraduate loans can be repaid in this way; loans made to parents of students (PLUS Loans) will not be eligible. Existing borrowers can be brought into the new system by having the Department of Education purchase existing loans from the private loan companies. There is a precedent for this: during the credit crunch, the Department of Education was authorized to buy loans from private servicers in order to free up capital so that more student loans could be made.

This is a system of loan repayment designed for the vast majority of former students—the 98 percent who borrow a manageable amount ($50,000 or less). For the few students who borrow unmanageable amounts, most of whom borrow through the private market, we advocate the following regulatory reforms. First, private loans should be dischargeable in bankruptcy. The protection from bankruptcy, established in 2005, gives lenders incentives to make loans even to students who are unlikely to be able to handle the payments, since the lender knows the borrower cannot ever escape the debt. Second, private lenders should not be allowed to use the label "student loan" for a loan that requires a cosigner or credit history. Removing the student loan label ensures that borrowers cannot confuse these loans with federal student loans and signals to students that they should borrow with caution. Third, students must exhaust federal lending options before taking out private loans. Some students take out private loans without exhausting their federal loan options, which reflects a lack of information on the part of the borrowers, as Stafford Loans are less costly than private loans.

This proposal can be implemented without adding to the federal deficit; in fact, it will likely save money for the federal government. The only major costs that the government would bear are those associated with administering repayment of the loans, which is currently handled by the private sector. These costs, however, can be more than offset by three provisions of this proposal. First, the federal deduction of loan interest would be eliminated for federal borrowers paying through the new system (which, in time, should be all student borrowers), saving $1 billion in tax expenditures. Second, the proposal eliminates existing contracts with private loan servicers, which currently cost about $360 million annually. Finally, as discussed above, the proposal eliminates the in-school subsidy, which will reduce by billions the cost of the federal loan program.

13
Measuring the Benefits of Income-Based Repayment for Graduate and Professional Students

Jason Delisle
New America

Alex Holt
New America

Kristin Blagg
Georgetown University

The federal government has maintained a student loan program since the 1960s, and since the early 1990s the program has been available to all undergraduate, subbaccalaureate, and graduate students without regard to family income. Since 2006, graduate students have been able to use the program to finance the entire cost of their educations as determined by the institution they attend (in any program, for any credential, and including living expenses) without limit (*Deficit Reduction Act of 2005*).

From a federal policy perspective, a government loan program is a logical tool to help ensure that people can obtain a postsecondary education. In essence, loans allow students to move some of the future earnings that they would gain from that education to the present to finance the education itself. The government's role in sponsoring such a program is sound on a theoretical basis as well: A robust private market for student lending is unlikely to develop because of information asymmetries and poor economies of scale (i.e., relatively small loans with multiple disbursements and long repayment terms); a private market would likely make credit most readily available to those who need it least (i.e., students from more affluent families or those attending elite institutions of higher education); and a private lending market would restrict credit availability in times of economic stress, the point at which demand for higher education tends to surge.

Despite its appeal, there is a downside to a loan arrangement for the student. If his future earnings are lower than expected or erratic, he may not be able to repay the loan on time or in full and would incur penalties, fees, accrued interest charges, a damaged credit history, etc. That problem falls away, however, if the student can repay the loan as a share of his income.

That reasoning led policymakers to add an income-based repayment plan to the federal loan program in the mid-1990s, coupling it with loan forgiveness, which was ultimately set in regulations at 25 years of payments (*Omnibus Budget Reconciliation Act of 1993*). That early version of income-based repayment, which remains available today, suffered from a number of limitations and has never been widely used.[1] Those limitations prompted student aid advocates to argue in 2006 that the program should be redesigned to make it more widely available and offer lower payments to borrowers.[2] Ultimately, lawmakers agreed and enacted the Income-Based Repayment program in 2007 and implemented it in 2009.

Under this version of the Income-Based Repayment (IBR) program (which this chapter refers to as Old IBR to distinguish it from an even more recent version of the program), borrowers make payments equal to 15 percent of their adjusted gross income after an exemption equal to 150 percent of the federal poverty guidelines adjusted for household size (see Table 13.1). Remaining debt is forgiven after 25 years of payments. All borrowers are eligible for the program if it would reduce their monthly payments below what they would pay under a 10-year fixed amortization, which is also known as the standard repayment plan.[3] Policymakers also added a new loan forgiveness provision when they enacted IBR: public service loan forgiveness (PSLF). Under PSLF, borrowers using IBR who work for most nonprofit organizations or any government position can have unpaid debt forgiven after 10 cumulative years of payments.[4]

In 2010, only months after borrowers could first enroll in Old IBR, President Obama proposed that Congress modify the program for all borrowers by reducing monthly payments to 10 percent of discretionary income and shortening the loan forgiveness term to 20 years of pay-

Table 13.1 Comparing Terms for New and Old Income-Based Repayment (IBR) Plans

Repayment term	Old IBR	New IBR
Eligible borrowers	All borrowers with federal student loans not in default	Borrowers who took out first federal loan on or after October 1, 2007, and also took out a loan on or after October 1, 2011; and all new borrowers as of October 1, 2011
Eligible loans	All federal student loans (except Parent PLUS loans)	Same
Income definition	Adjusted Gross Income (AGI) on prior year federal tax return; can exclude spouse's income if filing separately	Same
Exemption	150% of federal poverty guidelines adj. for household ($17,235 single, plus $6,030 ea. additional person, including spouse)	Same
Payment as share of income above exemption (annual)	15%	10%
Maximum payment regardless of income	Payment on original loan balance using a 10-year fixed monthly payment	Same
Public Service Loan Forgiveness eligibility	120 cumulative monthly payments (10 years) in qualified job	Same
General loan forgiveness eligibility (all enrollees)	25 years	20 years

SOURCE: Based on data from the U.S. Department of Education.

ments. All other terms under IBR would be left unchanged. Congress passed this proposal in early 2010 as part of a larger health care reform bill (*Health Care and Education Reconciliation Act of 2010*). While this law made the New IBR terms available to new borrowers as of 2014, the Obama administration used its authority under a different statute to accelerate the start date to December 2012 for new borrowers as of October 1, 2007.[5] This "bridge" program is called Pay As You Earn. This chapter refers to both Pay As You Earn and the IBR that begins for new borrowers in 2014 as New IBR. The terms of the two programs are virtually identical, with only one minor exception: Pay As You Earn includes a limit on how much interest can be capitalized at a certain point in repayment, but it does not limit how much interest can accrue. This is unlikely to have any effect on most borrowers, and a negligible effect on the limited universe of borrowers with high debt balances—over $50,000—who experience prolonged low incomes with sudden, large increases in incomes that are sustained.

In summary, the federal government has offered student loan borrowers repayment plans based on income since the early 1990s but later added the IBR plan and then modified it shortly thereafter to further reduce borrower payments. This chapter focuses on the most recent changes to the program.

UNDERSTANDING NEW IBR

To better understand how New IBR would affect borrowers over their entire repayment terms, in 2012 we developed a calculator that incorporates all of the repayment parameters and rules (i.e., income exemption, interest accrual, loan forgiveness, etc.) for both New and Old IBR to compare how the changes would affect different types of borrowers based on various debt and income scenarios. That is, our analysis examines how the program would work over a borrower's entire 20- or 25-year repayment term. Such an approach is the best way to understand how the multiple repayment terms in the program interact over many years with other factors such as inflation, interest accrual, income changes, and changes in household size.

Using the calculator, we analyze hundreds of hypothetical borrower scenarios (Delisle and Holt 2012). One of our main conclusions is that the changes to IBR made the program much more generous than was commonly understood, particularly for graduate students. Borrowers with debt from graduate school, despite earning high incomes, stand to have substantial debts forgiven. Under Old IBR, such a scenario would be highly unusual. (See Table 13.2 for a comparison.) Moreover, New IBR can work like tuition assistance for graduate students because a borrower can still qualify for substantial amounts of loan forgiveness, even when he earns an income that is average relative to national or peer incomes. Meanwhile, New IBR provides relatively small increases in benefits for undergraduate students and lower-income borrowers compared to Old IBR.[6]

Those findings are more thoroughly explained in Delisle and Holt (2012), but they can be described briefly with the following points. Graduate students stand to benefit the most from the changes because they can borrow federal student loans to finance their entire educations and then repay all federal student loans—from both undergraduate and graduate studies—as one balance under IBR, whereas undergraduate borrowers are subject to annual and aggregate borrowing limits. Under Old IBR, monthly payments and the 25-year term before loan forgiveness were sufficient to repay even large amounts of graduate student debt, but changes under New IBR reduce borrowers' monthly payments by 33 percent compared to Old IBR, and then shorten the repayment time before loan forgiveness by 5 years. Those changes result in a large increase in benefits for graduate students because of the rules on what they may borrow in federal loans.

For dependent undergraduates the payment reductions under New IBR increase benefits as well, but dependent undergraduate debt levels are not high enough such that New IBR results in significantly larger amounts of loan forgiveness compared to Old IBR.

Lastly, lower-income borrowers see little effect from the changes under New IBR, because the income exemption is the same under both plans, and these borrowers have too little income over that exemption such that the changes in the repayment rate and loan forgiveness term under New IBR do not translate into a large reduction in payments.

Table 13.2 Comparing a Borrower under Old and New IBR Plans

Starting loan balance: $65,000 at 6.0% interest

| | Repayment year | | | | | | Total | |
	1	5	10	15	20	25	payments	Forgiven
Income ($)	45,000	58,986	82,731	116,034	162,744	228,257		
Old IBR ($)								
Monthly payment	291	259	472	713	722	—	132,459	—
Loan balance	65,410	67,112	63,815	46,187	12,993	—		
New IBR ($)								
Monthly payment	194	173	315	475	694	—	88,045	55,817
Loan balance	66,574	72,908	77,210	73,241	55,817	—		

NOTE: Loan balance reflects principal and accrued unpaid interest at the end of the repayment year indicated. Borrower's income increases at 7 percent annually. Income reflects total income, but payments are calculated on the baiss of adjusted gross income, which is reduced by an assumed amount explained in Note 10 at the end of the chapter. The exemption is calculated for a household size of one for the first three years and a size of two each year thereafter to reflect a spouse.

SOURCE: Delisle and Holt (2012).

GRADUATE STUDENTS AND THE "NO MARGINAL COST THRESHOLD"

In this chapter, we delve more deeply into the benefits that New IBR will provide to graduate and professional students, using our prior work as a foundation. Our findings from that initial work suggest that the policy and market implications of the New IBR are significant in the graduate and professional education arena; namely, New IBR could act as a form of tuition assistance, as students borrow knowing that all or some of the incremental debt they incur will ultimately be forgiven. However, that work relied on somewhat generic (though plausible) debt and income scenarios, making it difficult to gauge the size and scope of the tuition-assistance effect and what types of degree programs could be most affected (Delisle and Holt 2012). Furthermore, our initial work did not factor in PSLF. That benefit applies to 25 percent of jobs in the economy, owing to the government's very broad definition of "public service" and makes the benefits we highlighted in our initial work several times larger because loan forgiveness occurs after only 10 years of payments (U.S. Department of Education Office of Federal Student Aid n.d.).

To build on our prior analysis, we develop income projections for individuals working in certain professions who have graduate and professional credentials. We also include the effects of PSLF in all of our analyses.

For the income estimates, we opt to estimate incomes by profession rather than lump together broader categories of graduate and professional degrees, such as all masters' of arts or all masters' of science. This allows for more distinctions in probable earnings between different professions. Moreover, many students who seek a graduate or professional degree do so to obtain employment or advancement in a defined field. For example, a student seeking a Juris Doctor typically intends to practice law or work in a field that requires that credential, and a student pursuing a master's of education likely intends to work in primary or secondary education. Thus, we can link specialized graduate and professional degrees to specific career and income paths. One limitation of this approach, however, is that it does not capture the incomes of borrowers who earn a degree in one area but are employed in another.

Obtaining complete and reliable information on the amounts that graduate students borrow for specific degrees and what specific programs cost is more problematic. Programs for the same graduate credential can have a range of costs, students can incur debt to finance a wide range of living costs, and they can attend part time or full time.[7] In a few cases we located debt figures by profession or specialized degree type, but most often those sources report only mean debt levels and understate the loan balances that borrowers would actually repay in New IBR because they do not include accrued interest or debt from undergraduate studies. Thus it is difficult to pinpoint the cost and debt incurred for a particular graduate or professional credential. However, to provide context for our analysis, we incorporate federal student loan debt levels for graduate and professional students by broad degree-type category as reported by the federal government in the 2012 National Postsecondary Student Aid Survey. (See Table 13.3.)

Instead of using cost or debt levels as the central focus of our analysis, we use a "no marginal cost threshold" (NMCT) measure. This places the analysis on what students would repay based on their projected incomes, not necessarily the amount that they borrow.

Table 13.3 Graduate Degree Categories and Debt Levels ($)

Degree by Dept. of Education survey category	Degree-profession profile	Debt level by percentile		
		25th	50th	75th
Education (any master's)	K-12 Teacher	23,000	42,000	69,000
Other master's degree	Accountant	29,000	49,000	85,000
	Reporter			
	Social Worker			
	Speech Pathologist			
Other master of science (MS)	Engineer	23,000	47,000	75,000
	Nurse			
Other health science degree	Pharmacist	98,000	132,000	199,000
	Veterinarian			
Law (LLB or JD)	Lawyer	86,000	140,000	191,000

NOTE: Debt figures reflect cumulative federal loan amount owed, principal and interest, from undergraduate and graduate studies for those who completed a degree in 2011–12, rounded to nearest $1,000.
SOURCE: U.S. Department of Education National Postsecondary Student Aid Survey 2012; Authors' calculations.

Because we already know the terms of New IBR and have built them into a calculator, we can determine how much an individual would repay on her student loans once we have estimated her future income over 20 years. That is, what she repays in total is a function of her income. We can also find the level of debt at which she ceases to incur any increases in her future loan payments if she borrows an additional dollar. Taking on more debt at that point increases only how much debt she has forgiven after 10 or 20 years, not her monthly or total payments.

The NMCT concept may best be understood in relation to a traditional loan. Under a traditional loan arrangement, the more a student borrows, the more she must repay. Under New IBR, for a set income level and path, there must be an amount of debt where that relationship ends, and the more a student borrows, the more she has forgiven.

This NMCT is a convenient indicator for identifying the implications of New IBR. If the NMCT is below what a graduate degree costs, then most borrowers holding those degrees will receive loan forgiveness. Schools could also raise prices with impunity, as those increases are borne by the federal government through loan forgiveness, and students would be encouraged to borrow for the full cost of attendance. Alternatively, an NMCT that is far below the typical cost of a graduate degree in a particular field might indicate that the New IBR is doing what its supporters wanted—it is subsidizing socially valuable credentials that a student's future income gains would not justify alone. There are a number of other ways to interpret the NMCT, and we highlight those in the discussion section of this chapter.

METHODOLOGY

Estimating Incomes by Profession and Credential

We selected 10 professions for our analysis: 1) lawyer, 2) pharmacist, 3) teacher, 4) accountant, 5) registered nurse, 6) social worker, 7) reporter (journalist), 8) engineer, 9) speech pathologist, and 10) veterinarian. The selection process aimed partly to present a wide range of professions that have varying earnings levels among the employment categories available in the data we used, and partly to capture graduate and professional programs that vary in cost.

To generate a 20-year income trajectory for each profession, we use age-based income data reported in the American Community Survey (ACS) for 2003–2011 for individuals who indicated that they worked in the specified profession and held a master's degree or higher level of education. The data do not allow us to confirm that the respondent held a degree that matches that profession; however, we selected professions where that would generally be the case (e.g., a lawyer with a Juris Doctor, a social worker with a Master of Social Work). Nevertheless, it is the income of individuals in a given profession that matters most for our analysis.

The income model roughly shows what a lawyer earns when she is 30 years old, when she is 31 years old, and so on. We assume all borrowers graduate and begin repaying their loans at age 27. Therefore, a 30-year-old lawyer is in her third year of loan repayment.[8] We generate two categories for each income profile, one at the 50th percentile and one at the 75th. Thus, the model roughly shows what a 30-year-old lawyer earns at the 50th and 75th percentiles for his profession.

Whereas a longitudinal data set would offer advantages over the ACS for developing our income projections, the available longitudinal data sets, such as the Bureau of Labor Statistics' National Longitudinal Survey of Youth or the Panel Study of Income Dynamics, are limited to broad profession categories or include too few respondents within a specific profession. The ACS data set, on the other hand, includes many individual professions with a large number of respondents in each and includes an indicator for level of education. That allows us to focus on individual professions and individuals with masters' or professional degrees rather than having to use more generic categories.

We chose to generate income estimates at the 50th and 75th percentiles because they give a sense of where the NMCT occurs for what might be considered a typical graduate in a given profession, and what it would be for a graduate who earns more than most of his peers, respectively. It is important to keep in mind that for borrowers who earn less than these amounts, the NMCT is lower. For graduates whom one could reasonably expect to earn below the 50th percentile (e.g., a teacher who plans to teach in a rural area, or graduates from the lowest-ranked law schools), the NMCT is also lower than the figures we stated.

Because we use data over the 2003–2011 period, we first adjust all figures for inflation and convert them to 2011 dollars. Then we inflate them again to match the future year in the borrower's repayment plan. Thus, the income projections begin in 2011, and a borrower's income in his 20th year of repayment is inflated to adjust for those 20 future years.

We also aggregate the earnings information because of the somewhat limited number of respondents in a given profession at a specific age. Therefore, we use five-year age ranges to approximate earnings by age and then interpolate and extrapolate income with increases for age. For example, we use the income information for veterinarians aged 30–34 to approximate the earnings of a 32-year-old veterinarian and income information for veterinarians aged 35–39 to approximate the earnings of a 37-year-old veterinarian. Then we interpolate incomes in the intervening years in even, incremental steps, where earlier years are lower and later years are incrementally higher.

That approach tends to produce smoother increases in incomes each year in a borrower's repayment term than individuals are likely to experience. When combined with the 2.5 percent annual inflation increases, our income projections show borrowers increasing their incomes every year in the repayment term based on both age and inflation. That effect also likely overstates borrowers' incomes because of issues such as negative income shocks that occur over an individual's life, although some of those effects should be captured in the data we used to build the models. However, biasing a borrower's income higher than it is likely to be in reality means our analysis *overestimates* what a borrower would pay on his student loans under New IBR, *underestimates* the amount of debt that would be forgiven, and it indicates that the NMCT for borrowing an additional dollar is likely *below* what we present. Table 13.25 (pp. 436–437) shows all of the income projections.

New IBR Calculator and Important Repayment Assumptions

The calculator we use to determine loan payments and the NMCT reflects all of the repayment rules for New IBR and several important assumptions and adjustments.[9] Annual payments are equal to 10 percent of a borrower's adjusted gross income (AGI). However, AGI tends to be lower than a borrower's stated income due to pretax fringe benefits and above-the-line deductions and credits. The calculator adjusts for those benefits by reducing total income to reflect an AGI figure.[10] We assume that all borrowers make IBR payments based only on their income, exclusive of any income from a spouse, as is allowed under New IBR.[11]

New IBR also reduces a borrower's AGI by an exemption amount equal to 150 percent of the federal poverty guidelines, based on household size. For this chapter, we assume that all borrowers have a household size of one for the first five repayment years and a household size of two each year thereafter to reflect a spouse (a larger household size increases the exemption).[12] The calculator increases the exemption by 2.5 percent each incremental repayment year to reflect adjustments for inflation.

New IBR includes a maximum payment cap based on how much debt a borrower has when entering repayment. This monthly payment cap is equal to the payment the borrower would make if he were paying his initial loan balance off on a 10-year amortization schedule. Therefore, a borrower's payment cannot exceed this level while enrolled in IBR, no matter how high his income. This payment cap is also the initial eligibility test for enrolling in IBR. If a borrower's payments are below this cap, he may enroll in New IBR, though if they later exceed it, he is not disqualified from IBR's other important benefit: loan forgiveness.

Consistent with the rules under New IBR, interest on the loan accrues and payments are first credited to unpaid accrued interest before principal. Unpaid accrued interest during repayment is not added to the borrower's principal balance (i.e., capitalized or compounded) unless and until his payments reach the capped payment discussed above.

We set the fixed interest rate on the borrower's debt at the weighted average of the rates on federal student loans (unsubsidized Stafford Loans and Grad PLUS), which were 6.8 percent and 7.9 percent, respectively, in the 2012–2013 school year. Those are still reasonable proxies, despite a recent change in law that will reduce those rates in the near term, because the rates are projected to rise in the near future above the 6.8 and 7.9 percent rates.[13] We assume the first $45,000 of debt a borrower incurs is unsubsidized Stafford Loans, and any above that is Grad PLUS, except for lawyers, pharmacists, registered nurses, and veterinarians, for which we assume the first $65,000 is unsubsidized Stafford Loans, reflecting the fact that borrowers with those degrees likely borrowed unsubsidized Stafford Loans for three, rather than two, years in their graduate studies. Unsubsidized Stafford Loans have lower interest rates, but those loans are subject to annual and aggregate limits. Students take out Grad PLUS Loans once they have reached the annual or aggregate unsubsidized Stafford Loan limits.

Outstanding principal and interest on the loans is forgiven after 10 years of payments for PSLF and 20 years for all other cases. Loan forgiveness at the 20-year mark is taxable, although estimated tax liability is excluded for the purposes of this chapter. We assume that lawmakers will make loan forgiveness tax free in the near future.

ANALYSIS PRESENTATION

Loan Repayment Tables by Profession and Income Category

We have arranged the results of our analysis in Tables 13.4–13.24. Table 13.4 is a summary table for all of the degree-profession categories.

There are sets of two tables for each degree-profession category (where each profession is linked to the most likely degree they were awarded), one for a borrower earning at the 50th percentile and one for a borrower earning at the 75th percentile in that degree-profession category. The "Debt level for completer" column states the cumulative undergraduate and graduate federal debt levels (including capitalized and noncapitalized interest) for program completers, of those who borrowed, reported in the 2011–2012 National Postsecondary Student Aid Study (NPSAS) database at the 25th, 50th, and 75th percentiles of indebtedness. The NPSAS data include general categories for graduate and professional programs, and we attempted to match the best NPSAS category with the degree-profession categories in this analysis.

The "Debt level for IBR no marginal cost" columns show the level of debt at which a student in the stated degree-profession category, earning at the percentile indicated in the table title, would bear no incremental cost in repayment if she borrowed an additional dollar. Under that heading, PSLF indicates where that point is for a borrower who qualifies for loan forgiveness after 10 years of payments under PSLF. We assume the borrower makes her qualifying payment consecutively and all in the first 10 years of repayment, although eligibility is based

Table 13.4 Debt Level for IBR No Marginal Cost Threshold ($)

	Loan Forgiveness Program			
	PSLF		20-year	
	Earnings percentile		Earnings percentile	
Degree/profession	50th	75th	50th	75th
Accountant	37,000	70,000	52,000	100,000
Engineer	50,000	74,000	88,000	113,000
Lawyer	54,000	116,000	86,000	179,000
Nurse	32,000	49,000	47,000	68,000
Pharmacist	70,000	82,000	91,000	114,000
Reporter	20,000	40,000	32,000	58,000
Social worker	17,000	27,000	26,000	41,000
Speech pathologist	22,000	31,000	32,000	46,000
K-12 teacher	16,000	25,000	26,000	41,000
Veterinarian	31,000	76,000	44,000	114,000

NOTE: When an accountant earning a master's degree accumulates $37,000 in federal student loans, borrowing an additional dollar does not increase his total payments on that debt, if he earns an income at the 50th percentile based on his age and qualifies for Public Service Loan Forgiveness (PSLF). If he earns at the 75th percentile, once he accumulates $70,000 in federal student loans, borrowing an additional dollar does not increase his total payments.

Borrower's debt is forgiven after 10 years of payments in IBR. For all other borrowers in IBR, debt is forgiven after 20 years of payments, denoted as "20-year" in this table. "No marginal cost" is the debt level at which a borrower repaying through IBR incurs no cost in borrowing an additional dollar above that debt level, excluding potential taxes that apply to amounts forgiven under IBR 20-year. No taxes apply to debt forgiven under PSLF.

SOURCE: Authors' calculations.

on cumulative payments at any point in the repayment term. The values under "20-year" indicate the NMCT for borrowers who do not qualify for PSLF and have their debt forgiven after 20 years of payments.

Lastly, on the left side of the table, "Total payments PSLF" and "Total payments 20-year" show the total principal and interest payments the borrower in the stated degree-profession category would make for the corresponding debt level indicated at the top of the column. The payments are discounted to the present at a rate of 2.5 percent.

As a rule, a borrower's total payments for a debt level above the NMCT will not exceed the payments she would make for a debt level at the NMCT. For example, if the NMCT is $61,000, the borrower's total payments will be the same if she leaves school with a loan balance of exactly that amount or any amount greater.

The following notes apply to Tables 13.5–13.24.

NOTE: Borrower's debt is forgiven after 10 years of payments in IBR. For all other borrowers in IBR, debt is forgiven after 20 years of payments, denoted as "20-yr" in this table.

[a]"Low" is 25th percentile, where 25 percent of degree completers finish with the stated debt level or less; "Mid" is 50th percentile; "High" is 75th percentile.

[b] Borrower incurs no cost in borrowing an additional dollar above the stated debt level, excluding potential taxes that apply to amounts forgiven under IBR 20-year. No taxes apply to debt forgiven under PSLF.

[c] Total payments under each plan are the present discounted value of all principal and interest payments made under that plan during the duration of the loan using 2.5 percent discount rate.

Table 13.5 Student Loan Payments ($) Using Income-Based Repayment Accountant with Master's Earning 75th Percentile by Age

	Debt level for completers[a]			Debt level for IBR no marginal cost[b]	
	Low	Mid	High	PSLF	20-yr
	29,000	49,000	85,000	70,000	100,000
Total payments PSLF[c]	Ineligible	53,470	59,462	59,462	—
Total payments 20-yr[c]	Ineligible	64,524	137,032	—	143,267

Table 13.6 Student Loan Payments ($) Using Income-Based Repayment Accountant with Master's Earning 50th Percentile by Age

	Debt level for completers[a]			Debt level for IBR no marginal cost[b]	
	Low	Mid	High	PSLF	20-yr
	29,000	49,000	85,000	37,000	52,000
Total payments PSLF[c]	34,608	37,908	37,908	37,908	—
Total payments 20-yr[c]	36,305	73,333	79,444	—	79,444

Table 13.7 Student Loan Payments ($) Using Income-Based Repayment Engineer with Master's Earning 75th Percentile by Age

	Debt level for completers[a]			Debt level for IBR no marginal cost[b]	
	Low	Mid	High	PSLF	20-yr
	23,000	47,000	75,000	74,000	113,000
Total payments PSLF[c]	Ineligible	54,779	66,612	66,612	—
Total payments 20-yr[c]	Ineligible	59,644	109,300	—	157,066

Table 13.8 Student Loan Payments ($) Using Income-Based Repayment Engineer with Master's Earning 50th Percentile by Age

	Debt level for completers[a]			Debt level for IBR no marginal cost[b]	
	Low	Mid	High	PSLF	20-yr
	23,000	47,000	75,000	50,000	88,000
Total payments PSLF[c]	Ineligible	47,715	48,090	48,090	—
Total payments 20-yr[c]	Ineligible	62,738	112,189	—	115,127

Table 13.9 Student Loan Payments ($) Using Income-Based Repayment Lawyer with JD Earning 75th Percentile by Age

	Debt level for completers[a]			Debt level for IBR no marginal cost[b]	
	Low	Mid	High	PSLF	20-yr
	86,000	140,000	191,000	116,000	179,000
Total payments PSLF[c]	92,057	100,435	100,435	100,435	—
Total payments 20-yr[c]	115,451	226,611	248,668	—	248,668

Table 13.10 Student Loan Payments ($) Using Income-Based Repayment Lawyer with JD Earning 50th Percentile by Age

	Debt level for completers[a]			Debt level for IBR no marginal cost[b]	
	Low	Mid	High	PSLF	20-yr
	86,000	140,000	191,000	54,000	86,000
Total payments PSLF[c]	47,661	47,661	47,661	47,661	—
Total payments 20-yr[c]	121,219	122,696	121,696	—	121,219

Table 13.11 Student Loan Payments ($) Using Income-Based Repayment Nurse with Master's Earning 75th Percentile by Age

	Debt level for completers[a]			Debt level for IBR no marginal cost[b]	
	Low	Mid	High	PSLF	20-yr
	23,000	47,000	75,000	49,000	68,000
Total payments PSLF[c]	Ineligible	49,409	49,535	49,535	—
Total payments 20-yr[c]	Ineligible	61,761	103,546	—	103,546

Table 13.12 Student Loan Payments ($) Using Income-Based Repayment Nurse with Master's Earning 50th Percentile by Age

	Debt level for completers[a]			Debt level for IBR no marginal cost[b]	
	Low	Mid	High	PSLF	20-yr
	23,000	47,000	75,000	32,000	47,000
Total payments PSLF[c]	Ineligible	35,112	35,112	35,112	—
Total payments 20-yr[c]	Ineligible	70,929	70,929	—	70,929

Table 13.13 Student Loan Payments ($) Using Income-Based Repayment Pharmacist with PharmD Earning 75th Percentile by Age

	Debt level for completers[a]			Debt level for IBR no marginal cost[b]	
	Low	Mid	High	PSLF	20-yr
	98,000	132,000	199,000	82,000	114,000
Total payments PSLF[c]	88,049	88,049	88,049	88,049	—
Total payments 20-yr[c]	140,742	179,107	179,107	—	179,107

Table 13.14 Student Loan Payments ($) Using Income-Based Repayment Pharmacist with PharmD Earning 50th Percentile by Age

	Debt level for completers[a]			Debt level for IBR no marginal cost[b]	
	Low	Mid	High	PSLF	20-yr
	98,000	132,000	199,000	70,000	91,000
Total payments PSLF[c]	57,956	57,956	57,956	57,956	—
Total payments 20-yr[c]	133,865	133,865	133,865	—	133,865

Table 13.15 Student Loan Payments ($) Using Income-Based Repayment Reporter with MA Earning 75th Percentile by Age

	Debt level for completers[a]			Debt level for IBR no marginal cost[b]	
	Low	Mid	High	PSLF	20-yr
	29,000	49,000	85,000	40,000	58,000
Total payments PSLF[c]	33,595	38,052	38,052	38.052	—
Total payments 20-yr[c]	36,904	73,342	82,852	—	82,852

Table 13.16 Student Loan Payments ($) Using Income-Based Repayment Reporter with MA Earning 50th Percentile by Age

	Debt level for completers[a]			Debt level for IBR no marginal cost[b]	
	Low	Mid	High	PSLF	20-yr
	29,000	49,000	85,000	20,000	32,000
Total payments PSLF[c]	20,234	20,234	20,234	20,234	—
Total payments 20-yr[c]	41,485	41,706	41,706	—	41,706

Table 13.17 Student Loan Payments ($) Using Income-Based Repayment Social Worker with MSW Earning 75th Percentile by Age

	Debt level for completers[a]			Debt level for IBR no marginal cost[b]	
	Low	Mid	High	PSLF	20-yr
	29,000	49,000	85,000	27,000	41,000
Total payments PSLF[c]	24,604	24,604	24,604	24,604	—
Total payments 20-yr[c]	41,213	56,815	56,815	—	56,815

Table 13.18 Student Loan Payments ($) Using Income-Based Repayment Social Worker with MSW Earning 50th Percentile by Age

	Debt level for completers[a]			Debt level for IBR no marginal cost[b]	
	Low	Mid	High	PSLF	20-yr
	29,000	49,000	85,000	17,000	26,000
Total payments PSLF[c]	14,027	14,027	14,027	14,027	—
Total payments 20-yr[c]	33,911	33,911	33,911	—	33,911

Table 13.19 Student Loan Payments ($) Using Income-Based Repayment Speech Pathologist with Master's Earning 75th Percentile by Age

	Debt level for completers[a]			Debt level for IBR no marginal cost[b]	
	Low	Mid	High	PSLF	20-yr
	29,000	49,000	85,000	31,000	46,000
Total payments PSLF[c]	34,012	34,315	34,315	34,315	—
Total payments 20-yr[c]	36,343	68,730	68,730	—	68,730

Table 13.20 Student Loan Payments ($) Using Income-Based Repayment Speech Pathologist with Master's Earning 50th Percentile by Age

	Debt level for completers[a]			Debt level for IBR no marginal cost[b]	
	Low	Mid	High	PSLF	20-yr
	29,000	49,000	85,000	22,000	32,000
Total payments PSLF[c]	22,726	22,726	22,726	22,726	—
Total payments 20-yr[c]	42,737	45,041	45,041	—	45,041

Table 13.21 Student Loan Payments ($) Using Income-Based Repayment K-12 Teacher with Master's Earning 75th Percentile by Age

	Debt level for completers[a]			Debt level for IBR no marginal cost[b]	
	Low	Mid	High	PSLF	20-yr
	23,000	42,000	69,000	25,000	41,000
Total payments PSLF[c]	23,964	24,149	24,149	24,149	—
Total payments 20-yr[c]	30,249	55,443	55,443	—	55,443

Table 13.22 Student Loan Payments ($) Using Income-Based Repayment K-12 Teacher with Master's Earning 50th Percentile by Age

	Debt level for completers[a]			Debt level for IBR no marginal cost[b]	
	Low	Mid	High	PSLF	20-yr
	23,000	42,000	69,000	16,000	26,000
Total payments PSLF[c]	23,964	24,149	24,149	24,149	—
Total payments 20-yr[c]	30,249	55,443	55,443	—	55,443

Table 13.23 Student Loan Payments ($) Using Income-Based Repayment Veterinarian with DVM Earning 75th Percentile by Age

	Debt level for completers[a]			Debt level for IBR no marginal cost[b]	
	Low	Mid	High	PSLF	20-yr
	98,000	132,000	199,000	76,000	114,000
Total payments PSLF[c]	71,166	71,166	71,166	71,166	—
Total payments 20-yr[c]	155,593	160,551	160,551	—	160,551

Table 13.24 Student Loan Payments ($) Using Income-Based Repayment Veterinarian with DVM Earning 50th Percentile by Age

	Debt level for completers[a]			Debt level for IBR no marginal cost[b]	
	Low	Mid	High	PSLF	20-yr
	98,000	132,000	199,000	31,000	44,000
Total payments PSLF[c]	34,475	34,475	34,475	34,475	—
Total payments 20-yr[c]	64,431	64,431	64,431	—	64,431

KEY FINDINGS AND DISCUSSION

Public Service Loan Forgiveness

The NMCT for borrowers who qualify for PSLF is one of the most significant findings from the analysis. It is important to understand that "public service" under PSLF is quite broad, and borrowers who might not be considered employed in traditional public service jobs will qualify for loan forgiveness after 10 years. Employment at any 501(c)(3) tax-exempt nonprofit qualifies, as does any government position (state, federal, local, and tribal). This is why the federal government estimates that 25 percent of all jobs in the economy would qualify (Consumer Financial Protection Bureau 2013).

For borrowers who qualify for PSLF, the point at which they bear no incremental cost in borrowing more is low relative to what many graduate and professional degrees cost, without even factoring in what students may borrow to pay for living costs, what they may have borrowed in undergraduate debt, or the interest they would accrue on their federal loans while in school. This suggests that through New IBR, the federal government has provided a very large source of tuition assistance for graduate and professional students who work in the governmental or not-for-profit sectors.

In fact, this tuition assistance is large enough that it could become common for the government to pay for a student's entire graduate education via loan forgiveness under PSLF, especially in some professions. Moreover, certain categories of students will pursue graduate degrees knowing that they will *only* work in PSLF-qualified employment, such as teachers and social workers. An example using the social worker profile helps illustrate this point.

Imagine a student who, having already accumulated a loan balance of $29,000 during her undergraduate studies, pursues a Master of Social Work and borrows the entire cost of the education, including living expenses. Assume she earns at the 75th percentile for a social worker with a master's degree by age for her first 10 years after graduate school. Because she began the program with debt well in excess of the NMCT ($23,000), every dollar she borrows will be forgiven by the federal government and will not increase her payments beyond those she would make on the debt she accumulated in undergraduate studies. This borrower need not earn an income that is unexpectedly low for this to be true. In fact, she can earn a relatively high income for a social worker with a master's degree, as this example reflects an income at the 75th percentile.

Note that for undergraduate students, the effects of New IBR and PSLF are much different. It would be impossible for an undergraduate student to fully finance an undergraduate degree through PSLF. Borrowers must incur costs for the initial amounts they borrow below the NMCT, and they will take out their initial loans pursuing an undergraduate degree. Furthermore, annual and aggregate loan limits in the federal loan program that apply to dependent undergraduates are generally set below or near the NMCT for all but the lowest-paid professions we profiled.

Stafford Loans Alone Allow for Significant Loan Forgiveness

Delisle and Holt (2012) show how high-income borrowers could qualify for loan forgiveness by amassing high-debt balances through

Table 13.25 Income Projections by Percentile for Degree-Profession Categories by Loan Repayment Year ($)

Repayment year	1	2	3	4	5	6	7	8	9
Accountant with master's									
50th percentile	59,017	62,644	66,415	70,336	74,411	78,647	82,169	85,819	89,599
75th percentile	73,544	79,842	86,410	93,255	100,390	107,822	114,104	120,632	127,416
Engineer with master's									
50th percentile	69,747	74,356	79,153	84,142	89,332	94,729	99,776	105,017	110,457
75th percentile	82,445	88,282	94,360	100,686	107,269	114,119	119,987	126,078	132,398
Lawyer with JD									
50th percentile	59,065	66,031	73,308	80,908	88,842	97,123	102,786	108,672	114,788
75th percentile	95,425	106,326	117,712	129,601	142,011	154,961	164,898	175,235	185,986
Nurse with master's									
50th percentile	54,842	58,462	62,228	66,146	70,221	74,459	77,197	80,025	82,947
75th percentile	72,876	77,591	82,496	87,598	92,903	98,419	101,843	105,377	109,023
Pharmacist with PharmD									
50th percentile	58,692	68,269	78,289	88,767	99,719	111,164	116,013	121,034	126,234
75th percentile	108,019	113,095	118,358	123,814	129,468	135,327	138,952	142,674	146,495
Reporter with master's									
50th percentile	39,660	42,419	45,293	48,283	51,394	54,631	55,849	57,094	58,365
75th percentile	53,070	58,167	63,485	69,032	74,817	80,849	85,211	89,741	94,444
Social worker with MSW									
50th percentile	24,131	28,821	33,730	38,867	44,240	49,857	51,586	53,371	55,212
75th percentile	37,955	42,269	46,774	51,478	56,389	61,512	64,330	67,250	70,276
Speech pathologist with master's									
50th percentile	49,359	50,373	51,407	52,461	53,536	54,631	55,766	56,923	58,103
75th percentile	60,729	62,439	64,196	66,003	67,859	69,767	71,772	73,832	75,951
K-12 teacher with master's									
50th percentile	34,671	36,775	38,964	41,238	43,603	46,059	48,391	50,810	53,321
75th percentile	43,541	46,126	48,812	51,604	54,505	57,519	60,558	63,713	66,988
Veterinarian with DVM									
50th percentile	62,133	63,551	64,968	66,386	68,128	69,869	71,611	73,352	75,094
75th percentile	85,585	92,579	99,868	107,465	112,933	118,608	124,496	130,604	136,940

NOTE: The table shows the 20-year income projections developed and used in this chapter. Loan payments under the Income Based Repayment plan are calculated using these income projections. All figures are in nominal dollars.

Table 13.25 (continued)

10	11	12	13	14	15	16	17	18	19	20
93,515	97,571	100,603	103,726	106,942	110,254	113,665	116,155	118,698	121,297	123,951
134,463	141,784	146,794	151,966	157,306	162,817	168,506	173,219	178,062	183,040	188,155
116,104	121,964	126,761	131,721	136,850	142,153	147,636	152,920	158,375	164,008	169,824
138,955	145,758	151,903	158,265	164,849	171,664	178,717	185,627	192,770	200,154	207,787
121,142	127,742	133,164	138,778	144,589	150,605	156,830	160,425	164,101	167,862	171,707
197,164	208,786	219,750	231,131	242,944	255,203	267,924	275,288	282,852	290,623	298,606
85,965	89,082	91,309	93,592	95,932	98,330	100,788	104,911	109,177	113,591	118,157
112,787	116,670	119,923	123,266	126,702	130,232	133,859	138,053	142,372	146,821	151,404
131,619	137,193	140,069	143,002	145,995	149,048	152,162	157,142	162,277	167,570	173,026
150,418	154,446	158,937	163,555	168,306	173,192	178,216	183,417	188,767	194,269	199,929
59,665	60,993	62,848	64,758	66,724	68,748	70,831	75,391	80,135	85,069	90,199
99,326	104,393	106,189	108,010	109,856	111,726	113,621	119,612	125,831	132,286	138,986
57,113	59,073	61,387	63,779	66,253	68,810	71,454	73,566	75,738	77,974	80,273
73,411	76,659	79,460	82,354	85,343	88,430	91,618	94,490	97,448	100,495	103,634
59,307	60,534	63,151	65,860	68,666	71,570	74,577	78,128	81,810	85,627	89,584
78,130	80,370	83,174	86,067	89,052	92,134	95,313	99,794	104,439	109,254	114,244
55,925	58,626	60,769	62,982	65,268	67,629	70,067	72,681	75,381	78,171	81,054
70,387	73,914	76,901	79,991	83,187	86,494	89,913	93,370	96,943	100,637	104,454
77,079	79,064	81,049	83,034	85,019	86,047	87,075	88,103	89,130	90,158	91,122
140,829	144,827	148,936	153,161	157,504	166,542	175,933	185,690	195,825	206,351	207,939

the federal Grad PLUS Program, which allows graduate students to borrow whatever a school charges (plus living costs as determined by the school) once they have exhausted the annual ($20,500) or aggregate ($138,500) Stafford Loan limit.

Some observers may therefore believe that New IBR only has implications for graduate education and borrowing when combined with Grad PLUS Loans. This analysis shows, however, that in many of the cases we profile, borrowers will reach the NMCT well before they would have to access Grad PLUS Loans. This is even more so the case if a borrower enters graduate school with a debt from undergraduate studies and repays the combined balance through New IBR.

For example, a student who borrows the maximum in undergraduate loans for a dependent over five years would enter graduate school with a balance of about $34,000 (including accrued interest and assuming he did not make any payments), and if he attends graduate school for two years and borrows the maximum in Stafford Loans, his combined loan balance (including accrued interest from both sets of loans) would total approximately $80,000 in Stafford Loans alone. That figure exceeds the NMCT for all but the highest-earning degree-profession categories that we profiled.

Declining Marginal Costs for More Debt

Even though our analysis focuses on the NMCT, as a borrower's debt level approaches that point, it is significant that the incremental cost of borrowing an additional dollar begins to decline. This effect occurs because some, but not all, of the added cost of borrowing more is forgiven. Thus, borrowers face declining costs in borrowing additional sums before their debt reaches the NMCT. It is as if the borrower faces a declining interest rate (and even a negative interest rate) the more he borrows as he approaches the NMCT.

For example, a lawyer earning at the 75th percentile by age, who repays his loans for 20 years under New IBR, pays a total of $226,611 (present value) and fully repays his loan when he enters repayment with a $140,000 balance at 7.65 percent interest; when he enters repayment with a balance of $179,000, or $39,000 more, his total payments increase by only $22,000 (present value) over the same 20-year repayment term. That is far less than what would be needed to fully repay the incremental $39,000 in debt plus interest over 20 years. Consequently, he has $67,000 forgiven (present value) after 20 years of payments when he borrows the additional amount. In short, borrowing more only marginally increases his costs, because much of the added cost is forgiven.

Payments for Median and High Debt Levels

In most of the cases we profiled, borrowers make payments under New IBR (PSLF or 20-year forgiveness) that are identical (or nearly identical) for median *and* high debt levels. That is because the NMCT for most of the cases we profile is close to median federal debt levels for borrowers who complete the specified graduate and professional programs according to federal data.

For example, a nurse with a master's degree earning at the 50th percentile by age would make the same payments on his loans if he left school with the median ($47,000) or the 75th percentile level ($75,000) of federal student loans for graduates with masters' of science.

This dynamic could have a significant impact on students' decisions about what schools to attend and how much to borrow. It could make attending an averaged-priced program the same cost as attending the highest-cost program, with the difference subsidized completely through loan forgiveness. Alternatively, a student who might consider using his own funds to finance some of his education, or work part time to finance his education, could decide that on the margin, whatever those choices would save him in future loan payments would simply be forgiven under New IBR and he should therefore borrow rather than use his own resources.

Schools also face altered incentives when borrower payments are the same for median and high debts. If a school is aware that the median amount of debt that students graduate with is above the NMCT for students who earn at the 75th percentile (or even higher), then any incremental price increases will be borne by the federal government through loan forgiveness, provided the students use federal loans to finance those costs. In such a scenario the school might take steps to inform students about this effect, making students insensitive to prices that exceed the NMCT, or the effects might simply work their way into the graduate school marketplace as schools raise prices without any drop-off in demand. If the cost of attendance is already above the

NMCT at a given program or school, then New IBR could artificially increase supply and demand irrespective of the labor market value of that graduate degree.

Implications for Scholarships and School-Provided Financial Aid

Some graduate and professional programs provide financial aid to certain students. Other organizations also offer scholarships for graduate and professional studies. New IBR may change whether, how, and to whom schools and other organizations provide this aid. Schools and scholarship providers may see the aid they are providing as supplanting loans that would have been forgiven by the federal government anyway. They may then put that money to other uses.

For example, a student who borrows $10,000 more than the NMCT for her degree-profession profile effectively receives a $10,000 grant from the federal government to finance her education. Her financial situation would be unchanged had she received the same amount from her school or a third party in the form of a scholarship.

Examples of Behavioral Changes in the Market

When scanning the market for examples of school and student responses to New IBR, it is important to keep in mind that the program has been available only since December 2012, the date at which eligible borrowers could first enroll. Moreover, the eligible cohorts of borrowers who would be out of school and in repayment—those who started borrowing more recently—is limited. Thus, student and school familiarity with the program is likely still in its very early stages. Even so, some early examples have emerged that illustrate how schools and students are responding to the benefits of New IBR.

Financial planners and consultants are helping clients understand the program, how to use it, and how to optimize the benefits it provides. This is not completely surprising given that the program is new and its benefits are not widely known. Also, many of the terms and rules for IBR are complicated and thus lend themselves to financial planning services, such as those for federal income tax preparation or retirement savings, where individuals can take actions that will reduce their monthly and total payments, significantly boosting the debt that they have forgiven, and thereby justifying fee-for-service financial planning.

Graduate and professional schools are also starting to inform current and prospective students about the benefits of New IBR. Most of these are focused on the benefits of PSLF. Many law schools offer special repayment programs for borrowers who use New IBR combined with PSLF, whereby the school pays a portion or all of a former student's loan payments as long as he earns below a certain income threshold. Georgetown's law school aggressively markets the benefits of its program to current and prospective students with seminars and other materials. A video recording of one such seminar includes testimonials from former students enrolled in the program who say the program allows them to take jobs with lower salaries and "ignore" debt balances, which often exceed $100,000.[14]

CONCLUSION AND POLICY RECOMMENDATIONS

The findings in this chapter show that the repayment terms policymakers designed for New IBR are unlikely to cause many graduate and professional students to fully repay their loans—even if they earn a competitive salary in their chosen careers—which will likely provide an incentive for graduate and professional students to borrow more rather than less, particularly for some professions. It should also make graduate students less sensitive to the price of a graduate or professional degree, allowing institutions to charge higher tuitions, especially for certain programs where borrowers could qualify for PSLF.

Policymakers need not completely roll back the changes made to IBR to mitigate these effects. In our 2012 paper (Delisle and Holt 2012) we demonstrated a limited approach to curtailing some of the benefits of New IBR. Our proposal would allow only the lowest-income borrowers (those earning less than 300 percent of the federal poverty guidelines) to make payments at 10 percent of income, require all others to pay 15 percent of their incomes above IBR's exemption, and require borrowers with higher debt levels to pay for longer before they receive loan forgiveness.

Alternatively, policymakers could allow all borrowers to pay 10 percent of their incomes but reduce New IBR's exemption to $10,000 for all borrowers from the current level of 150 percent of the federal poverty guidelines based on household size ($17,235 for a single person in 2013). All borrowers would qualify for loan forgiveness after 20 years of payments, except those with more than $50,000 in federal loans, who would qualify after 30 years of payments.

To address the extremely high subsidies and moral hazard issues inherent in PSLF, policymakers could simply cap the amount that can be forgiven under that benefit. Under current law, there is no limit.

Without changes like these, New IBR, along with PSLF, could have a very large impact on the graduate education marketplace and borrowing behavior in the coming years.

Notes

1. The program, called Income-Contingent Repayment, requires borrowers to make payments equal to 20 percent of adjusted gross income after an exemption equal to the federal poverty guidelines. Borrowers can often obtain much lower payments under other repayment options that are fully amortizing and not based on income by extending the duration of the loan and by making payments that slowly increase over time. Moreover, borrowers must have loans under the Direct Loan Program to use Income-Contingent Repayment, which up until about 2010 represented at most about 25 percent of loan issuance. The balance of the loans was made by private lenders and backed by the federal government but was not eligible for Income-Contingent Repayment.
2. The advocates' most compelling argument for modifying the program was that a borrower who defaulted on his loans and had his wages garnished by the U.S. Department of Education would pay roughly the same share of his income as under the Income-Contingent Repayment plan. (See Baum and Schwartz [2006], which was cited by advocates to make the case for payments based on smaller share of income than under the Income-Contingent Repayment option, and Shireman et al. [2006]).
3. For example, if a borrower's monthly payment based on a 10-year amortization schedule is $300, but her payments based on the IBR formula would be $290, she qualifies to enroll in IBR. If her income later increases such that her payments would exceed the amount she would pay on a 10-year amortization, then her payments are capped at $300 but she may remain enrolled in IBR and still qualifies for loan forgiveness after the required number of payments.
4. When Congress debated legislation to enact Old IBR in 2007, lawmakers focused exclusively on the loan forgiveness benefits of the program for borrowers in public

service jobs, PSLF. They viewed that provision as the main legislative change; few mentioned that the program would allow borrowers to make lower monthly payments than the Income-Contingent Repayment program in place at the time.

5. The Obama administration used the authority under a provision added to the Higher Education Act in 1993 that allows the Secretary of Education to offer an income-contingent repayment plan within certain parameters (20 U.S.C. § 1087e). A "new borrower" for purposes of the plan is someone who takes out a federal student loan for the first time on or after the specified date. For the Pay As You Earn plan, the borrower must also have taken out a loan on October 1, 2011, or after, or have become a new borrower on or after October 1, 2011. Someone who borrowed initially prior to that date but repaid the earlier loans in full before borrowing again on or after that date is also considered a "new borrower."

6. Undergraduates face relatively low limits in the federal loan program, thereby limiting the benefits of loan forgiveness. A dependent undergraduate borrower can borrow a maximum of $5,500 in her first year, $6,500 in her second, and $7,500 each year thereafter. The aggregate limit is $31,000. An independent undergraduate can borrow $4,000 more in the first two years and $5,000 more in later years, with an aggregate limit of $57,500. Note that borrowers can enter repayment with balances higher than the aggregate limit due to interest accrual. Additionally, a small share of undergraduate borrowers have federal Perkins Loans in addition to Stafford Loans, which may be repaid through New IBR as a consolidation loan. Perkins Loans do not count toward the aggregate loan limit for Stafford Loans. If eligible, certain students may therefore borrow $5,500 annually through the program, in addition to the Stafford limit, with a separate aggregate limit of $27,500. Borrowers with persistently low incomes make similar payments under both the Old and New IBR plans, owing to the exemption that is the same under both programs. Both Old and New IBR plans calculate a borrower's payments on income after an exemption equal to 150 percent of the federal poverty guidelines, adjusted for household size. If a borrower's income is below that threshold, then his payment is $0 regardless of which IBR he is using. Furthermore, borrowers with incomes slightly above the threshold make similar payments because 10 percent and 15 percent of the nonexempt income translates into only slightly different payments.

7. Students can finance their housing, food, transportation, and other costs using federal loans. Those costs are determined by the school itself with little to no parameters set by the federal government. A review of a number of graduate school programs' calculations suggests that the typical figure for such costs is $13,000 per year, though some schools set the figure as high as $25,000 per year.

8. IBR calculates a borrower's payments based on his prior year federal income tax return, and the program often updates his payments many months after his most recent tax return is filed. Therefore, a borrower will make payments under IBR that reflect his income in the prior year or even later, not his current income; that is, a 27-year-old borrower would make payments based on his income when he was age 25 or 26. Our analysis does not account for this lag and likely overstates the income and loan payments borrowers make.

9. The version of the New America IBR calculator used for this chapter is available in Microsoft Excel format at the URL below. Note that the calculator does not display loan payments in discounted present value. The analysis in this chapter reports loan payments displayed in the calculator in discounted present value using a constant discount rate of 2.5 percent. http://edmoney.newamerica .net/sites/newamerica.net/files/articles/NAF%20IBR%20Calculator%20with%20 PSLF%20for%20New%20IBR.xlsx (accessed April 22, 2014).

10. Income levels entered into the calculator that are less than $68,000 equate to an AGI of 90 percent of total income. Income between $68,001 and $100,000 equates to an AGI of 85 percent of total income. Income between $100,001 and $150,000 equates to an AGI of 95 percent of income. Income between $150,001 and $200,000 equates to an AGI of 98 percent of income. Income of $200,000 and above is not reduced. The calculator automatically increases those income brackets by 2.5 percent each successive year in the calculator. For example, the $68,000 income threshold at which point a borrower's AGI reflects 90 percent of total income increases by 2.5 percent per year so that in the second year it is $69,700, and so on. The rationale for those brackets is the following. Fringe benefits and the student loan interest deduction, even though small on an absolute basis, can easily reduce a borrower's income by a large percentage. The 90 percent threshold is conservative. As borrowers earn more, the threshold increases because these earners are more able to take advantage of fringe benefits, particularly pretax retirement contributions. At high incomes, the reduction is reduced because we assume that these borrowers have unearned income that partially or fully offsets any pretax fringe benefits or other above-the-line deductions and credits.

11. Borrowers would have to file a separate federal income tax return from their spouses to do this. While this may cause them to pay slightly more in income taxes, the reduced loan payments and increase in loan forgiveness far outweigh those costs.

12. Under the IBR rules, borrowers may include a spouse in their household size calculation, even if the couple files separate federal income tax returns. Children may be included in a borrower's household size if the borrower provides for more than half of a child's care, regardless of which spouse claims the child as a dependent on his or her tax return.

13. In 2012, Congress and the president amended the federal loan program such that interest rates on newly issued loans are based on the interest rates on 10-year Treasury notes plus a mark-up (*Bipartisan Student Loan Certainty Act of 2013*). Based on Congressional Budget Office estimates in 2013, interest rates on graduate Stafford Loans and Grad PLUS Loans will remain lower than rates in effect prior to enactment of the *Bipartisan Student Loan Certainty Act* only through 2015, after which they will remain above those rates.

14. Georgetown removed this video from its Web site after we published a post on the Higher Ed Watch blog regarding the Georgetown Law loan repayment program. The referenced footage can still be viewed on the *Ed Money Watch* blog. See Delisle and Holt (2013).

References

Baum, Sandy, and Saul Schwartz. 2006. *How Much Debt Is Too Much Debt? Defining Benchmarks for Manageable Student Debt.* New York: College Board. http://research.collegeboard.org/sites/default/files/publications/2012/9/researchinreview-2006-12-benchmarks-manageable-student-debt.pdf (accessed April 22, 2014).

Bipartisan Student Loan Certainty Act of 2013. Public L. No.113-28, 127 Stat. 506 (2013).

Consumer Financial Protection Bureau. 2013. "Public Service & Student Debt: Analysis of Existing Benefits and Options for Public Service Organizations." Washington, DC: Consumer Protection Financial Bureau. http://files.consumerfinance.gov/f/201308_cfpb_public-service-and-student-debt.pdf (accessed April 22, 2014).

Deficit Reduction Act of 2005. Public L. No. 109-171, 20 U.S.C. §8005 (2005).

Delisle, Jason, and Alex Holt. 2012. "Safety Net or Windfall: Examining Changes to Income-Based Repayment." Washington, DC: New America Foundation.

———. 2013. "Georgetown LRAP: In Their Own Words." *Ed Money Watch* (blog). http://edmoney.newamerica.net/blogposts/2013/georgetown_lrap_in_their_own_words-89258 (accessed April 22, 2014).

Health Care and Education Reconciliation Act of 2010. Public L. No. 111-152, §2213 (2010).

Omnibus Budget Reconciliation Act of 1993. Public L. No. 103-66, 20 U.S.C. 1087a, §4011 (1993).

Shireman, Robert, Lauren Asher, Ajita Talwalker, Shu-Ahn Li, Edie Irons, and Rowan Cota. 2006. "Addressing Student Loan Repayment Burdens." White paper. Washington, DC: The Project on Student Debt. http://projectonstudentdebt.org/files/pub/WHITE_PAPER_FINAL_PDF.pdf (accessed April 22, 2014).

U.S. Department of Education Office of Federal Student Aid. "Public Service Loan Forgiveness." Fact sheet. Washington, DC: U.S. Department of Education. http://studentaid.ed.gov/sites/default/files/public-service-loan-forgiveness.pdf (accessed April 22, 2014).

Authors

Pauline Abernathy is vice president at The Institute for College Access and Success.

Beth Akers is a fellow in the Brookings Institution's Brown Center on Education Policy.

Xiaoling Ang is an economist at the Consumer Financial Protection Bureau.

Lauren Asher is president at The Institute for College Access and Success.

Sandy Baum is a senior fellow at the Urban Institute and a research professor at the George Washington University Graduate School of Education and Human Development.

Kristin Blagg is a recent graduate of the Master of Public Policy program at Georgetown University.

Meta Brown is a senior economist at the Federal Reserve Bank of New York.

Stephanie Riegg Cellini is an associate professor at George Washington University and a faculty research fellow at the National Bureau of Economic Research.

Diane Cheng is a research analyst at The Institute for College Access and Success.

Matthew M. Chingos is a senior fellow in the Brookings Institution's Brown Center on Education Policy.

Debbie Cochrane is research director at The Institute for College Access and Success.

Rajeev Darolia is an assistant professor at the University of Missouri.

Jason Delisle is the director of the Federal Education Budget Project at New America.

Susan Dynarski is a professor at the University of Michigan.

Dora Gicheva is an assistant professor at the University of North Carolina, Greensboro.

Sara Goldrick-Rab is a professor at the University of Wisconsin–Madison.

Andrew Haughwout is a vice president and function head at the Federal Reserve Bank of New York.

Alice M. Henriques is an economist at the Federal Reserve Board of Governors.

Brad Hershbein is an economist at the W.E. Upjohn Institute for Employment Research.

Kevin M. Hollenbeck is vice president, senior economist, and director of publications at the W.E. Upjohn Institute for Employment Research.

Alex Holt is a policy analyst with the Education Policy Program at New America.

Dalié Jiménez is an associate professor at the University of Connecticut School of Law.

Robert Kelchen is an assistant professor at Seton Hall University.

Daniel Kreisman is an assistant professor at Georgia State University.

Donghoon Lee is a senior economist at the Federal Reserve Bank of New York.

Lance J. Lochner is a professor and director of the Canadian Imperial Bank of Commerce Centre for Human Capital and Productivity at the University of Western Ontario.

Joseph Mais is the Washington, D.C., office director and a senior policy analyst at The Institute for College Access and Success.

Alexander Monge-Naranjo is a research officer and economist at the Federal Reserve Bank of St. Louis and a visiting associate professor at Washington University in St. Louis.

Joelle Scally is a financial and economic analyst at the Federal Reserve Bank of New York.

Jeffrey Thompson is an economist at the Federal Reserve Board of Governors.

Jessica Thompson is a senior policy analyst at The Institute for College Access and Success.

Wilbert van der Klaauw is a senior vice president in the Microeconomic Studies Function at the Federal Reserve Bank of New York.

Discussants

Timothy J. Bartik, senior economist at the W. E. Upjohn Institute for Employment Research.

David Bergeron, vice president for postsecondary education at the Center for American Progress.

Eric Bettinger, associate professor of economics and education in the Stanford University School of Education.

John Bound, professor of economics at the University of Michigan.

Brian Cadena, assistant professor of economics at the University of Colorado.

Sarena Goodman, economist at the Board of Governors of the Federal Reserve System.

Brian Jacob, the Walter H. Annenberg Professor of Education Policy, and professor of economics and education at the University of Michigan.

Ben Keys, assistant professor at the University of Chicago Harris School of Public Policy.

Marta Lachowska, economist at the W.E. Upjohn Institute for Employment Research.

Caroline Ratcliffe, economist and senior fellow at the Urban Institute.

Jesse Rothstein, associate professor of public policy and economics at the University of California, Berkeley.

Lesley J. Turner, assistant professor of economics at the University of Maryland.

Index

The italic letters *f, n,* or *t* following a page number indicate a figure, note, or table on that page, respectively. Double letters mean more than one such item on a single page.

About the Institute

The W.E. Upjohn Institute for Employment Research is a nonprofit research organization devoted to finding and promoting solutions to employment-related problems at the national, state, and local levels. It is an activity of the W.E. Upjohn Unemployment Trustee Corporation, which was established in 1932 to administer a fund set aside by Dr. W.E. Upjohn, founder of The Upjohn Company, to seek ways to counteract the loss of employment income during economic downturns.

The Institute is funded largely by income from the W.E. Upjohn Unemployment Trust, supplemented by outside grants, contracts, and sales of publications. Activities of the Institute comprise the following elements: 1) a research program conducted by a resident staff of professional social scientists; 2) a competitive grant program, which expands and complements the internal research program by providing financial support to researchers outside the Institute; 3) a publications program, which provides the major vehicle for disseminating the research of staff and grantees, as well as other selected works in the field; and 4) an Employment Management Services division, which manages most of the publicly funded employment and training programs in the local area.

The broad objectives of the Institute's research, grant, and publication programs are to 1) promote scholarship and experimentation on issues of public and private employment and unemployment policy, and 2) make knowledge and scholarship relevant and useful to policymakers in their pursuit of solutions to employment and unemployment problems.

Current areas of concentration for these programs include causes, consequences, and measures to alleviate unemployment; social insurance and income maintenance programs; compensation; workforce quality; work arrangements; family labor issues; labor-management relations; and regional economic development and local labor markets.